ANNUAL EDITIONS

The Family 12/13

Thirty-Eighth Edition

EDITOR

Kathleen R. Gilbert
Indiana University

Kathleen Gilbert is a professor in the Department of Applied Health Science at Indiana University. She received a BA in Sociology and an MS in Marriage and Family Relations from Northern Illinois University. Her PhD in Family Studies is from Purdue University. Dr. Gilbert's primary areas of interest are loss and grief in a family context, trauma and the family, family process, and family diversity. She has published several books and articles in these areas.

Connect
Learn
Succeed™

ANNUAL EDITIONS: THE FAMILY, THIRTY-EIGHTH EDITION

Published by McGraw-Hill, a business unit of The McGraw-Hill Companies, Inc., 1221 Avenue
of the Americas, New York, NY 10020. Copyright © 2012 by The McGraw-Hill Companies, Inc.
All rights reserved. Printed in the United States of America. Previous edition(s) © 2010, 2009, and
2008. No part of this publication may be reproduced or distributed in any form or by any means,
or stored in a database or retrieval system, without the prior written consent of The McGraw-Hill
Companies, Inc., including, but not limited to, in any network or other electronic storage or
transmission, or broadcast for distance learning.

Some ancillaries, including electronic and print components, may not be available to customers
outside the United States.

This book is printed on acid-free paper.

Annual Editions® is a registered trademark of The McGraw-Hill Companies, Inc.

Annual Editions is published by the **Contemporary Learning Series** group within
The McGraw-Hill Higher Education division.

1 2 3 4 5 6 7 8 9 0 QDB/QDB 1 0 9 8 7 6 5 4 3 2 1

ISBN 978–0–07–805104–3
MHID 0–07–805104–5
ISSN 1092–4876 (Print)
ISSN 2162–1640 (Online)

Managing Editor: *Larry Loeppke*
Developmental Editor: *Dave Welsh*
Permissions Coordinator: *DeAnna Dausener*
Marketing Specialist: *Alice Link*
Project Manager: *Connie Oertel*
Design Coordinator: *Margarite Reynolds*
Buyer: *Susan K. Culbertson*
Cover Graphics: *Kristine Jubeck*

Compositor: Laserwords Private Limited
Cover Images: image100/Corbis (inset); Mark Steinmetz (background)

Editors/Academic Advisory Board

Members of the Academic Advisory Board are instrumental in the final selection of articles for each edition of ANNUAL EDITIONS. Their review of articles for content, level, and appropriateness provides critical direction to the editors and staff. We think that you will find their careful consideration well reflected in this volume.

ANNUAL EDITIONS: The Family 12/13
38th Edition

EDITOR

Kathleen R. Gilbert
Indiana University

ACADEMIC ADVISORY BOARD MEMBERS

Preface

In publishing ANNUAL EDITIONS we recognize the enormous role played by the magazines, newspapers, and journals of the public press in providing current, first-rate educational information in a broad spectrum of interest areas. Many of these articles are appropriate for students, researchers, and professionals seeking accurate, current material to help bridge the gap between principles and theories and the real world. These articles, however, become more useful for study when those of lasting value are carefully collected, organized, indexed, and reproduced in a low-cost format, which provides easy and permanent access when the material is needed. That is the role played by ANNUAL EDITIONS.

The purpose of *Annual Editions: The Family 12/13* is to bring to the reader the latest thoughts and trends in our understanding of the family, to identify current concerns as well as problems and potential solutions, and to present alternative views of family processes. The intent of this anthology is to explore intimate relationships as they are played out within the family and, in doing this, to reflect the family's evolving function and importance. The articles in this volume are taken from professional journals as well as other professionally oriented publications and popular lay publications aimed at both special populations and a general readership. The selections are carefully reviewed for their currency and accuracy.

In the current edition, a number of new articles have been added to reflect reviewers' comments on the previous edition. As the reader, you will note the tremendous range in tone and focus of these articles, from first-person accounts to reports of scientific discoveries as well as philosophical and theoretical writings. Some are more practical and applications-oriented, while others are more conceptual and research-oriented.

This anthology is organized to address many of the important aspects of family and family relationships. The first unit takes an overview perspective and looks at varied perspectives on the family. The second unit examines the beginning steps of relationship building as individuals go through the process of exploring and establishing connections. In the third unit, various methods of finding and maintaining a relationship balance, romantic as well as for other intimate relationships, are examined. Unit 4 is concerned with crises and ways in which these can act as challenges and opportunities for families and their members. Finally, the fifth unit takes an affirming tone as it looks at family strengths and ways of empowering families.

Annual Editions: The Family 12/13 is intended to be used as a supplemental text for lower-level, introductory marriage and family or sociology of the family classes, particularly when they tie the content of the readings to essential information on marriages and families, however they are defined. As a supplement, this book can also be used to update or emphasize certain aspects of standard marriage and family textbooks. Because of the provocative nature of many of the essays in this anthology, it works well as a basis for class discussion about various aspects of marriages and family relationships. This edition of *Annual Editions: The Family* contains websites that can be used to further explore topics addressed in the articles. These sites are cross-referenced by number in the *topic guide*.

I would like to thank everyone involved in the development of this volume. My appreciation goes to those who sent in article rating forms and comments on the previous edition as well as those who suggested articles to consider for inclusion in this edition. To all of the students in my Marriage and Family Interaction class who have contributed critiques of articles, I would like to say thanks.

Anyone interested in providing input for future editions of *Annual Editions: The Family* should complete and return the postage-paid *article rating form* at the end of this book. Your suggestions are much appreciated and contribute to the continuing quality of this anthology.

Kathleen R. Gilbert
Editor

Contents

UNIT 1
Evolving Perspectives on the Family

UNIT 2
Exploring and Establishing Relationships

The concepts in bold italics are developed in the article. For further expansion, please refer to the Topic Guide.

UNIT 3
Family Relationships

The concepts in bold italics are developed in the article. For further expansion, please refer to the Topic Guide.

The concepts in bold italics are developed in the article. For further expansion, please refer to the Topic Guide.

UNIT 4
Challenges and Opportunities

The concepts in bold italics are developed in the article. For further expansion, please refer to the Topic Guide.

The concepts in bold italics are developed in the article. For further expansion, please refer to the Topic Guide.

UNIT 5
Families, Now and into the Future

The concepts in bold italics are developed in the article. For further expansion, please refer to the Topic Guide.

The concepts in bold italics are developed in the article. For further expansion, please refer to the Topic Guide.

Correlation Guide

The *Annual Editions* series provides students with convenient, inexpensive access to current, carefully selected articles from the public press. **Annual Editions: The Family 12/13** is an easy-to-use reader that presents articles on important topics such as *family composition, love and sex, family stressors,* and many more. For more information on *Annual Editions* and other *McGraw-Hill Contemporary Learning Series* titles, visit www.mhhe.com/cls.

This convenient guide matches the units in **Annual Editions: The Family 12/13** with the corresponding chapters in three of our best-selling McGraw-Hill Family textbooks by Olson et al., Lauer/Lauer, and Miller.

Annual Editions: The Family 12/13	Marriages and Families: Intimacy, Diversity, and Strengths, 7/e by Olson et al.	Marriage and Family: The Quest for Intimacy, 8/e by Lauer/Lauer	Intimate Relationships, 6/e by Miller
Unit 1: Evolving Perspectives on the Family	**Chapter 1:** Perspectives on Intimate Relationships **Chapter 2:** Cultural Diversity: Family Strengths and Challenges **Chapter 3:** Understanding Marriage and Family Dynamics	**Chapter 1:** Marriage and Family in America: Needs, Myths, and Dreams	**Chapter 1:** The Building Blocks of Relationships
Unit 2: Exploring and Establishing Relationships	**Chapter 1:** Perspectives on Intimate Relationships **Chapter 4:** Communication and Intimacy **Chapter 6:** Sexual Intimacy	**Chapter 4:** Sexuality **Chapter 6:** Falling in Love **Chapter 7:** Selecting a Life Partner **Chapter 9:** The Challenge of Communication **Chapter 16:** Intimacy in Later Years	**Chapter 3:** Attraction **Chapter 5:** Communication **Chapter 8:** Love **Chapter 9:** Sexuality
Unit 3: Family Relationships	**Chapter 5:** Conflict and Conflict Resolution **Chapter 12:** Parenthood: Satisfaction and Challenge **Chapter 15:** Divorce, Single-Parent Families, and Stepfamilies	**Chapter 10:** Power and Conflict in Marriage **Chapter 14:** Separation and Divorce	**Chapter 11:** Conflict **Chapter 12:** Power and Violence **Chapter 13:** The Dissolution and Loss of Relationships
Unit 4: Challenges and Opportunities	**Chapter 5:** Conflict and Conflict Resolution **Chapter 8:** Managing Economic Resources **Chapter 13:** Midlife and Older Couples **Chapter 15:** Divorce, Single-Parent Families, and Stepfamilies **Chapter 16:** Strengthening Marriages and Families	**Chapter 13:** Family Crises **Chapter 14:** Separation and Divorce **Chapter 15:** Remarriage and Stepfamilies	**Chapter 13:** The Dissolution and Loss of Relationships **Chapter 14:** Maintaining and Repairing Relationships
Unit 5: Families: Now and into the Future	**Chapter 15:** Divorce, Single-Parent Families, and Stepfamilies	**Chapter 1:** Marriage and Family in America: Needs, Myths, and Dreams	**Chapter 1:** The Building Blocks of Relationships

Topic Guide

This topic guide suggests how the selections in this book relate to the subjects covered in your course. You may want to use the topics listed on these pages to search the Web more easily.

On the following pages a number of websites have been gathered specifically for this book. They are arranged to reflect the units of this Annual Editions reader. You can link to these sites by going to www.mhhe.com/cls

All the articles that relate to each topic are listed below the bold-faced term.

Abuse and neglect
15. Do We Need a Law to Prohibit Spanking?
22. Recognizing Domestic Partner Abuse
23. The Fatal Distraction: Forgetting a Child in the Backseat of a Car Is a Horrifying Mistake. Is It a Crime?
24. Role of Foster Family Belonging in Recovery from Child Maltreatment
33. Trust and Betrayal in the Golden Years

Aging
33. Trust and Betrayal in the Golden Years

Bereavement
36. Bereavement after Caregiving
37. A Family Undertaking
40. Helping Military Kids Cope with Traumatic Death

Biology
5. This Thing Called Love
10. Fats, Carbs and the Science of Conception
25. Children of Alcoholics: Risk and Resilience

Caregiving
34. Dealing *Day-to-Day* with Diabetes: A Whole Family Experience
35. The Positives of Caregiving: Mothers' Experiences Caregiving for a Child with Autism
36. Bereavement after Caregiving

Childcare/Child rearing
2. The Significant Dynamic Relationship between Globalization and Families
3. Matches Made on Earth: Why Family Values are Human Values
17. Parenting Gay Youth: Creating a Supportive Environment
21. Support and Empower Families of Children with Disabilities
46. Relative Happiness

Children
3. Matches Made on Earth: Why Family Values are Human Values
4. Family Partnerships That Count
12. Can Marriage Be Saved?
16. Children of Lesbian and Gay Parents: Psychology, Law and Policy
18. The Forgotten Siblings
19. Oh, Brother!
21. Support and Empower Families of Children with Disabilities
24. Role of Foster Family Belonging in Recovery from Child Maltreatment
25. Children of Alcoholics: Risk and Resilience
26. Impact of Family Recovery on Pre-Teens and Adolescents
31. Making Time for Family Time
39. Military Children and Families: Strengths and Challenges during Peace and War
40. Helping Military Kids Cope with Traumatic Death
46. Relative Happiness

Communication
28. Love but Don't Touch
42. Civil Wars
47. The Joy of Rituals: Simple Strategies for Strengthening Family Ties

Dating
6. She's Out There
8. Against All Odds
9. The Expectations Trap

Divorce
1. Marriage and Family in the Scandinavian Experience
41. A Divided House
42. Civil Wars
43. Estranged Spouses Increasingly Waiting Out Downturn to Divorce

Emotions
5. This Thing Called Love
15. Do We Need a Law to Prohibit Spanking?
36. Bereavement after Caregiving
47. The Joy of Rituals: Simple Strategies for Strengthening Family Ties
48. Rituals in Relationships

Family forms
1. Marriage and Family in the Scandinavian Experience
2. The Significant Dynamic Relationship between Globalization and Families
3. Matches Made on Earth: Why Family Values are Human Values
13. The Polygamists
17. Parenting Gay Youth: Creating a Supportive Environment
39. Military Children and Families: Strengths and Challenges during Peace and War
46. Relative Happiness
49. Where Is Marriage Going?

Family interaction
15. Do We Need a Law to Prohibit Spanking?
19. Oh, Brother!
20. Building on Strengths: Intergenerational Practice with African American Families
21. Support and Empower Families of Children with Disabilities
24. Role of Foster Family Belonging in Recovery from Child Maltreatment
38. Stressors Afflicting Families during Military Deployment
41. A Divided House
44. Get a Closer Look: 12 Tips for Successful Family Interviews
46. Relative Happiness
47. The Joy of Rituals: Simple Strategies for Strengthening Family Ties
48. Rituals in Relationships

Finances, family
1. Marriage and Family in the Scandinavian Experience
2. The Significant Dynamic Relationship between Globalization and Families
12. Can Marriage Be Saved?
30. The Opt-Out Myth
31. Making Time for Family Time
32. Finding New Balance
33. Trust and Betrayal in the Golden Years

Gay marriage
1. Marriage and Family in the Scandinavian Experience
16. Children of Lesbian and Gay Parents: Psychology, Law and Policy
46. Relative Happiness

Internet References

The following Internet sites have been selected to support the articles found in this reader. These sites were available at the time of publication. However, because websites often change their structure and content, the information listed may no longer be available. We invite you to visit www.mhhe.com/cls for easy access to these sites.

Annual Editions: The Family 12/13

General Sources

AARP (American Association of Retired Persons)
www.aarp.org

This major advocacy group for older people includes among its many resources suggested readings and Internet links to organizations that deal with social issues that may affect people and their families as they age.

Encyclopedia Britannica
www.britannica.com

This huge "Britannica Internet Guide" leads to a cornucopia of informational sites and reference sources on such topics as family structure, the family cycle, forms of family organization, and other social issues.

Planned Parenthood
www.plannedparenthood.org

Visit this well-known organization's home page for links to information on the various kinds of contraceptives (including outercourse and abstinence) and to discussions of other topics related to sexual and reproductive health.

Social Science Information Gateway
http://sosig.esrc.bris.ac.uk

This is an online catalog of Internet resources relevant to social science education and research. Sites are selected and described by a librarian or subject specialist.

Sympatico: HealthyWay: Health Links
www1.sympatico.ca/Contents/health

This Canadian site, which is meant for consumers, will lead you to many links that are related to sexual orientation. *Sympatico* also addresses aspects of human sexuality as well as reproductive health over the life span.

Child & Family Webguide
www.cfw.tufts.edu

Evaluates, describes and provides links to hundreds of sites containing child development research and practical advice.

UNIT 1: Evolving Perspectives on the Family

American Studies Web
www1.georgetown.edu/departments/american_studies

This site provides links to a wealth of resources on the Internet related to American studies, from gender to race and ethnicity to demography and population studies.

Anthropology Resources Page
www.usd.edu/anth

Many cultural topics can be accessed from this site from the University of South Dakota. Click on the links to find comparisons of values and lifestyles among the world's peoples.

POSSIBLE INCLUSIONS

Feminist Perspectives on Reproduction and the Family
http://plato.stanford.edu/entries/feminism-family/

This article discusses feminist viewpoints on the family.

Kearl's Guide to the Sociology of the Family
www.trinity.edu/MKEARL/family.html

Difficult to read due to poor web design, but a good overview of the many factors that impact the modern family, as well as many links to web resources.

Australian Institute of Family Studies
www.aifs.gov.au/

An Australian government site dedicated to disseminating information about the current state of the family

UNIT 2: Exploring and Establishing Relationships

Bonobo Sex and Society
http://songweaver.com/info/bonobos.html

This site, accessed through Carnegie Mellon University, contains an article explaining how a primate's behavior challenges traditional assumptions about male supremacy in human evolution. This interesting site is guaranteed to generate much spirited debate.

Go Ask Alice!
www.goaskalice.columbia.edu/index.html

This interactive site of the Columbia University Health Services provides discussion and insight into a number of personal issues of interest to college-age people and those younger and older.

The Kinsey Institute for Research in Sex, Gender, and Reproduction
www.indiana.edu/~kinsey

The purpose of this Kinsey Institute website is to support interdisciplinary research in the study of human sexuality.

Mysteries of Odor in Human Sexuality
www.pheromones.com

This is a commercial site with the goal of selling a book by James Kohl. Look here to find topics of interest to nonscientists about pheromones. Check out the diagram of "Mammalian Olfactory-Genetic-Neuronal-Hormonal-Behavioral Reciprocity and Human Sexuality" for a sense of the myriad biological influences that play a part in sexual behavior.

The Society for the Scientific Study of Sexuality
www.sexscience.org

The Society for the Scientific Study of Sexuality is an international organization dedicated to the advancement of knowledge about sexuality.

The Electronic Journal of Human Sexuality
www.ejhs.org/index.htm

This exclusively online journal publishes a variety of articles with the purpose of reaching an international audience. The section "research articles" is most useful, while "general interest" contains some opinion pieces.

Internet References

UNIT 3: Family Relationships

Child Welfare League of America
www.cwla.org

The CWLA is the largest U.S. organization devoted entirely to the well-being of vulnerable children and their families. This site provides links to information about such issues as teaching morality and values.

Coalition for Marriage, Family, and Couples Education
www.smartmarriages.com

CMFCE is dedicated to bringing information about and directories of skill-based marriage education courses to the public. It hopes to lower the rate of family breakdown through couple-empowering preventive education.

The National Academy for Child Development
www.nacd.org

The NACD, dedicated to helping children and adults reach their full potential, presents links to various programs, research, and resources into a variety of family topics.

National Council on Family Relations
www.ncfr.com

This NCFR home page leads to valuable links to articles, research, and other resources on issues in family relations, such as stepfamilies, couples, and children of divorce.

Positive Parenting
www.positiveparenting.com

Positive Parenting is an organization dedicated to providing resources and information to make parenting rewarding, effective, and fun.

SocioSite
www.pscw.uva.nl/sociosite/TOPICS/Women.html

Open this site to gain insights into a number of issues that affect family relationships. It provides wide-ranging issues pertaining to women and men, family and children, and more.

UNIT 4: Challenges and Opportunities

Alzheimer's Association
www.alz.org

The Alzheimer's Association, dedicated to the prevention, cure, and treatment of Alzheimer's and related disorders, provides support to afflicted patients and their families.

Modern Family or Modernized Family Traditionalism?: Master Status and the Gender Order in Switzerland
www.sociology.org/content/vol006.004/lwk.html

An article discussing traditional and current family dynamics, arguing that we are moving towards a more egalitarian family form.

Sociological Perspectives of Work and Family
www.scribd.com/doc/24528839/
Sociological-Perspectives-on-Work-and-Family

This article presents the challenges of work and family from four principle theoretical frameworks.

Child Welfare Information Gateway
www.childwelfare.gov/

Connects child welfare and related professionals to comprehensive information and resources to help protect children and strengthen families. Features the latest on topics from prevention to permanency, including child abuse and neglect, foster care, and adoption.

Child Rights Information Network
www.crin.org/

A clearinghouse of information and human rights advocacy organization related to global child labor.

UNIT 5: Families, Now and into the Future

National Institute on Aging
www.nih.gov/nia

UNIT 1

Evolving Perspectives on the Family

Unit Selections

1. **Marriage and Family in the Scandinavian Experience,** David Popenoe
2. **The Significant Dynamic Relationship between Globalization and Families,** Bahira Sherif Trask
3. **Matches Made on Earth: Why Family Values Are Human Values,** Nancie L. Gonzalez
4. **Family Partnerships That Count,** JoBeth Allen

Learning Outcomes

After reading this unit, you will be able to:

- Distinguish the differences between marriages and families in the United States and in Scandinavia.

- Describe the similarities of divorce in Swedish and American families.

- Interpret cultural impact of marriage and family in Scandinavia and the United States.

- Evaluate the role of policy on families.

- Describe the impact of globalization on families.

- Explain the impact of migration on families.

- Examine the impact of globalization on children.

- Recognize the social construction of "family values" in family and society.

- Identify the impact of religion in how family values are constructed.

- Illustrate the diversity of family values.

- Describe the importance of developing a partnership when working with families.

- Identify ways in which teachers can engage and work with parents and other family members.

- Analyze the different approaches used to work with a diverse population of children and families.

Student Website
www.mhhe.com/cls

Internet References

American Studies Web
www1.georgetown.edu/departments/american_studies
Anthropology Resources Page
www.usd.edu/anth
Feminist Perspectives on Reproduction and the Family
http://plato.stanford.edu/entries/feminism-family
Kearl's Guide to the Sociology of the Family
www.trinity.edu/MKEARL/family.html
Australian Institute of Family Studies
www.aifs.gov.au

Digital Vision

Our image of what family is and what it should be is a powerful combination of personal experience, family forms we encounter or observe, and attitudes we hold. Once formed, this image informs decision making and interpersonal interaction throughout our lives and has far-reaching effects: On an intimate level, it influences individual and family development as well as relationships both inside and outside the family; on a broader level, it affects legislation as well as social policy and programming. In many ways, this image can be positive. It can act to clarify our thinking and facilitate interaction with like-minded individuals. It can also be negative, because it can narrow our thinking and limit our ability to see that other ways of carrying out the functions of family have value. Their very differentness can make them seem "bad." In this case, interaction with others can be impeded because of contrasting views. This unit is intended to meet several goals with regard to perspectives on the family: (1) to sensitize the reader to sources of beliefs about the "shoulds" of the family—what the family should be and the ways in which family roles should be carried out, (2) to show how different views of the family can influence attitudes toward community responsibility and family policy, and (3) to show how views that dominate one's culture can influence awareness of ways of structuring family life. In the first reading, "Marriage and Family in the Scandinavian Experience," David Popenoe explores the differences and similarities in marriage and family experiences in the United States and Sweden. These comparisons provide information that may surprise the reader. Following this reading, Bahira Sherif Trask's article on "The Significant Dynamic Relationship between Globalization and Families" addresses these and other aspects of the family in terms of the effect of globalization on the form and function of families. Questions about what "family" is and the nature of family values are explored in "Matches Made on Earth." Collaboration between families and the schools is the focus of the final reading in this unit, "Family Partnerships. That Count."

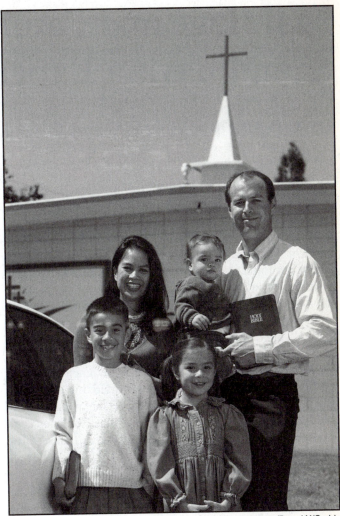

© SW Productions/Brand X/Corbis

Marriage and Family in the Scandinavian Experience

DAVID POPENOE

Many Americans have long had a ready answer to America's family problems: We should become more like Scandinavia. Whether the issues are work-family, teen sex, child poverty, or marital break-up, a range of Scandinavian family and welfare policies is commonly put forth with the assertion that, if only these could be instituted in America, family life in our nation would be improved significantly. But what can we in the United States really learn from Scandinavia? The Scandinavian nations are so small and demographically homogeneous that the idea of simply transferring their social policies to this country must be viewed as problematic. Sweden, for example, the largest Scandinavian nation and the one featured in this essay, has only 9 million people compared to our population of nearly 300 million. And how well have these policies actually worked in Scandinavia? As this essay will make clear, some of the Scandinavian family policies have, indeed, been quite successful on their own home ground. Yet aside from the potential non-transferability of these policies, by focusing so much attention on them we may be overlooking some even more important aspects of the Scandinavian family experience.

Sweden and the United States

It is now well known that there has been a weakening of marriage and the nuclear family in advanced, industrialized societies, especially since the 1960s. What is not well known is the surprising fact that the two nations that lead in this weakening are Sweden and the United States—two nations that stand at almost opposite extremes in terms of their socioeconomic systems. Let us look at one telling statistical measure. Defining the nuclear family as a mother and father living together with their own biological children, a good measure of nuclear familism in a society is the percentage of children under the age of 18 who live with both biological parents. This percentage for the United States is 63, the lowest among Western industrialized nations. The second from lowest is Sweden, at 73!

How is this possible? At the one socioeconomic extreme, Sweden has the strongest public sector, the highest taxes, and is the most secular. At the other, the United States has the weakest public sector, the lowest taxes, and is the most religious. Could these fundamental factors be mostly irrelevant to family change? And if so, what key factors are involved? As we shall see, the answer to this intellectual puzzle is to be found largely in the realm of a postmodern trend shared by both nations. But first we need to consider other family differences between the two nations. Two key differences stand out: in the United States more people marry, but they also divorce in large numbers; in Sweden, fewer people marry, but the Swedish divorce rate is a little lower than in the United States.

Here is the recent statistical record, beginning with Sweden. The Swedish marriage rate by the late 1990s was *one of the lowest in the world;* indeed, one of the lowest marriage rates ever recorded and considerably lower than the rates of other Western European nations. (Number of marriages per 1000 unmarried women in 2002—Sweden: 17.5; U.S.: 43.4. Unless otherwise noted, all statistics in this essay were gathered or computed by the National Marriage Project from official statistical sources in each nation.) If this rate holds, only about 60 percent of Swedish women today will "ever marry," compared to over 85 percent in the United States. This is a quite recent development. Not so long ago the two nations were quite similar: For the generation marrying in the 1950s, the figure for Sweden was 91 percent and for the United States 95 percent.

Sweden's low marriage rate does not mean that Swedes are living alone; rather, they are living together outside of marriage—another area in which Sweden has been in the vanguard. In fact, Sweden leads the Western nations in the degree to which nonmarital cohabitation has replaced marriage. The United States, on the other hand, has a lower rate of nonmarital cohabitation than all but the Catholic nations of southern Europe. About 28 percent of all couples in Sweden are cohabiting, versus 8 percent of all American couples. In Sweden, virtually all couples live together before marriage, compared to around two-thirds of couples currently in America. Many couples in Sweden don't marry even when they have children. In a recent opinion poll, Swedish young adults were asked whether it was OK to cohabit even after having children; 89 percent of women and 86 percent of men answered "yes."

Why is the Swedish marriage rate so low relative to other nations? In brief, because religion there is weak, a left-wing political ideology has long been dominant, and almost all governmental incentives for marriage have been removed. First, the religious pressure for marriage in Sweden is all but gone (although of the marriages that do occur, many are for vague religious reasons). Any religious or cultural stigma in Sweden against cohabitation is no longer in evidence; it is regarded as irrelevant to question whether a couple is married or just living together. Second, the political left wing throughout Europe has generally been antagonistic to strong families, based on a combination of feminist concerns about patriarchy and oppression, an antipathy toward a bourgeois social institution with traditional ties to nobility and privilege, and the belief that families have been an impediment to full equality. Finally, unlike in the United States, all government benefits in Sweden are given to individuals irrespective of their intimate relationships or family form. There is no such thing, for example, as spousal benefits in health care. There is also no joint-income taxation for married couples; all income taxation is individual.

Turning to the United States, if Sweden stands out for having the lowest marriage rate, the United States is notable for having the world's highest divorce rate. Given the divorce rates of recent years, the risk of a marriage ending in divorce in the United States is close to 50 percent, compared to a little over 40 percent in Sweden. Why is the American divorce rate so high relative to other nations? Mainly because of our relatively high ethnic, racial and religious diversity, inequality of incomes with a large underclass, and extensive residential mobility, each of which is associated with high divorce rates. Revealingly, if one looks at the divorce rate of the relatively homogeneous and Scandinavian-settled state of Minnesota, it is only slightly higher than that of Sweden. (Number of divorces per 1000 married women in 2002—Sweden: 13.7; Minnesota: 14.7; United States: 18.4.)

Another big divorce risk factor in America is marrying at a young age; the average U.S. ages of first marriage today are 25 for women and 27 for men, versus 31 and 33 in Sweden. As a more consumer-oriented and economically dynamic society, in addition, there is probably something about this nation that promotes a more throw-away attitude toward life. And let us not overlook the dominant influence of Hollywood and pop culture in general, with their emphasis on feel good and forget the consequences.

Of course, if people don't marry, they can't divorce. And that is one reason why, by certain measures, Sweden has a lower divorce rate. But if couples just cohabit they certainly can break up, and that is what Swedish nonmarital couples do in large numbers. It is estimated that the risk of breakup for cohabiting couples in Sweden, even those with children, is several times higher than for married couples. By one indication, in the year 2000 there were two-and-one-half separations or divorces per 100 children among married parents, almost twice that number among unmarried cohabiting parents living with their own biological children, and three times that number among cohabiting couples living with children from a previous relationship. (A recent study found that 50 percent of children born to a cohabiting couple in the United States see their parents' union end by age five, compared to only 15 percent of children born to a married couple. [Wendy D. Manning, Pamela J. Smock, and Debamm Majumdar, "The Relative Stability of Cohabiting and Marital Unions for Children," *Population Research and Policy Review* 23 (2004): 135–159].)

Already one of the highest in Western Europe, the Swedish divorce rate has been growing in recent years, while the U.S. rate has been declining. If we consider this convergence of divorce rates, and count both cohabiting couples and married couples, *the total family breakup rate in the two nations today is actually quite similar.*

So why, in view of the similarity of overall family breakup rates, are more Swedish than American children living with their biological parents? This is especially surprising in view of the fact that the Swedish nonmarital birth percentage is much higher than that of the United States (56 percent in Sweden vs. 35 percent in the U.S.). The main reason is that far more nonmarital births in Sweden, about 90 percent, are actually to biological parents who are living together but have not married, compared to just 40 percent in the United States. The great majority of nonmarital births in the U.S., 60 percent, are to truly single, non-cohabiting mothers. This discrepancy reflects the far higher rate of births in the United States to teenagers, the stage of life at which the father is least likely to remain involved with the mother and child. (Births per 1000 girls ages 15–19 in 2002—United States: 43; Sweden: 5.) The relatively high U.S. teen birthrate, in turn, is commonly accounted for by more teen sexual activity combined with less use of contraceptives. There is also a discrepancy between the two countries in that the United States has about twice Sweden's rate of "unwanted" children.

Having sketched out these noteworthy differences in family structure between the United States and Sweden, together with some causal explanations for the differences, what are some reasonable conclusions that can be drawn from the Scandinavian family experience?

The Decline of Marriage

If a society deinstitutionalizes marriage, as Sweden has done through its tax and benefit policies and the secularization of its culture, marriage will weaken. In addition, because most adults still like to live as couples, human pair-bonding doesn't disappear when this happens. Rather, the institution of marriage is replaced by nonmarital cohabitation—marriage lite. Then, if one institutionalizes nonmarital cohabitation in the laws and government policies, as Sweden has also done, making it the virtual equivalent of marriage, marriage will decline still further.

In the modern world, people are reluctant to make strong commitments if they don't have to; it's easier to hang loose. The problem is that society ends up with adult intimate relationships that are much more fragile. It is, indeed, surprising that Sweden has such a high level of couple breakup, because it is the kind of society—stable, homogeneous, and egalitarian—where one would expect such breakups to be minimal. Yet the high breakup level is testimony to the fragility of modern marriage in which most of the institutional bonds have been stripped away—economic dependence, legal definitions, religious sentiments, and family pressures—leaving marriage and other pair-bonds held together solely by the thin and unstable reed of affection.

The losers in this social trend, of course, are the children. They are highly dependent for their development and success in life on the family in which they are born and raised, and a convincing mass of scientific evidence now exists pointing to the fact that not growing up in an intact nuclear family is one of the most deleterious events that can befall a child. In Sweden, just as in the United States, children from non-intact families—compared to those from intact families—have two to three times the number of serious problems in life. We can only speculate about the extent of psychological damage that future generations will suffer owing to today's family trends. That the very low marriage rate and high level of parental breakup are such non-issues in Sweden, something which few Swedes ever talk about, should be, in my opinion, a cause there for national soul searching.

All that said, however, there are other important conclusions one can draw from the Scandinavian family experience. What most Americans don't realize is that, in a strict comparison, Scandinavia is probably preferable to the United States today as a place to raise young children. In other writings I have suggested that the ideal family environment for raising young children has the following traits: an enduring two-biological parent family that engages regularly in activities together, has developed its own routines, traditions and stories, and provides a great deal of contact time between adults and children. Surrounded by a community that is child friendly and supportive of parents, the family is able to develop a vibrant family subculture that provides a rich legacy of meaning and values for children throughout their lives. Scandinavians certainly fall short on the enduring two-biological-parent part of this ideal (yet even there they are currently ahead of the United States), but on the key ingredients of structured and consistent contact time between parents and their children in a family-friendly environment, they are well ahead of us.

In America today, the achievement of this ideal family environment requires what many parents are coming to consider a Herculean countercultural effort, one that involves trying to work fewer hours and adopting the mantra of "voluntary simplicity" for those who can afford it; turning off the TV set and avoiding popular culture; seeking employment in firms that have family-friendly policies such as flexible working hours; and residing in areas that are better designed for children and where the cost of living is lower. Families in Scandinavia need not be so countercultural to achieve these goals because the traits of the ideal childrearing environment are to a larger degree already built into their societies.

The Scandinavian societies tend to be "soft" or low-key, with much more leisure time and not so much frantic consumerism and economic striving as in the United States. Perhaps one could even say that they practice "involuntary simplicity." The average American would probably find life in Scandinavia rather uncomfortable due to high taxes, strict government regulation, limited consumer choice, smaller dwelling units, social conformity, and a soft work ethic, not to mention possible boredom. There are also growing concerns about the quality of education in Scandinavia. Moreover, the Scandinavian system may ultimately prove to be so counterproductive for economic growth that it becomes unsustainable. At any one time more than 20 percent of working-age Swedes are either on sick leave, unemployed, or have taken early retirement, and the nation has recently sunk to one of the lowest per capita income levels in Western Europe! (Reported in Sweden's leading newspaper, *Dagen's Nyheter,* on August 23, 2004.) But in the meantime, and compared to other modern nations, the system seems particularly good for the rearing of young children.

The Scandinavian childrearing advantage is probably as much cultural as governmental, as much due to the way Scandinavians think about children as to specific welfare state policies (although the two are, of course, interrelated.) Scandinavian culture has always been more child centered than the more individualistic Anglo societies. The emphasis in Scandinavian culture on nature and the outdoor environment, conflict-aversion, and even social conformity happens to be especially child friendly. Children benefit from highly structured, stable, and low-conflict settings. There are in Scandinavia many statues of children and mothers in public parks (in place of war heroes!), and planned housing environments are heavily oriented to pedestrian access and children's play. Scandinavian children even have their own Ombudsmen who represent them officially in the government and monitor children's rights and interests. Interestingly, Minnesota—the most Scandinavian-settled U.S. state—was recently ranked the number one state in the nation for child well-being by the Kids Count Data Book. (Annie E. Casey Foundation, 2004, Baltimore, MD).

Scandinavian Family Policies

The Scandinavian concern for children, sometimes even smacking of "traditional family values," is expressed in some areas that should surprise those Americans who think only of "decadent welfare states." For example, all Swedish married couples with children aged 16 and younger, should they want a divorce, have a six-month waiting period before a divorce becomes final. Most American states make no distinction in their divorce laws between couples with children and those without. In vitro fertilization in Sweden can be performed only if the woman is married or cohabiting in a relationship resembling marriage, and completely anonymous sperm donations are not allowed, whereas the practice of "assisted reproduction" in America goes virtually unregulated. And no Swedish abortion can take place after the 18th week of pregnancy, except under special circumstances and only with permission from the National Board of Health. The laws permitting abortion are much more liberal in the United States. Some of these positions are made possible, of course, by the fact that the Scandinavian societies are more homogeneous, unified, and less rights-oriented than the United States.

Just as in the United States at least up until welfare reform, welfare policies in Scandinavia have not been drawn up with an eye toward encouraging marriage and limiting family breakup, a very serious problem as noted above. There are relatively few economic disincentives to becoming a single parent in Sweden, in fact probably fewer than in any other society in the world. Nevertheless, many Scandinavian welfare-state policies have brought significant benefits to children and to childrearing families. Scandinavian family leave policies, especially, seem highly desirable for young children. Almost all mothers in Sweden, for example, and far more than in the United States, are at home with their infants up until age one—which is the critical year for mother-child connection. They have one year off from their jobs at 80 percent or more of their salary (and an additional six months at reduced salary), with a guarantee of returning to their old jobs or an equivalent when they reenter the labor force. Recently, two months leave has been set aside solely for fathers to take; if they don't take it, the benefit is lost. Because of these family-leave policies very few Swedish infants under the age of one are in day care or other out-of-home child care arrangement, a quite different situation from the United States. In addition, to help defray the expenses of childrearing, all Swedish parents receive a non-means-tested child allowance and there is also a means-tested housing allowance.

Beyond these benefits, Scandinavian mothers and fathers have far more flex-time from their work to be home with children during the growing-up years, and most women with young children work just part time. There are certainly fewer full-time, non-working, stay-at-home mothers in Sweden than in the United States, in fact almost none because it is economically prohibitive. But in actual parenting time—although good comparative data are unavailable—Sweden may well be in the lead. The larger number of stay-at-home moms in the United States is off-set by the larger number of full-time working mothers, many of whom return to work during their child's first year. It is of interest to note that many fewer Swedish women have top positions in the private sector than is the case in the United States, and this has long been a bone of contention for American feminists when they look at Sweden. By one recent analysis, only 1.5 percent of senior management positions are filled by women in Sweden, compared to 11 percent in the United States. The amount of time that Swedish mothers devote to child care clearly has affected their ability to rise in the private sector hierarchy of jobs, although this is off-set in some degree by their much stronger status in the public sector where a high percentage of the jobs are located.

As a result of welfare state policies child poverty in Sweden is virtually nonexistent (for the 1990s, 1 percent compared to 15 percent in the United States) and all children are covered by health insurance. These and related factors are doubtless of importance in placing Sweden at the top of the list of the best places in the world to live, surpassed only by Norway according to the Human Development Index prepared by the United Nations Development Program (2004), and based on income, life expectancy and education. The United States ranks well down the list, in eighth place, no doubt due in part to the fact that we have a different population mix than other nations.

Again, the two societies are such polar opposites, at least among Western nations, as we have indicated, that it is a mistake to think that what works in Sweden could necessarily be transplanted to the United States. Up to now, at least, the Scandinavian nations have had that strong sense of "brotherhood" or "sisterhood" that is required for a strong welfare state. The common sentiment has been that the high taxes are going for a good cause, "my fellow Swede." Indeed, the lack of outcry against high taxation in Scandinavia comes as a shock to most visiting Americans. To suggest that this communal spirit and attitude toward government and taxation could ever exist in the United States, with all its diversity and individualism, is to enter the realm of utopian thinking. Thus, it is unclear how many of these family policies could be implemented in the United States, and what their actual effect would be if they were.

This leaves us with a final conclusion from the Scandinavian family experience, a more general one. The fact that family breakdown has occurred so prevalently in both the United States and Scandinavia, two almost opposite socioeconomic systems, suggests that the root cause lies beyond politics and economics and even national culture in an overarching trend of modernity that affects all advanced, industrial societies. Basic to this trend is the growth of a modern form of individualism, the single-minded pursuit of personal autonomy and self-interest, which takes place at the expense of established social institutions such as marriage. It shows up in low marriage and high cohabitation rates in the Scandinavian societies, even though they are relatively communitarian. And it is expressed in high divorce and high solo parenting rates in the United States, despite our nation's relatively religious character.

One paramount family goal for modern societies today, put forward by many experts, is to create the conditions whereby an increasing number of children are able to grow up with their own two married parents. If this is a worthy goal, both Scandinavia and the United States have failed badly, and millions of children have been hurt. If we are to take seriously the record of recent history in these nations, the market economy on its own, no matter how strong, is unlikely to be of much help in achieving this goal. The wealthier we become, the weaker the family. But neither helpful, apparently, are the many governmental policies of the welfare state. They may help to soften the impact of family breakup, but the state appears relatively powerless to contain family decline and often even contributes to it. What we must look for, are ways to curtail the growth of modern individualism. While in Scandinavia the main thrust of such efforts probably should focus on resisting the anti-marriage influences of political ideologies and social policies, in the United States the issue is to find better ways to insulate marriage and the family from the pernicious effects of a self-interested market economy that is tethered increasingly to a coarsening popular culture.

Critical Thinking

1. What are the two key differences between U.S. and Swedish marriages?

2. According to Popenoe, one reason that the marriage rate is so low is due to religious pressures. Do you see these types of religious pressures in the United States?

3. Thinking about governmental influences on marriage, what do you see as benefits from federal and state governments, such as tax incentives in the United States, and weaknesses?

4. When comparing both cultures, where would you rather raise a family and why?

DAVID POPENOE is co-director of the National Marriage Project at Rutgers, The State University of New Jersey. He is author of *War Over the Family*, *Disturbing the Nest*, and *Private Pleasure, Public Plight* all available from Transaction.

The Significant Dynamic Relationship between Globalization and Families

BAHIRA SHERIF TRASK, PHD

Globalization is associated with profound changes for individuals and families in the United States and abroad. Some of these changes have been highlighted through the recent global economic recession. We are increasingly aware that economic downturns and governmental policies affect everyone's lives, often with unexpected consequences. Furthermore, rapid advances in communication and information technologies are changing the ways in which individuals connect, access information, and interact with each other. The farthest corners of the world now accessible, in ways that most of us were unable to imagine even just several years ago. All of these developments are related to globalization. Due to a number of factors however, in most people's minds, globalization remains primarily associated with economics and politics. In reality, globalization is closely related to both the major and day to day decisions that families make with respect to work issues, gender roles, the raising of children and care of the elderly, and moving and migration.

What Is Globalization?

Even though globalization is a complicated controversial phenomenon, there is some agreement that it refers to an economic and political process, and that it also entails a new form of connecting geographic and cultural distances. Globalization as a concept and a term, entered mainstream discussions in economics and political science from the mid-1990s onwards (Rodrik, 1997). With respect to globalization, of particular interest has been the flow of money and capital between countries, the changing role of governments vis a vis their citizenry, the increased movement and migration of individuals within and between countries, and the growth and expansion of multinational corporations and transnational organizations. However, despite the fact that individuals and families are affected by all of these issues, there has been remarkably little attention focused on the societal effects of globalization. This omission is important because it is specifically families, communities, and social life that are affected by globalization (Baars, Dannefer, Phillipson, & Walker, 2006).

Despite the lack of analyses of the effects of globalization on social life, individuals and families are directly and indirectly affected by globalizing processes all over the world. While family arrangements may vary, depending on place and time, some form of family or kin relationships characterize all societies. As individuals, families, communities, and societies increasingly become integrated into new complex globalized systems, their values, traditions, and relationships change (Parkin & Stone, 2004). Moreover, we often find that different groups of people react very differently to globalization. Globalization transmits new concepts about gender, work citizenship, identity, familial relationships, and women's and children's rights around the globe. In some cases, these concepts empower individuals and their families to change their lives, and in other cases, they are forced into situations that are disadvantageous and destructive. Also, in some places in the world, globalization is perceived as a form of enforced Westernization. The response to the assumption of dominance of Westernization is often nationalistic and fundamentalist. In an effort to preserve "traditional" values and beliefs, people turn back to what they believe are the authentic traditions and beliefs of their societies, sometimes even use violence to enforce their values.

Globalization and Migration

An important part of globalization is the movement of individuals within societies and across national borders. Migration is most commonly associated with seeking new work opportunities, but at times individuals and families migrate due to political and other social reasons. Specifically, international migration has led to a new type of family form, also known as transnational families. Transnational families are characterized by retaining roots in their home societies and simultaneously also creating new ties in their host countries. While proportionally to the world population, actual migration numbers are low (currently approximately 3 percent of the global population is on the move), modern migration has significant social effects. Most individuals migrate as families or in groups, and their residency in the new host society has a significant impact on both their country of origin, as well as the receiving society (Castles & Miller, 2003). For example, immigrants may be highly educated and possess important skills which benefit the receiving society but they also leave behind in their home countries what is commonly referred to as the "brain drain"—not enough highly educated people to take on important jobs that require education and skills, and could potentially improve the conditions in these countries. There are also other types of immigrants. For example, immigrants may be uneducated, poorer members of their home societies who leave and are then willing to take on the lowest level jobs in the host country. In either case, immigrants often send back extensive remittances (money to their relatives back home) that make a significant economic impact on their home societies.

Increasingly, transnational families are also associated with a phenomenon sometimes referred to as transnational mothering (Mortgan & Zippel, 2003). As service jobs in the industrialized world have multiplied, women from poorer countries are leaving their families behind in order to earn an income in other parts of the world. Women who leave their families to work abroad most often do this in order to help their families financially, and specifically to provide a future better life for their children. Many of these migrating women take on jobs associated with domestic labor such as cleaning houses and providing child and elder care. Most often women who migrate do so because there is a lack of economic opportunities in their home societies. However, this fact is often overlooked in political and academic discussions and analyses. Instead, because migrating women so often leave their children behind in their home countries, they are criticized and referred to as "negligent" or "uncaring" mothers by individuals in their host and home societies. Nevertheless, these women take on migration and its accompanying life styles and challenges and adapt their mothering styles with the hope of one day bettering the lives of their children. They usually make arrangements with their husbands (if there is a husband in the picture) and extended families to take care of their children while they are abroad. The growing phenomenon of transnational mothering illustrates that globalization can have significant impacts on family life that are not easily understood from a superficial perspective.

Globalization and Gender

As the migration example illustrates, globalization has had a profound effect on the lives of women, men, and children. It is worth noting that women as a group have been specifically and significantly impacted by globalizing processes. For example, for women around the world, there are today increasing chances for education, training, and work. In the West, specifically middle class women have seen new opportunities open up with respect to jobs, education, and equal rights over the last fifty years. Interestingly, in less developed countries, there has also been an increasing concern with the status of women. Some governments and international non-profits have set up training programs for poor and rural women in order to advance their lives. While these opportunities have not benefited all women, their very presence indicates that under the correct circumstances, globalizing forces can have positive effects on individuals' lives.

For the majority of women the world over, however, globalization has not necessarily improved their lives. Particularly

in the developing world, but also in parts of the industrialized world, we are increasingly seeing what is termed as the "feminization of the labor force." This term refers to the growing number of women who are working outside of the home in paid employment. Most of the time, these women are working in employment that is more flexible than traditional U.S. 8—5 jobs and in informal types of work that are part time and come without benefits. Both in the U.S. and other countries, this trend has been accompanied by a decrease in the types of jobs that have regularly been held by men—full time jobs with benefits for the whole family (Safa, 2002).

As an increasing number of women take on this type of work, and as more men lose their role as the primary breadwinner, gender roles and relationships are changing. We see this particularly in the United States, Canada, Australia, and Europe, where there has been an increase in new living arrangements such as cohabitation, a rising divorce rate, and out of wedlock births. Moreover, cross-cultural research reveals that as economic bonds in families are changing with an increased number of women working in the paid labor force, the concept of marriage is shifting in response. For example, as women are able to earn their own living, they are less likely to stay in destructive and abusive relationships, or they may choose not to marry at all. These changes have results in a global rise in divorce and an increase in female-headed households. As women's roles are changing, diverse family structures are becoming more common even in places such South East Asia and the Middle East, where cultural beliefs about traditional roles in families have long played a significant role in preserving certain aspects of those societies (Moghadam, 2003).

In a discussion about the changing roles of women and men, is also important to remember that millions of women worldwide do not have the same freedom with respect to making choices about their marriages, working outside of the home, and having control over their money, such as those that are available to middle class Western women. For many women, especially rural and low-income women, working outside of the home in the formal and informal labor force has not bettered their lives. Instead, these women now carry the double burden of working for pay and having to take care of the home, the children, the disabled, and the elderly.

Globalization has also had a serious impact on the roles of men. As a significant number of men have lost their jobs and their primary role as breadwinner/provider, they have had to adjust to new roles in the family. For example, middle class American men today are more likely to be involved with home responsibilities and child care than men in previous generations. However, these types of changes in family life have not necessarily occurred across the world. Instead, in some areas and in some cases, men have reacted with anger over the loss of what they perceive as their basic rights. In fact, there is some evidence that domestic violence rises in those places where men have been out of work for a significant period of time. Since most men the world over are raised to believe that men are to be the primary provider/breadwinner, when they lose that role, they may react in unexpected and at times violent ways. The clash of values that results from globalizing processes that draw women into the paid labor force conflicts with traditional values pertaining to the roles of women and men (Yan & Neal, 2006). Further, many of these conflicts are heightened through the spread of media and Internet images of the lives and rights of women in the West compared to those in other places.

Globalization and Children

While there is quite a bit of research on the relationship between globalization and women's changing roles, we know much less about the relationship between globalization and children. Globalization has produced and spread a popular vision of what childhood is supposed to be like, and what children should do with their time (Kuznesof, 2005). From a Western perspective, children need to be "protected" from harsh surroundings and complex situations, they should "play," and they ought to go to school. However, this concept of children and childhood does not fit neatly with the day to day realities of the lives of children in many parts of the world, raising complicated questions about universal concepts about the lives and rights of children.

Ideas about childhood and what children are like and what they are capable of are determined by the social context and the historical period in society in which they grow up. Historically, we have had very different beliefs about the capabilities of children. For example, during colonial times, children were raised very strictly and most children began learning a work related skill (usually through an apprenticeship) at a very young age (Malkki & Martin, 2003). In part, due to globalization, we have a very different situation today. Western, and specifically, American concepts about children and childhood are spreading to parts of the world where children live under very different conditions. For example, many contemporary children are growing up in war zones, areas ravaged by HIV/AIDS, and/or areas of extreme poverty. Under those conditions, children are unable to go to school and have no access to an easy, carefree childhood. Even here in the U.S., many children grow up in areas that are crime ridden and extremely poor. These conditions do not allow them to have the kind of childhood that is encouraged and promoted by so much of the current child pedagogy literature, raising complicated questions about the universal application of our ideas about children and childhood. What may be appropriate in one context, for example, for white middle class American children, may not be fit in any way the lives of street children in Brazil. While this was also true in the past, in the contemporary context information flows more easily between societies and places. And since the West tends to dominate information flows, we are increasingly setting the standard for what is appropriate—or at least what we feel is appropriate when it comes to children and childhood experiences.

Another complex issue arising out of our globalized context is the disputed topic of children's rights. Children's rights are closely related to debates on human rights, which many feel have been, by far, one of the most important aspects of a growing system of globally shared values (Kaufman, 2002). The concept of human rights encompasses the idea that the world's most vulnerable individuals including minorities, women, children, and the disabled should receive equal protection under the law. This is based on the idea that all people have a shared humanity, irrespective of their nationality. For much of recorded history, children from many societies were not accorded the status of being "fully human" and were allowed to be sold and exchanged as if they were possessions. However, over the course of the last century, this situation changed and culminated in the global adoption in 1989 of the Convention on the Rights of the Child. This convention entails the protection of the largest single group (children) that any legal document with respect to human rights has ever dealt with. By signing on, countries take on a legal obligation to ensure the "best interests of the child" and work towards the survival, development, and protection of their nations' children. According to the Convention, children have certain basic rights that include the right to life, to their own name and identity, to be raised within their own families or cultural groupings, to express their opinions, to be protected from abuse, and to have their privacy protected. Currently, the only two countries in the world that have not signed on to the Convention on the Rights of the Child are the United States and Somalia. Much of the opposition in the U.S. comes from individuals who believe that there are some basic conflicts between the Convention and the Constitution and due to the resistance of some religious and political conservatives. Moreover, certain factions in the U.S. worry that by signing on to an international legal document, the U.S. will be bound to external international control over what are deemed as domestic policies.

Closely related to the issue of children's rights is the complicated topic of child labor. Current statistics indicate that child labor is actually increasing instead of declining. The International Labor Organization (ILO) (2002) estimates that approximately 352 million five- to seventeen-year-olds around the globe work in some form, and that out of this group about two-thirds of young workers are defined as "child laborers." Most of these children work, primarily on family farms, in their families' households, in small manufacturing businesses, and in mining. Some children are also involved with the production of carpets, garments, furniture, textiles, and shoes (French & Wokutch, 2005). Included in the statistics on child labor are a small group of children around the world who live on the street and participate in a wide range of legal or illegal activities or are involved in prostitution.

Globalization and engagement with the Convention on the Rights of the Child has raised awareness about the issue of child labor. Images of children working in sweat shops and hard labor move across the Internet and the media easily and have raised, in particular, concerns in the West about the lives of children in other parts of the world. Even people who would usually not be that concerned with social justice issues have spoken out publicly and led crusades banning "third world labor practices." This has led to international boycotts of certain brands and corporations who supposedly rely on this type of exploitive behavior for the production of their goods. What is rarely understood in these debates is that there is a great deal of controversy about what constitutes child labor, and to what extent enforcing a Western type of childhood would actually benefit these children. Often the children who are engaged in child labor are doing so to support their families and kin groups because there is no other way for them to survive. For example, in certain parts of Africa, many children have lost both of their parents to the HIV/AIDS crisis. The only way for them and their siblings to make any kind of a living is for some members of the family, or even for all of them, to work at whatever employment is available. This is only one example, but it points to the fact that we need to be more sensitive about the contexts in which children live, and we need to allow for some variation in their personal circumstances.

The complexity of child labor disputes is further heightened by the conflicts over what exactly constitutes "work". There are some types of jobs such as working in mines that are clearly harmful to children's health. However, it is unclear if helping on the family farm is really physically and psychologically damaging to a teenager. Critics of universal labor laws argue that if a family's survival depends on children's work, and if they are not being placed in harm's way, it may actually have social and personal benefits to not enforce a uniform approach to child labor. In other words, we should institute some basic laws that ensure the safety of all children, but that with respect to work, certain types of labor should be permitted. Moreover, gender needs to be taken into account in these discussions. Often, depending on cultural context, it is girls who are taken out of school and asked to take over domestic responsibilities such as cooking and child care, while their mothers work outside of the home and their brothers go to school. Statistics on child labor often do not include these employed girls, because their duties are not understood to be "real work." However, it is clearly these girls, life chances that become permanently constrained due to their lack of education. Again, this indicates that we need to think carefully about enforcing universal concepts such as the rights of children and the prohibition of child labor. An approach that universalizes the needs, beliefs, and rights of all children can have unintended detrimental consequences, thus it is imperative that local conditions also be taken into account.

The Continuing Significance of Families

While this article has raised awareness about some of the complex issues that are faced by individuals and families, in a globalized context, it has also highlighted the fact that there is a close relationship between globalization and families. In all parts of the world, individuals, be they children or adults, still make decisions in the context of those that they consider to be family or they have a close, family-like bond to. Families act as a buffer between globalizing forces and the choices and challenges that individuals need to deal with (Edgar, 2004). However, globalization has varying effects and means different things depending on where people live and what their particular social, political, and economic situation is like. Globalization can allow individuals to be exposed to new ideas and resources; however, globalization can also mean that certain groups become poorer or are treated in a way that is not in synch with their particular culture or situation. Moreover, particularly in

non-Western concepts the whole family often functions specifically as an economic unit (Kelly, 2001). Decisions with respect to who works, what they do, and if they work near their home or in a far away locale is closely tied to family decision making and often family survival. Globalization has provided the venue for many people to seek out new opportunities. But it has also limited the options of others. For example, it is now possible for an unemployed nurse from the Philippines to find work in Hong Kong and send money back to her family. However, a family father from a small mid-Western industrial town may find that after twenty years of devoted employment, he is permanently laid off from his manufacturing site, because his job has been outsourced to China. Both of these trends are related to globalization, making it difficult to speak about globalization as either just a positive or a negative force in individuals' and families' lives. We can also not assume that globalization will lead to all families having similar lives and sharing the same tastes despite increasing global exposure to similar messages and goods. Instead, we need to realize that people live in very varied circumstances and that these local contexts are an important component for how global messages and products are received. Maybe most importantly, it is critical to understand that globalization is related to fast, intense social change. None of us are immune to these changes but our experiences will vary depending on where we live and what our particular circumstances may be.

References

Baars, J., Dannefer, D., Phillipson, C., & Walker, A. (2006). Introduction: Critical perspectives in social gerontology. In J. Baars, D. Dannefer, C. Phillipson, & A. Walker, (Eds.), *Aging, globalization and inequality: The new critical gerontology.* (pp. 1–16). Amityville, NY: Baywood Publishing.

Castles, S., & Miller, M. (2003). *The age of migration: International population movements in the modern world.* New York: Guilford Press.

Edgar, D. (2004). Globalization and Western bias in family sociology. In J. Scott, J. Treas, & M. Richards (Eds.), *The Blackwell companion to the sociology of families* (pp. 3–16). Malden, MA: Oxford University Press.

French, J.L., & Woktuch, R. E. (2005). Child workers, globalization, and international business ethics: A case study in Brazil's export-oriented shoe industry. *Business Ethics Quarterly, 15,* 615–640.

Kaufman, N. (2002). The status of children in international law. In N. Kauman & I. Rizzini, (Eds.), *Globalization and children: Exploring potentials for enhancing opportunities in the lives of children and youth,* (pp. 31–45.) New York: Springer.

Kelly, R.M. (2001). *Gender, globalization and democratization.* Lanham, MD: Rowman & Littlefield Publishers.

Kuznesof, E. (2005). The house, the street, global society: Latin American families and childhood in the twenty-first century. *Journal of Social History, 38,* 859–872.

Malkki, L., & Martin, E. (2003). Children and the gendered politics of globalization: In remembrance of Sharon Stephens. *American Ethnologist, 30,* 216–224.

Moghadam, V. (2003). A political explanation of the gendered division of labor in Japan. In M. Marchand & A. Runyan (Eds.),

Gender and global restructuring: Sightings, sites and resistances (pp. 99–115). London: Routledge.

Mortgan, K., & Zippel, K. (2003). "Paid to care: The origins and effects of care leave policies in Western Europe." *Social Politics: International Studies in Gender, State, and Society, 10,* 49–85.

Parkin, R., & Stone, L. (2004). *Kinship and family: An anthropological reader.* New York: Blackwell.

Rodrik, D. (1997). *Has globalization gone too far?* Washington, Institute for International Economics.

Safa, H. (2002). Questioning globalization: Gender and export processing in the Dominican Republic. *Journal of Developing Societies, 18,* 11–31.

Yan, R., & Neal, A. (2006). The impact of globalization on family relations in China. *International Journal of Sociology of the family, 32,* 113–125.

Critical Thinking

1. Describe globalization and how it impacts families.

2. If you were a mother who had to go to a different country to find work, would you be able to leave your children behind? What are your thoughts about the concept of transnational mothering?

3. Do you feel that globalization has had a greater impact on men or women?

4. Explain some of the human rights issues that were addressed in the article. If you were a policymaker, how would you address child labor?

5. What are some of the impacts from globalization between families in an industrialized nations such as the United States and poorer countries?

Matches Made on Earth
Why Family Values Are Human Values

Nancie L. Gonzalez

The term "family values," the importance of which fundamentalist Christians have been preaching for decades, continues to permeate religious and political printed matter and discussions in the United States today. The conservatives' concept of family values is generally characterized by abstinence from sex until marriage, which is then entered into with a like-minded individual of the opposite sex and is thereafter permanent and free from adultery. It is also expected that children will ensue, either through birth or adoption. In line with these prescriptions, proponents of traditional family values foment prejudice and activism against divorce, abortion, homosexuality, single-parent families, and even the choice not to have children. The fact that their efforts have become more intensive and intrusive lately can be explained, I believe, by the increasingly tolerant and diverse sexual, racial, and religious views and behavior of the American public at large.

The problem isn't that some people espouse conservative ideals of family, but that they promulgate them as the only way to live, looking down upon and often demonizing those with other values. Indeed, the family values crowd often refers to any who oppose its agenda as having no values at all. They support their ideals as based upon divine "truth" by quoting the Bible and rejecting scientific evidence that supports a different set of explanations for the existence and history of humankind. They repeatedly argue that more general social acceptance of other ways to live will endanger their own. This fear has inspired efforts for decades to influence our school boards and our local, state, and national governments to change text books, curricula, and the law to reflect socially conservative views. When these fail, parents turn to private schools or home schooling, and later enroll their offspring in one of the several conservative Christian colleges whose faculties and administrative personnel are vetted to make sure their values are religiously and politically "correct." The fact that some of these schools are admittedly training their graduates to seek public office or employment in state and national venues is further evidence of their intolerance, and their misunderstanding of the nature of society and culture.

Most of the idealistic family values held by conservative Christians today are not now nor have they ever been characteristic of the world at large. Statistics, as well as more informal evidence suggest that the so-called nontraditional behaviors they condemn are now common throughout the United States and much of the industrialized world, often despite laws forbidding them. Furthermore, such behaviors have existed in many parts of the world for centuries. The problem I see for humanists is to convince much of the conservative American public that these prejudices and fears are unwarranted on at least two grounds: 1) family values are the products of human sociocultural conditions, and cannot be attributed to either divine or biological imperatives, and 2) pluralism in marriage and family values should be expected in any large twenty-first century society as a result of technological advances that have made globalization both possible and perhaps inevitable.

If neither a deity nor our genes are wholly determinative, we must ask our conservative counterparts: what accounts for the vast panorama of intimate human bonding practices, either in the past, or today?

It may be useful to consider what social and biological scientists have concluded about the origin and nature of marriage and the family. All animals must struggle for self and species survival, which demands food, defense, reproduction, and care of newborns until they can care for themselves. Both genetics and learning are involved for all species, but only humans have created *social institutions* to help themselves in these endeavors. By social, I mean any kind of bonding with other humans to share in the food quest; to ward off environmental and other dangers; to reproduce, nurture, and educate the young; and to provide physical and psychological well-being for themselves, their children, and their neighbors. The specific characteristics of these institutions vary with the society; trial and error must have occurred over time, and some societies failed to persist. But those institutions that worked well became customary, "traditional," and thus value-laden. Children would be taught by example and by experience. But traditions change as cultural evolution occurs and as societies grow, develop new technologies, and increasingly influence each other. The young and the most pragmatically minded are likely to change with the times, yet there are always some who cling to the older ways—not that this is, in itself, dysfunctional, for the "old ways" still serve some purposes, and sometimes are reinstated or reinterpreted by succeeding generations.

Although marriage and the family have existed in all human societies and form the primary roots of all the particulars of family values everywhere, different societies have constructed their own definitions of incest; permissible marriage partners; appropriate sexual behavior before, during, and after marriage; "normal" and alternate sexual orientations; ideal post-marital residence; and composition of the ideal family and household, including what to do if too many children "appear," or if conception occurs at an inconvenient time. For example, marriages that we likely consider incestuous but others don't include marriage between first cousins, especially patrilateral parallel cousin marriage (where the children of two brothers marry) seen in some parts of the Middle East and Africa. Among some Bedouin cultures, there was even a stated preference for such a marriage. Similarly, cross-cousin marriage is widespread in many "tribal" societies, including the Yanomamo in South America.

Different societies have constructed their own definitions of incest appropriate sexual behavior, "normal" and alternate sexual orientations, and ideal post-marital residence.

Formal bonding or marriage rituals probably developed in very early human societies, since it was important then as now to confer legitimacy of the children in relation to membership in whatever social unit was pertinent (tribe, clan, patrilineage, matrilineage, nation-state, religious group, and so forth). Formal marriage also establishes rights of inheritance of property, as well as social position. In many societies, including our own, women, and to a lesser extent, men, are treated like adolescents until they marry.

Neither religious nor biological explanations for conservative family values take into account the fact that even the notion of two sexes is not, and probably never has been, biologically correct. We have no way to know whether prehistoric societies recognized inborn sexual variations, what the frequency of such variations might have been, or whether "different" newborns would even have been allowed to live. However, colonial travelers to America noted that some native cultures recognized the existence of some among them whose bodies, psyches, or both weren't comfortable living in either of the two primary gender roles of male or female. They called these people "two spirits" and provided a socially acceptable niche for them.

Homosexuality of different types has been documented throughout Western civilization since at least the ancient Greeks. However, only in the current century has the recognition developed in Western societies that sexual orientation is not merely a matter of differences in genitalia, and that it isn't a mere matter of choice. The growing acceptance of the idea that sexuality and sexual identity should not alter one's basic humanity and civil rights has led to changes in the laws in many countries, including the decriminalization of certain sex practices and the legalization of same-sex marriage. At the time of this writing, five U.S. states as well as the District of Columbia now allow gay and lesbian couples to marry, and in three more states same-sex marriages are recognized but not performed legally. Nine other states recognize certain legal rights of same-sex couples through civil unions, domestic partnerships, or reciprocal beneficiary laws. Still, these arrangements are only gradually becoming acceptable to the general public, and since same-sex marriage hasn't been documented as legal in any society in history, we shouldn't be surprised that it is and will remain controversial for some time. Nevertheless, it should now be added to the evidence we have for different kinds of marriage and family institutions.

Studies of pre-agricultural and pre-industrial societies, as well as continuing historical research over the past century have documented such a variety of marriage customs and rules that a God hypothesis would almost have to suggest an anthropological deity who understood that no single practice should be imposed upon all. However, the following discussion focuses not on the supernatural, but the natural ways in which human pair bonding and family formation have occurred. These include *monogamy* as the permanent or lifetime union of two persons, usually, but not always, of opposite sex. This was probably the most common marriage form for Paleolithic foragers, as was the nuclear family. However, that small unit had affinal relatives (we call them in-laws), some of whom lived together in what anthropologists call a band. As the noted nineteenth-century anthropologist Edward B. Tylor suggested, early societies had to "marry out or die out." Institutions promoting reproduction and care of the young were crucial to social survival.

Polygamy is often confused with *polygyny—the* union of one man with several wives—but polygamy also includes *polyandry—one* woman with several husbands. All of these forms, especially polygyny, were more typical of larger, more advanced societies based upon pastoralism, agriculture, or both. The advantages were to enlarge the family unit by drawing in more nubile and fertile women, while at the same time providing care for those who might no longer have been able to bear children. If the sex ratio, for whatever reason, was unbalanced, as it was among early converts to the Church of the Latter Day Saints, polygyny also was a way for new single young women to be immediately drawn in to an existing family. The custom was formally abolished by the Mormons in the early part of the twentieth century, but the family values created more than one hundred years earlier have held on for some.

Polyandry has been fairly rare, practiced primarily in the Himalayan regions of Nepal, Tibet, India, and Bhutan. It has also occurred in the Canadian Arctic, Nigeria, and Sri Lanka, and is known to have been present in some pre-contact Polynesian societies, though probably only among higher caste women. Some forms of polyandry appear to be associated with a perceived need to retain aristocratic titles or agricultural lands within kin groups, and/or because of the frequent absence, for long periods, of a man from the household. In Tibet the practice is particularly popular among the priestly Skye class but also among poor small farmers who can ill afford to divide their small holdings. As to the latter variety, as some males return to the household, others leave for a long time, so that there is usually one husband present. Fraternal polyandry occurs when multiple brothers share a common wife. This occurs in the pastoral Toda community in Southern India. Similarly, among the Tibetan Nyinba, anthropologist Nancy Levine described the strong bond between brothers as essential in creating a strong sense of family unity and keeping land holdings intact, thus preserving socioeconomic standing.

Group marriage involving multiple members of both sexes has sometimes been averred to have existed; however, there appears to be no reputable description of it in the anthropological or historical literature. In recent years a movement has arisen that produces something very similar to the idea of group marriage; the term *polyamory* has been offered to describe plural simultaneous attachments between and among people, including lesbian, gay, bisexual, and transgendered individuals (LGBTs). From the perspective of this writing, this may or may not be new under the sun, but it doesn't (yet?) constitute marriage.

Serial monogamy is perhaps the most common type of marriage known in much of the world today. Individuals in such unions may have only one spouse but, shedding that one, they may contract any number later—again, usually only one at a time, except in those societies that still accept and approve polygyny. Serial monogamy depends on the existence of easy divorce laws or more informal practices, such as what is generally called "living together." *Domestic partnerships* by law may or may not be considered marriages. In the United States persons of both the same and opposite sex have for some time entered into such unions, but those of opposite sex partners have generally received greater social acceptance, even without the legal protections, status, or financial benefits society offers to married couples.

Why do some people choose not to abide by the marriage rules of their own society? Obviously, reasons vary. Some think a trial marriage to be a good idea; others simply don't care about rules of any kind. A few may be prohibited from marrying because one or the other is already bound by a previous, legitimate union which can't be formally dissolved. And while others have simply adopted a more individualized lifestyle, some are still convinced of the values of marriage in a previous age (as in polygyny). In short, the choice of whether and whom to marry has increasingly been seen as a personal, individual decision, and it is no longer important to the functioning of the modern industrial state that all persons marry, unless they wish the state to adjudicate property or child custody rights.

Co-residence of the partners and the creation of a household are usually, but not always, typical in any kind of marriage. Yet households vary enormously in both size and composition, and usually, but not always, include some kind of family. In societies in which men must find work through short or long term emigration, *consanguineal households* have arisen that contain no married pair. Such a household is most often headed by an elderly woman, together with some of her sons and daughters and their children. The marital partners of these co-residential adults live elsewhere—often with their own mothers. The United States today is also seeing an increase in extended families moving in together due to economic constraints, as well as "single" parents who live with a partner.

A study by the Pew Research Center released in November, titled, "The Decline of Marriage and Rise of New Families," revealed changing attitudes about what constitutes a family. Among survey respondents, 86 percent said a single parent and child constitute a family; 80 percent considered an unmarried couple living together with a child a family; and 63 percent said a gay or lesbian couple raising a child is a family.

Obviously, the "traditional family" so highly valued by the religious right can't be considered as the typical American household today. Instead, the term "family" has taken on a much broader meaning to incorporate various combinations of persons of different genders, sexual orientations, and familial

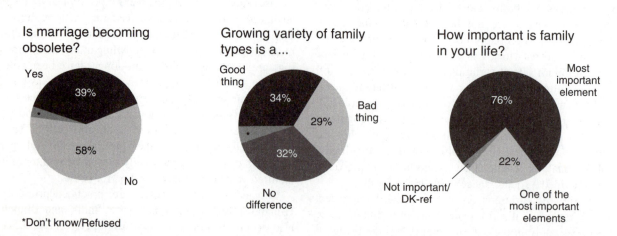

Data from the Pew Research Center's 2010 survey, "The Decline of Marriage and Rise of New Families"

or non-familial relationships living together, as in the refrigerator magnet that proclaims, "Friends Are the Family You Choose for Yourself."

We still, and always will, value the need to bond with others. Kinship remains one major way to do so, but social and geographical mobility have lessened its role as the most important tie that binds. Today it may be similar age groups, vocations, or philosophical views on the nature of the universe or of the hereafter that form the basis of relationships. People will continue to find or invent ways to get together, live together, and share what is important in life with others.

Does this mean that marriage and the family as we know it will likely disappear in the near future as Focus on the Family fears? Does the fact that many young people of various genders and sexual identities choose not to marry or stay married, nor to form traditional households augur the demise, or even the diminution in value of these institutions in our society? Should the legal sanctioning of same-sex marriage in any way affect the dignity of opposite-sex couples joined by similar ceremonies? I think not. Society has, for the most part, already accepted the newer bonding patterns described above—at least for persons of opposite sex.

Taking away any social stigma, LGBT couples will likely experience the same joys and struggles in marriage as straight couples do, thus proving that sexual orientation is irrelevant when it comes to pair-bonding. Although the ethnographic and historical evidence doesn't confirm that true marriages were ever legally sanctioned between persons thought to be of the same sex, present-day reminiscences and folklore suggest that love, sex, and companionship were known and accepted among them, and that untold numbers of people have lived in happy unions with persons perceived to be of the same sex for perhaps hundreds of years.

Finally, what about love and companionship? It is only in modern Western society that these have become the very most important components of marriage. There is no evidence that these occur only between spouses of opposing sex or gender. The idea that sexual activity is only appropriate between members of the opposite sex is a product of our cultural conditioning, born of the thousands of years when it was important to keep people focused on finding a mate of the opposite sex to ensure continued reproduction. The need for population control, rather than survival of the species or of any

specific society, makes this value irrelevant today, as it does for the idea that all marriages should produce children. Also, the extended family of yore is no longer functional in industrial society—today one does indeed marry the individual, not the whole family.

Sex is no longer seen as a major reward for contracting marriage, regardless of one's sexual orientation. Tests of virginity have disappeared as premarital sex with more than one partner has become more common and seems to be a largely irrelevant factor for many marriages, including the first. Yet, the fact that homosexual and lesbian partners engage in sexual activities without marriage is always seen as a disgrace, even for many of them who may share the traditional religious notion that unmarried sex is a sin.

As we continue to consider the nature and causes of the diversity of family values in the post-industrial, individualistic, global society in which we now live, I hope that the single set of specific rules of behavior promulgated by Focus on the Family and other such organizations comes to be seen as outmoded, even by the so-called moral majority. As the U.S. Constitution has always insisted, all citizens should have equal rights, so for those who find the "old ways" to their taste, we should wish them well, but plead with them not to damage the lives of those who choose to live or even to think differently, nor to forget that our nation was founded by outsiders and has continually accepted those from other cultures, and that we have, in fact, valued and profited by our diversity.

Critical Thinking

1. What are some of your family values? Where do your family values come from?

2. Do you feel that family values are a naturally occurring phenomena or are they learned from society and culture?

3. After reading this article are there some family values from your family of origin that differ now that you are in college?

4. What do you think about the author's question about, ". . . marriage and family as we know if disappearing"?

NANCIE L. GONZALEZ is Professor Emeritus of Anthropology at the University of Maryland. She has conducted ethnographic and ethnohistorical research on marriage and family patterns in a number of societies, including the American Southwest, the Caribbean, Central America, China, and the West Bank and has published widely since the 1960s. She is presently working on a memoir dealing with changes in marriage and family patterns as revealed in letters and diaries from five generations of her own family. She lives in Richmond, Virginia.

Family Partnerships That Count

How can schools meaningfully engage families in supporting student learning?

JoBeth Allen

Uptown High School's Mardi Gras Carnival, organized by the 21-person Parent Advisory Council, is a fun family event that raises nearly $1,000 each year.

Midtown Elementary teachers reach their goal of 100 percent participation in parent-teacher conferences, in which they strive to convey all the important information about programs, test scores, and grades in only 15 minutes.

Downtown Middle School draws more than half of its families to Technology Night. Parents walk through impressive exhibits of student projects and then enjoy refreshments in the cafeteria, converted to a student-run Cyberspace Café.

Which of these endeavors to "involve parents" contribute to student learning?

To start a conversation about this question at your school, you might want to gather a group of educators, students, and family members to brain storm a list of everything the school does to involve families. If you're like most schools, it will be an impressive list. Next, put each item in one of three categories: Builds Deep Relationships; Supports Student Learning; or Does Neither (But We Keep Doing It Anyway). Finally, examine the activities in the first two columns and ask, Which families are benefiting? Which families are not?

Contrary to the prevailing myth, when parents or guardians walk into school, their children's learning does not automatically increase. Mattingly, Radmila, McKenzie, Rodriguez, and Kayzar (2002) analyzed 41 parent involvement programs. They concluded that some things we count as parental that Count involvement—being room parents, signing behavior reports, attending PTA meetings, and so on—don't improve student achievement. So what does?

Henderson and Mapp (2002) examined 80 studies on parental involvement, preschool through high school, throughout the United States. They concluded that family involvement was likely to increase student achievement when that involvement was connected to academic learning. Let's look at three important approaches they identified: building respectful relationships, engaging families in supporting learning at home, and addressing cultural differences.

Building Respectful Relationships
Family Funds of Knowledge

Horses. That was the common thread Kathy Amanti noticed from home visits with three families in her multiage bilingual classroom. She learned that Carlos's father was teaching his sons how to care for and ride the family's three horses; that Fernando rode and cared for horses each summer when he stayed with his grandparents in Mexico; and that the Rivera family had gathered to watch a videotape of a relative riding in a horse race in Sonoyta, Mexico.

Surveying the rest of her class, Amanti found a great deal of interest in and knowledge about horses. Together, she and her students designed an interdisciplinary unit on horses, which included taking a field trip to Carlos's home, observing a parent shoeing a horse, and viewing the Riveras' video. Families were resources on individual projects as well, helping students study Spanish explorers; the history of saddles; local horse ordinances; horse anatomy; measurement (converting hands to inches and feet); and horse gestation and evolution.

Amanti was one of a group of teachers and professors who worked with Mexican and Yaqui Indian families in Tucson, Arizona (Gonzáles, Moll, & Amanti, 2005). These educators challenged the deficit model and developed a powerful alternative: learning about and incorporating family *funds of knowledge* into the classroom. Teachers studied the history of their border community. They visited homes and entered into conversations—*not* scripted interviews—centering on family and work history (border crossings, extended families, religious traditions, work experiences); household activities (gardening, home and car repair, caring for children, recreation); and parents' views of their roles (raising children, languages spoken at home, schooling).

The home visits enabled teachers and families to build *confianza* (mutual trust) and to create *reciprocity* (a healthy partnership in which teachers and parents give in ways that support one another and support the student). The teachers learned that all families have important experiences, skills, and knowledge that teachers can tap into. The teachers also became more knowledgeable about how their students learned outside school. For example, in many Mexican and Yaqui families, children are active participants and ask questions that guide their own learning, skills not always encouraged at school.

Throughout the year, teachers met in study groups to discuss what they learned and to create thematic units that built on their community's funds of knowledge. They learned that families had a wealth of knowledge about ranching, farming, mining, and construction. In the area of business, they knew about appraising, renting and selling, labor laws, and building codes. Household management acumen included budgeting, child care, cooking, and repair. Many had knowledge of both contemporary and folk medicine for people and animals. Religious knowledge included rituals; texts (especially the Bible); and moral and ethical understandings.

We've seen how Kathy Amanti incorporated family funds of knowledge into meaningful learning that went beyond the classroom. Here's another example of the way learning with and from families can support student achievement.

Teacher-Parent Partnerships for Learning

Antonio was 13, had a broad vocabulary, and was fluent in oral Spanish and English. He had been homeless for five years, and his family frequently moved. He stopped reading specialist Paula Murphy in the hall one day, asking, "I need help in reading. Can I go to your class?"

Paula started making home visits to Antonio's family at the shelter, at a friend's apartment, and at other temporary housing. She learned that his mother and stepfather helped him with homework; his mother wrote short stories, provided emotional support, and encouraged him to do well in school. Paula designed a reading program that actively involved his parents. She engaged in regular communication with the family. She also intervened with the district so Antonio could stay in her school when the family moved. In one year, Antonio's reading and writing skills improved significantly. Paula reflected,

> As a Puerto Rican . . . I felt that sharing the culture and the language of my Latino students was enough to understand their world. . . . I learned I know nothing about growing up poor, homeless, and in an environment of violence. . . . I learned of my responsibility to understand not only my students' ethnic culture, but their community culture as well. (Murphy, 1994, p. 87)

Although there is no substitute for the personal relationships and deep understanding of family knowledge developed in home visits, it's not always possible for teachers to visit every student's home on a regular basis. But there's another way of learning about a student's life outside of school—hand her a camera!

Photographs of Local Knowledge Sources (PhOLKS)

I was part of a teacher study group in Georgia that used photography to learn about family funds of knowledge (Allen et al., 2002). The PhOLKS group served a culturally, linguistically, and economically diverse student population. Educators in our group were African American, Colombian, and European American; Christian and Jewish; originally from the Northeast, Midwest, and South; with childhoods from poor to privileged. This diversity was essential in mediating our understanding of cultural differences.

With a small grant, we paid for three 35mm cameras, film, and processing for each classroom. We invited students to photograph what was important to them in their homes and neighborhoods. Teachers prepared students by analyzing photographic essays, sharing photographs of their own lives outside school, and inviting parents who enjoyed photography to help students learn how to see through the camera's eye. English as a second language teacher Carmen Urdanivia-English read from her photo-illustrated memoir about growing up in Colombia and then invited a reporter from the local Spanish-language newspaper to show students ways to document family and community histories.

Students took cameras home on a rotating schedule, charged with capturing their out-of-school lives. Teachers invited students and family members to write or dictate stories about their photos. Parents and guardians contributed descriptions, memories, poetry, letters, and personal stories.

Cyndy, a white teacher, worried about Kenesha, a black student who often slept in class. Other teachers at the school said her mother was never involved and had been in special education when she attended the school. When Kenesha took her photo journal home with an invitation to write about the pictures, her mother wrote,

> My daughter name is Kenesha. . . . She is very sweet all the teacher and people love her because she is understanding and nice, polite, sweet, listen, smart. She have her good days & bad days but she is the sweetest child you like to spend time with. . . . Members of the church love to hear her sing she sings so good you love her. She like to read and talk a lot. She loves dogs. She like to play with dolls. She love her new baby brother. (Allen et al., 2002, p. 317)

Cyndy and Kenesha's mother began communicating frequently through notes and phone calls. Mom wanted to know how Kenesha was doing. She promised to make sure Kenesha got more sleep.

One photograph, one invitation, and one letter did not change Kenesha's life. The family still struggled, and so did Kenesha—but now there was a partnership working together to teach her.

Engaging Families in Supporting Learning at Home

The parental support that made a difference for Antonio and Kenesha did not involve parents coming into the classroom, yet the parent-teacher-student relationships affected not only the students' participation in the classroom community but also their learning. That was also the case for the students of two primary-grade teachers with whom I worked in Georgia.

School-Home Reading Journals

I learned about genuine family-school partnerships from Betty Shockley and Barbara Michalove, 1st and 2nd grade teachers (respectively) who invited parents and other family members to join them in teaching their children to read and write.

Betty, Barbara, and I are European American, middle-class, experienced educators who joined in partnership with families in a high-poverty, predominantly black school. To connect home and school literacy learning, Betty and Barbara designed family-school connections including, among other practices, school-home reading journals.

Teachers and families exchanged reading journals all year. Children took home these spiral-bound or sewn notebooks two or three times a week along with books from the classroom libraries. Parents or others in the family sustained a remarkable commitment to read with their children, talk about the books, and write together in the journals.

Betty and Barbara honored the families' investment of time by responding to every entry, as we see from these excerpts from the journal of Lakendra's mother, Janice:

Janice: In the story "I Can Fly" Lakendra did very good. Her reading was very good. And maybe she's ready to move on to . . . a book with a few more words. If you think so also. (9/30)

Betty: I agree. She can read more difficult books but like everybody, young readers enjoy reading things that are easy for them too. (10/1)

Janice: In the story of the Halloween Performance, Lakendra seem to have some problems with many of the words. Maybe she get a story with too many difficult words for her right now. But still I enjoyed her reading. Thank You. Janice (10/2)

Betty: When you get ready to read together each night, you might begin by asking Lakendra, Do you want to read your book to me or do you want me to read to you? Sometimes after you read even a more difficult book, she may ask to read it after you. Let her be the leader. One of the most important things about sharing books together is talking about them together. Thanks. (10/3)

Janice: Lakendra was very excited about the books she chose to read to me. So excited she read them over and over again. And I was so pleased. Maybe last night she did want me to read the story to her I don't know but I will ask her from now on. Because she was a little upset that she didn't know a lot of the words. And I don't ever want her to feel pressured. Thanks. Janice (10/3) (Shockley, Michalove, & Allen, 1995, pp. 42–43)

This kind of extended written communication, which did not involve enlisting parents to solve discipline problems or to sign reading logs, established deep relationships that supported emerging readers and writers at home as well as at school in ways neither teacher nor parent could have accomplished alone. Without ever entering the school, parents became members of the classroom community.

Addressing Cultural Differences

We are all cultural beings shaped by time and place, religion and race, language and gender, and a host of other ongoing influences. In my work with educators, we use a number of strategies as a springboard for conversations among parents and teachers of diverse cultural backgrounds.

For example, drawing maps of childhood neighborhoods, or *memory maps* (Frank, 2003), might take place during a home visit, or in a classroom, or during a whole-school event such as a family night. Each participant draws an annotated map of his or her childhood neighborhood(s). Next, in small groups that include both teachers and families, participants walk one another through their neighborhood maps. Participants at one school had had very different childhood experiences: One of us made daily trips to the corner grocery store in Philadelphia; one rarely left the farm until he was in high school; one moved from a small town in Mexico and learned English at the Boys and Girls Club. We were amazed at the differences as well as the similarities (for example, "Back then it was safe for a child to go to the store alone").

Neighborhood maps may lead to stories of schooling. Each teacher and parent writes down or draws two memories of schooling, one positive and one negative. The sharing of these stories is often quite intense. It's important for parents to know that teachers have both kinds of memories; many parents may believe that all teachers had only positive, successful school experiences. Conversely, teachers need to learn about parents' positive memories as well as the "ghosts at the table," Sara Lawrence-Lightfoot's (2003) expression for those memories from their own schooling that haunt parents and hover over the conference table when parents and teachers try to talk about a student.

A third and potentially deeper exploration of cultural understanding occurs through developing cultural memoirs. Family members—including students—and teachers can ask themselves, Who am I as a cultural being and what are the influences in my life that have made me who I am? These are some ways to approach this project with families:

- *Read and discuss cultural memoirs.* A great place to start is by reading and discussing memoirs deeply contextualized in time and place, such as *All Over But the Shoutin',* by Rick Bragg (Pantheon, 1997), or *The House on Mango Street,* by Sandra Cisneros (Vintage, 1989). Busy parents and teachers may appreciate shorter memoirs from popular magazines, television biopics, or radio broadcasts such as National Public Radio's StoryCorps.

- *Gather photographs and other cultural artifacts.* Go through those boxes, albums, and digital files asking, What were my cultural influences in terms of race, social class, gender, ethnicity, geographic region, religion, nationality, language/dialect, sexual orientation, schooling, physical or mental health or ability, and family structure?
- *Share cultural memoirs.* Create a form to represent your multicultured self, such as a poem, scrapbook, telenovela, photo essay, iMovie, or picture book. Some teachers and parents create classroom coffee house atmospheres and invite families in during the school day, in the evening, or on Saturday to share memoirs. Find out from parents what works for them, and consider holding two or three events so everyone can participate. You might plan one meeting for adults only, but remember that students love hearing their parents' and teachers' stories, too.

Educators and family members begin to understand cultural differences when they share their lives and make connections that build a foundation of respect and trust. When we make culture central to creating family-school partnerships, we acknowledge differences with respect, marvel at similarities, and open up dialogue about how to support each student as a unique learner.

Educators and family members begin to understand cultural differences when they share their lives.

A Starting Point

We've examined funds of knowledge, home visits, photography, reading journals, and other ways teachers have engaged families in creating positive learning experiences for students at home and in the classroom. Any of these practices could be a starting point. But let me suggest another logical place to start. Go back to that list you made of your school's parent involvement activities: Builds Deep Relationships; Supports Student Learning; Does Neither (But We Keep Doing It Anyway).

What are you already doing that you can build on? What might you do with your equivalent of Uptown High School's Mardi Gras Carnival—that fun tradition that doesn't really build relationships or support student learning? In addition to striving for high parent participation in conferences as Midtown Elementary does, what if you held student-led conferences, focusing only on student learning? How could you involve parents in the preparation for a Technology Night event? Perhaps students could interview their parents and grandparents about changes in technology in their lifetimes, how they use technology in their jobs, and the pros and cons of various aspects of technology. Parents might engage with students in studying the effects of technology on global warming by surveying their home, work, and community settings to assess how much energy is used to run computers, cell phones, and other technologies.

How will you create opportunities *with* families?

How will you create opportunities *with* families that really improve and deepen student learning?

References

Allen, J., Fabregas, V., Hankins, K., Hull, G., Labbo, L., Lawson, H., et al. (2002). PhOLKS lore: Learning from photographs, families, and children. *Language Arts, 79*(4), 312–322.

Frank, C. (2003). Mapping our stories: Teachers' reflections on themselves as writers. *Language Arts, 80*(3), 185–195.

Gonzáles, N., Moll, L., & Amanti, C. (Eds.). (2005). *Funds of knowledge: Theorizing practices in households, communities, and classrooms.* Mahwah, NJ: Erlbaum.

Henderson, A., & Mapp, K. (2002). *A new wave of evidence: The impact of school, family, and community connections on student achievement.* Austin, TX: Southwest Educational Development Laboratory.

Lawrence-Lightfoot, S. (2003). *The essential conversation: What parents and teachers can learn from each other.* New York: Random House.

Mattingly, D. J., Radmila, P., McKenzie, T. L., Rodriguez, J. L., & Kayzar, B. (2002). Evaluating evaluations: The case of parent involvement programs. *Review of Education Research, 72*(4), 549–576.

Murphy, P. (1994). Antonio: My student, my teacher. *Language Arts, 1*(2), 75–88.

Shockley, B., Michalove, B., & Allen, J. (1995). *Engaging families: Connecting home and school literacy communities.* Portsmouth, NH: Heinemann.

Critical Thinking

1. What are other ways that you would engage families as a teacher that were not listed in the article?
2. Explain the importance of developing partnerships with families and the community.
3. When thinking back to your own childhood, can you remember activities schools used to work with families?
4. Why is it important to develop an understanding of a family's culture other than your own?
5. What are the benefits of developing family partnerships within schools?

JoBeth Allen is Professor, Department of Language and Literacy Education, University of Georgia, Athens; jobethal@uga.edu. She is the author of *Creating Welcoming Schools: A Practical Guide to Home-School Partnerships with Diverse Families* (Teachers College Press, 2007).

UNIT 2

Exploring and Establishing Relationships

Unit Selections

Learning Outcomes

After reading this unit, you will be able to:

- Explain the science behind love, including lust, romance, and attachment.
- Recognize the cultural aspects of love and marriage.
- Describe the role of behaviors when people are in love.
- Explain the science behind love, including lust, romance, and attachment.
- Recognize the cultural aspects of love and marriage.
- Describe the role of behaviors when people are in love.
- Explain the trends in couples around love and sexual intimacy.
- Examine some of the major themes in the study of intimate relationships.
- Identify the linkages between length of courtship and marriage.
- Discuss some of the reasons why couples who are too slow or too quick to wed are more likely to divorce.
- Compare couples who marry with less dating time to couples with more time dating.
- Describe how culture impacts happiness within relationships.
- Identify how couples can protect themselves from exterior influences that strains their relationship.
- Identify the role of diet and exercise plays in fertility.
- Describe the types of foods impact pregnancy.
- Analyze other factors that contribute to infertility.
- Describe seven common assumptions about parenting.
- Translate how these seven beliefs translate to new parents.
- Demonstrate the given advice when working with new parents.

Student Website

www.mhhe.com/cls

Internet References

Bonobo Sex and Society
http://songweaver.com/info/bonobos.html

Go Ask Alice!
www.goaskalice.columbai.edu/index.html

The Kinsey Institute for Research in Sex, Gender, and Reproduction
www.indiana.edu/~kinsey

Mysteries of Odor in Human Sexuality
www.pheromones.com

The Society for the Scientific Study of Sexuality
www.sexscience.org

The Electronic Journal of Human Sexuality
www.ejhs.org/index.htm

By and large, we are social animals, and as such, we seek out meaningful connections with other humans. John Bowlby, Mary Ainsworth, and others have proposed that this drive toward deep connections is biologically based and is at the core of what it means to be human. However it plays out in childhood and adulthood, the need for connection, to love and be loved, is a powerful force moving us to establish and maintain close relationships. As we explore various possibilities, we engage in the complex business of relationship building. In doing this, many processes occur simultaneously: Messages are sent and received; differences are negotiated; assumptions and expectations are or are not met. The ultimate goals are closeness and continuity. How we feel about others and what we see as essential to these relationships play an important role in our establishing and maintaining relationships. In this unit, we look at factors that underlie the establishment of relationships as well as the beginning stages of relationships.

The first subsection takes a broad look at factors that influence the building of meaningful connections and at the beginning stages of adult relationships. The first essay, "This Thing Called Love" takes a cross-cultural perspective on the nature of romantic love. Among its interesting and controversial suggestions is that passionate love has a natural lifespan and shares characteristics with obsessive compulsive disorder. In "She's Out There," Kyle Western presents suggestions for men on how to attract women and to build a romantic relationship. The next essay goes on to discuss "24 Things Love and Sex Experts Are Dying to Tell You"—key pieces of information for couples.

In the second subsection, several aspects of the choice of a mate are examined. "Against All Odds" explores the concept of "instant relationships" and "The Expectations Trap" examines the impact of expectations on the choice we make regarding life partners.

The third subsection looks at pregnancy and the next generation. "Fats, Carbs and the Science of Conception" explores new research on the role of diet, exercise, and weight control in fertility. The final article in this section, "Baby Survival Guide. 7 Truths That'll Keep You Sane," discusses seven truths that both

© Glowimages/SuperStock

help parents to deal with the stress of raising a baby while also benefitting their child.

This Thing Called Love

Lauren Slater

My husband and I got married at eight in the morning. It was winter, freezing, the trees encased in ice and a few lone blackbirds balancing on telephone wires. We were in our early 30s, considered ourselves hip and cynical, the types who decried the institution of marriage even as we sought its status. During our wedding brunch we put out a big suggestion box and asked people to slip us advice on how to avoid divorce; we thought it was a funny, clear-eyed, grounded sort of thing to do, although the suggestions were mostly foolish: Screw the toothpaste cap on tight. After the guests left, the house got quiet. There were flowers everywhere: puckered red roses and fragile ferns. "What can we do that's really romantic?" I asked my newly wed one. Benjamin suggested we take a bath. I didn't want a bath. He suggested a lunch of chilled white wine and salmon. I was sick of salmon.

What can we do that's really romantic? The wedding was over, the silence seemed suffocating, and I felt the familiar disappointment after a longed-for event has come and gone. We were married. Hip, hip, hooray. I decided to take a walk. I went into the center of town, pressed my nose against a bakery window, watched the man with flour on his hands, the dough as soft as skin, pushed and pulled and shaped at last into stars. I milled about in an antique store. At last I came to our town's tattoo parlor. Now I am not a tattoo type person, but for some reason, on that cold silent Sunday, I decided to walk in. "Can I help you?" a woman asked.

"Is there a kind of tattoo I can get that won't be permanent?" I asked.

"Henna tattoos," she said.

She explained that they lasted for six weeks, were used at Indian weddings, were stark and beautiful and all brown. She showed me pictures of Indian women with jewels in their noses, their arms scrolled and laced with the henna markings. Indeed they were beautiful, sharing none of the gaudy comic strip quality of the tattoos we see in the United States. These henna tattoos spoke of intricacy, of the webwork between two people, of ties that bind and how difficult it is to find their beginnings and their elms. And because I had just gotten married, and because I was feeling a post wedding letdown, and because I wanted something really romantic to sail me through the night, I decided to get one.

"Where?" she asked.

"Here," I said. I laid my hands over my breasts and belly.

She raised her eyebrows. "Sure," she said.

I am a modest person. But I took off my shirt, lay on the table, heard her in the back room mixing powders and paints. She came to me carrying a small black-bellied pot inside of which was a rich red mush, slightly glittering. She adorned me. She gave me vines and flowers. She turned my body into a stake supporting whole new gardens of growth, and then, low around my hips, she painted a delicate chain-linked chastity belt. An hour later, the paint dry, I put my clothes back on, went home to film my newly wed one. This, I knew, was my gift to him, the kind of present you offer only once in your lifetime. I let him undress me.

"Wow," he said, standing back.

I blushed, and we began.

We are no longer beginning, my husband and I. This does not surprise me. Even back then, wearing the decor of desire, the serpentining tattoos, I knew they would fade, their red-clay color bleaching out until they were gone. On my wedding day I didn't care.

I do now. Eight years later, pale as a pillowcase, here I sit, with all the extra pounds and baggage time brings. And the questions have only grown more insistent. Does passion necessarily diminish over time? How reliable is romantic love, really, as a means of choosing one's mate? Can a marriage be good when Eros is replaced with friendship, or even economic partnership, two people bound by bank accounts?

Let me be clear: I still love my husband. There is no man I desire more. But it's hard to sustain romance in the crumb-filled quotidian that has become our lives. The ties that bind have been frayed by money and mortgages and children, those little imps who somehow manage to tighten the knot while weakening its actual fibers. Benjamin and I have no time for chilled white wine and salmon. The baths in our house always include Big Bird.

If this all sounds miserable, it isn't. My marriage is like a piece of comfortable clothing; even the arguments have a feel of fuzziness to them, something so familiar it can only be called home. And yet . . .

In the Western world we have for centuries concocted poems and stories and plays about the cycles of love, the way it morphs and changes over time, the way passion grabs us by our flung-back throats and then leaves us for something saner.

If *Dracula*—the frail woman, the sensuality of submission—reflects how we understand the passion of early romance, the *Flintstones* reflects our experiences of long-term love: All is gravel and somewhat silly, the song so familiar you can't stop singing it, and when you do, the emptiness is almost unbearable.

We have relied on stories to explain the complexities of love, tales of jealous gods and arrows. Now, however, these stories—so much a part of every civilization—may be changing as science steps in to explain what we have always felt to be myth, to be magic. For the first time, new research has begun to illuminate where love lies in the brain, the particulars of its chemical components.

Anthropologist Helen Fisher may be the closest we've ever come to having a doyenne of desire. At 60 she exudes a sexy confidence, with corn-colored hair, soft as floss, and a willowy build. A professor at Rutgers University, she lives in New York City, her book-lined apartment near Central Park, with its green trees fluffed out in the summer season, its paths crowded with couples holding hands.

Fisher has devoted much of her career to studying the biochemical pathways of love in all its manifestations: lust, romance, attachment, the way they wax and wane. One leg casually crossed over the other, ice clinking in her glass, she speaks with appealing frankness, discussing the ups and downs of love the way most people talk about real estate. "A woman unconsciously uses orgasms as a way of deciding whether or not a man is good for her. If he's impatient and rough, and she doesn't have the orgasm, she may instinctively feel he's less likely to be a good husband and father. Scientists think the fickle female orgasm may have evolved to help women distinguish Mr. Right from Mr. Wrong."

One of Fisher's central pursuits in the past decade has been looking at love, quite literally, with the aid of an MRI machine. Fisher and her colleagues Arthur Aron and Lucy Brown recruited subjects who had been "madly in love" for an average of seven months. Once inside the MRI machine, subjects were shown two photographs, one neutral, the other of their loved one.

What Fisher saw fascinated her. When each subject looked at his or her loved one, the parts of the brain linked to reward and pleasure—the ventral tegmental area and the caudate nucleus—lit up. What excited Fisher most was not so much finding a location, an address, for love as tracing its specific chemical pathways. Love lights up the caudate nucleus because it is home to a dense spread of receptors for a neurotransmitter called dopamine, which Fisher came to think of as part of our own endogenous love potion. In the right proportions, dopamine creates intense energy, exhilaration, focused attention, and motivation to win rewards. It is why, when you are newly in love, you can stay up all night, watch the sun rise, run a race, ski fast down a slope ordinarily too steep for your skill. Love makes you bold, makes you bright, makes you run real risks, which you sometimes survive, and sometimes you don't.

I first fell in love when I was only 12, with a teacher. His name was Mr. McArthur, and he wore open-toed sandals and sported a beard. I had never had a male teacher before, and I thought it terribly exotic. Mr. McArthur did things no other teacher dared to do. He explained to us the physics of farting. He demonstrated how to make an egg explode. He smoked cigarettes at recess, leaning languidly against the side of the school building, the ash growing longer and longer until he casually tapped it off with his finger.

What unique constellation of needs led me to love a man who made an egg explode is interesting, perhaps, but not as interesting, for me, as my memory of love's sheer physical facts. I had never felt anything like it before. I could not get Mr. McArthur out of my mind. I was anxious; I gnawed at the lining of my cheek until I tasted the tang of blood. School became at once terrifying and exhilarating. Would I see him in the hallway? In the cafeteria? I hoped. But when my wishes were granted, and I got a glimpse of my man, it satisfied nothing; it only inflamed me all the more. Had he looked at me? Why had he not looked at me? When would I see him again? At home I looked him up in the phone book; I rang him, this in a time before caller ID. He answered.

"Hello?" Pain in my heart, ripped down the middle. Hang up. Call back. "Hello?" I never said a thing.

Once I called him at night, late, and from the way he answered the phone it was clear, even to a prepubescent like me, that he was with a woman. His voice fuzzy, the tinkle of her laughter in the background. I didn't get out of bed for a whole day.

Sound familiar? Maybe you were 30 when it happened to you, or 8 or 80 or 25. Maybe you lived in Kathmandu or Kentucky; age and geography are irrelevant. Donatella Marazziti is a professor of psychiatry at the University of Pisa in Italy who has studied the biochemistry of lovesickness. Having been in love twice herself and felt its awful power, Marazziti became interested in exploring the similarities between love and obsessive-compulsive disorder.

She and her colleagues measured serotonin levels in the blood of 24 subjects who had fallen in love within the past six months and obsessed about this love object for at least four hours every day. Serotonin is, perhaps, our star neurotransmitter, altered by our star psychiatric medications: Prozac and Zoloft and Paxil, among others. Researchers have long hypothesized that people with obsessive-compulsive disorder (OCD) have a serotonin "imbalance." Drugs like Prozac seem to alleviate OCD by increasing the amount of this neurotransmitter available at the juncture between neurons.

Marazziti compared the lovers' serotonin levels with those of a group of people suffering from OCD and another group who were free from both passion and mental illness. Levels of serotonin in both the obsessives' blood and the lovers' blood were 40 percent lower than those in her normal subjects. Translation: Love and obsessive-compulsive disorder could have a similar chemical profile. Translation: Love and mental illness may be difficult to tell apart. Translation: Don't be a fool. Stay away.

Of course that's a mandate none of us can follow. We do fall in love, sometimes over and over again, subjecting ourselves, each time, to a very sick state of mind. There is hope, however, for those caught in the grip of runaway passion—Prozac. There's nothing like that bicolored bullet for damping down the sex drive and making you feel "blah" about the buffet. Helen

Fisher believes that the ingestion of drugs like Prozac jeopardizes one's ability to fall in love—and stay in love. By dulling the keen edge of love and its associated libido, relationships go stale. Says Fisher, "I know of one couple on the edge of divorce. The wife was on an antidepressant. Then she went off it, started having orgasms once more, felt the renewal of sexual attraction for her husband, and they're now in love all over again."

Psychoanalysts have concocted countless theories about why we fall in love with whom we do. Freud would have said your choice is influenced by the unrequited wish to bed your mother, if you're a boy, or your father, if you're a girl, Jung believed that passion is driven by some kind of collective unconscious. Today psychiatrists such as Thomas Lewis from the University of California at San Francisco's School of Medicine hypothesize that romantic love is rooted in our earliest infantile experiences with intimacy, how we felt at the breast, our mother's face, these things of pure unconflicted comfort that get engraved in our brain and that we ceaselessly try to recapture as adults. According to this theory we love whom we love not so much because of the future we hope to build but because of the past we hope to reclaim. Love is reactive, not proactive, it arches us backward, which may be why a certain person just "feels right." Or "feels familiar." He or she is familiar. He or she has a certain look or smell or sound or touch that activates buried memories.

Love and obsessive-compulsive disorder could have a similar chemical profile. Translation: Love and mental illness may be difficult to tell apart. Translation: Don't be a fool. Stay away.

When I first met my husband, I believed this psychological theory was more or less correct. My husband has red hair and a soft voice. A chemist, he is whimsical and odd. One day before we married he dunked a rose in liquid nitrogen so it froze, whereupon he flung it against the wall, spectacularly shattering it. That's when I fell in love with him. My father, too, has red hair, a soft voice, and many eccentricities. He was prone to bursting into song, prompted by something we never saw.

However, it turns out my theories about why I came to love my husband may be just so much hogwash. Evolutionary psychology has said good riddance to Freud and the Oedipal complex and all that other transcendent stuff and hello to simple survival skills. It hypothesizes that we tend to see as attractive, and thereby choose as mates, people who look healthy. And health, say these evolutionary psychologists, is manifested in a woman with a 70 percent waist-to-hip ratio and men with rugged features that suggest a strong supply of testosterone in their blood. Waist-to-hip ratio is important for the successful birth of a baby, and studies have shown this precise ratio signifies higher fertility. As for the rugged look, well, a man with a good dose of testosterone probably also has a strong immune system and so is more likely to give his partner healthy children.

Perhaps our choice of mates is a simple matter of following our noses. Claus Wedekind of the University of Lausanne in Switzerland did an interesting experiment with sweaty T-shirts. He asked 49 women to smell T-shirts previously worn by unidentified men with a variety of the genotypes that influence both body odor and immune systems. He then asked the women to rate which T-shirts smelled the best, which the worst. What Wedekind found was that women preferred the scent of a T-shirt worn by a man whose genotype was most different from hers, a genotype that, perhaps, is linked to an immune system that possesses something hers does not. In this way she increases the chance that her offspring will be robust.

It all seems too good to be true, that we are so hardwired and yet unconscious of the wiring. Because no one to my knowledge has ever said, "I married him because of his B.O." No. We say, "I married him (or her) because he's intelligent, she's beautiful, he's witty, she's compassionate." But we may just be as deluded about love as we are when we're *in* love. If it all comes down to a sniff test, then dogs definitely have the edge when it comes to choosing mates.

Why doesn't passionate love last? How is it possible to see a person as beautiful on Monday, and 364 days later, on another Monday, to see that beauty as bland? Surely the object of your affection could not have changed that much. She still has the same shaped eyes. Her voice has always had that husky sound, but now it grates on you—she sounds like she needs an antibiotic. Or maybe you're the one who needs an antibiotic, because the partner you once loved and cherished and saw as though saturated with starlight now feels more like a low-level infection, tiring you, sapping all your strength.

Studies around the world confirm that, indeed, passion usually ends. Its conclusion is as common as its initial flare. No wonder some cultures think selecting a lifelong mate based on something so fleeting is folly. Helen Fisher has suggested that relationships frequently break up after four years because that's about how long it takes to raise a child through infancy. Passion, that wild, prismatic insane feeling, turns out to be practical after all. We not only need to copulate; we also need enough passion to start breeding, and then feelings of attachment take over as the partners bond to raise a helpless human infant. Once a baby is no longer nursing, the child can be left with sister, aunts, friends. Each parent is now free to meet another mate and have more children.

Biologically speaking, the reasons romantic love fades may be found in the way our brains respond to the surge and pulse of dopamine that accompanies passion and makes us fly. Cocaine users describe the phenomenon of tolerance: The brain adapts to the excessive input of the drug. Perhaps the neurons become desensitized and need more and more to produce the high—to put out pixie dust, metaphorically speaking.

Maybe it's a good thing that romance fizzles. Would we have railroads, bridges, planes, faxes, vaccines, and television if we were all always besotted? In place of the ever evolving technology that has marked human culture from its earliest tool use, we would have instead only bonbons, bouquets, and birth control. More seriously, if the chemically altered state induced by romantic love is akin to a mental illness or a drug-induced euphoria, exposing yourself for too long could result in psychological damage. A good sex life can be as strong as Gorilla Glue, but who wants that stuff on your skin?

Once upon a time, in India, a boy and a girl fell in love without their parents' permission. They were from different castes, their relationship radical and unsanctioned. Picture it: the sparkling sari, the boy in white linen, the clandestine meetings on tiled terraces with a fat, white moon floating overhead. Who could deny these lovers their pleasure, or condemn the force of their attraction?

Their parents could. In one recent incident a boy and girl from different castes were hanged at the hands of their parents as hundreds of villagers watched. A couple who eloped were stripped and beaten. Yet another couple committed suicide after their parents forbade them to marry.

Anthropologists used to think that romance was a Western construct, a bourgeois by-product of the Middle Ages. Romance was for the sophisticated, took place in cafés, with coffees and Cabernets, or on silk sheets, or in rooms with a flickering fire. It was assumed that non-Westerners, with their broad familial and social obligations, were spread too thin for particular passions. How could a collectivist culture celebrate or in any way sanction the obsession with one individual that defines new love? Could a lice-ridden peasant really feel passion?

Easily, as it turns out. Scientists now believe that romance is panhuman, embedded in our brains since Pleistocene times. In a study of 166 cultures, anthropologists William Jankowiak and Edward Fischer observed evidence of passionate love in 147 of them. In another study men and women from Europe, Japan, and the Philippines were asked to fill out a survey to measure their experiences of passionate love. All three groups professed feeling passion with the same searing intensity.

But though romantic love may be universal, its cultural expression is not. To the Fulbe tribe of northern Cameroon, poise matters more than passion. Men who spend too much time with their wives are taunted, and those who are weak-kneed are thought to have fallen under a dangerous spell. Love may be inevitable, but for the Fulbe its manifestations are shameful, equated with sickness and social impairment.

In India romantic love has traditionally been seen as dangerous, a threat to a well-crafted caste system in which marriages are arranged as a means of preserving lineage and bloodlines. Thus the gruesome tales, the warnings embedded in fables about what happens when one's wayward impulses take over.

Today love marriages appear to be on the rise in India, often in defiance of parents' wishes. The triumph of romantic love is celebrated in Bollywood films. Yet most Indians still believe arranged marriages are more likely to succeed than love marriages. In one survey of Indian college students, 76 percent said they'd marry someone with all the right qualities even if they weren't in love with the person (compared with only 14 percent of Americans). Marriage is considered too important a step to leave to chance.

Studies around the world confirm that, indeed, passion usually ends. No wonder some cultures think selecting a lifelong mate based on something so fleeting is folly.

Renu Dinakaran is a striking 45-year-old woman who lives in Bangalore, India. When I meet her, she is dressed in Western-style clothes—black leggings and a T-shirt. Renu lives in a well-appointed apartment in this thronging city, where cows sleep on the highways as tiny cars whiz around them, plumes of black smoke rising from their sooty pipes.

Renu was born into a traditional Indian family where an arranged marriage was expected. She was not an arranged kind of person, though, emerging from her earliest days as a fierce tennis player, too sweaty for saris, and smarter than many of the men around her. Nevertheless at the age of 17 she was married off to a first cousin, a man she barely knew, a man she wanted to learn to love, but couldn't. Renu considers many arranged marriages to be acts of "state-sanctioned rape."

Renu hoped to fall in love with her husband, but the more years that passed, the less love she felt, until, at the end, she was shrunken, bitter, hiding behind the curtains of her in-laws' bungalow, looking with longing at the couple on the balcony across from theirs. "It was so obvious to me that couple had married for love, and I envied them. I really did. It hurt me so much to see how they stood together, how they went shopping for bread and eggs."

Exhausted from being forced into confinement, from being swaddled in saris that made it difficult to move, from resisting the pressure to eat off her husband's plate, Renu did what traditional Indian culture forbids one to do. She left. By this time she had had two children. She took them with her. In her mind was an old movie she'd seen on TV, a movie so strange and enticing to her, so utterly confounding and comforting at the same time, that she couldn't get it out of her head. It was 1986. The movie was *Love Story*.

"Before I saw movies like *Love Story*, I didn't realize the power that love can have," she says.

Renu was lucky in the end. In Mumbai she met a man named Anil, and it was then, for the first time, that she felt passion. "When I first met Anil, it was like nothing I'd ever experienced. He was the first man I ever had an orgasm with. I was high, just high, all the time. And I knew it wouldn't last, couldn't last, and so that infused it with a sweet sense of longing, almost as though we were watching the end approach while we were also discovering each other."

When Renu speaks of the end, she does not, to be sure, mean the end of her relationship with Anil; she means the end of a certain stage. The two are still happily married, companionable, loving if not "in love," with a playful black dachshund they bought together. Their relationship, once so full of fire, now seems to simmer along at an even temperature, enough to keep them well fed and warm. They are grateful.

"Would I want all that passion back?" Renu asks. "Sometimes, yes. But to tell you the truth, it was exhausting."

From a physiological point of view, this couple has moved from the dopamine-drenched state of romantic love to the relative quiet of an oxytocin-induced attachment. Oxytocin is a hormone that promotes a feeling of connection, bonding. It is released when we hug our long-term spouses, or our children. It is released when a mother nurses her infant. Prairie voles, animals with high levels of oxytocin, mate for life. When scientists block oxytocin receptors in these rodents, the animals don't form monogamous bonds and tend to roam. Some researchers speculate that autism, a disorder marked by a profound inability to forge and maintain social connections, is linked to an oxytocin deficiency. Scientists have been experimenting by treating autistic people with oxytocin, which in some cases has helped alleviate their symptoms.

In long-term relationships that work—like Renu and Anil's—oxytocin is believed to be abundant in both partners. In long-term relationships that never get off the ground, like Renu and her first husband's, or that crumble once the high is gone, chances are the couple has not found a way to stimulate or sustain oxytocin production.

"But there are things you can do to help it along," says Helen Fisher. "Massage. Make love. These things trigger oxytocin and thus make you feel much closer to your partner."

Well, I suppose that's good advice, but it's based on the assumption that you still want to have sex with that boring windbag of a husband. Should you fake-it-till-you-make-it?

"Yes," says Fisher. "Assuming a fairly healthy relationship, if you have enough orgasms with your partner, you may become attached to him or her. You will stimulate oxytocin."

This may be true. But it sounds unpleasant. It's exactly what your mother always said about vegetables: "Keep eating your peas. They are an acquired taste. Eventually, you will come to like them."

But I have never been a peas person.

I t's 90 degrees on the day my husband and I depart, from Boston for New York City, to attend a kissing school. With two kids, two cats, two dogs, a lopsided house, and a questionable school system, we may know how to kiss, but in the rough and tumble of our harried lives we have indeed forgotten how to *kiss*.

The sky is paved with clouds, the air as sticky as jam in our hands and on our necks. The Kissing School, run by Cherie Byrd, a therapist from Seattle, is being held on the 12th floor of a run-down building in Manhattan. Inside, the room is whitewashed; a tiled table holds bottles of banana and apricot nectar, a pot of green tea, breath mints, and Chapstick. The other Kissing School students—sometimes they come from as far away as Vietnam and Nigeria—are sprawled happily on the bare floor, pillows and blankets beneath them. The class will be seven hours long.

Byrd starts us off with foot rubs. "In order to be a good kisser," she says, "you need to learn how to do the foreplay before the kissing." Foreplay involves rubbing my husband's smelly feet, but that is not as bad as when he has to rub mine. Right before we left the house, I accidentally stepped on a diaper the dog had gotten into, and although I washed, I now wonder how well.

"Inhale," Byrd says, and shows us how to draw in air.

"Exhale," she says, and then she jabs my husband in the back. "Don't focus on the toes so much," she says. "Move on to the calf."

Byrd tells us other things about the art of kissing. She describes the movement of energy through various chakras, the manifestation of emotion in the lips; she describes the importance of embracing all your senses, how to make eye contact as a prelude, how to whisper just the right way. Many hours go by. My cell phone rings. It's our babysitter. Our one-year-old has a high fever. We must cut the long lesson short. We rush out. Later on, at home, I tell my friends what we learned at Kissing School: We don't have time to kiss.

A perfectly typical marriage. Love in the Western world.

Luckily I've learned of other options for restarting love. Arthur Aron, a psychologist at Stony Brook University in New York, conducted an experiment that illuminates some of the mechanisms by which people become and stay attracted. He recruited a group of men and women and put opposite sex pairs in rooms together, instructing each pair to perform a series of tasks, which included telling each other personal details about themselves. He then asked each couple to stare into each other's eyes for two minutes. After this encounter, Aron found most of the couples, previously strangers to each other, reported feelings of attraction. In fact, one couple went on to marry.

Novelty triggers dopamine in the brain, which can stimulate feelings of attraction. So riding a roller coaster on a first date is more likely to lead to second and third dates.

Fisher says this exercise works wonders for some couples. Aron and Fisher also suggest doing novel things together, because novelty triggers dopamine in the brain, which can stimulate feelings of attraction. In other words, if your heart flutters in his presence, you might decide it's not because you're anxious but because you love him. Carrying this a step further, Aron and others have found that even if you just jog in place and then meet someone, you're more likely to think they're attractive. So first dates that involve a nerve-racking activity, like riding a roller coaster, are more likely to lead to second and third dates. That's a strategy worthy of posting on Match.com. Play some squash. And in times of stress—natural disasters, blackouts, predators on the prowl—lock up tight and hold your partner.

In Somerville, Massachusetts, where I live with my husband, our predators are primarily mosquitoes. That needn't stop us from trying to enter the windows of each other's soul. When I propose this to Benjamin, he raises an eyebrow.

"Why don't we just go out for Cambodian food?" he says.

"Because that's not how the experiment happened."

As a scientist, my husband is always up for an experiment. But our lives are so busy that, in order to do this, we have to make a plan. We will meet next Wednesday at lunchtime and try the experiment in our car.

On the Tuesday night before our rendezvous, I have to make an unplanned trip to New York. My husband is more than happy to forget our date. I, however, am not. That night, from my hotel room, I call him.

"We can do it on the phone," I say.

"What am I supposed to stare into?" he asks. "The keypad?"

"There's a picture of me hanging in the hall. Look at that for two minutes. I'll look at a picture I have of you in my wallet."

"Come on," he says.

"Be a sport," I say. "It's better than nothing."

Maybe not. Two minutes seems like a long time to stare at someone's picture with a receiver pressed to your ear. My husband sneezes, and I try to imagine his picture sneezing right along with him, and this makes me laugh.

Another 15 seconds pass, slowly, each second stretched to its limit so I can almost hear time, feel time, its taffy-like texture, the pop it makes when it's done. Pop pop pop. I stare and stare at my husband's picture. It doesn't produce any sense of startling intimacy, and I feel defeated.

Still, I keep on. I can hear him breathing on the other end. The photograph before me was taken a year or so ago, cut to fit my wallet, his strawberry blond hair pulled back in a ponytail. I have never really studied it before. And I realize that in this picture my husband is not looking straight back at me, but his pale blue eyes are cast sideways, off to the left, looking at something I can't see. I touch his eyes. I peer close, and then still closer, at his averted face. Is there something sad in his expression, something sad in the way he gazes off?

I look toward the side of the photo, to find what it is he's looking at, and then I see it: a tiny turtle coming toward him. Now I remember how he caught it after the camera snapped, how he held it gently in his hands, showed it to our kids, stroked its shell, his forefinger moving over the scaly dome, how he held the animal out toward me, a love offering. I took it, and together we sent it back to the sea.

Critical Thinking

1. Do you think that love can be explained by science? If not, how would you explain love?

2. When looking at today's media, do you feel that they play a role in how we see love?

3. Why do some people feel in need to be married and stay married?

4. Does passion diminish over time? Are there causes that were not mentioned in the article?

5. Which theoretical perspective do you agree with: Freud, evolutionary, unexplainable, or scientific? Why?

She's Out There

KYLE WESTERN

Will you meet her? In times of economic distress, women seek emotional safe havens. Here are 13 places—and reasons—she's looking for you.

The saddest thing you will ever see in a bar is the lights on at closing time. It's the moment you realize that although you've been bankrolling her martinis since midnight, she won't be going home with you. And why should she? You're a stranger, and this is just a game. When the filaments flicker on, the fantasy ends.

"Men are possessed by the myth of the pickup," says David Grazian, Ph.D., an associate professor of sociology at the University of Pennsylvania and the author of *On the Make: The Hustle of Urban Nightlife.* It's in their heads that these bars and clubs are "teeming with anonymous females who are dying to have sex with any guy who is confident enough to talk to them." The reality is that less than 6 percent of women report having had sex with their partners within two days or less of meeting them, and less than 20 percent of adults say they first met their most recent sexual partner in a bar. Perhaps it's the nasty stigma of nightlife: A survey of 1,034 women by StrategyOne, a market research agency, reveals that nearly one in four women would be embarrassed to admit that she met a mate in a bar.

So why does the alcohol-soaked pickup scene still exist? Aside from the obvious reasons (tequila, vodka, rum), there's a surprising one as well: inexperience. Men are new to this 21st-century version of the boy-meets-girl game. In 1970, the median age for marriage was 23 for men and 21 for women. Today it's 28 and 26. "It used to be that people felt they'd somehow missed out if they didn't have a spouse by the time they graduated college," says David Popenoe, Ph.D., founder and codirector of the National Marriage Project and a professor emeritus of sociology at Rutgers University. "Today, people feel they need to establish themselves economically first." The postponement of "I do" means most men will be single in their 20s, a trend that populates the bar scene and empties the church aisles.

The real world of dating is rough on men. The risk and onus of rejection are almost always on them, because men initiate about 80 percent of encounters. And the competition is brutal for men in their 20s and 30s: For every 100 unmarried women there's an average of 113 unmarried men, according to the U.S. Census Bureau. And those men just aren't doing the job. The Pew Research Center found that about half of young singles reported going on no more than one date in the three months prior to its survey, and 55 percent of singles who were looking for love said it was hard to meet people.

But the situation doesn't have to be that bleak. In fact, there's no better time to be single than during an economic recession. A recent eHarmony survey found that one in four single women say that financial stress has increased their interest in a relationship. Compare that with the 61 percent of men who say money worries are causing stress in their love lives. Look at it this way: More women are on the market, and they're primed to connect. But men are looking to meet them over $12 martinis—and are going home alone and broke. There's an opening here for you: Think patterns, not people. Forget the pickup lines and rely on the new rules of attraction. We can help you with the odds.

RULE 1 Build Your Romantic Network

You're 227 percent more likely to meet a potential girlfriend through a friend or family member rather than in a bar, at the gym, or on the street.

Malcolm Parks, Ph.D., knows the secret to meeting women: Don't.

Instead, meet people.

Parks, a University of Washington communication researcher and author of *Personal Relationships & Personal Networks,* has determined that 75 percent of the people who dated extensively the year before said they had help from a friend. In their corner is what Parks calls "the social proximity effect," which holds that the probability of two people meeting is directly proportional to the number of contacts they share. In other words, more friends means more female referrals. "Our research has shown that two-thirds of people who initiate a romantic relationship had met at least one of the dozen or so members of their partner's closest social network prior to meeting their partner for the first time," says Parks, "and nearly half had met two or three." If you know Tom, and Tom knows Betty, then there's a greater chance you'll meet Betty. And if Tom also knows Susan, Heather, and Kimberly . . . well, then you owe Tom a fruit basket.

The potential is there, but the problem is that most men's social networks are too small or too stale to be effective. The average guy would have difficulty mustering enough friends to round out a Fave 5, according to a 2006 survey in the American Sociological Review. In fact, our close social networks have shrunk by almost a third since 1985.

But it's not just the friend famine that's starving our sex lives. Socially inbred crews are detrimental, too. "In a tightly knit group, you know the same people," says Parks. "Your friends can't introduce you to women you don't already know." That's why access to a new resource, whether it's an unadvertised job opening, a lead on a house listing, or an introduction to a woman you might click with, is more likely to come through casual friends than close ones. It's what social network theorists call "the strength of weak ties," and the greater the number of unique casual connections you have, the better positioned you are to benefit. These types of people are essentially network bridges, says Parks.

They connect you to women you might not otherwise have met through your close friends. The secret isn't blind dates and setups; it's party invites and casual introductions.

The beauty of forging weak ties is that while others hunt, you gather. To be successful, you need to continually meet new people outside your existing circles in order to find quantity and diversity in new links. All connections have potential. For example, you may have written off the guy with a wife or live-in girlfriend, but he's the money ball. According to a 2003 study in Social Networks, dating couples share 20 percent to 25 percent of their friends, but that percentage increases to 50 when they start living together. The result: His network is likely to be populated with more women after he moves in with her.

We'll supply the fertile meeting grounds. You find the equivalents in your town, and the potential mates who gather there.

Weak-Tie Strongholds

Dallas Sport and Social Club Coed Kickball

Team play encourages what sociologists call "situational generalization"—in other words, positive circumstances help people click. "When people are working toward a shared outcome, they're more likely to grow closer together," says Parks. Recreational outfits make it easy to form new connections because individuals can sign up and be assigned to a team without needing to know anyone.

ImprovBoston Theatre Performance Classes

Sharing a funny experience can help reduce tension among strangers, according to a 2004 study in Personal Relationships. And improv class will sharpen communications with everyone you encounter.

Durham Bulls Athletic Park (Durham, NC)

For the cost of a Yankees ticket (or less), you and your friends can each grab a multigaine package featuring up to 13 MLB minor-league affiliates. Rooting for team sports can boost testosterone levels—yours as well as hers. And T is the libido hormone, so if your team wins, you both win. Try this: Split the cost of an extra package with your friends, and then take turns

inviting someone new. It'll expand your weak ties, and the presence of friends creates a "celebrity effect" that can be as desirable as attractiveness or wealth.

Meetup Volunteer Groups

Selflessness is sexy. A 2008 study published in the *British Journal of Psychology* showed that women consider altruism more important in a mate than men do. To show your selfless stuff, try joining a Meetup volunteer group (volunteerism.meetup.com). This network serves a variety of causes, allows you to select groups with members who share your interests, and lets you see who has signed up for which projects.

RULE 2 Let Chaos Be Your Wingman

Less than 1 percent of women say they met their current partner because they were neighbors, compared with 22 percent of women who say their man is from a different part of town.

When a team of two physicists and a human-network scientist tells you your life is bland, you know you're in trouble. Northeastern University researchers took their dig in a 2008 study in the journal *Nature*, after they tracked the movements of 100,000 cellphone users for six months. Their finding: People are predictable. Nearly half of their human lab rats kept to a maze that was little more than 6 miles wide, and 83 percent mostly stayed within a 37-mile radius. And they tended to spend the majority of their time in five or fewer places.

The result: dating pools the size of shot glasses.

In the United States, there's an average of only seven single women between the ages of 20 and 44 per square mile. Now consider your "spots," the places you usually go despite the presence of equivalent alternatives: your Starbucks, your bank branch, your dry cleaner, your gym, your grocery store. These are embedded destinations in other people's travel itineraries, too, meaning they're also their "spots." If everyone repeats routines, as the Northeastern University research suggests, the rate at which you encounter new women plummets.

If you stick to a 6-mile orbit, your romantic trajectory is stunted as well. "In the stock market, diversification is critical to reducing risk," says Amir Aczel, Ph.D., a former professor of mathematics and statistics at Bentley University near Boston and author of *Chance*. "In dating, the same rule applies. You should vary the places you go, and when you go there. This diversification will result in increased probability of meeting women who respond well to you."

Consider these tweaks to your routine.

Chaos Corners

Santa Monica Farmers' Market

Bust out of supermarket hell to join the communal ambience of a farmers' market, where you can tap into a spirit of sociability, exploration, and inquisitiveness. Engage her over the Asian pears, and she'll thank you for the rest of her life. To find a market near you, go to localharvest.org.

Yelp

Yelp.com's 5 million local reviews can lead you to a dry cleaner, cafe, barbershop, or bookstore where all the cool people go. Post your own reviews and you may meet a fellow critic. The social-networking functions of the site allow readers to swap private messages, post public comments, and classify deserving reviews as funny, useful, or cool, so you can navigate them accordingly.

Waterloo Records (Austin, Texas)

Research suggests that people are more attracted to potential partners who share their musical tastes. Itunes has revolutionized the music landscape, but for many passionate music lovers, it can't replace the places like Waterloo and the 700 other independent record stores across the country. Go to recordstoreday .com to find a shop near you.

Ikea

Researchers note that shopping trips are fueled by social motives, including the desire for new communal experiences. Big-box stores are socially fertile: More than 10 million people pass through Ikea every week, and U.S. consumers spend an average of 2 to 3 hours each visit. And at Ikea, traffic moves one way, creating a natural movement and pacing that makes it easy to stroll and engage. Think about store or mall flow the next time you're shopping, and patronize spots, like the Apple store, that make kibitzing part of the experience. If you're the active type, L.L. Bean or REI might be a better bet.

RULE 3 Use Spare Time as Showtime

Approximately one-fifth of couples first met in public places. But as available free time plummets, you may not get out enough.

You're just about as likely to meet a woman during Sunday service at church as you are during "Sexy Saturday" at a club. The takeaway isn't that you need to find God to find a woman. You simply need to be with people, wherever they may gather.

Your time to do that is shrinking, according to a 2008 Harris Interactive poll. Americans have just 16 hours a week—down 20 percent from 2007—that are all theirs. With leisure time scarce, many men make the mistake of blocking off a weekend night for dating, says Paul Dobransky, M.D., a Chicago psychiatrist and the director of DoctorPaul.net. "Their lack of success is due to their hyperfocused approach," says Dr. Dobransky. "They see meeting women as something that is done rather than something that naturally happens, which is the way women view it."

The single women are waiting, but they're not doing it in front of an LCD screen, where you're more likely to be most nights. On any given day, more women attend or host social events, volunteer, join religious functions, practice hobbies, or go shopping, while the average single guy is home, pathetically

alone. Compared with single women, single men spend 45 minutes more a day watching TV and about 20 minutes more on the computer.

It's a surprisingly detrimental decision. A 2008 study in Social Indicators Research reveals that unhappy people watch 30 percent more TV every day than very happy people. "It's possible that TV causes people to be unhappy because it pushes aside time for activities with long-term benefits," says study author John Robinson, Ph.D., a professor of sociology at the University of Maryland and director of the Americans' Use of Time Project. "Or TV viewing is an outlet for people who are already unhappy."

Whatever the case, the consequences are clear: If you shut down socially during the week, you're severely undermining your efforts and personal satisfaction. You'll have more success with women if you aim to collect experiences rather than phone numbers. Consider these connection points.

Showtime Showcases

First Fridays at the Natural History Museum of Los Angeles County

In a 2008 University of Iowa survey, women ranked a man's intelligence and education higher than his good looks and financial prospects. On the first Friday of the month, stuffy cultural mainstays unbutton their starched shirts a bit, offering gallery tours, cocktails, hors d'oeuvres, and music.

Movies in the Parks (Chicago)

In the summer, the park district invites citizens to pull up a blanket and watch movies. The air is warm with conviviality. Many cities offer similar programs. If yours doesn't, volunteer to start one and meet artsy types and wealthy sponsors as you set it up.

Mile High Music Festival

"The rhythmic pulse of music lets listeners synchronize with one another, which can increase group cohesion," says Michael Cunningham, Ph.D., a psychologist and professor of communication at the University of Louisville. Concerts are good, but music festivals attract a more diverse crowd because of the different acts and transcend the behavioral norms of everyday life. Visit festivalfinder.com for events near you.

Philadelphia Punk Rock Flea Market

Odd? Sure, and that's the point. If you want to meet interesting people, you need to do interesting things.

Bank of America Chicago Marathon

No, she's not waiting for you at mile marker 19. The real appeal here is the free training program held several days a week. Studies show that when we anticipate future experiences with someone, we focus on that person's positive qualities to better ensure that those upcoming experiences will be pleasant ones. Go to marathonguide.com for a list of races near you. No training program? Join a local running club.

Critical Thinking

1. What were some of the places in the article that you thought you might use to find a date?

2. Do you feel that in times of recession that people are less likely to meet in bars or restaurants? Why or why not?

3. After reading this article would you suggest one of these ideas to a friend? Why or why not?

4. Why do you think that meeting someone through friends is such a good idea?

5. How comfortable would you be meeting someone at a music festival or museum?

24 Things Love and Sex Experts Are Dying to Tell You

ELLISE PIERCE

At REDBOOK, we're dedicated to helping you get the most out of every part of your life—*especially* your love life. That's why we created the REDBOOK Love Network, a brain trust of today's top authorities on relationships, to provide you with the best, most current info on the ins and outs, and ups and downs, of sex and love. Here, our experts share the essential pieces of advice every couple needs.

1 Never Underestimate the Power of a Compliment

"Every day, tell your partner about one thing they did that you appreciate. Everybody is quick to let their partner know what they didn't do right, and what made you angry. Make sure you balance this with what they do that pleases you. From the small things to the big things, the more you say 'Thank you,' the more of what makes you happy will come your way."

—Jane Greer, PhD, couples therapist and author of *Gridlock: Finding the Courage to Move On in Love, Work, and Life*

2 Sex: Just Do It

"Have sex—even when you don't want to! Many times, arousal comes before desire. Once you get going, you'll probably find yourself enjoying it. And the more you experience sex, the more your body will condition itself to want it. You'll feel more sensual and energized, and your partner will pick up on this sexy change."

—Laura Berman, PhD, director of the Berman Center in Chicago and author of *The Passion Prescription*

3 Listen More, Talk Less

"Communication is 85 percent listening and 15 percent talking. The more you listen, the more you'll enhance communication. Try getting out of the house, taking a long walk without your cell phones, and just looking into your partner's eyes and listening to him. It's an amazing thing in a relationship when you truly feel listened to!"

—Neil Clark Warren, PhD, founder of eHarmony.com and author of *Falling in Love for All the Right Reasons*

4 Sweep Your Problems (The Little Ones) Under the Rug

"It really is okay to drop certain subjects and not even come back to them. People think this means you're avoiding key issues. But for everyday little things, successful couples agree to ignore the small problems. It's not worth the aggravation to insist on winning everything."

—David Wexler, PhD, executive director of the Relationship Training Institute in San Diego and author of *When Good Men Behave Badly*

5 Treat Your Love Like a Cherished Friendship

"The happiest couples relate to each other with respect, affection, and empathy. They choose their words carefully, avoiding the most poisonous relationship behaviors—criticism, defensiveness, contempt, and stonewalling—and feel emotionally connected."

—John Gottman, PhD, cofounder of the Gottman Institute in Seattle and author of *10 Lessons to Transform Your Marriage*

6 To Change Your Relationship, Change Yourself

"In most relationships, we think, I'm right, you're wrong, and I'll try to convince you to change. The truth is, if one person changes, the relationship changes. People say, 'Why do I have to change?' But when I show them how to tip over the first domino, their only question is, "Why did I wait so long?"

—**Michele Weiner-Davis, couples therapist and author of** *The Sex-Starved Marriage*

7 Watch out for Harsh Comments—They Hit Harder Than You Think

"When you're tired or frustrated, it's easy to slip into being critical of your partner. But remember, negative expressions and comments and behaviors hold much more weight than positive interactions. Make sure that for every one negative interaction, you have five positive interactions to counteract it—a touch, a laugh, a kiss, an act of love, a compliment."

—**Scott Haltzman, MD, Psychiatrist and author of** *The Secrets of Happily Married Men*

8 Don't Knock It Till You've Tried It . . . Twice

"Try being adventurous in bed. Even if you don't like something, give it at least two chances before you give up on it—it may grow on you!"

—**Laura Berman, PhD**

9 Be the First to Offer the Olive Branch

"Often when there's a problem, each person will wait for the other to take the initiative to work things out. But the longer you wait, the more frustrated you both get and the worse you feel. Try making the first move to break a stalemate. It doesn't mean that you're giving in. You're getting the ball rolling, rather than being stuck."

—**Norman Epstein, PhD, marriage researcher and family therapist at the University of Maryland**

10 How to Be a Couple and Still Be Free

Give the love you want to get. "Put out lots of love and appreciation and doing your share, and you're much more likely to get it back. Put out demands and complaining, and you'll get that back too."

—**Tina B. Tessina, PhD, couples therapist and author of** *How to Be a Couple and Still Be Free*

11 Fight for Your Love

"I've never seen a decent marriage where there wasn't a lot of conflict. Conflict is always the result of uniqueness, the differences between two people rubbing up against each other. Lots of people try to shut themselves down in order to avoid conflict, but any two people living full and vibrant lives are going to clash at some point. If you manage it carefully and thoughtfully, conflict can actually give your marriage a shot of energy. You can have a broader, fuller, more interesting relationship."

—**Neil Clark Warren, PhD**

12 Sex Matters; Couple Time Matters Even More

"Often couples focus on scheduling sex and working very hard on their sex life, and they don't get anywhere. But when they focus instead on spending time together— going to the movies, working on a project together—then often a better sex life will grow out of that."

—**Ian Kerner, PhD, sex therapist and author of** *She Comes First* **and** *He Comes Next*

13 Don't Get Caught up in Right or Wrong

"It's easy to fall into a power struggle of who's right and who's wrong, but that prevents you from actually solving the real problem. You're not going to be punished for being wrong, so don't worry about who's right—work together to solve the problem."

—**Tina B. Tessina, PhD**

14 Feed Your Relationship

"People often make their own needs a first priority, and then say they can't get what they want out of the relationship. It's like going to your garden and saying,

'Feed me,' and you haven't put any plants in the ground. Make your relationship your first priority. Maybe your relationship needs more time, more vacation. Maybe you need to put in more positive statements or more moments of connection. Become partners in taking care of this relationship. If you get couples engaged in a mutual project, which is their relationship, no matter what they come up with, it's good. It's the working together that does it."

—Harville Hendrix, PhD, founder/
director of Imago Relationship
International and author of
Getting the Love You Want

15 Words Are Like Food—Nurture Each Other with Good Ones

"Say things such as 'I love you,' 'I really appreciate that,' 'I'd love to hear your thoughts about. . . you name it.' And use more empathetic words, like, 'It seems like you're struggling with this.' You'll communicate genuineness and respect, and make your partner feel loved."

—Alan Hovestadt, EdD, president of the
American Association for Marriage
and Family Therapy

16 Never Mind Equality; Focus on Fairness

"Everything doesn't have to be 50/50. Having a sense that each person is doing what's fair—even if it's not always equal—is what really makes a happy marriage. That applies not just to housework, but to the relationship itself."

—Barbara Dafoe Whitehead, PhD,
codirector of the National Marriage
Project at Rutgers University

17 Remember That You Were Partners before You Were Parents

"If you have children, don't forget about your own connection and relationship and put everything into the children. Make relating to each other one-on-one—not just as parents, but as lovers a priority."

—Lou Paget, sex educator
and author of The Great Lover
Playbook

18 Learn How to Communicate without Saying a Word

"We are profoundly affected by touch, both physically and emotionally. Happy couples touch each other frequently. A caring touch offers a simple acknowledgment of your partner, saying, 'Way to go' or 'I know that was difficult for you,' without words."

—Alan Hovestadt, EdD

19 Pay Back Your Partner Using His or Her Currency

"Each of us wants our mate to pay us back for our contributions, to give us positive reinforcement. But this payment needs to be in currency that we recognize. A wife may say, 'The way I show I care is that I make his bed every day,' but if he doesn't even notice that, it's ineffective. Get to know what your partner is looking for and make sure you speak his language."

—Scott Haltzman, MD

20 Draw on Your Successes as a Couple

"One way to bring out the best in a relationship is to focus on what you've done right in the past. For example, if you're trying to break a habit of bickering a lot, think back to a time when you were bickering but ended it differently, with humor or by dropping it or in some other way. Every couple has a big hat of experiences when they handled things well, and it's important to draw on this catalog of successes, rather than just focusing on the times when things ended negatively."

—David Wexler, PhD

21 Dream a Big Dream for Your Relationship

"When two people dream a great dream for their marriage, they typically see their relationship take a dramatic step in the direction of that dream. Start dreaming big—envision where you want your lives and your relationship to be in 10 years. Then let yourself be inspired by these dreams to make whatever changes are necessary to live these dreams out."

—Neil Clark Warren, PhD

22 See Things through Each Other's Eyes

"A lot of conflict comes from always putting a negative spin on what your partner does. Instead of telling yourself that your partner is being thoughtless or irritating, try to think about it from the other person's point of view—ask yourself, What is going on inside that would make him or her act that way? The behavior might still be a problem, but being aware of your partner's intention can change how you view the problem, and make it easier to communicate about it."

—David Wexler, PhD

23 Cultivate Trust to Grow Intimacy

"Trust issues are like sparks in a dry forest—you want to deal with them as fast as you can, whether it's something major, like an affair, or something smaller, like a wife sharing intimate things about her marriage with her best friend. You have to remove the reasons for lack of trust so that you can both feel safe sharing yourselves deeply."

—Neil Clark Warren, PhD

24 Never Lose Sight of the Romance

"It's important to keep setting aside time for romance. It doesn't always mean that you have to go out for dinner or take a trip. Be imaginative. In fact, I think it's better to have little romantic episodes more often than to have one romantic blowout a year. You want this romantic feeling to be threaded through all your days, so it becomes part of the lifeblood of the marriage."

—Barbara Dafoe Whitehead, PhD

Critical Thinking

1. Describe the top three pieces of "advice" in the article that you thought were important and why.

2. In #4, Wexler encourages couples to "drop certain subjects and not even come back to them." What are some instances where you have drop an issue with your partner? How did you decide to let that issue go?

3. Were there any "things" that you did not agree with and why?

4. Were there any pieces of advice that were missing from the list that you would add?

5. Name one piece of advice that you would put into practice in a current or former relationship and why.

Against All Odds

Anne Kingston

Last month, Jillian Harris packed up her bags and moved from Vancouver to Chicago to live with her fiancé, Ed Swiderski, whom she'd known all of nine weeks before giddily agreeing to marry him; they plan to wed within the year. The couple's warp-speed romance, one of several Harris was juggling on the last season of *The Bachelorette,* was served up like spray cheese on crackers to a fixated audience of millions. The 29-year-old gushed about her instant connection with the 30-year-old Swiderski on *Live with Regis and Kelly* in July: "We had that one date when everything came together," she said. "I knew I could not let him go ever."

As psychotic as that statement sounds, it's the linga franca of the whirlwind courtship, a phenomenon far more fascinating in reality than any on faux "reality" programming. Lately there's been a crop of them. Earlier this year, the 70-year-old writer Joyce Carol Oates married Charles Gross, a professor of psychology at Princeton less than a year after her husband of 47 years, with whom she'd had a happy marriage, died. In January, the *National Post* columnist Diane Francis wed John Beck, the CEO of the construction conglomerate Aecon Group, knowing him less than four months. The couple, both in their 60s, met at a dinner thrown by the conservative think tank the Fraser Institute, which, when you think about it, is the perfect forum for finding Mr. or Ms. Right: Beck, who arrived late, ended up in the only available empty chair, next to Francis. The opinionated pundit declines to comment on her personal life, but in an email response to a question from the *Globe and Mail* about the relationship's rapid progression, she wrote: "When it's right you just know it."

The French coined the term *coup de foudre* to describe the love-at-first-sight thunderbolt—fitting, given the impetuous history of its current first couple, 53-year-old Nicolas Sarkozy and 41-year-old Carla Bruni, the supermodel turned songstress. "I was in love at first sight," Bruni told *Vanity Fair* about meeting France's president at a dinner party in 2007. "I was really surprised by him, by his youth, his energy, his physical charm—which you could not actually see so much on television—his charisma." The pair wed in February 2008, less than three months after that fateful night. It was the first marriage for Bruni, who's famed for her sexual conquests, the third for Sarkozy, also known for making amorous leaps.

The certainty, that "I just knew" that underlines the whirlwind marriage, inspires wonder—and cynicism given the wreckage it can leave in its wake. Hollywood provides the most celebrated examples, the most madcap being Pamela Anderson's and Mötley Crüe member Tommy Lee's three-year nuptial spectacle that kicked off in a pheromone haze on a Mexican beach in 1995: Anderson, in a bridal bikini, married the drummer some 96 hours after they were introduced. Then there is the actress Kate Walsh, who crowed about becoming engaged to 20th Century Fox executive Alex Young in May 2007 after knowing him weeks. "I know—I'm literally living the dream," she told *People* magazine. "But you know when you know." The couple wed in September 2007; 15 months later, the marriage was kaput and Walsh is now living the nightmare of a messy public divorce.

Emily Yoffe, the Washington-based writer who's the "Prudence" of *Slate*'s popular advice column "Dear Prudence," believes the love-at-first-sight model can create pressure, and unrealistic expectations. "There are so many paths to falling in love," she says. She gets letters from people who say they're with a wonderful person and are the happiest they've ever been but don't feel the big romantic "This is it!" so common in chick flicks and reality shows: "And I can never be sure if it's 'You're in this genuine boredom' or 'You have this stupid Hollywood thing in your head about what it should be and you're going to miss what real life is.'"

Marriage counsellors too are critical of "instant" relationships, observing they're often animated by delusion and projection. "I see so much of the damage caused by people blindly connecting, rushing through the stages of commitment, and not creating the solid basis a true relationship needs," says Tina Tessina, a marriage therapist and author in Long Beach, Calif.

Programs like *The Bachelorette* foster the myth that love is an instantaneous emotion, says Mary-Lou Galician, who teaches media analysis and criticism at Arizona State University. "We all have had that feeling and then found out what a dreadful mistake it was," she says. "Real love takes time."

Still, enough inspiring examples exist that suggest a quick impulse to marry can be prescient, even shrewd. Exhibit A is lawyer, political operative and University of Toronto chancellor David Peterson and his wife, Shelley, an actress and author: the couple knew one another only 2½ months before they married in London, Ont., in January 1974. He was 29, she was 21. She didn't know what his religious background was, whether his grandparents were alive or whether or not he wanted children, Shelley Peterson admits: "There were a lot of things we hadn't figured out." Thirty-five years, three children and one grandchild later, the former Ontario premier calls the flight to the altar "the smartest thing I ever did." His wife is equally effusive: "I'm more in love with him now than I was then," she says. "I find that astonishing."

Peterson says he was smitten the first time he saw his future wife on stage. He finagled her phone number and called repeatedly. She had no interest in meeting him, she says: "I didn't need more men in my life." Finally she agreed to lunch. "I thought 'I'll just get this over with. One hour, that's it.'"

By the time the soup course came, David Peterson was "head over heels in love," he says: "She was perfect, gorgeous, funny." She too was taken: "I thought he was lovely and intriguing. I thought, 'This is somebody I need to get to know.'" Shelley Peterson speaks of their marriage as inevitable. "There wasn't a moment I wanted to marry him," she says. "It was more that there just wasn't any other thing to do except to marry him."

Waiting wasn't an option, he says: "How could you wait? It's like a cat catching a mouse: you just jump on it. Everyone knew she was perfect. The only question was whether I was good enough for her."

Her friends and family were less enthusiastic. "But I was quite sure," she says. "And on the other hand I felt that if it didn't turn out to be a good idea I could get out of it."

Catherine Burton, a marriage and family therapist in Dallas, has said that couples who move quickly because they've found someone with stellar spouse qualities—being even-tempered, respectful and thoughtful—tend to have stronger marriages. The Petersons' example supports this theory; they both speak of enduring qualities in the other. "I recognized a sincerity, a belief in humanity, an optimism—a lot of things that never change in a person," she says. He praises her character: "She's the most empathetic person, deeply moral, she has a deep knowledge of the world and what's important." Love flourishes only with mutual respect, they agree. They've told their own children never to settle for a relationship that isn't joyful and passionate. "We tell them it's far better to be alone than in an even slightly unhappy relationship," Shelley Peterson says.

But she knows luck played a part. "How would I know that David was all of the things I hoped he was?" she says. "I couldn't know that. I believe I was extraordinarily lucky that the wilful passion I felt as a 21-year-old didn't end in terrible disaster." Her husband agrees: "But there's also brains in it and you have to work on it."

Research on courtship, surprisingly, contradicts the conventional wisdom that the longer the courtship, the more stable the union. The expert in the field is Ted Huston, a professor of human ecology at the University of Texas who set up a project in 1978 that, for decades, followed 168 couples from their newlywed days. He concludes marital happiness is less a result of a courtship's length than its quality: harmonious courtships tend to presage happy marriages; turbulent ones foreshadow problems. He found that the closer a couple's courtship is to the average length of two years, four months, the more successful their marriage will be. Couples very quick or very slow to wed are more likely to divorce, though those who married in a whirlwind tended to remain married longer, which he attributes to the fact that they start off on such an

emotional high they're reluctant to give it up. Those with more drawn-out courtships often hope marriage will improve their relationship; when it doesn't, they quickly conclude it isn't going to work.

Tessina says she has seen successful marriages after quick courtships: "It can work, if both people are really committed to building a life together, and not just to 'being happy' or getting their own individual needs met," she says. Still, she tells couples to slow down and discuss the serious issues: "They can find out pretty quickly if they have enough shared values."

That's the advice Emily Yoffe gives as "Prudence." "My reaction is: 'What's the rush?'" she says. "Wait at least a year—you'll go through the seasons, you'll have had the holiday issues. Also, you'll want to have your first fight. Sometimes it takes quite a while for masks to drop."

Yet she made the marital leap almost as quickly as Bruni and Sarkozy did; she married *Washington Post* writer John Mintz in 1994 within four months of meeting him. She was 38, had never married, and was living in Los Angeles. Mintz was a 41-year-old widower, living in Washington. Their circles overlapped: Yoffe had lived in Washington and they had mutual friends. Yoffe had dated one of Mintz's friends in L.A. When he told her about Mintz's devotion to his wife during her long illness she was impressed. She didn't know at the time that the friend was turning to Mintz for advice when the relationship began to falter. Mintz, who'd been widowed and single for five years, found himself becoming intrigued by Yoffe. "After a while, John was thinking to himself, 'I have a conflict of interest here: she sounds perfect for me,'" Yoffe says with a laugh. When Yoffe and the friend stopped seeing one another, Mintz called her. After several conversations, he concocted a reason to visit L.A. for business. Yoffe recalls telling her mother that she wasn't sure she wanted to move back to Washington. "My mother said, 'What are you talking about? You haven't even gone out with him yet!' But she didn't understand what this was about, that the stakes were high," she says.

Their maturity was a benefit, Yoffe believes: "We just knew. But we knew in a way that had I been 24 I wouldn't have known." They also knew the attraction was more than lust: "We couldn't stop talking: it's one thing if you can't stop the other 'i-n-g'; that's great but it burns out fast."

Yoffe speaks of the easy comfort and calm many quick-to-marry couples experience, what some refer to as "being home," absent the common "Will he call me?" dating angst. "We were able to read one another and realize we're not on first-date best behavior. We got each other's jokes. I felt he got me, I got him." Six weeks later, standing in the dairy section of a Washington supermarket, they decided to marry. "For us there was a rush," she says. "We wanted to try to have kids. The clock was ticking." Today, the couple are the happily married parents of a 13-year-old daughter.

Older couples often know what they need from a partner, says Tessina, which can help them figure out more quickly if their relationship will succeed, though not always: "Some just repeat the same old mistakes." What counts more, she says, is "emotional maturity."

Yet having the clock ticking literally can spur couples on, as was the case with 61-year-old Shirley Griff, a real estate agent in Thorold, Ont., who married Bill Coates, also 61, in November 2007, six months to the day after they met through an online dating site. Griff's 30-year marriage ended in 2002. Coates, a professional stamp collector, was divorced after a 24-year marriage. They met for lunch at one o'clock. Griff recalls tearing herself away at 4:15 for a 4:30 appointment. "We just spent so much time together and have so much in common," she says. "We're two days apart in age. We're both Pisces." His devotion to his mother impressed her: "To me that's a sign he's going to be appreciative of you as well." He also clicked with her two adult children, who teased her about the suddenness of the wedding, she says, which in part was spurred by their desire that Coates's 92-year-old mother be there: "My daughter asked me: 'Are you pregnant, Mom?'"

Waiting didn't make sense, Griff says. "It didn't seem it would prove anything to us, like it would be any different."

Such is the logic from inside the whirlwind courtship. Outside it's another matter. Asked what he'd say to his children if they announced they were marrying someone they had known for a matter of weeks, the happily married David Peterson is adamant: "I'd tell them they were crazy."

Critical Thinking

1. What are some of the reasons why couples are not spending as much time dating before marriage?

2. What do you feel is a reasonable time for couples to date before getting married?

3. List some of the characteristics of the successful relationships in the article. Are these characteristics that are found in any couple?

4. Do you feel that age is a factor in quicker marrying times? What age do you want to be married by and why?

The Expectations Trap

Much of the discontent couples encounter today is really culturally inflicted, although we're conditioned to blame our partners for our unhappiness. Yet research points to ways couples can immunize themselves against unseen pressures now pulling them apart.

HARA ESTROFF MARANO

Six years, ten months, and eight days into their marriage, Sam and Melissa blew apart. Everyone was stunned, most of all the couple themselves. One day she was your basic stressed-out professional woman (and mother of a 3-year-old) carrying the major financial burden of their household. The next day she was a betrayed wife. The affair Sam disclosed detonated a caterwaul of hurt heard by every couple in their circle and her large coterie of friends and family. With speed verging on inevitability, the public knowledge of their private life commandeered the driver's seat of their own destiny. A surge of support for Melissa as the wronged woman swiftly isolated Sam emotionally and precluded deep discussion of the conditions that had long alienated him. Out of respect for the pain that his mere presence now caused, Sam decamped within days. He never moved back in.

It's not clear that the couple could have salvaged the relationship if they had tried. It wasn't just the infidelity. "We had so many background and stylistic differences," says Sam. "It was like we came from two separate cultures. We couldn't take out the garbage without a Geneva Accord." Constant negotiation was necessary, but if there was time, there was also usually too much accumulated irritation for Melissa to tolerate. And then, opening a public window on the relationship seemed to close the door on the possibility of working through the disappointments, the frustrations, the betrayal.

Within weeks, the couple was indeed in discussions—for a divorce. At least they both insisted on mediation, not litigation, and their lawyers complied. A couple of months, and some time and determination later, they had a settlement. Only now that Sam and Melissa have settled into their mostly separate lives, and their daughter appears to be doing well with abundant care from both her parents, are they catching their respective breaths—two years later.

Americans value marriage more than people do in any other culture, and it holds a central place in our dreams. Over 90 percent of young adults aspire to marriage—although fewer are actually choosing it, many opting instead for cohabitation. But no matter how you count it, Americans have the highest rate of romantic breakup in the world, says Andrew J. Cherlin, professor of sociology and public policy at Johns Hopkins. As with Sam and Melissa, marriages are discarded often before the partners know what hit them.

"By age 35, 10 percent of American women have lived with three or more husbands or domestic partners," Cherlin reports in his recent book, *The Marriage-Go-Round: The State of Marriage and the Family in America Today.* "Children of married parents in America face a higher risk of seeing them break up than children born of unmarried parents in Sweden."

With general affluence has come a plethora of choices, including constant choices about our personal and family life. Even marriage itself is now a choice. "The result is an ongoing self-appraisal of how your personal life is going, like having a continual readout of your emotional heart rate," says Cherlin. You get used to the idea of always making choices to improve your happiness.

The constant appraisal of personal life to improve happiness creates a heightened sensitivity to problems that arise in intimate relationships.

The heightened focus on options "creates a heightened sensitivity to problems that arise in intimate relationships." And negative emotions get priority processing in our brains. "There are so many opportunities to decide that it's unsatisfactory," says Cherlin.

It would be one thing if we were living more satisfied lives than ever. But just gauging by the number of relationships wrecked every year, we're less satisfied, says Cherlin. "We're carrying over into our personal lives the fast pace of decisions and actions we have everywhere else, and that may not be for the best." More than ever, we're paying attention to the most volatile parts of our emotional makeup—the parts that are too reactive to momentary events to give meaning to life.

More than ever, we're paying attention to the most volatile parts of our emotional makeup—parts that are too reactive to momentary events to give meaning to life.

Because our intimate relationships are now almost wholly vehicles for meeting our emotional needs, and with almost all our emotions invested in one relationship, we tend to look upon any unhappiness we experience—whatever the source—as a failure of a partner to satisfy our longings. Disappointment inevitably feels so *personal* we see no other possibility but to hunt for individual psychological reasons—that is, to blame our partners for our own unhappiness.

But much—perhaps most—of the discontent we now encounter in close relationships is culturally inflicted, although we rarely interpret our experience that way. Culture—the pressure to constantly monitor our happiness, the plethora of choices surreptitiously creating an expectation of perfection, the speed of everyday life—always climbs into bed with us. An accumulation of forces has made the cultural climate hostile to long-term relationships today.

Attuned to disappointment and confused about its source, we wind up discarding perfectly good relationships. People work themselves up over "the ordinary problems of marriage, for which, by the way, they usually fail to see their own contributions," says William Doherty, professor of family sciences at the University of Minnesota. "They badger their partners to change, convince themselves nothing will budge, and so work their way out of really good relationships." Doherty believes it's possible to stop the careering disappointment even when people believe a relationship is over.

It's not going to happen by putting the genie back in the bottle. It's not possible to curb the excess of options life now offers. And speed is a fixture of the ongoing technological revolution, no matter how much friction it creates in personal lives. Yet new research points to ways that actually render them irrelevant. We are, after all, the architects of our own passions.

The Purpose of Marriage

Marriage probably evolved as the best way to pool the labor of men and women to enable families to subsist and assure that children survive to independence—and data indicate it still is. But beyond the basics, the purpose of marriage has shifted constantly, says Stephanie Coontz, a historian at Washington's Evergreen State College. It helps to remember that marriage evolved in an atmosphere of scarcity, the conditions that prevailed for almost all of human history. "The earliest purpose of marriage was to make strategic alliances with

---

Case Study
Stephen and Christina

Five years into his marriage, not long after the birth of his first son, most of Stephen G.'s interactions with his wife were not pleasant. "I thought the difficulties would pass," he recalls. "My wife, Christina, got fed up faster and wanted me to leave." He was traveling frequently and finances were thin; she'd gone back to school full-time after having worked until the baby was born. "Very few needs were being met for either of us. We were either yelling or in a cold war."

They entered counseling to learn how to co-parent if they indeed separated. "It helped restore our friendship: At least we could talk civilly. That led to deeper communication—we could actually listen to each other without getting defensive. We heard that we were both hurting, both feeling the stress of new parenthood without a support system of either parents or friends. We could talk about the ways we weren't there for each other without feeling attacked. It took a lot longer for the romance to return."

Stephen, now 37, a sales representative for a pharmaceutical company in San Francisco, says it was a time of "growing up. I had to accept that I had new responsibilities. And I had to accept that my partner, now 38, is not ideal in every way although she is ideal in many ways. But her short temper is not enough of a reason to leave the relationship and our two kids. When I wish she'd be different, I have to remind myself of all the ways she is the person I want to be with. It's not something you 'get over.' You accept it."

---

other people, to turn strangers into relatives," says Coontz. "As society became more differentiated, marriage became a major mechanism for adjusting your position."

It wasn't until the 18th century that anyone thought that love might have anything to do with marriage, but love was held in check by a sense of duty. Even through the 19th century, the belief prevailed that females and males had different natures and couldn't he expected to understand each other well. Only in the 20th century did the idea take hold that men and women should be companions, that they should be passionate, and that both should get sexual and personal fulfillment from marriage.

We're still trying to figure out how to do that—and get the laundry done, too. The hassles of a negotiated and constantly renegotiated relationship—few wish a return to inequality—assure a ready source of stress or disappointment or both.

From We to Me

Our mind-set has further shifted over the past few decades, experts suggest. Today, the minute one partner is faced with dissatisfaction—feeling stressed-out or neglected, having

Case Study
Susan and Tim

Susan Pohlman, now 50, reluctantly accompanied her workaholic husband on a business trip to Italy believing it would be their last together. Back home in Los Angeles were their two teenagers, their luxurious home, their overfurnished lives—and the divorce lawyer she had contacted to end their 18-year marriage.

They were leading such parallel lives that collaboration had turned to competition, with fights over things like who spent more time with the kids and who spent more time working. But knocked off balance by the beauty of the coast near Genoa toward the end of the trip, Tim asked, out of the blue, "What if we lived here?" "The spirit of this odd day overtook me," recalls Susan. At 6 P.M. on the evening before departure, they were shown a beautiful apartment overlooking the water. Despite knowing no Italian, they signed a lease on the spot. Two months later, with their house sold, they moved with their kids to Italy for a year.

"In L.A. we were four people going in four directions. In Italy, we became completely dependent on each other. How to get a phone? How to shop for food? Also, we had no belongings. The simplicity forced us to notice the experiences of life. Often, we had no idea what we were doing. There was lots of laughing at and with each other." Susan says she "became aware of the power of adventure and of doing things together, and how they became a natural bridge to intimacy."

Both Pohlmans found Italy offered "a more appreciative lifestyle." Says Susan: "I realized the American Dream was pulling us apart. We followed the formula of owning, having, pushing each other. You have all this stuff but you're miserable because what you're really craving is interaction." Too, she says, American life is exhausting, and "exhaustion distorts your ability to judge problems."

Now back in the U.S. and living in Arizona, the Pohmans believe they needed to remove themselves from the culture to see its distorting effects. "And we needed to participate in a paradigm shift: 'I'm not perfect, you're not perfect; let's not get hung up on our imperfections.'" But the most powerful element of their move could be reproduced anywhere, she says: "The simplicity was liberating."

a partner who isn't overly expressive or who works too hard or doesn't initiate sex very often—then the communal ideal we bring to relationships is jettisoned and an individualistic mentality asserts itself. We revert to a stingier self that has been programmed into us by the consumer culture, which has only become increasingly pervasive, the current recession notwithstanding.

Psychologically, the goal of life becomes *my* happiness. "The minute your needs are not being met then you appropriate the individualistic norm," says Doherty. This accelerating consumer mind-set is a major portal through which destructive forces gain entry and undermine conjoint life.

"Marriage is for *me*" is the way Austin, Texas, family therapist Pat Love puts it. "It's for meeting *my* needs." It's not about what *I do,* but how it makes me *feel.*

Such beliefs lead to a sense of entitlement: "I deserve better than I'm getting." Doherty sees that as the basic message of almost every advertisement in the consumer culture. You deserve more and we can provide it. You begin to think: This isn't the deal I signed up for. Or you begin to feel that you're putting into this a lot more than you're getting out. "We believe in our inalienable right to the intimate relationships of our choice," says Doherty.

In allowing such free-market values to seep into our private lives, we come to believe that a partner's job is, above all, to provide pleasure. "People do not go into relationships because they want to learn how to negotiate and master difficulties," observes Brown University psychiatrist Scott Haltzman. "They want the other person to provide pleasure." It's partner as service provider. The pleasure bond, unfortunately, is as volatile as the emotions that underlie it and as hollow and fragile as the hedonic sense of happiness.

The Expectations Trap: Perfection, Please

If there's one thing that most explicitly detracts from the enjoyment of relationships today, it's an abundance of choice. Psychologist Barry Schwartz would call it an *excess* of choice—the tyranny of abundance. We see it as a measure of our autonomy and we firmly believe that freedom of choice will lead to fulfillment. Our antennae are always up for better opportunities, finds Schwartz, professor of psychology at Swarthmore College.

Just as only the best pair of jeans will do, so will only the best partner—whatever that is. "People walk starry-eyed looking not into the eyes of their romantic partner but over their romantic partner's shoulder, in case there might be somebody better walking by. This is not the road to successful long-term relationships." It does not stop with marriage. And it undermines commitment by encouraging people to keep their options open.

Like Doherty, Schwartz sees it as a consequence of a consumer society. He also sees it as a self-fulfilling phenomenon. "If you think there might be something better around the next comer, then there will be, because you're not fully committed to the relationship you've got."

It's naïve to expect relationships to feel good every minute. Every relationship has its bumps. How big a bump does it have to be before you do something about it? As Hopkins's Cherlin says, if you're constantly asking yourself whether you should leave, "there may be a day when the answer is yes. In any marriage there may be a day when the answer is yes."

One of the problems with unrestrained choice, explains Schwartz, is that it raises expectations to the breaking point.

A sense of multiple alternatives, of unlimited possibility, breeds in us the illusion that perfection exists out there, somewhere, if only we could find it. This one's sense of humor, that one's looks, another one's charisma—we come to imagine that there will be a package in which all these desirable features coexist. We search for perfection because we believe we are entitled to the best—even if perfection is an illusion foisted on us by an abundance of possibilities.

If perfection is what you expect, you will always be disappointed, says Schwartz. We become picky and unhappy. The cruel joke our psychology plays on us, of course, is that we are terrible at knowing what will satisfy us or at knowing how any experience will make us feel.

> **A sense of multiple alternatives, of unlimited possibility, breeds in us the illusion that the perfect person is out there waiting to be found.**

If the search through all possibilities weren't exhausting (and futile) enough, thinking about attractive features of the alternatives not chosen—what economists call opportunity costs—reduces the potential pleasure in whatever choice we finally do make. The more possibilities, the more opportunity costs—and the more we think about them, the more we come to regret any choice. "So, once again," says Schwartz, "a greater variety of choices actually makes us feel worse."

Ultimately, our excess of choice leads to lack of intimacy. "How is anyone going to stack up against this perfect person who's out there somewhere just waiting to be found?" asks Schwartz. "It creates doubt about this person, who seems like a good person, someone I might even be in love with—but who knows what's possible *out* there? Intimacy takes time to develop. You need to have some reason to put in the time. If you're full of doubt at the start, you're not going to put in the time."

Moreover, a focus on one's own preferences can come at the expense of those of others. As Schwartz said in his 2004 book, *The Paradox of Choice: Why More Is Less,* "most people find it extremely challenging to balance the conflicting impulses of freedom of choice on the one hand and loyalty and commitment on the other."

And yet, throughout, we are focused on the partner we want to have, not on the one we want—or need—to be. That maybe the worst choice of all.

Disappointment—or Tragedy?

The heightened sensitivity to relationship problems that follows from constantly appraising our happiness encourages couples to turn disappointment into tragedy, Doherty contends.

Inevitably, images of the perfect relationship dancing in our heads collide with our sense of entitlement; "I'm entitled to the best possible marriage." The reality of disappointment becomes intolerable. "It's part of a cultural belief system that says we are entitled to everything we feel we need."

Through the alchemy of desire, wants become needs, and unfulfilled needs become personal tragedies. "A husband who isn't very expressive of his feelings can be a disappointment or a tragedy, depending on whether it's an entitlement," says Doherty. "And that's very much a cultural phenomenon." We take the everyday disappointments of relationships and treat them as intolerable, see them as demeaning—the equivalent of alcoholism, say, or abuse. "People work their way into 'I'm a tragic figure' around the ordinary problems of marriage." Such stories are so widespread, Doherty is no longer inclined to see them as reflecting an individual psychological problem, although that is how he was trained—and how he practiced for many years as an eminent family therapist. "I see it first now as a cultural phenomenon."

First Lady Michelle Obama is no stranger to the disappointment that pervades relationships today. In *Barack and Michelle: Portrait of an American Marriage,* by Christopher Anderson, she confides how she reached a "state of desperation" while working full-time, bringing in the majority of the family income, raising two daughters, and rarely seeing her husband, who was then spending most of his week away from their Chicago home as an Illinois state senator, a job she thought would lead nowhere while it paid little. "She's killing me with this constant criticism," Barack complained. "She just seems so bitter, so angry all the time." She was annoyed that he "seems to think he can just go out there and pursue his dream and leave all the heavy lifting to me."

But then she had an epiphany: She remembered the guy she fell in love with. "I figured out that I was pushing to make Barack be something I wanted him to be for me. I was depending on him to make me happy. Except it didn't have anything to do with him. I needed support. I didn't necessarily need it from Barack."

Certainly, commitment narrows choice. But it is the ability to remember you really do love someone—even though you may not be feeling it at the moment.

Commitment is the ability to sustain an investment, to honor values over momentary feelings. The irony, of course, is that while we want happiness, it isn't a moment-by-moment experience; the deepest, most enduring form of happiness is the result of sustained emotional investments in other people.

Architects of the Heart

One of the most noteworthy findings emerging from relationship research is that desire isn't just something we passively feel when everything's going right; it develops in direct response to what we do. Simply having fun together, for example, is crucial to keeping the sex drive alive.

But in the churn of daily life, we tend to give short shrift to creating positive experiences. Over time, we typically become more oriented to dampening threats and insecurities—to resolving conflict, to eliminating jealousy, to banishing problems. But the brain is wired with both a positive and negative motivational system, and satisfaction and desire demand keeping the brain's positive system well-stoked.

Even for long-term couples, spending time together in novel, interesting, or challenging activities—games, dancing, even conversation—enhances feelings of closeness, passionate love, and satisfaction with the relationship. Couples recapture the excitement of the early days of being in love. Such passion naturally feeds commitment.

From Michelle to Michelangelo

Important as it is to choose the right partner, it's probably more important to *be* the right partner. Most people are focused on changing the wrong person in the relationship; if anyone has to change in a relationship, it's you—although preferably with the help of your partner.

Important as it is to choose the right partner, it's probably more important to *be* the right partner. We focus on changing the wrong person.

Ultimately, "Marriage is an inside job," Pat Love told the 2009 Smart Marriages Conference. "It's internal to the person. You have to let it do its work." And its biggest job is helping individuals grow up. "Marriage is about getting over yourself. Happiness is not about focusing on yourself." Happiness is about holding onto your values, deciding who you are and being that person, using your particular talent, and investing in others.

Unfortunately, says Margin family therapist and *PT* blogger Susan Pease Gadoua, not enough people today are willing to do the hard work of becoming a more mature person. "They think they have a lot more choices. And they think life will be easier in another relationship. What they don't realize is that it will be the same relationship—just with a different name."

The question is not how you want your partner to change but what kind of partner and person you want to be. In the best relationships, not only are you thinking about who you want to be, but your partner is willing to help you get there. Psychologist Caryl E. Rusbult calls it the Michelangelo phenomenon. Just as Michelangelo felt the figures he created were already "in" the stones, "slumbering within the actual self is an ideal form," explains Eli Finkel, associate professor of psychology at Northwestern University and frequent Rusbult collaborator. Your partner becomes an ally in sculpting your ideal self, in bringing out the person you dream of becoming, leading you to a deep form of personal growth as well as long-term satisfaction with life and with the relationship.

Case Study
Patty and Rod

Patty Newbold had married "a really great guy," but by the time their 13th anniversary rolled around, she had a long list of things he needed to change to make the marriage work. At 34, she felt depressed, frantic—and guilty, as Rod was fighting a chronic disease. But she had reached a breaking point, "I read my husband my list of unmet needs and suggested a divorce," even though what she really wanted was her marriage back. "I wanted to feel loved again. But it didn't seem possible."

Newbold has had a long time to think about that list. Her husband died the next day, a freak side effect of his medications. "He was gone, but the list remained. Out of perhaps 30 needs, only one was eased by losing him. I was free now to move the drinking glasses next to the sink."

As she read through the list the morning after he died, she realized that "marriage isn't about my needs or his needs or about how well we communicate about our needs. It's about loving and being loved. *Life* is about meeting (or letting go of) my own *needs. Marriage* is about loving another person and receiving love in return. It suddenly became oh so clear that receiving love is something I make happen, not him." And then she was flooded with memories of all the times "I'd been offered love by this wonderful man and rejected it because I was too wrapped up in whatever need I was facing at the time."

Revitalized is "a funny word to describe a relationship in which one party is dead," she reports, "but ours was revitalized. I was completely changed, too," Everything she learned that awful day has gone into a second marriage, now well into its second decade.

It takes a partner who supports your dreams, the traits and qualities you want to develop—whether or not you've articulated them clearly or simply expressed vague yearnings. "People come to reflect what their partners see in them and elicit from them," Finkel and Rusbult report in *Current Directions in Psychological Science.*

Such affirmation promotes trust in the partner and strengthens commitment. And commitment, Rusbult has found, is a key predictor of relationship durability. "It creates positive bias towards each other," says Finkel. "It feels good to achieve our goals. It's deeply satisfying and meaningful." In addition, it immunizes the relationship against potential distractions—all those "perfect" others. Finkel explains, "It motivates the derogation of alternative partners." It creates the perception—the illusion—that even the most attractive alternative partners are unappealing. Attention to them gets turned off—one of the many cognitive gymnastics we engage in to ward off doubts.

Like growth, commitment is an inside job. It's not a simple vow. Partners see each other in ways that enhance their connection and fend off threats. It fosters the perception that the relationship you're in is better than that of others. It breeds the inclination to react constructively—by accommodation—rather than destructively when a partner does something inconsiderate. It even motivates that most difficult of tasks, forgiveness for the ultimate harm of betrayal, Rusbult has shown.

It is a willingness—stemming in part from an understanding that your well-being and your partner's are linked over the long term—to depart from direct self-interest, such as erecting a grudge when you feel hurt.

The Michelangelo phenomenon gives the lie to the soul mate search. You can't find the perfect person; there is no such thing. And even if you think you could, the person he or she is today is, hopefully, not quite the person he or she wants to be 10 years down the road. You and your partner help each other become a more perfect person—perfect, that is,

according to your own inner ideals. You are both, with mutual help, constantly evolving.

Critical Thinking

1. Describe some of the influences that culture has on happiness within marriages.
2. In the case study of Stephen and Christina, what do you think were some of the causes of the friction in their relationship?
3. What are some ways that couples can keep their relationship from becoming strained?
4. List some of the expectations that you have or had in a relationship. Did you see any in the reading?
5. Do you think that there is a trend in today's society that marriage should be perfect? Why or why not?

Fats, Carbs and the Science of Conception

In a groundbreaking new book, Harvard researchers look at the role of diet, exercise, and weight control in fertility. Guarantee: You will be surprised.

JORGE E. CHAVARRO, MD, WALTER C. WILLETT, MD, AND PATRICK J. SKERRETT

Every new life starts with two seemingly simple events. First, an active sperm burrows into a perfectly mature egg. Then the resulting fertilized egg nestles into the specially prepared lining of the uterus and begins to grow. The key phrase in that description is "seemingly simple." Dozens of steps influenced by a cascade of carefully timed hormones are needed to make and mature eggs and sperm. Their union is both a mad dash and a complex dance, choreographed by hormones, physiology and environmental cues.

A constellation of other factors can come into play. Many couples delay having a baby until they are financially ready or have established themselves in their professions. Waiting, though, decreases the odds of conceiving and increases the chances of having a miscarriage. Fewer than 10 percent of women in their early 20s have issues with infertility, compared with nearly 30 percent of those in their early 40s. Sexually transmitted diseases such as chlamydia and gonorrhea, which are on the upswing, can cause or contribute to infertility. The linked epidemics of obesity and diabetes sweeping the country have reproductive repercussions. Environmental contaminants known as endocrine disruptors, such as some pesticides and emissions from burning plastics, appear to affect fertility in women and men. Stress and anxiety, both in general and about fertility, can also interfere with getting pregnant. Add all these to the complexity of conception and it's no wonder that infertility is a common problem, besetting an estimated 6 million American couples.

It's almost become a cliché that diet, exercise and lifestyle choices affect how long you'll live, the health of your heart, the odds you'll develop cancer and a host of other health-related issues. Is fertility on this list? The answer to that question has long been a qualified "maybe," based on old wives' tales, conventional wisdom—and almost no science. Farmers, ranchers and animal scientists know more about how nutrition affects fertility in cows, pigs and other commercially important animals than fertility experts know about how it affects reproduction in humans. There are small hints scattered across medical journals, but few systematic studies of this crucial connection in people.

We set out to change this critical information gap with the help of more than 18,000 women taking part in the Nurses' Health Study, a long-term research project looking at the effects of diet and other factors on the development of chronic conditions such as heart disease, cancer and other diseases. Each of these women said she was trying to have a baby. Over eight years of follow-up, most of them did. About one in six women, though, had some trouble getting pregnant, including hundreds who experienced ovulatory infertility—a problem related to the maturation or release of a mature egg each month. When we compared their diets, exercise habits and other lifestyle choices with those of women who readily got pregnant, several key differences emerged. We have translated these differences into fertility-boosting strategies.

At least for now, these recommendations are aimed at preventing and reversing ovulatory infertility, which accounts for one quarter or more of all cases of infertility. They won't work for infertility due to physical impediments like blocked fallopian tubes. They may work for other types of infertility, but we don't yet have enough data to explore connections between nutrition and infertility due to other causes. And since the Nurses' Health Study doesn't include information on the participants' partners, we weren't able to explore how nutrition affects male infertility. From what we have gleaned from the limited research in this area, some of our strategies might improve fertility in men, too. The plan described in The Fertility Diet doesn't guarantee a pregnancy any more than do in vitro fertilization or other forms of assisted reproduction. But it's virtually free, available to everyone, has no side effects, sets the stage for a healthy pregnancy, and forms the foundation of a healthy eating strategy for motherhood and beyond. That's a winning combination no matter how you look at it.

Slow Carbs, Not No Carbs

Once upon a time, and not that long ago, carbohydrates were the go-to gang for taste, comfort, convenience and energy. Bread, pasta, rice, potatoes—these were the highly recommended, base-of-the-food-pyramid foods that supplied us with half or more of our calories. Then in rumbled the Atkins and South Beach diets. In a scene out of George Orwell's "1984," good became bad almost overnight as the two weight-loss juggernauts turned carbohydrates into dietary demons, vilifying them as the source of big bellies and jiggling thighs. Following the no-carb gospel, millions of Americans spurned carbohydrates in hopes of shedding pounds. Then, like all diet fads great and small, the no-carb craze lost its luster and faded from prominence.

It had a silver lining, though, and not just for those selling low-carb advice and products. All the attention made scientists and the rest of us more aware of carbohydrates and their role in a healthy diet. It spurred several solid head-to-head comparisons of low-carb and low-fat diets that have given us a better understanding of how carbohydrates affect weight and weight loss. The new work supports the growing realization that carbohydrate choices have a major impact—for better and for worse—on the risk for heart disease, stroke, type 2 diabetes and digestive health.

New research from the Nurses' Health Study shows that carbohydrate choices also influence fertility. Eating lots of easily digested carbohydrates (fast carbs), such as white bread, potatoes and sugared sodas, increases the odds that you'll find yourself struggling with ovulatory infertility. Choosing slowly digested carbohydrates that are rich in fiber can improve fertility. This lines up nicely with work showing that a diet rich in these slow carbs and fiber before pregnancy helps prevent gestational diabetes, a common and worrisome problem for pregnant women and their babies. What do carbohydrates have to do with ovulation and pregnancy?

More than any other nutrient, carbohydrates determine your blood-sugar and insulin levels. When these rise too high, as they do in millions of individuals with insulin resistance, they disrupt the finely tuned balance of hormones needed for reproduction. The ensuing hormonal changes throw ovulation off-kilter.

Knowing that diet can strongly influence blood sugar and insulin, we wondered if carbohydrate choices could influence fertility in average, relatively healthy women. The answer from the Nurses' Health Study was yes. We started by grouping the study participants from low daily carbohydrate intake to high. One of the first things we noticed was a connection between high carbohydrate intake and healthy lifestyles.

Women in the high-carb group, who got nearly 60 percent of their calories from carbs, ate less fat and animal protein, drank less alcohol and coffee, and consumed more plant protein and fiber than those in the low-carb group, who got 42 percent of calories from carbohydrates. Women in the top group also weighed less, weren't as likely to smoke and were more physically active. This is a good sign that carbohydrates can be just fine for health, especially if you choose good ones.

The *total* amount of carbohydrate in the diet wasn't connected with ovulatory infertility. Women in the low-carb and high-carb groups were equally likely to have had fertility problems. That wasn't a complete surprise. As we described earlier, different carbohydrate sources can have different effects on blood sugar, insulin and long-term health.

Evaluating total carbohydrate intake can hide some important differences. So we looked at something called the glycemic load. This relatively new measure conveys information about both the amount of carbohydrate in the diet and how quickly it is turned to blood sugar. The more fast carbs in the diet, the higher the glycemic load. (For more on glycemic load, go to health.harvard.edu/newsweek.) Women in the highest glycemic-load category were 92 percent more likely to have had ovulatory infertility than women in the lowest category, after accounting for age, smoking, how much animal and vegetable protein they ate, and other factors that can also influence fertility. In other words, eating a lot of easily digested carbohydrates increases the odds of ovulatory infertility, while eating more slow carbs decreases the odds.

Because the participants of the Nurses' Health Study complete reports every few years detailing their average daily diets, we were able to see if certain foods contributed to ovulatory infertility more than others. In general, cold breakfast cereals, white rice and potatoes were linked with a higher risk of ovulatory infertility. Slow carbs, such as brown rice, pasta and dark bread, were linked with greater success getting pregnant.

Computer models of the nurses' diets were also revealing. We electronically replaced different nutrients with carbohydrates. Most of these substitutions didn't make a difference. One, though, did. Adding more carbohydrates at the expense of naturally occurring fats predicted a decrease in fertility. This could very well mean that natural fats, especially unsaturated fats, improve ovulation when they replace easily digested carbohydrates.

In a nutshell, results from the Nurses' Health Study indicate that the *amount* of carbohydrates in the diet doesn't affect fertility, but the *quality* of those carbohydrates does. Eating a lot of rapidly digested carbohydrates that continually boost your blood-sugar and insulin levels higher can lower your chances of getting pregnant. This is especially true if you are eating carbohydrates in place of healthful unsaturated fats. On the other hand, eating whole grains, beans, vegetables and whole fruits—all of which are good sources of slowly digested carbohydrates—can improve ovulation and your chances of getting pregnant.

Eating whole grains, beans, vegetables and whole fruits—all sources of 'slow carbs'—can improve ovulation and chances of pregnancy.

Balancing Fats

In 2003, the government of Denmark made a bold decision that is helping protect its citizens from heart disease: it essentially banned trans fats in fast food, baked goods and other commercially prepared foods. That move may have an unexpected effect—more little Danes. Exciting findings from the Nurses' Health Study indicate that trans fats are a powerful deterrent to ovulation and conception. Eating less of this artificial fat can improve fertility, and simultaneously adding in healthful unsaturated fats whenever possible can boost it even further.

Women, their midwives and doctors, and fertility researchers have known for ages that body fat and energy stores affect reproduction. Women who don't have enough stored energy to sustain a pregnancy often have trouble ovulating or stop menstruating altogether. Women who have too much stored energy often have difficulty conceiving for other reasons, many of which affect ovulation. These include insensitivity to the hormone insulin, an excess of male sex hormones and overproduction of leptin, a hormone that helps the body keep tabs on body fat.

A related issue is whether *dietary* fats influence ovulation and reproduction. We were shocked to discover that this was largely uncharted territory. Until now, only a few studies have explored this connection. They focused mainly on the relationship between fat intake and characteristics of the menstrual cycle, such as cycle length and the duration of different phases of the cycle. In general, these studies suggest that more fat in the diet, and in some cases more saturated fat, improves the menstrual cycle. Most of these studies were very small and didn't account for total calories, physical activity or other factors that also influence reproduction. None of them examined the effect of dietary fat on fertility.

The dearth of research in this area has been a gaping hole in nutrition research. If there is a link between fats in the diet and reproduction, then simple changes in food choices could offer delicious, easy and inexpensive ways to improve fertility. The Nurses' Health Study research team looked for connections between dietary fats and fertility from a number of different angles. Among the 18,555 women in the study, the total amount of fat in the diet wasn't connected with ovulatory infertility once weight, exercise, smoking and other factors that can influence reproduction had been accounted for. The same was true for cholesterol, saturated fat and monounsaturated fat—none were linked with fertility or infertility. A high intake of polyunsaturated fat appeared to provide some protection against ovulatory infertility in women who also had high intakes of iron, but the effect wasn't strong enough to be sure exactly what role this healthy fat plays in fertility and infertility.

Trans fats were a different story. Across the board, the more trans fat in the diet, the greater the likelihood of developing ovulatory infertility. We saw an effect even at daily trans fat intakes of about four grams a day. That's less than the amount the average American gets each day.

Eating more trans fat usually means eating less of another type of fat or carbohydrates. Computer models of the nurses' diet patterns indicated that eating a modest amount of trans fat (2 percent of calories) in place of other, more healthful nutrients like polyunsaturated fat, monounsaturated fat or carbohydrate would dramatically increase the risk of infertility. To put this into perspective, for someone who eats 2,000 calories a day, 2 percent of calories translates into about four grams of trans fat.

That's the amount in two tablespoons of stick margarine, one medium order of fast-food french fries or one doughnut.

Fats aren't merely inert carriers of calories or building blocks for hormones or cellular machinery. They sometimes have powerful biological effects, such as turning genes on or off, revving up or calming inflammation and influencing cell function. Unsaturated fats do things to improve fertility—increase insulin sensitivity and cool inflammation—that are the opposite of what trans fats do. That is probably why the largest decline in fertility among the nurses was seen when trans fats were eaten instead of monounsaturated fats.

The Protein Factor

At the center of most dinner plates sits, to put it bluntly, a hunk of protein. Beef, chicken and pork are Americans' favorites, trailed by fish. Beans lag far, far behind. That's too bad. Beans are an excellent source of protein and other needed nutrients, like fiber and many minerals. And by promoting the lowly bean from side dish to center stage and becoming more inventive with protein-rich nuts, you might find yourself eating for two. Findings from the Nurses' Health Study indicate that getting more protein from plants and less from animals is another big step toward walking away from ovulatory infertility.

Scattered hints in the medical literature that protein in the diet may influence blood sugar, sensitivity to insulin and the production of insulin-like growth factor-1—all of which play important roles in ovulation—prompted us to look at protein's impact on ovulatory infertility in the Nurses' Health Study.

We grouped the participants by their average daily protein intake. The lowest-protein group took in an average of 77 grams a day; the highest, an average of 115 grams. After factoring in smoking, fat intake, weight and other things that can affect fertility, we found that women in the highest-protein group were 41 percent more likely to have reported problems with ovulatory infertility than women in the lowest-protein group.

When we looked at animal protein intake separately from plant protein, an interesting distinction appeared. Ovulatory infertility was 39 percent more likely in women with the highest intake of animal protein than in those with the lowest. The reverse was true for women with the highest intake of plant protein, who were substantially less likely to have had ovulatory infertility than women with the lowest plant protein intake.

That's the big picture. Computer models helped refine these relationships and put them in perspective. When total calories were kept constant, adding one serving a day of red meat, chicken or turkey predicted nearly a one-third increase in the risk of ovulatory infertility. And while adding one serving a day of fish or eggs didn't influence ovulatory infertility, adding one serving a day of beans, peas, tofu or soybeans, peanuts or other nuts predicted modest protection against ovulatory infertility.

Eating more of one thing means eating less of another, if you want to keep your weight stable. We modeled the effect that juggling the proportions of protein and carbohydrate would have on fertility. Adding animal protein instead of carbohydrate was related to a greater risk of ovulatory infertility. Swapping 25 grams of animal protein for 25 grams of carbohydrates upped the risk by nearly 20 percent. Adding plant protein instead of carbohydrates was related to a lower risk of ovulatory infertility. Swapping 25 grams of plant protein for 25 grams of carbohydrates shrank the risk by 43 percent. Adding plant protein instead of animal protein was even more effective. Replacing 25 grams of animal protein with 25 grams of plant protein was related to a 50 percent lower risk of ovulatory infertility.

These results point the way to another strategy for overcoming ovulatory infertility—eating more protein from plants and less from animals. They also add to the small but growing body of evidence that plant protein is somehow different from animal protein.

Milk and Ice Cream

Consider the classic sundae: a scoop of creamy vanilla ice cream crisscrossed by rivulets of chocolate sauce, sprinkled with walnuts and topped with a spritz of whipped cream. If you are having trouble getting pregnant, and ovulatory infertility is suspected, think of it as temporary health food. OK, maybe that's going a bit too far. But a fascinating finding from the Nurses' Health Study is that a daily serving or two of whole milk and foods made from whole milk—full-fat yogurt, cottage cheese, and, yes, even ice cream—seem to offer some protection against ovulatory infertility, while skim and low-fat milk do the opposite.

The results fly in the face of current standard nutrition advice. But they make sense when you consider what skim and low-fat milk do, and don't, contain. Removing fat from milk radically changes its balance of sex hormones in a way that could tip the scales against ovulation and conception. Proteins added to make skim and low-fat milk look and taste "creamier" push it even farther away.

It would be an overstatement to say that there is a handful of research into possible links between consumption of dairy products and fertility. The vanishingly small body of work in this area is interesting, to say the least, given our fondness for milk, ice cream and other dairy foods. The average American woman has about two servings of dairy products a day, short of the three servings a day the government's dietary guidelines would like her to have.

The depth and detail of the Nurses' Health Study database allowed us to see which foods had the biggest effects. The most potent fertility food from the dairy case was, by far, whole milk, followed by ice cream. Sherbet and frozen yogurt, followed by low-fat yogurt, topped the list as the biggest contributors to ovulatory infertility. The more low-fat dairy products in a woman's diet, the more likely she was to have had trouble getting pregnant. The more full-fat dairy products in a woman's diet, the less likely she was to have had problems getting pregnant.

Our advice on milk and dairy products might be criticized as breaking the rules. The "rules," though, aren't based on solid science and may even conflict with the evidence. And for solving the problem of ovulatory infertility, the rules may need tweaking. Think about switching to full-fat milk or dairy products as a temporary nutrition therapy designed to improve your chances of becoming pregnant. If your efforts pay off, or

if you stop trying to have a baby, then you may want to rethink dairy—especially whole milk and other full-fat dairy foods—altogether. Over the long haul, eating a lot of these isn't great for your heart, your blood vessels or the rest of your body.

Before you sit down to a nightly carton of Häagen-Dazs ("*The Fertility Diet* said I needed ice cream, honey"), keep in mind that it doesn't take much in the way of full-fat dairy foods to measurably affect fertility. Among the women in the Nurses' Health Study, having just one serving a day of a full-fat dairy food, particularly milk, decreased the chances of having ovulatory infertility. The impact of ice cream was seen at two half-cup servings a week. If you eat ice cream at that rate, a pint should last about two weeks.

Equally important, you'll need to do some dietary readjusting to keep your calorie count and your waistline from expanding. Whole milk has nearly double the calories of skim milk. If you have been following the U.S. government's poorly-thought-out recommendation and are drinking three glasses of milk a day, trading skim milk for whole means an extra 189 calories a day. That could translate into a weight gain of 15 to 20 pounds over a year if you don't cut back somewhere else. Those extra pounds can edge aside any fertility benefits you might get from dairy foods. There's also the saturated fat to consider, an extra 13 grams in three glasses of whole milk compared with skim, which would put you close to the healthy daily limit.

Aim for one to two servings of dairy products a day, both of them full fat. This can be as easy as having your breakfast cereal with whole milk and a slice of cheese at lunch or a cup of whole-milk yogurt for lunch and a half-cup of ice cream for dessert. Easy targets for cutting back on calories and saturated fat are red and processed meats, along with foods made with fully or partially hydrogenated vegetable oils.

Once you become pregnant, or if you decide to stop trying, going back to low-fat dairy products makes sense as a way to keep a lid on your intake of saturated fat and calories. You could also try some of the nondairy strategies for getting calcium and protecting your bones. If you don't like milk or other dairy products, or they don't agree with your digestive system, don't force yourself to have them. There are many other things you can do to fight ovulatory infertility. This one is like dessert—enjoyable but optional.

The Role of Body Weight

Weighing too much or too little can interrupt normal menstrual cycles, throw off ovulation or stop it altogether. Excess weight lowers the odds that in vitro fertilization or other assisted reproductive technologies will succeed. It increases the chances of miscarriage, puts a mother at risk during pregnancy of developing high blood pressure (pre-eclampsia) or diabetes, and elevates her chances of needing a Cesarean section. The dangers of being overweight or underweight extend to a woman's baby as well.

Weight is one bit of information that the participants of the Nurses' Health Study report every other year. By linking this information with their accounts of pregnancy, birth, miscarriage and difficulty getting pregnant, we were able to see a strong connection between weight and fertility. Women with the lowest and highest Body Mass Indexes (BMI) were more likely to have had trouble with ovulatory infertility than women in the middle. Infertility was least common among women with BMIs of 20 to 24, with an ideal around 21.

Keep in mind that this is a statistical model of probabilities that links weight and fertility. It doesn't mean you'll get pregnant only if you have a BMI between 20 and 24. Women with higher and lower BMIs than this get pregnant all the time without delay or any medical help. But it supports the idea that weighing too much or too little for your frame can get in the way of having a baby.

We call the range of BMIs from 20 to 24 the fertility zone. It isn't magic—nothing is for fertility—but having a weight in that range seems to be best for getting pregnant. If you aren't in or near the zone, don't despair. Working to move your BMI in that direction by gaining or losing some weight is almost as good. Relatively small changes are often enough to have the desired effects of healthy ovulation and improved fertility. If you are too lean, gaining five or 10 pounds can sometimes be enough to restart ovulation and menstrual periods. If you are overweight, losing 5 percent to 10 percent of your current weight is often enough to improve ovulation.

Being at a healthy weight or aiming toward one is great for ovulatory function and your chances of getting pregnant. The "side effects" aren't so bad, either. Working to achieve a healthy weight can improve your sensitivity to insulin, your cholesterol, your blood pressure and your kidney function. It can give you more energy and make you look and feel better.

While dietary and lifestyle contributions to fertility and infertility in men have received short shrift, weight is one area in which there has been some research. A few small studies indicate that overweight men aren't as fertile as their healthy-weight counterparts. Excess weight can lower testosterone levels, throw off the ratio of testosterone to estrogen (men make some estrogen, just as women make some testosterone) and hinder the production of sperm cells that are good swimmers. A study published in 2006 of more than 2,000 American farmers and their wives showed that as BMI went up, fertility declined. In men, the connection between increasing weight and decreasing fertility can't yet be classified as rock solid. But it is good enough to warrant action, mainly because from a health perspective there aren't any downsides to losing weight if you are overweight. We can't define a fertility zone for weight in men, nor can anyone else. In lieu of that, we can say to men who are carrying too many pounds that shedding some could be good for fertility and will be good for overall health.

The Importance of Exercise

Baby, we were born to run. That isn't just the tagline of Bruce Springsteen's anthem to young love and leavin' town. It's also a perfect motto for getting pregnant and for living a long, healthy life. Inactivity deprives muscles of the constant push and pull they need to stay healthy. It also saps their ability to respond to insulin and to efficiently absorb blood sugar. When that leads to too much blood sugar and insulin in the bloodstream, it endangers

ovulation, conception and pregnancy. Physical activity and exercise are recommended and even prescribed for almost everyone—except women who are having trouble getting pregnant. Forty-year-old findings that too much exercise can turn off menstruation and ovulation make some women shy away from exercise and nudge some doctors to recommend avoiding exercise altogether, at least temporarily. That's clearly the right approach for women who exercise hard for many hours a week and who are extremely lean. But taking it easy isn't likely to help women who aren't active or those whose weights are normal or above where they should be. In other words, the vast majority of women.

Some exciting results from the Nurses' Health Study and a handful of small studies show that exercise can be a boon for fertility. These important findings are establishing a vital link between activity and getting pregnant. Much as we would like to offer a single prescription for conception-boosting exercise, however, we can't. Some women need more exercise than others, for their weight or moods, and others are active just because they enjoy it. Some who need to be active aren't, while a small number of others may be too active.

Instead of focusing on an absolute number, try aiming for the fertility zone. This is a range of exercise that offers the biggest window of opportunity for fertility. Being in the fertility zone means you aren't overdoing or underdoing exercise. For most women, this means getting at least 30 minutes of exercise every day. But if you are carrying more pounds than is considered healthy for your frame (i.e., a BMI above 25), you may need to exercise for an hour or more. If you are quite lean (i.e., your BMI is 19 or below), aim for the middle of the exercise window for a few months. Keep in mind that the fertility zone is an ideal, not an absolute. Hospital delivery rooms are full of women who rarely, or never, exercise. Not everyone is so lucky. If you are having trouble getting pregnant, then maybe the zone is the right place for you.

Whether you classify yourself as a couch potato or an exercise aficionado, your fertility zone should include four types of activity: aerobic exercise, strength training, stretching and the activities of daily living. This quartet works together to control weight, guard against high blood sugar and insulin, and keep your muscles limber and strong. They are also natural stress relievers, something almost everyone coping with or worrying about infertility can use.

Exercise has gotten a bad rap when it comes to fertility. While the pioneering studies of Dr. Rose Frisch and her colleagues convincingly show that too much exercise coupled with too little stored energy can throw off or turn off ovulation in elite athletes, their work says nothing about the impact of usual exercise in normal-weight or overweight women. Common sense says that it can't be a big deterrent to conception. If it were, many of us wouldn't be here. Our ancestors worked hard to hunt, forage, clear fields and travel from place to place. Early *Homo sapiens* burned twice as many calories each day as the average American does today and were fertile despite it—or because of it.

Results from the Nurses' Health Study support this evolutionary perspective and show that exercise, particularly vigorous exercise, actually improves fertility. Exercising for at least

30 minutes on most days of the week is a great place to start. It doesn't really matter how you exercise, as long as you find something other than your true love that moves you and gets your heart beating faster.

Critical Thinking

1. Besides diet and exercise, what are some other contributing factors to infertility?

2. Why may be some reasons behind there not being a "fertility diet" for men?

3. After reading this article, what elements of the fertility diet have you seen in the current dieting trends?

Jorge E. Chavarro and **Walter C. Willett** are in the Department of Nutrition at the Harvard School of Public Health. **Patrick J. Skerrett** is editor of the Harvard Heart Letter. For more information, go to health.harvard.edu/newsweek or thefertilitydiet.com.

Acknowledgments—Adapted from *The Fertility Diet* by Forge E. Chavarro, MD, ScD, Walter C. Willett, MD, Dr. P.H., and Patrick F. Skerrett. Adapted by permission from The McGraw-Hill Companies, Inc. Copyright © 2008 by the President and Fellows of Harvard College.

Originally from Chapter 4 of *The Fertility Diet* (McGraw-Hill, 2007) by Jorge E. Chavarro, Walter C. Willett, and Patrick J. Skerrett, pp. 54–62 excerpt. Copyright © 2007 by Jorge E. Chavarro, Walter C. Willett, and Patrick J. Skerrett. Reprinted by permission of The McGraw-Hill Companies.

Baby Survival Guide
7 Truths That'll Keep You Sane

Maura Rhodes

A week or so after I had my first baby, my friend Susan stopped by—just in the nick of time: Will had been crying for what felt like hours and nothing I did helped. Susan, who'd just had her second daughter, calmly scooped up my inconsolable newborn and did a sort of combo side-to-side swaying and up-and-down jostling that magically lulled him out of Waa-Waa Land.

I've had three kids since then, and Susan's "mommy jig" has been a lifesaver with every one of them. But I never would have known it if I hadn't let her help me out—and that's exactly why she, and I, and other moms who've been there want you to remember these seven rules:

1 Asking for Help Does Not Make You Incompetent

Precisely the opposite, in fact. Sometimes, there's no other way to get from point A to point B. Even if there is, getting there alone can take twice as long and make you crazy.

Kim Ganier of Huntington Beach, California, was always a self-sufficient person—until her first baby, Laci (now 3), was a week old and Ganier found herself doing laundry while "someone else was sitting in my glider and cuddling my baby. The lightbulb went on," she says. After that, visitors were put to work so Ganier could enjoy Laci. Her advice now: Speak up, be specific about what you need, and say yes when offered help of any kind. "You'll feel guilty at first, but you'll get over it," she says.

It'll be easier if you remember that someday you will reciprocate—if not to the particular mom who helped you out, then to another. Several months ago, I was having dinner out with my kids when the mom at the next table asked if I had an extra diaper. I happily handed one over. Sure enough, not long after that, I discovered I'd forgotten to bring a clean swim diaper to the pool and had to go begging from lounge chair to lounge chair for a spare. A better-prepared mom than I saved the day.

So never let guilt or embarrassment or even your ego get in the way of accepting help. Improvising a diaper is a lot harder than returning a favor.

2 Babies Don't Need as Much New Stuff as You Think

They seem to outgrow everything from stretchies to bassinets overnight, so why stock up? "I wish someone had told me not to buy cutesy, expensive clothes for my newborn," says Kristine Shuler, mom of 3-year-old Kaylee in Baroda, Michigan. "Little did I know she would spend most of the time in T-shirts from Target. She didn't wear half the clothes I bought!"

There are two lessons here: First, take your time when deciding what you'll really need. Do a little research, make a list, and stick with it. (*Parenting Magazine's Baby Must-Haves* book is a great resource for teasing out what to buy and what to skip, by the way.) Second, as tempting as it is to buy everything fresh and new and adorable for your first baby—resist. Some items, like swings and bouncy seats, are used for such short periods of time that they never see much wear and tear. Can you borrow from a friend? If not, check out Craigslist.org or Freecycle.org.

Marilyn Sklar swears by a children's resale store in her town. "When my daughter, Raquel, was born, I started buying gently used clothes from there. Later, I brought in some of Raquel's clothing and took an in-store credit to purchase more," says the mom of two in Phoenix. "Now I recycle that way whenever possible. We're saving money and being green!"

3 Getting a Baby to Sleep Is Worth the Trouble

This is a matter of basic maternal math: baby zzz's = mommy zzz's. Veteran moms will tell you that figuring out, early on, how to get your baby to go to sleep, stay asleep, and take regular naps is key to getting through that entire first year. "Being sleep-deprived is a fact of life, but the sooner you get sleep figured out, the better," says Michelle Wilkins, a mom of three in Blacksburg, Virginia.

For Theresa Cole, mom of Ethan, 5, and Jordan, 1, in Kansas City, Missouri, the trick is to get your newborn used to falling asleep on his own: "Think twice about feeding your baby to put him to sleep. He's a clean slate, waiting to learn how to do things. If you teach him he can only drift off with a boob or bottle in his mouth, that's the only way he will—even at two in the morning. And, seriously, who wants to deal with that every night for the next couple of years?"

I'm a firm believer in consistency. When my third baby was 9 months old and not taking decent naps during the day, I came up with some new routines. I stopped letting him catnap in the car while I ran errands, and planned outings around his naptime, to make sure he could go down in his crib. I also turned his room into a sleep haven (blackout shades, white-noise machine). Pretty soon he was napping twice a day, and snoozing better at night, too. To keep daytime noise to a minimum, Jamie Pearson, mom of Avery, 7, and Max, 5, in Palo Alto, California, adds this tip: "Make a diplomatic front-door sign that says, 'Baby napping. Please visit us another time.'"

4 Competitive Parenting: Not Cool

Of course you already know that babies develop at their own pace. And of course you know there's more to your baby than when he hits milestones. But when it seems like every kid in the playgroup except yours is sitting up or saying "Mama," it can take all your willpower to act like you just don't care.

It's totally understandable to compare. But for the sake of your sanity, it's worth trying to stop. "I made the conscious decision to believe the experts who said that the spectrum of normalcy was wide," says Susie Sonneborn Blim, a mom of three in Montclair, New Jersey. "I also stopped hanging out with moms who were constantly boasting about or obsessing over their babies' milestones, because that played a huge part in how caught up I got with comparing my baby to other babies."

Pearson had a similar tactic: "When Avery wasn't the first—or second, or third—baby in my mothers' group to crawl, I told myself that the impatient, intense, irritable babies were always the early crawlers and walkers," she says. "I kept these theories to myself, of course!"

If you're truly worried that your baby is falling behind, bring it up with your pediatrician. She should be your go-to expert when it comes to your child's health and development—not the bragging, pitying other moms.

5 You and Your Baby Don't Have to Be Joined at the Hip

Experts say: Being touched, held, carried, and cuddled is vital to a baby's development. Moms answer back: There's nothing more delicious than touching, holding, carrying, and cuddling a baby—to a point. When it's clear that you and/or your baby need a break from each other, take it. This is especially true when your infant's wailing or your pre-toddler's whining is about to push you over the edge. Hand her to Daddy or send out an SOS to a friend or relative.

There's nothing more delicious than cuddling a baby—to a point. So take a break.

If there's no one you can call on for help, take a tip from Christine Klepacz, a mom of two in Bethesda, Maryland. "When your baby is crying and you could burst into tears yourself, or when you're just overwhelmed, it's okay to put her in her crib for a while and sit by yourself. She's safe, and sometimes she needs time away from you, too. It's okay. We all do it!"

It's equally important to carve out time for yourself regularly—not just when you're about to go off the deep end. If there's one thing Jennifer Geddes, a *Parenting* staffer and mom of two girls, learned during the first year, it's that "you have to take a few minutes for yourself here and there. It's essential to being a happy and healthy mom. I was so concerned with attending to my daughter's needs that I neglected my own. I barely ate, slept, or left the house," she says.

If you're thinking, "Yeah, right—I can barely get a shower," wait: It's doable. You just have to plan ahead, be creative, and adjust your definition of what constitutes a relaxing break. Where, prebaby, you were used to spur-of-the-moment shopping sprees or on-a-whim workouts, you might find, like Marilyn Sklar, that your idea of a good time now is "a glass of wine and a good book after the children are in bed." Or a brisk walk in the morning before they get up. Me, I swear by weekend matinees. I can get a lot of regenerative mileage out of two hours by myself in a cozy, dark theater with a bag of popcorn, lost in a great story onscreen.

6 The Best Baby Stage Is the One You're In

"They grow up so fast." The reason you'll hear this from everyone and her grandmother: It's true. Kim Lavergne of Nashville, mom of 2-year-old Justin, remembers feeling like time was crawling after he was born. "In reality, the days go by so fast that the next thing you know, your child is no longer a baby," she says. "I've learned to cherish and enjoy the time I spend with Justin."

Charlene Kochensparger of Centerville, Ohio, who has a daughter and a son, seconds that. "First-time parents tend to wish the time away—'I can't wait for her to crawl, walk, talk'—and not enjoy the moment," she says.

The time slipped away from Loretta Sehlmeyer of Dix Hills, New York, because she was so focused on being a perfect parent to her son, Christian, now 4. "I fretted so much over caring for him that I missed the entire experience. I honestly didn't notice that my baby was growing and changing a little bit each day. I spent a lot of time looking at him, but I was way too distracted to actually see him," she says. "So take some time each day, real time, to hold your baby and do nothing else but use your senses to connect with him. Smell his sweetness, and look at those tiny fingers and toes and amazing little nose."

7 There's No One Else Like You

Only a handful of babycare rules are written in stone (specifically, those having to do with health and safety—like, you really should always put a baby to sleep on his back). Most everything else is up for interpretation. "It's great to read up, solicit opinions, and listen respectfully to advice you haven't asked for," says Michelle Wilkins. "But you know your baby and yourself best. You'll know when an idea resonates."

Adds Chantel Fry, mom of Dylan, 3, and Madalyn, 7 months, in Pittsburgh: "You're going to be different than the next mom. Not better, not worse—because you do the best you can, and if at the end of the day your child has laughed, and is clean and fed, you can go to sleep knowing that you did what is expected of you." No matter how you did those things, exactly, you can be proud that you're inventing your own special way of being a mom.

Critical Thinking

1. What are some of the social barriers that new parents face when asking for help from others?

2. If you were to rank the 7 truths in order of importance, what would that look like? Explain your rationale for the ranking.

3. Of the 7 truths, which one do you feel is the most essential for new parents and which one is most essential for seasoned parents to remember?

MAURA RHODES, a mom of four, is a contributing editor at *Parenting*.

UNIT 3
Family Relationships

Unit Selections

Learning Outcomes

After reading this unit, you will be able to:

- Describe the societal influences on marriage.
- Explain the current trends of marriage in families.
- Analyze the impact of marriage on children.
- Evaluate the role of public policy in marriage.
- Define polygamy.
- Identify the origins of polygamy in the United States.
- Explain the association between religious beliefs and polygamy.
- Identify the influence parents have on their child's behavior.
- Describe the common ways that parents "fail" in raising their children.
- Analyze the role parenting style has on children's behavior.
- Describe the emotional impact that spanking has on children as a form of punishment.
- Evaluate the reasons why parent should not use spanking as a form of punishment.
- Explain how gay parenting has affected their children.
- Describe the experiences of youth who come out to their parents.
- Understand the importance of educating parents about homosexuality and their children.
- Identify some of the myths related to homosexuality.
- Identify the impact of sibling relationships on an individual.
- Describe the significance of birth order.
- Analyze the impact of sibling type relationships among couples.
- Identify competition between siblings.
- Describe the influence of age distribution on sibling relationships.
- Indicate the roles that siblings had in the family.
- Describe the influence of sibling relationships on individuals within the family.
- Explain the perceptions of parent–child relationships between siblings.

- Identify competition between siblings.
- Describe the influence of age distribution on sibling relationships.
- Indicate the roles that siblings had in the family
- Describe the influence of sibling relationships on individuals within the family.
- Identify the strengths that African American families have as a result of intergenerational practice.
- Describe the resources that African American families have through intergenerational relationships.
- Examine how intergenerational family relationship influence cultural values.
- Define Family-Centered Support services.
- Explain types of family support and family empowerment.
- Identify the ways in which professionals can work with families who have children with disabilities.

Student Website
www.mhhe.com/cls

Internet References

Child Welfare League of America
www.cwla.org
Coalition for Marriage, Family, and Couples Education
www.smartmarriages.com
The National Academy for Child Development
www.nacd.org
National Council on Family Relations
www.ncfr.com
Positive Parenting
www.positiveparenting.com
SocioSite
www.pscw.uva.nl/sociosite/TOPICS/Women.html

And they lived happily ever after. . . . The romantic image conjured up by this well-known final line from fairy tales is not reflective of the reality of family life and relationship maintenance. The belief that somehow love alone should carry us through is pervasive. In reality, maintaining a relationship takes dedication, hard work, and commitment.

We come into relationships, regardless of their nature, with fantasies about how things ought to be. Partners, spouses, parents, children, siblings, and others—all family members have at least some unrealistic expectations about each other. It is through the negotiation of their lives together that they come to work through these expectations and replace them with other, it is hoped, more realistic ones. By recognizing and acting on their own contribution to the family, members can set and attain realistic family goals. Tolerance and acceptance of differences can facilitate this process as can competent communication skills. Along the way, family members need to learn new skills and develop new habits of relating to each other. This will not

© Ariel Skelley/Getty Images

be easy, and, try as they may, not everything will be controllable. Factors both inside and outside the family may impede their progress. Even before we enter a marriage or other committed relationship, attitudes, standards, and beliefs influence our choices. Increasingly, choices include whether we should commit to such a relationship. From the start of a committed relationship, the expectations both partners have of their relationship have an impact, and the need to negotiate differences is a constant factor. Adding a child to the family affects the lives of parents in ways that they could previously only imagine. Feeling under siege, many parents struggle to know the right way to rear their children. These factors can all combine to make child rearing more difficult than it might otherwise have been. Other family relationships also evolve, and in our nuclear-family-focused culture, it is possible to forget that family relationships extend beyond those between spouses and parents and children.

The initial subsection presents a number of articles regarding marital and other committed relationships, decisions about whether one wants to enter such a relationship, and ways of balancing multiple and often competing roles played by today's couples, who hope to fulfill individual as well as relationship needs. It is a difficult balancing act to cope with the expectations and pressures of work, home, children, and relational intimacy. The first article, "Can Marriage Be Saved?" argues that, in fact, marriage, for American society at large, is not at risk. What is of concern is marriage as an institution among disadvantaged groups. The second article in this section addresses plural marriage. "The Polygamists" examines a conservative community in which plural marriage is the norm.

The next subsection examines the parent/child relationship. In the first article, "Good Parents, Bad Results," looks at eight errors that well-meaning parents make and ways to avoid them. The next article, "Do We Need a Law to Prohibit Spanking?" addresses the fact that, although research strongly supports the drawbacks of corporal punishment, legislation may be necessary to end a practice that is commonly seen as relatively benign. "Children of Lesbian and Gay Parents" comes to the conclusion that sexual orientation of parents has no effect on the development and well-being of their children The next reading, "Parenting Gay Youth: Creating Supportive Environment," counters common myths associated with homosexuality and provides information on how parents can support their lesbian, gay, bisexual, or transgendered child.

The third and final subsection looks at other family relationships. "The Forgotten Siblings" draws attention to the fact that, in research on family, siblings receive little or no attention. "Oh, Brother!" addresses sibling rivalry and the ways in which this may influence sibling and other relationships through life. "Building on Strengths: Intergenerational Practice with African American Families" explores the uniquely strong ties found within African American families. The final article in this section, "Support and Empower Families of Children with Disabilities" uses a family strengths perspective in suggesting a number of ways to support and empower families of children with disabilities.

Can Marriage Be Saved?

FRANK FURSTENBERG

A growing number of social scientists fear that marriage may be on the rocks and few doubt that matrimony, as we have known it, has undergone a wrenching period of change in the past several decades. Andrew Cherlin, a leading sociologist of the family, speaks of "the de-institutionalization of marriage," conceding a point to conservative commentators who have argued that marriage and the family have been in a state of free-fall since the 1960s.

Western Europe has experienced many of the same trends—declining rates of marriage, widespread cohabitation, and rising levels of nonmarital childbearing—but has largely shrugged them off. By contrast, concern about the state of marriage in the United States has touched a raw, political nerve. What ails marriage and what, if anything, can be done to restore this time-honored social arrangement to its former status as a cultural invention for assigning the rights and responsibilities of reproduction, including sponsorship and inheritance?

On the left side of the political spectrum, observers believe that the institutional breakdown of marriage has its roots in economic and social changes brought about by shifts in home-based production, structural changes in the economy, and the breakdown of the gender-based division of labor—trends unlikely to be reversed. The other position, championed by most conservatives, is that people have lost faith in marriage because of changes in cultural values that could be reversed or restored through shifts in the law, changes in administrative policies and practices, and public rhetoric to alter beliefs and expectations.

The Bush administration is trying to put into place a set of policies aimed at reversing the symptoms of retreat from marriage: high rates of premarital sex, nonmarital childbearing, cohabitation, and divorce. Do their policies make sense and do they have a reasonable prospect of success? To answer this question, I want to begin with the trends that Americans, including many social scientists, have found so alarming and then turn to the question of how much public policy and what kinds of policies could help to strengthen marriage.

Demographic Changes and Political Interpretations

When compared to the 1950s, the institution of marriage seems to be profoundly changed, but is the middle of the twentieth century an appropriate point of comparison? It has been widely known since the baby boom era that the period after the Second World War was unusual demographically: the very early onset of adult transitions; unprecedented rates of marriage; high fertility; an economy that permitted a single wage earner to support a family reasonably well; and the flow of federal funding for education, housing, and jobs distinguished the 1950s and early 1960s as a particular historical moment different from any previous period and certainly different from the decades after the Vietnam War era. For a brief time, the nuclear family in the United States and throughout much of Europe reigned supreme.

If we use the middle of the twentieth century as a comparison point, it might appear that we have been witnessing a deconstruction of the two-parent biological family en masse. But such a view is historically shortsighted and simplistic. The nuclear family, though long the bourgeois ideal, had never been universally practiced, at least as it was in the middle of the last century. Only in the 1950s—and then for a very brief time—did it become the gold standard for what constitutes a healthy family. Indeed, sociologists at that time fiercely debated whether this family model represented a decline from the "traditional" extended family. Even those who argued against this proposition could not agree whether this family form was desirable ("functional" in the language of the day) or contained fatal flaws that would be its undoing.

During the 1960s and 1970s, anthropological evidence indicated that family diversity is universal, and findings from the new field of historical demography revealed that families in both the East and the West had always been changing in response to economic, political, demographic, and social conditions. In short, the nuclear family was cross-culturally and historically not "the natural unit" that many wrongly presume today.

Although it was widely known that the family had undergone considerable changes from ancient times and during the industrial revolution, that family systems varied across culture, and that social-class differences created varied forms of the family within the same society, it was not until the 1960s, when historians began to use computers to analyze census data, that the extent of this variation came into clearer focus. For the first time, family scholars from several disciplines could see the broad outlines of a new picture of how family forms and functions are intimately related to the social, cultural, and perhaps especially the economic contexts in which household and kinship systems are embedded.

From this evidence, students of the family can assert three points. First, no universal form of the family constitutes the appropriate or normative arrangement for reproduction, nurturance, socialization, and economic support. Both across and within societies, family forms, patterns, and practices vary enormously. Second, change is endemic to all family systems, and at least in the West, where we have the best evidence to date, family systems have always been in flux. Typically, these changes create tensions and often ignite public concern. Since colonial times, the family has been changing and provoking public reaction from moralists, scientists, and, of course, public authorities. Finally, family systems do not evolve in a linear fashion but become more or less complex and more elemental in different eras or among different strata of society depending on the economic and social conditions to which families must adapt.

Does this mean that we are seeing a continuation of what has always been or something different than has ever occurred in human history—the withering of kinship as an organizing feature of human society? The decline of marriage suggests to some that this round of change is unique in human history or that its consequences for children will be uniquely unsettling to society.

Many scholars weighed in on these questions. It is fair to say that there are two main camps: (1) those who have decided that the family is imperiled as a result of changes in the marriage system, a position held by such respectable social scientists as Linda Waite, Norvel Glenn, and Judith Wallerstein; and (2) those who remain skeptical and critical of those sounding the alarm, a position held by the majority of social scientists. Many in this second camp take seriously the concerns of the "alarmists" that children's welfare may be at risk if the current family regime continues. Still, they doubt that the family can be coaxed back into its 1950s form and favor adaptations in government policy to assist new forms of the family—an approach followed by most European nations.

S ome portion of those skeptics are not so alarmed by changes in the family, believing that children's circumstances have not been seriously compromised by family change. They contend that children's well-being has less to do with the family form in which they reside than the resources possessed to form viable family arrangements. Lacking these resources (material and cultural), it matters little whether the children are born into a marriage, cohabitation, or a single-parent household, because they are likely not to fare as well as those whose parents possess the capacity to realize their goals.

I place myself in this latter group. Of course, children will fare better when they have two well-functioning, collaborative parents than one on average, but one well-functioning parent with resources is better than two married parents who lack the resources or skills to manage parenthood. Moreover, parents with limited cultural and material resources are unlikely to remain together in a stable marriage. Because the possession of such psychological, human, and material capital is highly related to marital stability, it is easy to confuse the effects of stable marriage with the effects of competent parenting. Finally, I believe that the best way to foster marriage stability is to support children with an array of services that assist parents and children, regardless of the family form in which they reside.

Marriage and Good Outcomes for Children

A huge number of studies have shown that children fare better in two-biological-parent families than they do in single-biological-parent families, leading most family researchers to conclude that the nuclear family is a more effective unit for reproduction and socialization. Yet this literature reveals some troubling features that have not been adequately examined by social scientists. The most obvious of these is that such findings rule out social selection.

If parents with limited resources and low skills are less likely to enter marriage with a biological parent and remain wed when they do (which we know to be true), then it follows that children will do worse in such single-parent households than in stable marriages. We have known about this problem for decades, but researchers have not been equipped adequately to rule out selection. The standard method for doing so is by statistically controlling for prior differences, but this method is inadequate for ruling out differences because it leaves so many sources of selection unmeasured, such as sexual compatibility, substance abuse, and so on. Newer statistical methods have been employed to correct for unmeasured differences, but strong evidence exists that none of these techniques is up to the challenge. Nevertheless, it is *theoretically* possible to examine social experiments such as those being mounted in the marriage-promotion campaign and assess their long-term effects on children.

Another useful approach is to examine macro-level differences at the state or national level that would be less correlated with social selection and hence more revealing of the impact of marriage arrangements on children's well-being. To date, there is little evidence supporting a correlation between family form and children's welfare at the national level. Consider first the historical data showing that children who grew up in the 1950s (baby boomers) were not notably free of problem behavior. After all, they were the cohort who raised such hell in the 1960s and 1970s. From 1955 to 1975, indicators of social problems among children (test scores, suicide, homicide, controlled-substance use, crime) that can be tracked by vital statistics all rose. These indicators accompanied, and in some cases preceded rather than followed, change in the rates of divorce, the decline of marriage, and the rise of nonmarital childbearing during this period. Conversely, there is no evidence that the cohort of children who came of age in the 1990s and early part of this century is doing worse than previous cohorts because these children are more likely to have grown up in single-parent families. Of course, compensatory public policies or other demographic changes such as small family size, higher parental education, or lower rates of poverty may have offset the deleterious effects of family form, but such an explanation concedes that family form is not as potent a source of children's well-being as many observers seem to believe.

We might also gain some purchase on this issue by comparing the success of children under different family regimes. Do the countries with high rates of cohabitation, low marriage, high divorce, and high nonmarital fertility have the worst outcomes for children? We don't know the answer to this question, but we do know that various indicators of child well-being—health, mental health, educational attainment—do show higher scores in Northern than in Southern Europe. They appear to be linked to the level of investment in children, not the family form (which is certainly more intact in Southern Europe). Still, this question deserves more attention than it has received.

Significantly, many of the countries that continue to adhere to the nuclear model have some of the world's lowest rates of fertility—a problem that seems worse in countries with very low rates of nonmarital childbearing. I am not claiming that nonmarital childbearing is necessarily desirable as a social arrangement for propping up fertility, but it is a plausible hypothesis that nonmarital childbearing helps to keep the birth rate up in countries that would otherwise be experiencing a dangerously low level of reproduction.

Finally, it is important to recognize that family change in the United States (and in most Western countries, it appears) has not occurred evenly among all educational groups. In this country, marriage, divorce, and nonmarital childbearing have jumped since the 1960s among the bottom two-thirds of the educational distribution but have not changed much at all among the top third, consisting, today, of college graduates and postgraduates. Though marriage comes later to this group, they are barely more likely to have children out of wedlock, have high levels of marriage, and, if anything, lower levels of divorce than were experienced several decades ago. In other words, almost all the change has occurred among the segment of the population that has either not gained economically or has lost ground over the past several decades. Among the most socially disadvantaged and most marginalized segments of American society, marriage has become imperiled and family conditions have generally deteriorated, resulting in extremely high rates of union instability. The growing inequality in the United States may provide some clues for why the family, and marriage in particular, is not faring well and what to do about it.

Marriage and Public Policy

The logic of the Bush administration's approach to welfare is that by promoting and strengthening marriage, children's well-being, particularly in lower-income families will be enhanced. At first blush, this approach seems to make good sense. Economies of scale are produced when two adults live together. Two parents create healthy redundancies and perhaps help build social capital both within the household and by creating more connections to the community. The prevalence of marriage and marital stability is substantially higher among well-educated and more stably employed individuals than among those with less than a college education and lower incomes. Wouldn't it be reasonable to help the less educated enjoy the benefits of the nuclear family?

There are several reasons to be skeptical of this policy direction. First, we have the experience of the 1950s, when marriages did occur in abundance among low-income families. Divorce rates were extremely high during this era, and many of these families dissolved their unions when they had an opportunity to divorce because of chronic problems of conflict, disenchantment, and scarcity. In my own study of marriages of teen parents in the 1960s, I discovered that four out of every five women who married the father of their children got divorced before the child reached age eighteen; the rate of marital instability among those who married a stepfather was even higher. Certainly, encouraging marriage among young couples facing a choice of nonmarital childbearing or wedlock is not an easy choice when we know the outcome of the union is so precarious. If divorce is a likely outcome, it is not clear whether children are better off if their parents marry and divorce than remain unmarried, knowing as we do that family conflict and flux have adverse effects on children's welfare.

What about offering help to such couples before or after they enter marriage? This is a good idea, but don't expect any miracles from the current policies. Strong opposition exists to funding sustained and intensive premarital and postmarital counseling among many proponents of marriage-promotion programs. Conservative constituencies largely believe that education, especially under the aegis of religious or quasi-religious sponsorship is the best prescription for shoring up marriage. Yet, the evidence overwhelmingly shows that short-term programs that are largely didactic will not be effective in preserving marriages. Instead, many couples need repeated bouts of help both before and during marriage when they run into difficult straits. Most of these couples have little or no access to professional counseling.

The federal government has funded several large-scale experiments combining into a single program marital education or counseling *and* social services including job training or placement. These experiments, being conducted by the Manpower Research Demonstration Corporation, will use random assignment and have the best hope of producing some demonstrable outcomes. Yet, it is not clear at this point that even comprehensive programs with sustained services will be effective in increasing partner collaboration and reducing union instability.

There is another approach that I believe has a better prospect of improving both children's chances and probably at least an equal chance of increasing the viability of marriages or marriage-like arrangements. By directing more resources to low-income children regardless of the family form they live in, through such mechanisms as access to quality child care, health care, schooling, and income in the form of tax credits, it may be possible to increase the level of human, social, and psychological capital that children receive. And, by increasing services, work support, and especially tuition aid for adolescents and young adults to attend higher education, Americans may be able to protect children from the limitations imposed by low parental resources. Lending this type of assistance means that young adults are more likely to move into higher paying jobs and acquire through education the kinds of communication and problem-solving skills that are so useful to making marriage-like relationships last.

When we invest in children, we are not only likely to reap the direct benefits of increasing human capital but also the indirect benefits that will help preserve union stability in the next generation. This approach is more likely to increase the odds of success for children when they grow up. If I am correct, it probably follows that direct investment in children and youth has a better prospect of strengthening marriage and marriage-like relationships in the next generation by improving the skills and providing the resources to make parental relationships more rewarding and enduring.

So it comes down to a choice in strategy: invest in strengthening marriage and hope that children will benefit or invest in children and hope that marriages will benefit. I place my bet on the second approach.

Critical Thinking

1. What do you feel has the greatest impact on married couples today? Cultural norms, values, beliefs, etc.?
2. How does the evolution of demographics influence families today?
3. What role does government play in family life? Should policy be made to influence marriage?
4. If you were a policymaker, what types of policies would you implement to strengthen marriage?

FRANK FURSTENBERG, Zellerbach Family Professor of Sociology at the University of Pennsylvania, has written extensively on children, families, and public policy. His most recent book is *On the Frontier of Adulthood* (co-edited with Rick Settersten and Ruban Rumbaut), University of Chicago Press, 2005.

The Polygamists

A sect that split from the Mormons allows multiple wives, expels "lost boys," and heeds a jailed prophet.

SCOTT ANDERSON

The first church members arrive at the Leroy S. Johnson Meeting House in Colorado City, Arizona, at about 6 P.M. Within a half hour the line extends out the front doors, down the side of the building, and out into the parking lot. By seven, it stretches hundreds of yards and has grown to several thousand people—the men and boys dressed in suits, the women and girls in Easter egg–hued prairie dresses.

The mourners have come for a viewing of 68-year-old Foneta Jessop, who died of a heart attack a few days ago. In the cavernous hall Foneta's sons form a receiving line at the foot of her open casket, while her husband, Merril, stands directly alongside. To the other side stand Merril's numerous other wives, all wearing matching white dresses.

Foneta was the first wife.

Colorado City is a town with special significance for those of Foneta's faith. Together with its sister community of Hildale, Utah, it is the birthplace of the Fundamentalist Church of Jesus Christ of Latter-Day Saints (FLDS), a polygamous offshoot of the Mormon Church, or LDS. Here in the 1920s and '30s, a handful of polygamous families settled astride the Utah-Arizona border after the leadership of the Mormon Church became increasingly determined to shed its polygamous past and be accepted by the American mainstream. In 1935 the church gave settlement residents an ultimatum: renounce plural marriage or be excommunicated. Practically everyone refused and was cast out of the LDS.

At the memorial service for Foneta, her husband and three sons give testimonials praising her commitment to the covenant of plural marriage, but there is an undertone of family disharmony, with vague references by Merril Jessop to his troubled relationship with Foneta. No one need mention that one of Merril's wives is missing. Carolyn Jessop, his fourth wife, left the household in 2003 with her eight children and went on to write a best-selling book on her life as an FLDS member. She describes a cloistered environment and tells of a deeply unhappy Foneta, an overweight recluse who fell out of favor with her husband and slept her days away, coming out of her room only at night to eat, do laundry, and watch old Shirley Temple movies on television.

At the conclusion of the service, most of the congregation walk over to the Isaac Carling cemetery for a graveside observance. I assume the enormous turnout—mourners have come in from FLDS communities in Texas, Colorado, and British Columbia—stems from the prominent position Foneta's husband holds: Merril Jessop is an FLDS leader and the bishop of the large chapter in West Texas. But Sam Steed, a soft-spoken, 37-year-old accountant acting as my guide, explains that elaborate funerals are a regular occurrence. "Probably between 15 and 20 times a year," he says. "This one is maybe a little bigger than most, but even when a young child dies, you can expect three or four thousand people to attend. It's part of what keeps us together. It reminds us we're members of this larger community. We draw strength from each other."

Few Americans had heard of the FLDS before April 2008, when law enforcement officials conducted a raid on a remote compound in West Texas known as the Yearning for Zion Ranch. For days after, television viewers witnessed the bizarre spectacle of hundreds of children and women—all dressed in old-fashioned prairie dresses, with elaborately coiffed hair—being herded onto school buses by social workers and police officers.

That raid had been spurred by phone calls to a domestic violence shelter, purportedly from a 16-year-old girl who claimed she was being sexually and physically abused on the ranch by her middle-aged husband. What lent credibility to the calls was that the residents of YFZ Ranch were disciples of the FLDS and its "prophet," Warren Jeffs, who had been convicted in a Utah court in 2007 for officiating at the marriage of a 14-year-old girl to a church member.

The raid made for gripping television, but it soon became clear that the phone calls were a hoax. And although authorities had evidently anticipated a violent confrontation like the 1993 shoot-out at the Branch Davidian compound in Waco—SWAT teams were brought in, along with an armored personnel carrier—the arsenal at the YFZ Ranch consisted of only 33 legal firearms. A Texas appeals court later found that authorities had not met the burden of proof for the removal of the more than 400 children, and most were returned to their families within two months.

Yet after interviewing teenagers who were pregnant or had children, Texas authorities began investigating how many under-age girls might have been "sealed" to older men. (Plural marriages are performed within the church and are not legal.) The result: Twelve church members, including Warren Jeffs, were indicted on charges ranging from bigamy to having sex with a minor. The first defendant to stand trial, Raymond Jessop, was convicted of one charge last November. Trials of the other defendants are scheduled to take place over the coming year.

From the Bluff behind his Hildale home, Joe Jessop has a commanding view of the Arizona Strip, an undulating expanse of sagebrush and piñon-juniper woodland that stretches south of the Utah border all the way to the northern rim of the Grand Canyon, some 50 miles away. Below are the farm fields and walled compounds of Hildale and Colorado City, which Joe refers to collectively by their old name, Short Creek. "When I first came to Short Creek as a boy, there were just seven homes down there," says Joe, 88. "It was like the frontier."

Today, Short Creek is home to an estimated 6,000 FLDS members—the largest FLDS community. Joe Jessop, a brother of Merril, has contributed to that explosive growth in two very different ways. With the weathered features and spindly gait of a man who has spent his life outdoors and worked his body hard, he is the community's undisputed "water guy," a self-taught engineer who helped with the piping of water out of Maxwell Canyon back in the 1940s. He's had a hand in building the intricate network of waterlines, canals, and reservoirs that has irrigated the arid plateau in the decades since.

A highly respected member of the FLDS, Joe is also the patriarch of a family of 46 children and—at last count—239 grandchildren. "My family came to Short Creek for the same reason as everyone else," he says, "to obey the law of plural marriage, to build up the Kingdom of God. Despite everything that's been thrown our way, I'd say we've done a pretty good job."

Members of the faith describe the life that the Jessops and other founding families have built as idyllic, one in which old-fashioned devotion and neighborly cooperation are emphasized and children are raised in a wholesome environment free of television and junk food and social pressures. Critics, on the other hand, see the FLDS as an isolated cult whose members, worn down by rigid social control, display a disturbing fealty to one man, the prophet Warren Jeffs—who has claimed to be God's mouthpiece on Earth.

To spend time in Hildale and Colorado City is to come away with a more nuanced view. That view is revealed gradually, however, due to the insular nature of the community. Many of the oversize homes are tucked behind high walls, both to give children a safe place to play and to shield families from gawking Gentiles, as non-Mormons are known. Most residents avoid contact with strangers. *National Geographic* was given access to the community only on the approval of the church leadership, in consultation with the imprisoned Warren Jeffs.

In keeping with original Mormon teachings, much of the property in Hildale and Colorado City is held in trust for the church. Striving to be as self-sufficient as possible, the community grows a wide variety of fruits and vegetables, and everyone, including children, is expected to help bring in the yield. Church members also own and operate a number of large businesses, from hotels to tool and machine manufacturers. Each Saturday, men gather at the meetinghouse to go over a roster of building and maintenance projects around town in need of volunteers. In one display of solidarity, the men built a four-bedroom home, from foundation to roof shingles, in a single day.

This communal spirit continues inside the polygamous home. Although living arrangements vary—wives may occupy different wings of a house or have their own granny cottages—the women tend to carve out spheres of influence according to preference or aptitude. Although each has primary responsibility for her own children, one wife might manage the kitchen, a second act as schoolteacher (virtually all FLDS children in Hildale and Colorado City are homeschooled), and a third see to the sewing. Along with instilling a sense of sorority, this division of labor appears to mitigate jealousy.

"I know it must seem strange to outsiders," says Joyce Broadbent, a friendly woman of 44, "but from my experience, sister wives usually get along very well. Oh sure, you might be closer to one than another, or someone might get on your nerves occasionally, but that's true in any family. I've never felt any rivalry or jealousy at all."

Joyce is a rather remarkable example of this harmony. She not only accepted another wife, Marcia, into the family, but was thrilled by the addition. Marcia, who left an unhappy marriage in the 1980s, is also Joyce's biological sister. "I knew my husband was a good man," Joyce explains with a smile as she sits with Marcia and their husband, Heber. "I wanted my sister to have a chance at the same kind of happiness I had."

Not all FLDS women are quite so sanguine about plural marriage. Dorothy Emma Jessop is a spry, effervescent octogenarian who operates a naturopathic dispensary in Hildale. Sitting in her tiny shop surrounded by jars of herbal tinctures she ground and mixed herself, Dorothy admits she struggled when her husband began taking on other wives. "To be honest," she says, "I think a lot of women have a hard time with it, because it's not an easy thing to share the man you love. But I came to realize this is another test that God places before you—the sin of jealousy, of pride—and that to be a godly woman, I needed to overcome it."

What seems to help overcome it is an awareness that a woman's primary role in the FLDS is to bear and raise as many children as possible, to build up the "celestial family" that will remain together for eternity. It is not uncommon to meet FLDS women who have given birth to 10, 12, 16 children. (Joyce Broadbent is the mother of 11, and Dorothy Emma Jessop of 13.) As a result, it's easy to see why this corner of the American West is experiencing a population explosion. The 400 or so babies delivered in the Hildale health clinic every year have resulted in a median age of just under 14, in contrast with 36.6 for the entire U.S. With so many in the community tracing their lineage to a handful of the pioneering families, the same few names crop up over and over in Hildale and Colorado City, suggesting a murkier side to this fecundity: Doctors in Arizona say a severe form of a debilitating disease called fumarase deficiency, caused by a recessive gene, has become more prevalent in the community due to intermarriage.

The collision of tradition and modernity in the community can be disorienting. Despite their old-fashioned dress, most FLDS adults have cell phones and favor late-model SUVs. Although televisions are now banished, church members tend to be highly computer literate and sell a range of products, from soaps to dresses, via the Internet. When I noticed how few congregants wore glasses, I wondered aloud if perhaps a genetic predisposition for good eyesight was at work. Sam Steed laughed lightly. "No. People here are just really into laser surgery."

The principle of plural marriage was revealed to the Mormons amid much secrecy. Dark clouds hovered over the church in the early 1840s, after rumors spread that its founder, Joseph Smith, had taken up the practice of polygamy. While denying the charge in public, by 1843 Smith had shared a revelation with his closest disciples. In this "new and everlasting covenant" with God, plural wives were to be taken so that the faithful might "multiply and replenish the earth."

After Smith was assassinated by an anti-Mormon mob in Illinois, Brigham Young led believers on an epic 1,300-mile journey west to the Salt Lake Basin of present-day Utah. There the covenant was at last publicly revealed and with it, the notion that a man's righteousness before God would be measured by the size of his family; Brigham Young himself took 55 wives, who bore him 57 children.

But in 1890, faced with the seizure of church property under a federal antipolygamy law, the LDS leadership issued a manifesto announcing an end to plural marriage. That certainly didn't end the practice, and the LDS's tortured handling of the issue—some church leaders remained in plural marriages or even took on new wives after the manifesto's release—contributed to the schism between the LDS and the fundamentalists.

"The LDS issued that manifesto for political purposes, then later claimed it was a revelation," says Willie Jessop, the FLDS spokesman. "We in the fundamentalist community believe covenants are made with God and are not to be manipulated for political reasons, so that presents an enormous obstacle between us and those in the LDS mainstream."

Upholding the covenant has come at a high price. The 2008 raid on the YFZ Ranch was only the latest in a long list of official actions against polygamists—persecutions for simply adhering to their religious principles, in the eyes of church members—that are integral to the FLDS story. At various times both Utah and Arizona authorities attempted to crack down on the Short Creek community: in 1935, in 1944, and most famously, in 1953. In that raid some 200 women and children were hauled to detention centers, while 26 men were brought up on polygamy charges. In 1956 Utah authorities seized seven children of Vera Black, a Hildale plural wife, on grounds that her polygamous beliefs made her an unfit mother. Black was reunited with her children only after agreeing to renounce polygamy.

Melinda Fischer Jeffs is an articulate, outgoing woman of 37, and she gives an incredulous laugh when describing what she's read about the FLDS. "Honestly, I can't even recognize it!" the mother of three exclaims. "Most all of what appears in the media, it makes us sound like we're somehow being kept against our will."

Melinda is in a unique position to understand the conflicting views of this community. She is a plural wife to Jim Jeffs, one of the prophet's nephews and an elder in the FLDS. But she is also the daughter of Dan Fischer, a former FLDS member who has emerged as one of the church leadership's most vociferous critics. In 2008 Fischer testified before a U.S. Senate committee about alleged improprieties within the FLDS, and he now heads an organization that works with people who have been kicked out of the church or who have "escaped." When Fischer broke with the church in the 1990s, his family split apart too; today 13 of his children have left the FLDS, while Melinda and two of her half siblings have renounced their father.

"And that is not an easy thing," Melinda says softly, "obviously, because I still love my father. I pray all the time that he will see his errors—or at least, stop his attacks on us."

If there is one point on which FLDS defenders and detractors might agree, it is that most of the current troubles can be traced to when its leadership passed to the Jeffs family, in 1986. Until then, the FLDS had been a fairly loosely run group led by an avuncular man named Leroy Johnson, who relied on a group of high priests to guide the church. That ended when Rulon Jeffs took over following Johnson's death. After being declared the prophet by the community, Rulon solidified the policy of one-man rule.

Charges that a theocratic dictatorship was taking root in the Arizona Strip grew louder when, after Rulon's death in 2002, the FLDS was taken over by his 46-year-old son, Warren. Assuming the role of the prophet, Warren first married several of his father's wives—and then proceeded to wed many more women, including, according to Carolyn Jessop, eight of Merril Jessop's daughters. Although many FLDS men have multiple wives, the number of wives of those closest to the prophet can reach into the double digits. A church document called the Bishop's Record, seized during the Texas raid, shows that one of Jeffs's lieutenants, Wendell Nielsen, claims 21 wives. And although the FLDS would not disclose how many plural wives Warren Jeffs has taken (some estimate more than 80), at least one was an underage girl, according to a Texas indictment.

Although the issue of underage marriage within the church has garnered the greatest negative media attention, Dan Fischer has championed another cause, the so-called Lost Boys, who have left or been forced from the community and wound up fending for themselves on the streets of Las Vegas, Salt Lake City, and St. George, Utah. Fischer's foundation has worked with 300 such young men, a few as young as 13, over the past seven years. Fischer concedes that most of these boys were simply "discouraged out," but he cites cases where they were officially expelled, a practice he says increased under Jeffs.

Fischer attributes the exodus partly to a cold-blooded calculation by church leaders to limit male competition for the pool of marriageable young women. "If you have men marrying 20, 30, up to 80 or more women," he says, "then it comes down to biology and simple math that there will be a lot of other men who aren't going to get wives. The church says it's kicking these boys out for being disruptive influences, but if you'll notice, they rarely kick out girls."

Equally contentious has been the FLDS restoration of an early Mormon policy of transferring the wives and children of a church member to another man. Traditionally, this was done upon the death of a patriarch so that his widows might be cared for, or to rescue a woman from an abusive relationship. But critics argue that under Jeffs this "reassignment" became one more weapon to hold over the heads of those who dared step out of line.

Determining who is unworthy has been the exclusive province of the prophet. When in January 2004 Jeffs publicly ordered the expulsion of 21 men and the reassignment of their families, the community acquiesced. Jeffs's diary, also seized during the Texas raid, reveals a man who micromanaged the community's every decision, from chore assignments and housing arrangements to who married whom and which men were ousted—all directed by revelations Jeffs received as he slept. He claimed that God guided his every action, no matter how small. One diary entry reads: "The Lord directed that I go to the sun tanning salon and get sun tanned more evenly on their suntanning beds."

In 2005 a Utah court transferred control of the trust that oversees much of the land in Hildale and Colorado City from the FLDS leadership to a state-appointed fiduciary; the church is currently waging a campaign to recover control of the trust. As for Jeffs, after spending over a year on the lam avoiding legal issues in Utah—and earning a spot on the FBI's Ten Most Wanted list—he was caught and is currently serving a ten-year-to-life sentence as an accomplice to rape. He awaits trial on multiple indictments in Arizona and Texas. The 11 other church members awaiting trial in Texas include Merril Jessop, who was indicted for performing the marriage of Jeffs to an underage girl.

Yet Jeffs's smiling portrait continues to adorn the living room of almost every FLDS home. In his absence, his lieutenants have launched a fierce defense of his leadership. While conceding that underage marriages did occur in the past, Donald Richter, contributor to one of the official FLDS websites, says the practice has now been stopped. As for the Lost Boys, he argues that both the numbers involved and the reasons for the expulsions have been greatly exaggerated by the church's enemies. "This is only done in the most extreme cases," Richter says, "and never for the trivial causes they're claiming. And anyway, all religious groups have the right to expel people who won't accept their rules."

Certainly Melinda Fischer Jeffs hasn't been swayed by the ongoing controversy. "Warren is just the kindest, most loving man," she says. "The image that has been built up about him

by the media and his enemies is just unrecognizable to who he really is." Like other church members, Melinda has ready answers for most of the accusations leveled against Jeffs and is especially spirited in defending the policy of reassignment. According to her, it is almost always initiated at the request of a wife who has been abandoned or abused. This is debatable. In his diary Jeffs recounts reassigning the wives of three men, including his brother David, because God had shown him that they "couldn't exalt their ladies, had lost the confidence of God." One of his brother's wives had difficulty accepting the news and could barely bring herself to kiss her new husband. "She showed a great spirit of resistance, yet she went through with it," Jeffs records. "She needs to learn to submit to Priesthood."

Yet Melinda's defense of Jeffs underscores one of the most curious aspects of the polygamous faith: the central role of women in defending it. This is not new. In Brigham Young's day a charity rushed to Utah to establish a safe house for polygamous women seeking to escape this "white slavery"; that house sat virtually empty. Today FLDS women in the Hildale–Colorado City area have ample opportunity to "escape"—they have cell phones, they drive cars, there are no armed guards keeping them in—yet they don't.

Undoubtedly one reason is that, having been raised in this culture, they know little else. Walking away means leaving behind everything: the community, one's sense of security, even one's own family. Carolyn Jessop, the plural wife of Merril Jessop who did leave the FLDS, likens entering the outside world to "stepping out onto another planet. I was completely unprepared, because I had absolutely no life skills. Most women in the FLDS don't even know how to balance a checkbook, let alone apply for a job, so contemplating how you're going to navigate in the outside world is extremely daunting."

It would seem there's another lure for women to stay: power. The FLDS women I spoke with tended to be far more articulate and confident than the men, most of whom seemed paralyzed by bashfulness. It makes sense when one begins to grasp that women are coveted to "multiply and replenish the earth," while men are in extraordinary competition to be deemed worthy of marriage by the prophet. One way to be deemed worthy, of course, is to not rock the boat, to keep a low profile. As a result, what has all the trappings of a patriarchal culture, actually has many elements of a matriarchal one.

There are limits to that power, of course, for it is subject to the dictates of the prophet. After hearing Melinda's stout defense of Jeffs, I ask what she would do if she were reassigned.

"I'm confident that wouldn't happen," she replies uneasily.

"But what if it did?" I ask. "Would you obey?"

For the only time during our interview, Melinda grows wary. Sitting back in her chair, she gives her head a quarter turn to stare at me out of the corner of one eye.

On a sunny afternoon in March 2009, Bob Barlow, a friendly, middle-aged member of the FLDS, gives me a tour of the YFZ Ranch in West Texas. The compound consists of about 25 two-story log-cabin-style homes, and a number of workshops and factories are scattered over 1,700 acres. At the center sits a gleaming white stone temple. It is remarkable what the residents have created from the hardscrabble plain. With heavy machinery, they literally made earth out of the rocky terrain, crushing stone and mixing it with the thin topsoil. They planted orchards and gardens and lawns and were on their way to creating a self-sufficient community amid the barren landscape. All that ground to a halt after the 2008 raid.

"The families are slowly coming back now," Barlow says. "We'll come out the other side of this better and stronger than before."

I suspect he's right. So many times in the history of Mormon polygamy the outside world thought it had the movement on the ropes only to see it flourish anew. I'm reminded of this one afternoon in Colorado City when I speak with Vera Black. Now 92 and in failing health, Vera is the woman whose children were taken from her by Utah authorities in 1956 and returned only after she agreed to renounce polygamy. Within days of making that promise, she was back in Short Creek with her children and had renewed her commitment to the everlasting covenant.

Now living with her daughter Lillian, Vera lies in a daybed as her children gather around. Those children are now in their 50s and 60s, and as they recount the story of their long-ago separation—both from their mother and their faith—several weep, as if the pain were fresh.

"I had to make that promise," Vera says, with a smile, "but I crossed my fingers while I did it."

Critical Thinking

1. How do you view the FLDS communities and their beliefs on polygamy?

2. In your opinion, should government outlaw polygamy? Why or why not?

3. Does polygamy threaten traditional marriage?

4. Do you believe that law enforcement should investigate polygamist families?

5. What are some of the benefits of polygamy and the costs of polygamy?

6. In reading this article, how does polygamy impact children growing up in these families?

7. Thinking of the current media's portrayal of polygamy, such as *Big Love* and *Sister Wives,* does that make polygamy more acceptable?

From *National Geographic*, Vol. 217, No. 2, February 2010, pp. 34–57. Copyright © 2010 by National Geographic Society. Reprinted by permission.

Good Parents, Bad Results

Science is providing proof of where Mom and Dad go wrong.

NANCY SHUTE

Does your 3-year-old throw a five-alarm tantrum every time you drop him off at day care? Does "you're so smart!" fail to inspire your 8-year-old to turn off *Grand Theft Auto IV* and tackle his math homework? Do the clothes remain glued to your teenager's bedroom floor, along with your antisocial teenager, no matter how much you nag or cajole? Being a parent has never been easy—just ask your own. But in this day of two-earner couples and single parents, when 9-year-olds have cellphones, 12-year-olds are binge drinking and having oral sex, and there is evidence that teens are more fearful and depressed than ever, the challenges of rearing competent and loving human beings are enough to make a parent seek help from Supernanny. Actually, there is something better: science.

Researchers have spent decades studying what motivates children to behave and can now say exactly what discipline methods work and what don't: Call it "evidence-based parenting." Alas, many of parents' favorite strategies are scientifically proven to fail. "It's intuitive to scream at your child to change their behavior, even though the research is unequivocal that it won't work," says Alan Kazdin, a psychologist who directs the Yale Parenting Center and Child Conduct Clinic. Other examples:

- Yelling and reasoning are equally ineffective; kids tune out both.
- Praise doesn't spoil a child; it's one of the most powerful tools that parents can use to influence a child's actions. But most parents squander praise by using it generically—"you're so smart" or "good job!"—or skimping.
- Spanking and other harsh punishments ("You're grounded for a month!") do stop bad behavior but only temporarily. Punishment works only if it's mild, and it is far outweighed by positive reinforcement of good behavior.

As yet, few of the bestselling books and videos that promise to turn surly brats into little buttercups make use of this knowledge. That may be because the research goes on in academia—at Yale, at Vermont's Behavior Therapy and Psychotherapy Center, and at the University of Washington's Parenting Clinic, for example. Surprisingly, many family therapists and parenting educators aren't up to speed on the research, either, so that parents who seek professional help won't necessarily get the most proven advice. Case in point: Just 16 programs designed for treating kids with disruptive behavior have been proven "well established" in randomized clinical trials, according to a review led by Sheila Eyberg at the University of Florida and published in the January *Journal of Clinical Child and Adolescent Psychology*. Kazdin, who for years has pushed clinical psychologists to adopt evidence-based methods, published a book for parents earlier this year: *The Kazdin Method for Parenting the Defiant Child*. Other lab-tested tomes include *Parenting the Strong-Willed Child* by Rex Forehand and Nicholas Long and *The Incredible Years* by Carolyn Webster-Stratton.

These discipline programs are grounded in classical behavioral psychology—the positive reinforcement taught in Psych 101. Researchers have run randomized controlled trials on all the nuances of typical parent-child interactions and thus can say just how long a timeout should last to be effective or how to praise a 13-year-old so that he beams when he takes out the trash. Who knew that effectively praising a child in order to motivate her has three essential steps? They are: 1) Praise effusively, with the enthusiasm of a Powerball winner. 2) Say exactly what the child did right. 3) Finish with a touch or hug.

What else can parents learn from the science? Researchers say these are the biggest common boo-boos:

1. Parents Fail at Setting Limits

It would be hard to find a parent who doesn't agree that setting and enforcing rules are an essential part of the job description. Yet faced with whining, pouting, and tantrums, many parents cave. "The limited time you have with your kids, you want to make it ideal for them," says Forehand, a professor of psychology at the University of Vermont whose evidence-based program is outlined in his book. "As a result, we end up overindulging our kids."

Faced with whining and pouting, many parents cave. Result: domestic inferno.

A Good Parent's Dilemma: Is It Bad to Spank?

Plenty of people argue for an occasional swat

Last year, the California Legislature considered criminalizing the spanking of toddlers. But at least half of parents, and according to some surveys as many as 94 percent, consider a swat on the bottom to be an appropriate form of discipline. "spanking has worked very well for us," says Tim Holt, a 45-year-old insurance agent and the father of four children, ages 4 to 13, in Simpsonville, S.C., who notes that he and his wife spank very rarely. He recalls spanking his 7-year-old son, Scott, after Scott hit his brother in the head with a shoe and then lied to his father about it. "I pulled Scott aside. We discussed what he had done: Why is it wrong? What does God's law say? That we don't take our anger out on others." Then Holt put Scott over his knee and smacked him on his pants with a plastic glue stick. "It's something that gets his attention and provides a little bit of pain to his bottom."

Proponents include James Dobson, a psychologist and founder of Focus on the Family, who likens squeezing a child's shoulder or spanking his behind to discomfort that "works to shape behavior in the physical world." He writes in *The New Dare to Discipline:* "The minor pain that is associated with this deliberate misbehavior tends to inhibit it. . . . A boy or girl who knows love abounds at home will not resent a well-deserved spanking." But the subject generates more heat than just about any other child-rearing issue. Sweden banned spanking in 1979. The United Nations Committee on the Rights of the Child has been seeking a ban on corporal punishment worldwide since 1996.

The evidence. The debate roils academia, too. Murray Straus, a professor of sociology at the University of New Hampshire, says 110 studies have linked spanking to increased misbehavior in childhood as well as adult problems such as increased spousal abuse and depression. In February, Straus published research linking being spanked in childhood with an adult preference for sadomasochistic sex. Straus acknowledges that most of today's parents were themselves spanked as children but says that since spanking is no more effective than other discipline methods and can cause harm it's not worth the misery. Other researchers, including Diana Baumrind, a psychologist at the University of California-Berkeley, have found that children who were spanked occasionally had no more behavior problems than children who were never spanked. But Baumrind says regular reliance on physical punishment, as well as "impulsive and reactive spanking," causes harm to a child. The bottom line: Proponents of either position can come up with enough evidence to support their belief—but not enough to convince the other side.

Demonizing spanking may leave some parents feeling they must avoid *any* discipline that makes a child feel bad, says Lawrence Diller, a developmental pediatrician in Walnut Creek, Calif., who works with children with attention deficit hyperactivity disorder. He speculates that a more coherent disciplinary approach that includes an occasional well-timed swat can make the overall system more effective and could "make the difference in whether your child will be on Ritalin or not. You don't have to spank. But if you're using spanking as one of array of tools to get control of your kid, you're not hurting them in the long term."

—N.S.

But, paradoxically, not having limits has been proven to make children *more* defiant and rebellious, because they feel unsafe and push to see if parents will respond. Research since the 1960s on parenting styles has found that a child whose mom and dad are permissive is more likely to have problems in school and abuse drugs and alcohol as teenagers. "Parents ask their 1-year-olds what they want for dinner now," says Jean Twenge, an associate professor of psychology at San Diego State University and author of *Generation Me.* "No one ever said that a generation or two ago." Using surveys dating back to the 1930s, Twenge has found significant increases in reported symptoms of depression and anxiety among today's children and teenagers, compared with earlier generations. Suniya Luthar, a psychologist at Columbia University Teachers College, reported in 2003 that children who are showered with advantages are more likely to be depressed and anxious and to abuse drugs and alcohol than the norm. Luthar says that's probably because those children are under a lot of pressure to achieve at school and think that their parents value their achievements more than themselves. They also feel isolated from their parents.

Rule-setting works best when parents give simple, clear commands and discuss the family rules with kids well in advance of a conflict, according to Robert Hendren, a professor of psychiatry at the Medical Investigation of Neurodevelopmental Disorders Institute at the University of California-Davis and president of the American Academy of Child and Adolescent Psychiatry. A common recommendation for parents who fear coming off as a meanie: Let the child choose between two options when either choice is acceptable to the parent. A half-hour of Nintendo right after school, then homework? All homework before game time?

Consistency is also key. "I have to be very strict with myself and go over and tell him the rules and walk away," says Lauren Jordan, a stay-at-home mom in Essex Junction, Vt., whose 4-year-old son, Peter, would scream and hit Jordan and her husband, Sean, then kick the wall during timeout. "It felt out of control." Jordan signed up with Vermont's Behavior Therapy and Psychotherapy Center to learn Forehand's five-week process.

The first week was spent just "attending" to Peter, watching him play and commenting without telling the preschooler what to do. "He *loved* it," says Jordan, whose older son has autism and has required an outsize share of her energy. "I realized at that point that he needs this one-on-one attention." Jordan then had to learn to ignore Peter's minor bad behavior (such as screaming for attention while Mom is on the phone) and to not rush in to scold him during a timeout. "Consistency is the key. It's not easy," Jordan says. "But it's made our home a much happier place."

2. They're Overprotective

Teachers, coaches, and psychotherapists alike have noticed that parents today can't stand to see their children struggle or suffer a setback. So they're stepping in to micromanage everything from playground quarrels to baseball team positions to grades. Even bosses aren't immune. One owner of a New York public relations firm says he has gotten E-mails from parents telling him that's he's making their child work too much. The child in question is in his 20s.

"Many well-meaning parents jump in too quickly," says Robert Brooks, a clinical psychologist in Needham, Mass., and coauthor of *Raising Resilient Children*. "Resilient children realize that sometimes they will fail, make mistakes, have setbacks. They will attempt to learn from them." When parents intercede, Brooks says, "it communicates to the kid that 'I don't think you're capable of dealing with it.' We have to let kids experience the consequences of their behavior."

Otherwise, they may grow afraid to try. "I see a lot of kids who seem really unmotivated," says Kristen Gloff, 36, a clinical and school social worker in the Chicago area. "It's not that they're lazy. They don't want to fail."

3. They Nag. Lecture. Repeat. Then Yell.

If one verbal nudge won't get a kid to come to dinner, 20 surely will. Right? In fact, there's abundant evidence that humans tune out repeated commands. "So many parents think they have to get very emotionally upset, yell, threaten, use sarcasm," says Lynn Clark, a professor emeritus of psychology at Western Kentucky University and author of *SOS Help for Parents*. "The child imitates that behavior, and you get sassy talk."

Nagging also gives children "negative reinforcement," or an incentive—parental attention—to keep misbehaving. "I was kind of ignoring the good behavior, and every time he did something wrong, I would step in and give him attention," says Nancy Ailes, a 46-year-old stay-at-home mom in East Haven, Conn. She was frustrated with her 9-year-old son, Nick, who would melt down and throw things if the day's schedule changed, drag his feet about cleaning his room or doing homework, and call her "bad Mommy" if she complained.

Parent management training this spring at the Yale Child Conduct Center taught Ailes and her husband how to use positive reinforcement instead—to praise Nick immediately and enthusiastically. Now, when Nick is picking up his toys in the family room, she sits down, watches, and says: "Wow, that looks really nice!"

Ailes and her husband, David, also learned how to set up a reward system with points that Nick can cash in for Yu-Gi-Oh cards and Game Boy time and to back up the system with timeouts for bad behavior. Within three weeks, Ailes says, Nick had made a complete turnaround. "Instead of doing things that make people unhappy," she says, "you do things that make them happy!"

4. They Praise Too Much— and Badly

It seems like a truism that praising children would make them feel good about themselves and motivate them to do better. But parents don't give children attaboys as often as they think, Kazdin says. And when they do, it's all too often either generic ("good job!") or centered on the person, not the task ("you're so smart!"). This kind of praise actually makes children less motivated and self-confident. In one experiment by Carol Dweck, a psychologist now at Stanford University, fifth graders who were praised for being intelligent, rather than making a good effort, actually made less of an effort on tests and had a harder time dealing with failure.

"It's so common now for parents to tell children that they're special," says Twenge. That fosters narcissism, she says, not self-esteem. Twenge thinks parents tell a child "You're special" when they really mean "You're special to me." Much better in every way, she says, to just say: "I love you."

5. They Punish Too Harshly

Although spanking has been deplored by child-development experts since the days of Dr. Spock in the 1940s, as many as 90 percent of parents think it's OK to spank young children, according to research by Murray Straus, a professor of sociology at the University of New Hampshire (more on the spanking controversy in the box). Kazdin and other behavioral researchers say parents commonly punish far more harshly than they need to.

After all, it's not supposed to be about payback, though that's often what's going on, says Jamila Reid, codirector of the Parenting Clinic at the University of Washington. The clinic's "The Incredible Years" program has been found in seven studies to improve children's behavior. "Often parents come looking for bigger sticks. We tell parents the word discipline means 'teach.' It's something to teach a child that there's a better way to respond."

Consider the fine art of the timeout. Parents often sabotage timeouts by lecturing or by giving hugs, according to Sheila Eyberg, a professor of psychology at the University of Florida. Her Parent-Child Interaction Therapy is used in many mental health clinics. Forehand and other researchers have spent many hours observing the use of timeout as a disciplinary strategy to determine exactly what makes it effective. The key finding: Discipline works best when it's immediate, mild, and brief, because it's then associated with the transgression and doesn't breed more anger and resentment. A timeout should last for just a few minutes, usually one minute for each year of age of the child.

Teenagers who have outgrown timeouts shouldn't lose a privilege for more than a day. Beyond that, the child's attitude shifts from regretting bad behavior to resenting the parent. "The punishment business isn't just ineffective," Kazdin says. "It leads to avoidance and escape. It puts a little wedge in the relationship between parent and child." Long groundings also make it more likely that the parents will relent after a few days. Better,

Kazdin says, to ask the child to practice good behavior, such as fixing something he damaged, in order to win privileges back.

6. They Tell Their Child How to Feel

Most parenting books focus on eradicating bad behavior. But in study after study, empathy for other people leads the list of qualities that people need to successfully handle relationships at school, at work, and in the family. Children need to think about how their own feelings will be affected by what they do, as well as the feelings of others, says Myrna Shure, a developmental psychologist at Drexel University and author of *Raising a Thinking Child*. "That is what will inhibit a child from hurting others, either physically or emotionally."

And parents, by telling children "you're fine" or "don't cry," deny children the chance to learn those lessons. "The child learns empathy through being empathized with," says Stanley Greenspan, a child psychiatrist in Chevy Chase, MD, whose most recent book, *Great Kids,* tells parents how to help their child develop 10 essential qualities for a happy life. Empathy, creativity, and logical thinking top the list. A simple "We're so sorry, we know how it feels" is enough.

"Modeling empathic behavior is really very important," says James Windell, a counselor with the juvenile court system in Oakland County, Mich., and author of *8 Weeks to a Well-Behaved Child*. "How you respond to your children's needs sets the stage. It's really easy to be a supportive parent when they bring home a straight-A report card. When they get a bad grade, that's when they really need our support."

7. They Put Grades and SATs Ahead of Creativity

An overemphasis on good grades can also distort the message about how and what children should learn. "We like kids to learn rules, and we want them to learn facts," says Greenspan. "We're impressed when they can read early or identify their shapes. It's much harder for us to inspire them to come up with a creative idea." Children who can think creatively are more likely to be able to bounce back if their first idea doesn't work. They also know it can take time and patience to come up with a good solution. The goal, says Greenspan, is not to have a child who knows how to answer questions but one who will grow up to ask the important questions.

Parents can help their children become independent thinkers by asking open-ended questions like: Can you think of another way to solve the problem with your teammate? Or ask a whining preschooler: Can you think of a different way to tell me what you want?

8. They Forget to Have Fun

"When I talk to families that aren't functioning so well, and I ask, how often do you laugh together, they say: We haven't laughed together for a long time," says Hendren. Those little signs of love and connection—a laugh, a song shared in the car—are, he says, signs of health.

Critical Thinking

1. After reading this article, were there "boo-boos" that your parents made in your upbringing?
2. How did you feel about the author's opinion about spanking?
3. Is there such a thing as being overprotective and what are reasonable limits for each developmental stage?
4. What constitutes punishing too harshly and emotional or physical abuse?
5. Of the eight "boo-boos" listed in the article, which do you feel is most important if you were advising new parents?

From *U.S. News & World Report,* June 23, 2008, pp. 59–62, 64. Copyright © 2008 by U.S. News & World Report, LP. Reprinted by permission via Wright's Media.

Do We Need a Law to Prohibit Spanking?

Murray Straus, PhD

The proposal by a member of the California legislature to prohibit spanking and other corporal punishment of children age three and younger has attracted nationwide interest—and outrage. Newspapers around the country published editorials about it. I read many of them, and all opposed the proposal. The two main objections are that spanking children is sometimes necessary and that it is an unprecedented and horrible example of government interference in the lives of families. The editorials usually also say or imply that "moderate" spanking does not harm children. These objections accurately represent the beliefs of most Americans, but they are not accurate representations of the scientific evidence on the effectiveness and side effects of spanking. They are also historically inaccurate about government interference in the family.

The research on the effectiveness of spanking shows that it does work to correct misbehavior. But the research also shows that spanking does not work better than other modes of correction and control, such as time out, explaining, and depriving a child of privileges. Moreover, the research clearly shows that the gains from spanking come at a big cost. These include weakening the tie between children and parents, and increasing the probability that the child will hit other children, hit their parents, and as adults hit a dating or marital partner. Spanking also slows down mental development and lowers the probability of a child doing well in school and in college. There have been more than a hundred studies of these side effects of spanking, and there is over 90% agreement between them. There is probably no other aspect of parenting and child behavior where the results are so consistent.

Despite this overwhelming evidence, few believe that "moderate" spanking harms children, including few psychologists. It seems to contradict their own experience and that of their children. They say "I was spanked and I was not a violent kid and I did well in school." That is correct, but the implication that spanking is harmless is not correct. Like smoking, spanking is a "risk factor"—not a one-to-one cause of problems. About a third of heavy smokers die of a smoking related disease. That is gruesome, but it also means that two thirds can say "I smoked all my life and I am OK." Does that mean smoking is OK? No, it just means that they are one of the lucky two thirds. Similarly, when someone says "I was spanked and I am OK," that is

correct. However, the implication that spanking is harmless is not correct. The correct implication is that they are one of the lucky majority, rather than one of those harmed by spanking.

The large and consistent body of evidence on the harmful side effects of spanking is also not believed because because so few get to know about it.

Another reason the evidence is not believed is because the harm from spanking occurs down the road. Parents can see that the spanked child stopped what they were doing wrong. They cannot see the harmful effects that occur months or years later.

The large and consistent body of evidence on the harmful side effects of spanking is also not believed because so few get to know about it. I analyzed the content of ten child psychology textbooks published in the 1980's, ten in the 1990's, and ten published since 2000. These giant textbooks averaged only half a page on spanking, despite the fact that almost all American toddlers are spanked. None reported the fact that over 90% of the studies found harmful side-effects. Or putting it the other way around, none let their readers know that children who are not spanked, rather than being out of control brats, are more likely than spanked children to be well behaved and to have fewer psychological problems. This may be the best kept secret of American child psychology.

What about no-spanking legislation being an unprecedented interference in the family? Until the 1870's husbands had the right to use corporal punishment to correct an "errant wife." When the courts started to rule that this aspect of the common law was no longer valid, it was regarded by many as an outrageous interference in what should be a private family matter. Government now prohibits "physically chastisting an errant wife" and prohibits many other things to protect family members and to enhance the stability of the family, starting with prohibiting marriage at an early age.

The proposed California law, however, has two major problems. First, it applies only to children age three and younger. Therefore it has the ironic implication of endorsing the hitting of older children. A second irony is that this law would be doing the very thing it wants parents not to do—use harsh punishment to correct misbehavior. A better model is the 1979 Swedish no-spanking law. It has no criminal penalty. The purpose of that type of law is to set a standard for how children should be treated, and to make money available to educate the public about these standards and to provide services to help parents who are having enough difficulty with their children that they spank. The Swedish law has proven to be very effective. Spanking children has declined tremendously. Opponents of the law feared that Swedish children would be "running wild." The opposite has happened. Youth crime rates, drug use, and suicide have all decreased.

Fifteen nations now prohibit spanking by parents. There is an emerging consensus that this is a fundamental human right for children. The United Nations committee charged with implementing the Charter of Children's Rights is asking all nations to prohibit spanking. Never spanking will not only reduce the risk of delinquency and mental health problems, it will also bring to children the right to be free of physical attacks in the name of discipline, just as wives gained that human right a century and a quarter ago.

Critical Thinking

1. Should there be a law to prohibit spanking and why?

2. What are some reasons that parents give for using spanking to punish their child?

3. What are some of the harmful side effects from spanking a child?

4. Who should be allowed to spank children? Schools, caregivers who are not the parents, anyone?

5. What do you think of the following statement, "My parents spanked me and I turned out ok"?

MURRAY A. STRAUS, PhD, has studied spanking by large and representative samples of American parents for thirty years. He is the author of *Beating the Devil out of Them: Corporal Punishment in American Families and Its Effects on Children* (Transaction Press, 2001). He has been president of three scientific societies including the National Council on Family Relations, and an advisor to the National Institutes of Health and the National Science Foundation. He can be reached at 603 862-2594 or by email at murray.straus@unh.edu. Much of his research on spanking can be downloaded from http://pubpages.unh.edu/~mas2.

NCFR Report, *Family Focus Section,* volume FF34, June 2007. Used by permission. Copyright 2007.

Children of Lesbian and Gay Parents

Psychology, Law and Policy

Does parental sexual orientation affect child development, and if so, how? Studies using convenience samples, studies using samples drawn from known populations, and studies based on samples that are representative of larger populations all converge on similar conclusions. More than two decades of research has failed to reveal important differences in the adjustment or development of children or adolescents reared by same-sex couples compared to those reared by other-sex couples. Results of the research suggest that qualities of family relationships are more tightly linked with child outcomes than is parental sexual orientation.

CHARLOTTE J. PATTERSON

Does parental sexual orientation affect child development, and if so, how? This question has often been raised in the context of legal and policy proceedings relevant to children, such as those involving adoption, child custody, or visitation. Divergent views have been offered by professionals from the fields of psychology, sociology, medicine, and law (Patterson, Fulcher, & Wainright, 2002). While this question has most often been raised in legal and policy contexts, it is also relevant to theoretical issues. For example, does healthy human development require that a child grow up with parents of each gender? And if not, what would that mean for our theoretical understanding of parent–child relations? (Patterson & Hastings, in press) In this article, I describe some research designed to address these questions.

Early Research

Research on children with lesbian and gay parents began with studies focused on cases in which children had been born in the context of a heterosexual marriage. After parental separation and divorce, many children in these families lived with divorced lesbian mothers. A number of researchers compared development among children of divorced lesbian mothers with that among children of divorced heterosexual mothers and found few significant differences (Patterson, 1997; Stacey & Biblarz, 2001).

These studies were valuable in addressing concerns of judges who were required to decide divorce and child custody cases, but they left many questions unanswered. In particular, because the children who participated in this research had been born into homes with married mothers and fathers, it was not obvious how to understand the reasons for their healthy development. The possibility that children's early exposure to apparently heterosexual male and female role models had contributed to healthy development could not be ruled out.

When lesbian or gay parents rear infants and children from birth, do their offspring grow up in typical ways and show healthy development? To address this question, it was important to study children who had never lived with heterosexual parents. In the 1990s, a number of investigators began research of this kind.

An early example was the Bay Area Families Study, in which I studied a group of 4- to 9-year-old children who had been born to or adopted early in life by lesbian mothers (Patterson, 1996, 1997). Data were collected during home visits. Results from in-home interviews and also from questionnaires showed that children had regular contact with a wide range of adults of both genders, both within and outside of their families. The children's self-concepts and preferences for same-gender playmates and activities were much like those of other children their ages. Moreover, standardized measures of social competence and of behavior problems, such as those from the Child Behavior Checklist (CBCL), showed that they scored within the range of normal variation for a representative sample of same-aged American children. It was clear from this study and others like it that it was quite possible for lesbian mothers to rear healthy children.

Studies Based on Samples Drawn from Known Populations

Interpretation of the results from the Bay Area Families Study was, however, affected by its sampling procedures. The study had been based on a convenience sample that had been assembled by word of mouth. It was therefore impossible to rule out the possibility that families who participated in the research were especially well adjusted. Would a more representative sample yield different results?

To find out, Ray Chan, Barbara Raboy, and I conducted research in collaboration with the Sperm Bank of California

(Chan, Raboy, & Patterson, 1998; Fulcher, Sutfin, Chan, Scheib, & Patterson, 2005). Over the more than 15 years of its existence, the Sperm Bank of California's clientele had included many lesbian as well as heterosexual women. For research purposes, this clientele was a finite population from which our sample could be drawn. The Sperm Bank of California also allowed a sample in which, both for lesbian and for heterosexual groups, one parent was biologically related to the child and one was not.

We invited all clients who had conceived children using the resources of the Sperm Bank of California and who had children 5 years old or older to participate in our research. The resulting sample was composed of 80 families, 55 headed by lesbian and 25 headed by heterosexual parents. Materials were mailed to participating families, with instructions to complete them privately and return them in self-addressed stamped envelopes we provided.

Results replicated and expanded upon those from earlier research. Children of lesbian and heterosexual parents showed similar, relatively high levels of social competence, as well as similar, relatively low levels of behavior problems on the parent form of the CBCL. We also asked the children's teachers to provide evaluations of children's adjustment on the Teacher Report Form of the CBCL, and their reports agreed with those of parents. Parental sexual orientation was not related to children's adaptation. Quite apart from parental sexual orientation, however, and consistent with findings from years of research on children of heterosexual parents, when parent–child relationships were marked by warmth and affection, children were more likely to be developing well. Thus, in this sample drawn from a known population, measures of children's adjustment were unrelated to parental sexual orientation (Chan et al., 1998; Fulcher et al., 2005).

Even as they provided information about children born to lesbian mothers, however, these new results also raised additional questions. Women who conceive children at sperm banks are generally both well educated and financially comfortable. It was possible that these relatively privileged women were able to protect children from many forms of discrimination. What if a more diverse group of families were to be studied? In addition, the children in this sample averaged 7 years of age, and some concerns focus on older children and adolescents. What if an older group of youngsters were to be studied? Would problems masked by youth and privilege in earlier studies emerge in an older, more diverse sample?

Studies Based on Representative Samples

An opportunity to address these questions was presented by the availability of data from the National Longitudinal Study of Adolescent Health (Add Health). The Add Health study involved a large, ethnically diverse, and essentially representative sample of American adolescents and their parents. Data for our research were drawn from surveys and interviews completed by more than 12,000 adolescents and their parents at home and from surveys completed by adolescents at school.

Parents were not queried directly about their sexual orientation but were asked if they were involved in a "marriage, or marriage-like relationship." If parents acknowledged such a relationship, they were also asked the gender of their partner. Thus, we identified a group of 44 12- to 18-year-olds who lived with parents involved in marriage or marriage-like relationships with same-sex partners. We compared them with a matched group of adolescents living with other-sex couples. Data from the archives of the Add Health study allowed us to address many questions about adolescent development.

Consistent with earlier findings, results of this work revealed few differences in adjustment between adolescents living with same-sex parents and those living with opposite-sex parents (Wainright, Russell, & Patterson, 2004; Wainright & Patterson, 2006). There were no significant differences between teenagers living with same-sex parents and those living with other-sex parents on self-reported assessments of psychological well-being, such as self-esteem and anxiety; measures of school outcomes, such as grade point averages and trouble in school; or measures of family relationships, such as parental warmth and care from adults and peers. Adolescents in the two groups were equally likely to say that they had been involved in a romantic relationship in the last 18 months, and they were equally likely to report having engaged in sexual intercourse. The only statistically reliable difference between the two groups—that those with same-sex parents felt a greater sense of connection to people at school—favored the youngsters living with same-sex couples. There were no significant differences in self-reported substance use, delinquency, or peer victimization between those reared by same- or other-sex couples (Wainright & Patterson, 2006).

Although the gender of parents' partners was not an important predictor of adolescent well-being, other aspects of family relationships were significantly associated with teenagers' adjustment. Consistent with other findings about adolescent development, the qualities of family relationships rather than the gender of parents' partners were consistently related to adolescent outcomes. Parents who reported having close relationships with their offspring had adolescents who reported more favorable adjustment. Not only is it possible for children and adolescents who are parented by same-sex couples to develop in healthy directions, but—even when studied in an extremely diverse, representative sample of American adolescents—they generally do.

These findings have been supported by results from many other studies, both in the United States and abroad. Susan Golombok and her colleagues have reported similar results with a near-representative sample of children in the United Kingdom (Golombok et al., 2003). Others, both in Europe and in the United States, have described similar findings (e.g., Brewaeys, Ponjaert, Van Hall, & Golombok, 1997).

The fact that children of lesbian mothers generally develop in healthy ways should not be taken to suggest that they encounter no challenges. Many investigators have remarked upon the fact that children of lesbian and gay parents may encounter anti-gay sentiments in their daily lives. For example, in a study of 10-year-old children born to lesbian mothers, Gartrell, Deck, Rodas, Peyser, and Banks (2005) reported that a substantial minority had encountered anti-gay sentiments among their peers. Those who had had such encounters were likely to report having felt angry, upset, or sad about these experiences. Children of lesbian and gay parents may be exposed to prejudice against their parents in some settings, and this may be painful for them, but evidence for the idea that such encounters affect children's overall adjustment is lacking.

Conclusions

Does parental sexual orientation have an important impact on child or adolescent development? Results of recent research provide no evidence that it does. In fact, the findings suggest that parental sexual orientation is less important than the qualities of family relationships. More important to youth than the gender of their parent's partner is the quality of daily interaction and the strength of relationships with the parents they have.

One possible approach to findings like the ones described above might be to shrug them off by reiterating the familiar adage that "one cannot prove the null hypothesis." To respond in this way, however, is to miss the central point of these studies. Whether or not any measurable impact of parental sexual orientation on children's development is ever demonstrated, the main conclusions from research to date remain clear: Whatever correlations between child outcomes and parental sexual orientation may exist, they are less important than those between child outcomes and the qualities of family relationships.

Although research to date has made important contributions, many issues relevant to children of lesbian and gay parents remain in need of study. Relatively few studies have examined the development of children adopted by lesbian or gay parents or of children born to gay fathers; further research in both areas would be welcome (Patterson, 2004). Some notable longitudinal studies have been reported, and they have found children of same-sex couples to be in good mental health. Greater understanding of family relationships and transitions over time would, however, be helpful, and longitudinal studies would be valuable. Future research could also benefit from the use of a variety of methodologies.

Meanwhile, the clarity of findings in this area has been acknowledged by a number of major professional organizations. For instance, the governing body of the American Psychological Association (APA) voted unanimously in favor of a statement that said, "Research has shown that the adjustment, development, and psychological well-being of children is unrelated to parental sexual orientation and that children of lesbian and gay parents are as likely as those of heterosexual parents to flourish" (APA, 2004). The American Bar Association, the American Medical Association, the American Academy of Pediatrics, the American Psychiatric Association, and other mainstream professional groups have issued similar statements.

The findings from research on children of lesbian and gay parents have been used to inform legal and public policy debates across the country (Patterson et al., 2002). The research literature on this subject has been cited in amicus briefs filed by the APA in cases dealing with adoption, child custody, and also in cases related to the legality of marriages between same-sex partners. Psychologists serving as expert witnesses have presented findings on these issues in many different courts (Patterson et al., 2002). Through these and other avenues, results of research on lesbian and gay parents and their children are finding their way into public discourse.

The findings are also beginning to address theoretical questions about critical issues in parenting. The importance of gender in parenting is one such issue. When children fare well in two-parent lesbian-mother or gay-father families, this suggests that the gender of one's parents cannot be a critical factor in child development. Results of research on children of lesbian and gay parents cast doubt upon the traditional assumption that gender is important in parenting. Our data suggest that it is the quality of parenting rather than the gender of parents that is significant for youngsters' development.

Research on children of lesbian and gay parents is thus located at the intersection of a number of classic and contemporary concerns. Studies of lesbian- and gay-parented families allow researchers to address theoretical questions that had previously remained difficult or impossible to answer. They also address oft-debated legal questions of fact about development of children with lesbian and gay parents. Thus, research on children of lesbian and gay parents contributes to public debate and legal decision making, as well as to theoretical understanding of human development.

References

American Psychological Association (2004). Resolution on sexual orientation, parents, and children. Retrieved September 25, 2006, from www.apa.org/pi/lgbc/policy/parentschildren.pdf

Brewaeys, A., Ponjaert, I., Van Hall, E.V., & Golombok, S. (1997). Donor insemination: Child development and family functioning in lesbian mother families. *Human Reproduction, 12,* 1349–1359.

Chan, R.W., Raboy, B., & Patterson, C.J. (1998). Psychosocial adjustment among children conceived via donor insemination by lesbian and heterosexual mothers. *Child Development, 69,* 443–457.

Fulcher, M., Sutfin, E.L., Chan, R.W., Scheib, J.E., & Patterson, C.J. (2005). Lesbian mothers and their children: Findings from the Contemporary Families Study. In A. Omoto & H. Kurtzman (Eds.), *Recent research on sexual orientation, mental health, and substance abuse* (pp. 281–299). Washington, DC: American Psychological Association.

Gartrell, N., Deck., A., Rodas, C., Peyser, H., & Banks, A. (2005). The National Lesbian Family Study: 4. Interviews with the 10-year-old children. *American Journal of Orthopsychiatry, 75,* 518–524.

Golombok, S., Perry, B., Burston, A., Murray, C., Mooney-Somers, J., Stevens, M., & Golding, J. (2003). Children with lesbian parents: A community study. *Developmental Psychology, 39,* 20–33.

Patterson, C.J. (1996). Lesbian mothers and their children: Findings from the Bay Area Families Study. In J. Laird & R.J. Green (Eds.), *Lesbians and gays in couples and families: A handbook for therapists* (pp. 420–437). San Francisco: Jossey-Bass.

Patterson, C.J. (1997). Children of lesbian and gay parents. In T. Ollendick & R. Prinz (Eds.), *Advances in clinical child psychology* (Vol. 19, pp. 235–282). New York: Plenum Press.

Patterson, C.J. (2004). Gay fathers. In M.E. Lamb (Ed.), *The role of the father in child development* (4th ed., pp. 397–416). New York: Wiley.

Patterson, C.J., Fulcher, M., & Wainright, J. (2002). Children of lesbian and gay parents: Research, law, and policy. In B.L. Bottoms, M.B. Kovera, & B.D. McAuliff (Eds.), *Children, social science and the law* (pp. 176–199). New York: Cambridge University Press.

Patterson, C.J., & Hastings, P. (in press). Socialization in context of family diversity. In J. Grusec & P. Hastings (Eds.), *Handbook of socialization*. New York: Guilford Press.

Stacey, J., & Biblarz, T.J. (2001). (How) Does sexual orientation of parents matter? *American Sociological Review, 65,* 159–183.

Wainright, J.L., Russell, S.T., & Patterson, C.J. (2004). Psychosocial adjustment and school outcomes of adolescents with same-sex parents. *Child Development, 75,* 1886–1898.

Wainright, J.L., & Patterson, C.J. (2006). Delinquency, victimization, and substance use among adolescents with female same-sex parents. *Journal of Family Psychology, 20,* 526–530.

Critical Thinking

1. Do you believe that children of same-sex parents turn out differently from children from opposite-sex parents? Explain.

2. Is there a trend toward greater acceptance of same-sex parenting? If so, explain why you believe this is so.

Address correspondence to **CHARLOTTE J. PATTERSON,** Department of Psychology, P.O. Box 400400, University of Virginia, Charlottesville, VA 22904; e-mail: cjp@virginia.edu.

From *Current Directions in Psychological Science,* October 2006, pp. 241–244. Copyright © 2006 by the Association for Psychological Science. Reprinted by permission of Sage Publications via Rightslink.

Parenting Gay Youth: Creating a Supportive Environment

LINDA GOLDMAN

Parenting gay children can be challenging, rewarding and ultimately life changing. The level of acceptance of sexual orientation and gender identity by fathers and mothers can detract from or expand a child's healthy growth and development in countless ways. Too many of our LGBT (lesbian, gay bisexual, and transgender) youth face emotional isolation, rejection, and complete withdrawal from parents that lead many to depression, drugs and alcohol and even homelessness.

As a teacher and counselor in the public school system for 20 years, I witnessed LGBT students exposed to sexual harassment, bullying and victimization issues, and emotional and physical abuse that create an unsafe educational environment. As a therapist for 25 years, I have come to see the struggles gay youth face by living with societal stereotyping that becomes internalized homophobia and sexual prejudice projected from the heterosexual world. Consequentially, they then face the additional trauma of hate crimes, abandonment and parental rejection. All of these challenges are a breeding ground for low self-esteem, depression and suicide ideation. And, as a parent of a gay child, I have very personally experienced the challenges LGBT young people face in coming out and then suddenly being out in very uncharted territory. Positive parental attitudes and understanding can be of the utmost importance to ensure healthy outcomes.

"Mom, Dad, I'm Gay!"

Hearing the words "Mom, Dad, I think I am gay" can be life changing for many parents. Within an instant of hearing these words, their preconceived image, dreams and future expectations of their child are dramatically reshaped. Parents can choose to be supportive—this is still the same child they have always loved—and they can grow with their children as they venture into lives with LGBT relationships.

All too often, young people look to parents to be their ultimate support, but, unfortunately, parents cannot overcome the hurdles of prejudice. Ultimately, many mothers and fathers distance, alienate and disown their children because of their sexual orientation or gender identity.

Mom, Dad, I think I am gay.

Some young people would choose isolation or death rather than disclose to their parents, while others feel they are the only people they can turn to. The level of trust is immense as a child who has inwardly struggled with sexual orientation or gender identity decides to confide in his or her parents.

Clearly, parental responses to a child's gay disclosure can range along a continuum from complete rejection to extreme activism. Points on this continuum vary, grow and evolve as the nature of the relationship and deeper understandings emerge. Parental alienation can reinforce self-hatred, isolation and suicidal ideation; indeed, parental rejection can be life threatening.

Parent Education

As parents begin to become an integral part of their child's disclosure of being gay, it is important that they examine their own feelings and thoughts. Many mothers and fathers, even the most liberal, are surprised at their hidden prejudice and challenging ideas, as they felt they were devoid of bigotry until they found their own child to be homosexual.

Often, parents have been bombarded with cultural stereotypes and outdated information. When their daughters and sons disclose their sexual orientation or gender identity, distress and misinformation may surface. Educating families on LGBT issues includes establishing clear language, creating strategies for empowerment, dispelling outdated myths and providing information on resources and supports.

Myth 1. Homosexuality is linked with problems in a child's relationship with parents, such as a domineering or possessive mother and an ineffectual or hostile father.

LGBT individuals are no more likely to be smothered by maternal love than heterosexuals, nor were they more neglected by fathers or sexually abused.

Myth 2. Homosexuality involves a fear or hatred of people of the other sex, leading individuals to direct their sexual desires toward members of their own sex.

LGBT youth are very capable of warm friendships and loving ties with both the opposite and same sex and appear to have positive feelings toward both.

Myth 3. Homosexuality is a choice.

Reframing the assumption that "there is a choice to sexual orientation" and transforming this assumption to "there is no choice for the homosexual adolescent" begins the evolutionary trend leading to acceptance of homosexuality as being a state one is born into.

Myth 4. Homosexuality is caused when children were victimized, seduced, molested or sexually assaulted by an adult homosexual. There is no biological basis for homosexuality.

New research indicates that sexual orientation is at least partly biological, as the brain may differ with sexual orientation. This research affirms the possibility of homosexuality not being linked to sexual abuse as a child. Some researchers indicate evidence of a genetic component to homosexuality as well as the influence of prenatal hormones.

Myth 5. Homosexuality is a mental disorder. In 1973, the American Psychiatric Association removed the term homosexuality from the list of mental and emotional disorders stating sexual orientation is not a disorder. Therefore, it does not need to be cured.

Myth 6. Homosexual men are pedophiles. There is constant confusion over the use of the term pedophilia, which properly refers to offenses against or attraction to prepubescent children. There is no inherent connection between an adult's sexual orientation and her or his propensity for transgressions against children. There is no factual basis for organizations to avoid hiring homosexual or bisexual people on the basis of their sexual orientation for positions that involve responsibility for or supervision of children, adolescents or adults.

Myth 7. LGBT parents raise their children to be homosexual. The myth that LGBT parents will raise their children as homosexual has not been validated by experience or research.

Support

Often, parents feel alone, as they assume no other friends, relatives or mothers and fathers of their child's friends are living the experience of having a LGBT child. Finding a support group with other parents is of great help. They begin to see many of their thoughts and feelings are very common, and they have companions who understand.

Resources for LGBT Youth, Families and Friends

COLAGE: Children of Lesbians and Gays Everywhere
1550 Bryant St. Suite 830
San Francisco, California 94103
415-861-5437
www.colage.org

Family Acceptance Project: Cesar E. Chavez Institute
San Francisco State University
3004-16th St. #301
San Francisco, CA 94103
fap@sfsu.edu

Family Diversity Projects, Inc.
PO Box 1246
Amherst, MA 01004-1246
413-256-0502
www.lovemakesafamily.org

Family Pride Coalition
P.O. Box 65327
Washington, DC 20035-5327
www.familypride.org
202-331-5015

Gay and Lesbian Parents
Coalition International
PO Box 50360
Washington, DC 20091
202-583-8029
www.GLPCI.org

GLSEN: Gay, Lesbian and Straight Educational Network
90 Broad Street
New York, NY 10004
212-727-0135
www.glsen.org

L.A. Gay and Lesbian Center
McDonald/Wright Building
1625 N. Schrader Boulevard
Los Angeles, CA 90028-6213
www.lagaycenter.org
323-993-7400

Human Rights Campaign (HRC)
919 18th St. NW #800
Washington, DC 20006
800-777-4723
www.hrc.org

PFLAG: Parents, Families and Friends of Lesbians and Gays
1726 M St. NW, Suite 400
Washington, DC. 20036
202-467 8180
www.pflag.org

Organizations such as PFLAG (Parents, Families and Friends of Lesbian and Gays) are essential in providing parents with ongoing support to help them explore issues involving gay children.

On the other hand, parental support can be a major force in children's well-being as they step out and reveal with others that their son or daughter is gay, lesbian, bisexual or transgender. The enormous trust that children display in sharing what had been hidden for so long is a powerful tool in building a strong bond. Their ability to create a secure environment is paramount for their child's well being. The following are interventions adults can create to facilitate a comfortable and safe atmosphere:

- Create a supportive environment.
- Educate parents, students, school personnel and community and health professionals.
- Develop a sense of community by becoming involved with LGBT related organizations.
- Engage LGBT role models as identifiable supports and mentors for gay youth.
- Maintain firm boundaries and clear limits against any slurs or abusive words or actions.
- Distinguish between simplistic and negative media stereotyping and supportive films, TV, newspaper articles and music portraying LGBT relationships in a real and thoughtful way.
- Construct language that elicits acceptance and understanding of LGBT issues and expresses equality.

Conclusion

Parents of gay youth want for their children the same things all parents want for their children. They want to see their daughters and sons in a meaningful love relationship, becoming productive members of society and achieving a creative family life. Parents can become educated on the myths of homosexuality and the outdated cultural indoctrination they have unconsciously absorbed. They can become involved in group supports such as PFLAG that allow mothers and fathers a safe forum for coming out too.

Parents can become involved in joining their children in being open about their child's sexual orientation or gender identity. Ultimately, parents can become advocates seeking freedom and equal rights for all young people and speaking out against sexual bias and prejudice. The goal of each and every mother and father is not merely acceptance, but a total embracing of their children and their lives free from judgment and filled with loving support.

References

Bernstein, A. B., MacNeil, R. Introduction, DeGeneres, B. Forward. (2003). *Straight parents, gay children.* New York: Thunder's Mouth Press.

DeGeneres, B. (1999). *Love Ellen.* New York: William Morrow and Co. p. 326.

Goldman, L. (2008). *Coming out, coming in: Nurturing the well-being and inclusion of gay youth in mainstream society.* Taylor and Francis Publishers. pp. 1–329.

Herek, G. (2006) "Facts about homosexuality and child molestation", 12/03/05. pp. 1–16. http://psychology.ucdavis.edu/rainbow/html/facts_molestation.html.

Herek, G. (2006b). Legal recognition of same-sex relationships in the United States: A social science perspective. *American Psychologist,* 61 (6) pp. 607–621.

Kitts, R. Gay adolescents and suicide: Understanding the association. *Adolescence,* Fall 2005, 40, 159, Research Library Core. pp. 621–628.

Lindley, L., & Reininger, B., Support for instruction about homosexuality in South Carolina public schools. *The Journal of School Health,* Jan. 2001; 71, 1; Health Module pp. 17–22.

Myers, D. (2005). *Exploring psychology: Sixth edition in modules.* New York, NY: Worth Publishers. pp. 396–401.

National Youth Advocacy Coalition. (March/April 2003). A blueprint for justice, Washington, DC. Poverty and Race Research and Action Council Journal (PRRAC).

Pawelski, J., Perrin, E., Foy, J. Allen, C., Crawford, J., Del Monte, M., Kaufman, M., Klein, J., Smith, K., Springer, S., Tanner, J., & Vickers, D. (July 2006). The effects of marriage, civil union, and domestic partnership laws on the health and well-being of children. *PEDIATRICS.* Vol 118, No. 1, pp. 349–364.

Saltzburg, S. (January/2004). Learning that an adolescent child is gay or lesbian: The parent experience. Social Work. 49.1. Research Library Core. pp. 109–118.

Savage, T., Harley, D. & Nowak, T. (Spring, 2005). Applying social empowerment strategies as tools for self-advocacy in counseling lesbian and gay male clients. *Journal of Counseling and Development.* Vol. 83. pp. 131–137.

Critical Thinking

1. What does the research say about the origin of sexual orientation?
2. After reading this article, are there myths that you believed?
3. How would you react if your child came out to you?
4. Why is it so important for parents to accept their child's sexual orientation?
5. Explain the importance of supporting gay children.

LINDA GOLDMAN is a Fellow in Thanantology: Death, Dying, and Bereavement (FT) with an MS degree in counseling and Master's Equivalency in early childhood education. She is a Licensed Clinical Professional Counselor (LCPC) and a National Board for Certified Counselors (NBCC). She worked as a teacher and counselor and currently has a private grief therapy practice in Chevy Chase, MD. She works with children, teenagers, families with prenatal loss and grieving adults and shares workshops, courses and trainings on children and grief and trauma and currently teaches as adjunct faculty in the Graduate Program of Counseling at Johns Hopkins University. She has also taught on the faculty at the U. of MD. School of Social Work and lectured at many other universities including Penn State University, Buffalo School of Social Work, University of North Carolina and The National Changhua University of Education in Taiwan, as well as numerous schools systems throughout the country. She teaches the course on "Working with LGBT Youth" at the University of Maryland School of Social Work and Child Welfare Administration. She was named by the *Washingtonian* magazine as one of the top therapists in the MD, VA, DC area (1998) and again as a therapist to go to after the terrorist attacks in 2001. Linda contributed in many ways after 9/11, including writing articles and book chapters, playing a strong role in the TAPS (Tragedy Assistance Program for Survivors) response team at the Pentagon Family Assistance Center and conducting workshops about children and is the recipient of the "The Tenth Global Concern of Human Life Award 2007."

The Forgotten Siblings

In this article I wish to argue that the qualities and dynamics of sibling relationships may have been overlooked in family therapy. In overlooking them, we have also overlooked a significant feature in the emotional life of children. I would like to suggest that sibling relationships are where children practise identity. In these relationships we can learn how to be one in a group. Family Therapy treatment may not make enough use of the dynamic of the sibling relationship.

SALLY YOUNG

Family therapists have prided themselves on their peripheral vision. Part of the claim of systemic therapy is to see the 'big picture.' In terms of families, this often means seeing the whole family. At the very least, it means that the therapist must take into account the existence and importance of family viewpoints other than those represented in the therapy room. However, it could be contended that our primary focus has been on the parent-child relationship and that the sibling relationship is on the periphery. At worst these relationships may have been taken for granted rather than analysed.

In the course of writing this article I opened many relationship and psychology books and looked up 'sibling' in the index. What was interesting was how few references there were, and that usually the word 'sibling' was coupled with 'rivalry.' That in itself was disquieting, in that it suggests that the rivalry in sibling relationships has been emphasised above other emotional dynamics.

Siblings engage in multiple, complex interactions over many years, and in the process they learn much, and could be said to 'practise' many positions they will later take in adult life and relationships. From a lifespan perspective, sibling relationships are often the longest-lasting relationships we have—outlasting relationships with parents, partners, and our own offspring. Here are some key 'sibling learnings':

- That love and hate can quickly follow each other; this is the precursor to ambivalence, where a mixture of feelings can be tolerated together.
- That we can *feel* 'murderous,' but also come to know that we would not *act* on this: an important experience in differentiating thought and action.
- That there is a thin line between a tight hug and a strangle, that we can come to know about our desire to hurt, that in this way we become aware of our own potential for cruelty and our own potential to manage this.
- That we get to be alone together (Winnicott, 1958).
- That we can hate a sibling at home but defend him/her outside the home. That loyalty and honour involve the ability to manage our own ambivalence.
- That being a parent's favourite can ultimately be as burdensome as not being the favourite.
- That we can never overtake our older siblings—a challenge to our magical thinking.
- That we can imitate, anticipate, or dread, the developmental stages that we see our older siblings go through.
- That our sibling relationships offer an invisible continuity throughout our lives, although the grievances, the jealousy, and the competitiveness may be lifelong as well.

In the past couple of years, I have noticed a resurgence of interest in sibling relationships in the systemic and psychodynamic literature. *The Journal of Family Psychology* devoted a special edition to sibling relation-ships in 2005. This special edition emphasises the need for further research in this complex area, but looks at the state of the evidence for sibling relationships in the development of psychopathology. Juliet Mitchell's book. *Siblings* (2003) and *The Importance of Sibling Relationships in Psychoanalysis* (2003) by Prophecy Coles are another two examples. All in different ways suggest that our culture emphasises 'vertical relationships' and marginalises horizontal relationships such as those with our siblings. Sibling relationships are the prototype of peer and later collegial relationships. This idea attracted me as I have long felt that families, classrooms and workplaces survive on the capacity of individuals to find peers, as well protectors, in the face of the inevitable predators. Judy Dunn writes:

> There are powerful arguments for viewing siblings as potentially developmentally important: Their daily contact and familiarity, their emotionally uninhibited relationship, and the impact of sharing parents all suggest that the relationship may have a developmental influence (2005: 654).

Some scenarios come to mind.

Scenario 1

Sharon is a 17-year-old girl, who has a turbulent history. Her brother Mark is a source of great suffering for her. She feels tormented and intimidated by him. The intensity of their arguments has the quality of lovers' tiffs but without the love. One night, Sharon falls back on the familiar solution of cutting herself, as if in search of the lifeblood of her pain. Mark uncharacteristically tries to stop her. Sharon uncharacteristically does stop. Later in a session she says 'I stopped, as it was such a shock that he cared whether I lived'.

Scenario 2

Kathleen is in her forties. Suddenly and unexpectedly her eldest brother dies of a coronary. She awakes in the night anxious about her own mortality. The thought that she is one step closer to death strikes her: a rung has been removed in the ladder of mortality. Somewhere it reflects how deep the sense of sibling order is in her mind. As if some unconscious law dictates we must all die in timely order? Instead, reality declares an untimely disorder.

I would now like to look at theoretical constructions of sibling relationships.

As suggested earlier, 'sibling rivalry' is often the only aspect of sibling relationships to receive attention, and has become somewhat clichéd. Perhaps it is worth revisiting. Rivalry is often seen as negative and destructive, yet it can be a positive spur to development. Circular questioning in family therapy often illustrates that there is more than rivalry in sibling relationships, and that siblings can understand each other well, particularly when it comes to issues of the familiar war between parents and children.

Nonetheless it is important not to deny the power and at times the secession between siblings. I think

aggressive feelings between siblings are much less repressed than those between parents and children. Juliet Mitchell writes:

> I believe we have minimized or overlooked entirely the threat to our existence as small children that is posed by the new baby who stands in our place or the older child who was there before us (2003: xv).

She suggests there is little difference between the tantrumming two-year-old who feels left out by the attention given to the baby, and the hysteria of adult life. In both, she argues the demand is 'Look at me, I am unique, there is only room for me!'

Perhaps all of us in family work have come across individuals who cannot bear the sharing of emotional space that is needed in families, and in family therapy. Juliet argues that beneath this is something that may have its roots in traumatic sibling rivalry; that is, the threat of annihilation by the other, even if that annihilation is figurative rather than actual—a child feels obliterated just by the fact of its sibling's existence. Mitchell goes on to speak about the triumph which psychopaths feel in obliterating the other.

Both Mitchell and Coles argue that theoretically we have overemphasised the Oedipal complex, and as a result have looked vertically (at child–parent relationships) rather than horizontally (at the child–child level). The equivalent of this could be most graphically seen in the structural school of family therapy (Minuchin, 1974). Also the strategic school (Haley, 1976) places enormous emphasis on parental–child relationship. In family therapy perhaps this goes with the understandable stress on parents being parents, taking on their parental authority and functioning in an aware manner. All this I agree with completely, yet is it the complete story?

The danger of the parentified child is something we are all alert to. Yet many of us see single-parent families under stress, where it is necessary for the family's survival that a child carries some parental functions. I wonder if one aspect that may test the difference between functional and dysfunctional parentification is how the parent manages the differences in roles between the siblings. For instance, is it still clear that the child is a child carrying some parental functions, as opposed to being mother's partner, which can only promote aggression and rivalry between the siblings?

Psychodynamic authors suggest that siblings who are very rivalrous may reflect unresolved sibling conflict in the parent's family of origin. In my work in CYMHS, I am struck with how often a parent will, on exploration, reflect a concern that a child will be like a troublesome uncle or aunt. The parent's childhood experiences of their sibling are echoed in the child's behaviour. The child is seen like a sibling, and the parent often attempts to be like or very unlike their own parents, in the management of the sibling ghost. Byng-Hall calls this the replicative or corrective script (Byng-Hall, 1995).

The Development of Group Psychology

I think one of the most powerful areas that have been overlooked in sibling relationships is the power of identification. In childhood, it is an important experience to feel part of a group and be able to step inside the shoes of another. Mary Target (2002) refers to research that suggests that younger siblings are slightly better at reading the intentions of older siblings than their older siblings are, given that they are born into a sibling order with big sister or big brother predecessors. Peter Fonagy and Mary Target's work's (2003) highlights the concept of 'mentalisation' in emotional development. This is really the capacity to think about thinking and feeling, in ourselves and others. They suggest this capacity is vital for us in digesting the realities of our internal and external lives. The people we have the most practice in interpreting/ thinking about in childhood are our siblings. After all, we often spend the most time with them, in the timeless world of childhood.

It is worth reflecting on how powerfully siblings 'wind each other up,' so equally, they bear witness to each other's emotional worlds. Siblings can bring each other alive. In theory, circular questioning may access these understandings. However, this depends on a level of verbalisation that may be beyond many children, and perhaps we need to find a 'play equivalent' of this technique to access these understandings between siblings. These sibling insights may be accessed through projective games such as the Bear Cards (St. Lukes Innovative Resources) and family drawings.

Michael Rutter's studies of children from Romanian orphanages who had been adopted in England indicated that these traumatised children, from horrific institutional situations, like to be with babies—as though the baby gives them back their lost baby selves (Mitchell: 227). Similarly, one can see in many families the way in which a new baby can regenerate a capacity for feelings in siblings and in parents.

Juliet Mitchell writes of having the experience of being part of a group and not feeling annihilated by it (Mitchell, 2003: 52). Sibling relationships give us an early but important experience of being the same but different, which is an experience we have whenever we are in a group. Clearly, our parents are central in managing this experience. The capacity to be in a group is something that we have psychologically undervalued.

Stuart Twemlow (2001), in his research on bullying in schools, stresses the significance of the group, comparing schools with high and low rates of bullying. What he discovered to be the significant factor is what is called the bystander affect. If, when a victim was being bullied, the rest of the group acted as passive bystanders, this was oxygen for the bullying—it inflamed it; if the others were not prepared to be passive, but expressed a point of view, the bullying diminished. Our preparedness to participate in group life is vital, in personal life and in a democracy. In families, whether a troubled sibling is left isolated, or feels some connectedness with a sibling, is often predictive of how likely the family is to respond positively to treatment. Perhaps all family work on some level is looking for the capacity to imaginatively identify with the other.

Prophecy Coles writes:

> Emde, surveying research on infant development to date . . . suggests we need a new concept of the 'we' ego. That is children by the age of three had developed an executive sense of 'we', of the other being with them which gave them increased sense of power and control (Coles, 2003: 76).

Emde says:

> It is perhaps ironic that in our age, so preoccupied with narcissism and self, we are beginning to see a different aspect of psychology, a 'we' psychology in addition to a self psychology . . . This represents a pro-found change in our world view (Coles, 2003: 76).

The Significance of Birth Order

From Adler to the more recent work by Sulloway in his book *Born to Rebel,* theorists have asserted the determinative effects of birth order, though others have argued that these effects are exaggerated, or non-existent. Sulloway hypothesises that the eldest is more authoritarian, having lost something by his displacement by his younger siblings, and the youngest is more likely to rebel, having the security of being the baby of the family. This strikes me as over-deterministic.

However, each individual will experience and interpret family dynamics differently. Siblings growing up in the same family may report very different experiences. Research has indicated that inter-family experiences may be almost as diverse as between-family experiences (Richardson & Richardson, 1990). The differences in family experiences might partly be due to parental expectations, which vary depending on birth order. In their seminal book *Separate Lives: Why Sibling Are So Different,* Robert Plomin and Judy Dunn argue that despite siblings being brought up in the same environment, the environment only *seems* the same. Each sibling perceives their family environment differently, which explains why they turn out so different. I also wonder if a factor in identity formation is the experience of feeling individual through differentiation from one's sibling.

Michael Duffy's joint biography of politicians Mark Latham and Tony Abbott points out that

> . . . each is the eldest child of four children, the others being three girls, each had parents who were enormously ambitious for their only son, and each was as highly competitive and aggressive in sport as they were to be in Federal parliament (Fitzgerald, 2004: 11).

Whether it is completely accurate or not, this description gives a sense of the complex mixture of personality, sibling order, parental expectations and gender mix in families.

In fact, I wonder if one of the many insufficiently understood dynamics in sibling relationships is gender. Being a child with siblings of the other gender is a primary experience of a gendered relationship. Perhaps a test of this is the difference in associations in the public mind between brotherly love, sisterly love and love between a brother and a sister. I recall seeing a mother who had three sons, but who described having only sisters in her family of origin. Despite having a good relationship with her husband, she says 'I just don't understand boys.' I thought that she felt that without brothers, she had missed out on an imaginative understanding of boys, an understanding 'from the inside out,' in the way a sibling might.

Birth order can have determinative effects; take, for example, the case of the eldest child, accorded a special place with a grandparent, as the first grandchild. Yet many other factors can mitigate these effects. For instance, school gives children another chance with their peers. A youngest child who is the 'baby' at home may find herself being able to take a leadership role at school, in this way finding a possibility of being taken seriously by others and by herself.

It is important not to leave out the single child, frequently called the only child. For myself this has associations of 'only an only' child, as if the very description raises an idea of a disappointment that there aren't more children. Miriam Cosic, in her book *Only Child,* argues that culturally the drawbacks of being an only child have been overstated. Perhaps we may potentially envy the only child for not having to share! Single children frequently imagine what happened to the possibility of other children. Family therapists will be increasingly challenged to adapt when the single child family becomes more common. I think one particular difficulty is that the child then has no potential child witnesses or allies in the therapy room. Perhaps

when the family has only one child, the onus on the therapist is increased, to join with the child and allow him/her to remain a child, not a pseudo-adult in the sessions.

Single children frequently imagine what happened to the possibility of other children.

It is not unusual for children to carry the fantasy of a twin as a comforting solution to isolation. For example, Mary is complaining with great intensity about her troublesome little brother. He is indeed troublesome but something in her complaints makes me feel there is more. 'Do you wish you had a sister?' I ask. What then emerges is a very full imagining of a twin sister with whom she could play soccer. Later in the session it was possible for her to have some more hopeful imaginings of when her *brother* could manage to play soccer with her.

The Ghosts in the Nursery

We are generally alert to the influence of the parent's childhood lying like a shadow over their parenting. However, many children, too, carry ghosts—the ghosts of their sibling experiences, which can sometimes include a sibling's mental disturbance. The most poetic description I have found has been in the Oliver Sacks' autobiography, in which he describes the psychotic breakdown of his brother Michael, when Oliver was 12.

> Michael could no longer sleep or rest, but agitatedly strode to and fro in the house, stamping his feet, glaring, hallucinating, shouting. I became terrified of him, for him, of the nightmare which was becoming reality for him, the more so as I could recognize similar thoughts and feelings in myself, even though they were hidden locked up in my own depths. What would happen to Michael, and would something similar happen to me, too? It was at this time that I set up my own lab in the house, and closed the doors, closed my ears against Michael's madness. It was at this time that I sought for (and sometimes achieved) an intense concentration, a complete absorption in the worlds of mineralogy and chemistry and physics, in science—focusing on them, holding myself together in the chaos. It was not that I was indifferent to Michael; I felt a passionate sympathy for him, I half-knew what he was going through, but I had to keep a distance also, create my own world from the neutrality and beauty of nature, so that I would not be swept into the chaos, the madness, the seduction, of his (Sacks, 2001: 186).

It is not easy to deal with a child's trauma about a disturbed sibling. I have sometimes seen siblings who have such a fear of madness or emotionality, that it can be difficult to find a therapeutic engagement to support them. However, a timely family session can provide a forum for siblings to speak of their distress, and this can help rescue the parents from focusing only on the disturbed sibling.

> Rose is 13 years old. Her elder sister. Sara, has early symptoms of anorexia nervosa. Both parents are understandably preoccupied with Sara's mental and physical health. When asked in a family session how this affects her, Rose says, 'I just come home from school and go to my room. The talk is always about Sara'. Her parents are initially shocked, and Mother says she feels the same as Rose, unheard above the worry about Sara. A few minutes later we are again talking about Sara, but Mother and Rose have noticeably faded into the background. It seems important to draw attention that what happens in the family's daily life is happening in the session.

I am very fond of the idea, borrowed from physics, that in a family system, every action has an opposite and equal reaction. I have been struck many times over the years by how siblings tend towards either identifying with each other or individuating by being opposite. Often a conduct-disordered teenager who takes inadequate responsibility, somewhere has a sibling who takes too much responsibility. I think it often happens that the reactions to each other can be seen on the internalising–externalising spectrum. By this I mean that one child may 'internalise' his/her emotional life, perhaps by being withdrawn and depressive, and the other sibling may 'externalise' by being actively disobedient, showing aggression, doing drugs, and the like. Perhaps this 'equal and opposite' phenomenon could be a worthy area of further research, as if proven it would give further support to the systemic model of intervention.

> Harry is part of a large single-parent family. They are a poor family, struggling to keep their heads above water. Harry has an explosive temper that is frightening to everyone in the family. Harry is seen as following in the footsteps of his father's violence. When Harry explodes it reminds everyone in the family of the terrors of the past. Jean, the eldest girl in the family, stands up to Harry, trying to support her mother. Harry hates this, saying to Jean 'You are not my mother'. One day Jean unexpectedly runs away, perhaps in search of a childhood. Later she returns, wanting to live with the family. The family work is about helping Harry free himself from his identification with his father, but also to allow Jean

to be a big sister, not to replay a mother fighting with a father.

The siblings of children with special needs themselves have particular needs. Kate Strohm's book. *Siblings: Brothers and Sisters of Children with Special Needs,* vividly describes her own experience of growing up with a sister who had cerebral palsy. This work assisted in the development of a website www.siblingsaustralia.org.au, which provides information and Internet support to siblings. On this site, children whose siblings have special needs can talk about the dangers of lack of information about the disability, and their feelings of isolation, resentment and grief. The Internet chat room functions as a cyberspace sibling group for these young people. Anecdotal evidence suggests that siblings of special needs children sometimes become health professionals, so this may be pertinent to the professional reader.

Family Sessions as 'Commissions for Truth, Justice and Reconciliation'

I have long been struck by how significant the concept of fairness is in psychological life. An article by the British analyst Eric Rayner (Rayner, 2000: 153) drew my attention the preoccupation with fairness, in both therapy and everyday life. For instance, in writing this article, my wish to create case examples that would suit my argument might conflict with my wish to do justice to those involved, even if only in my imagination. It strikes me that the original arena for this fight for justice is the sibling group, and subsequently the playground. The oft-heard retort of childhood, 'S'not fair', echoes this preoccupation.

I think family therapy has a forgotten but useful sibling, anthropology. The anthropological attitude is very valuable in its enquiry into meaning, rituals and events. Sometimes we will be dealing with hostile 'warring tribes.' And in certain situations the anthropological attitude allows us not to feel compelled to be the agents of change, and can allow a more respectful attitude towards the family, so that they can create solutions within their own culture.

This idea of justice for multiple voices is exemplified by Helen Garner:

> I went to visit my four sisters, carrying a tape recorder and my imagined map of my family. It was unsettling to learn that each sister has her own quite individual map of that territory: the mountains and rivers are in different places, the borders are differently constituted and guarded, the history and politics and justice system of the country are different according to who's talking (Garner, 1997: vi).

In a very poetic way, Garner is alerting us to the trauma of growing up and dealing with competing claims within the same psychological territory. Since I decided to write this article I have been much more consciously asking children about their relationship about their siblings. This list is my attempt at the top 10 complaints:

1. *She gets into my things and sometimes breaks them.* This seems to be the precursor to:
2. *She gets under my skin.*
3. *It's not fair, he gets away with murder.*
4. *She is such a goody-goody.*
5. *Mum and Dad don't know what she gets up to.*
6. *He's the favourite.*
7. *I wish they were dead* [and they are not].
8. *They get all the attention.*
9. *He stinks.*
10. *She spends all her time in front of the mirror.*

I have found that surprisingly often, *the acknowledgement of some feeling of unfairness* seems to take the heat out of the anger, as if the child has felt that no one sees his or her point of view, that a sense of internal justice has been lost. This fight for justice happens in families and between couples as well. I think we do not do it psychological justice if we only call it a 'power struggle.' The apparent tussle for 'power' conceals a deeper concern with fairness.

Couples

Perhaps as a part of my recent focus on siblings, it is has been striking me that over time a sibling-type dynamic can develop in couple relationships. This has positive features, such as companionship and knowing each other very well. But it can also embody negative aspects, such as knowing each other too well, and being able to get under each other's skin. From this point of view, I wonder if the wish for space within a couple is sometimes the wish *to feel less like siblings* and hence to recapture some desire. I think sometimes the ghost of sibling relationships is enacted within these couples.

Mr X was the eldest child in his family. He has been married to Mrs X for 30 years, and she was the youngest child in her family. In the early stages of their relationship, some of his protective capacities were attractive to Mrs X. Gradually, however, she has come to feel restricted in the relationship as though she can never grow up, as though she always remains the little sister. Of course this description of their relationship would not do justice to its other dynamics. Yet to ignore this aspect would mean one

might never uncover what their sibling roles had meant in their identity formation, leaving them feeling stuck forever in an unfair childhood.

Conclusion

Throughout this paper, I have tried to argue that our sibling relationships have a power and dynamism of their own, not to be tidied away as a shadow of the parent–child relationship. Family therapy may not have paid enough attention to this dynamic, both theoretically and technically. Perhaps the question of 'Where are the siblings?' is an extension of Catherine Sanders' comment that has there been 'a recurrent failure to embrace children as clients' (2003: 177). A recent family therapy book by Robert Sanders (2004), *Sibling Relationships: Theory and Issues for Practice* may be testimony to a growing interest within family therapy. Sanders raises many dilemmas for practice such as the question of siblings in care being kept together and of course the danger of assuming we know what is best without assessing the uniqueness of any sibling relationship.

One area ripe for investigation is the actual history of this neglect of conceptualisation of sibling relationships, across all therapies. I wonder if unspoken assumptions that siblings are rivalrous and destructive has meant we potentially neglect the value of these early 'we' relationships. Ironically as systemic therapists, have we neglected the group experience of siblings as a subsystem? Has there been a therapeutic reenactment of the saying, 'Two's company, three is a crowd'?

References

Byng-Hall, J., 1995. *Rewriting Family Scripts,* NY, Guilford.

Coles, P., 2003. *The Importance of Sibling Relationships in Psychoanalysis,* London, Karnac.

Cosic, M., 1999. *Only Child; A Provocative Analysis of the Impact of being an Only Child,* Sydney, Lansdowne.

Dunn, J., 2005. Commentary: Siblings in their Families, *Journal of Family Psychology,* 19, 4: 654–657.

Dunn. J. & Plomin, R., 1990. *Separate Lives: Why Siblings Are So Different.* NY, Basic.

Fitzgerald, R., 2004. Review of Michael Duffy, *Abbott and Latham: The Lives and Rivalry of Two of the Finest Politicians of their Generation,* Sydney, Random House, 2004, *Sydney Morning Herald,* Spectrum Section: 11, August 14–15, 2004.

Fonagy, P. & Target, M., 2003. *Psychoanalytic Theories, Perspectives from Developmental Psychopathology,* London, Whurr.

Garner, H., 1997. A Scrapbook, An Album. In J. Sauers (Ed.), *Brothers and Sisters: Intimate Portraits of Sibling Relationships,* Melbourne, Random House.

Minuchin, S., 1974. *Families and Family Therapy,* London, Tavistock.

Mitchell, Juliet, 2003. *Siblings,* Cambridge, Polity Press.

Rayner, E., 2000. In M. Whelan (Ed.), *Mistress of Her Own Thoughts: Ella Freeman Sharpe and the Practice of Psychoanalysis,* London, Rebus Press.

Richardson, R. W. & Richardson, L. A., 1990. *Birth Order and You,* North Vancouver, British Columbia, Self-Counsel Press.

Sacks, O., 2001. *Uncle Tungsten,* NY, Picador.

Sanders, C., 2003. Living up to our Theory: Inviting Children to Family Sessions, *ANZJFT,* 24, 4: 177–182.

Sanders, R., 2004. *Sibling Relationships: Theory and Issues for Practice,* NY, Macmillan.

Sauers, J., 1997. *Brothers and Sisters: Intimate Portraits of Sibling Relationships,* Melbourne, Random House.

Sulloway, F., 1996. *Born to Rebel: Birth Order, Family Dynamics and Creative Lives,* NY, Random House.

Target, M., 2002. Adolescent Breakdown, A Developmental Perspective [Videotape of Lecture], Sydney. NSW Institute of Psychoanalytic Psychotherapy.

Twemlow. S., 2001. An Innovative Psychodynamically Influenced Approach to Reduce School Violence, *Journal of American Academy of Child and Adolescent Psychiatry,* 40, 3 (March): 741–785.

Winnicott, D., 1958. The Capacity to be Alone, *International Journal of Psychoanalysis,* 39, 5: Sept–Oct: 416–420.

Critical Thinking

1. What is your relationship with your siblings like? If you are an only child, do you have sibling-type relationships with other family members or friends?

2. Reflecting on your own sibling relationships, how do those relationships impact your other relationships?

3. Do you think that birth order is significant? If so, how and why?

4. When reading about the top 10 complaints of sibling relationships, what ones did you identify with most and why?

5. If birth order is significant, what does this mean for only children?

SALLY YOUNG is a Senior Social Worker at Greenslopes Child and Youth Mental Health Clinic, 34 Curd St. Brisbane 4120: yngs@bigpond.com. An earlier version of this paper was presented at the Australian Family Therapy Conference in Brisbane in 2004.

Oh, Brother!

Siblings are born to compete for parental attention, and the **strategies** they use wind up **encoded** in personality. Small wonder it can take a **lifetime** to work out sibling relationships.

HARA ESTROFF MARANO

He set the standard for my lifelong attraction to younger men," says Isadora Alman of her brother, her only sibling, 5½ years her junior. "I can't remember one occasion on which we fought. If one of us was to be punished, the other would immediately jump in: 'Oh, no, it was my fault.' Our relationship became part of the way I love people."

Of course, Alman notes, "It helped that we never lived under the same roof after I turned 13 and went off to boarding school" and that they now live on opposite coasts. It also helped that her baby brother was promised to *her.* "He was *my* baby. I was prepared for him. There was no sense of competition."

Their bond is sealed by something unquantifiably stronger than genes or geography—a shared sense of the absurd. "We're both word people," she explains. So the emails they exchange once or twice a week revel in outrageous puns and the verbal mishaps of others.

As a marriage and family therapist in Alameda, California, Alman knows from countless hours in the consulting room that she and her brother are lucky exceptions. Sibling strife is often the rule, at least at some point in life.

Not only may parents treat young offspring unequally, giving rise to sibling resentments that can long outlast the parents themselves, there is evidence that competition among siblings to distinguish themselves from each other is an inevitable—and necessary—part of family life. Sibling strife allows for the emergence of distinct personalities and identities.

Despite siblings' power to inflame, they are the longest-lasting relationships many of us ever have. Others may help us become who we are, but no one else knows us from the beginning to the end, and that longevity can be humbling.

Whether siblings cycle through our lives or call every week, we are almost always conscious they are there. We carry deep within a sense of shared fate. What's more, often quite unthinkingly, we tend to replicate our roles relative to them in work and even love. Whether we like them or not, siblings are forever.

The Sibling Trajectory

The 82 percent of Americans with siblings typically spend their early years interacting with each other far more than with outsiders. That changes as they grow, expand their range of contacts, and hit new stages of development. In early adolescence, the sibling bond naturally sheds some of its intensity as exciting new relationships open up outside the family and intimacy takes a great leap forward with agemates of both sexes. In early adulthood, siblings—especially sisters, bound by their penchant for self-disclosure—may come together to share resources.

As siblings get beyond their 20s, pair off with partners, move, and establish their own families, the bond generally goes into hibernation. "It's not a key relationship even if you like each other," reports Heidi Riggio, assistant professor of psychology at California State University Los Angeles. "We care; it's just that we're so busy raising our families." Distance becomes more a determinant of sibling emotional closeness. Unless, of course, there's a crisis.

At 44, Shanley Wells is the oldest of three. "Because of our age distribution—my brother and sister are five and six years younger—we seemed to be raised in two different families'," she reports. "Our memories are different, our knowledge of our parents is different—but we did have the same parents!" Wells grew up in a traditional family with a stay-at-home mother. But when she was in college, her father left, and her siblings grew up with a single, working mother. One result, she says, is that her sister became a strong feminist.

Wells was not close to her siblings growing up in Memphis. "They were close in age and knew a lot of the same people. I always felt out of the loop." To her, both siblings were "a general annoyance. We fought a lot. For years my brother and I had our younger sister convinced that she was bought at a children's farm in Kentucky. He even drew up a certificate of purchase." Wells believes that in taking their frustrations out on each other, she and her siblings were reflecting the tensions in their parents' marriage.

Nor was Wells a role model for her siblings: "I was angry and rebellious." Wells moved to the Midwest. Ten years ago, her sister also moved to the Midwest, and the two became much closer. "I felt more secure," Wells confides. "I had my own sense of self. What happened when we were kids didn't matter anymore." Eventually, their brother also moved to the Midwest.

And then last year, their mother died, totally unexpectedly, at a relatively young 68. "That pulled us together," Wells reports. "Formerly, we all stayed in touch through my mother. But my brother, busy with his work and children, has vowed not to let life whiz by without contact. He's really trying. We now have a plan to all travel together, with our spouses, once a year."

The Long Arm of Influence

Sibling relations are so durable because they are close—"often uncomfortably close," in the words of British developmental psychologist Judy Dunn. What's more, they are children's first relational experiences, the ones that shape their social and self-understanding for life. And without any prompting from adults, they tend to be highly emotionally charged. They turn everyday family life into a daily drama for young ones, each of whom is vying for a starring role.

No one has limned this territory better than Dunn, professor of child development at the Institute of Psychiatry in London, who has studied siblings in their natural habitat, the home. Starting from a very early age—before 12 months—children exhibit a highly sophisticated social understanding.

They are extraordinarily sensitive to differences in affection, in warmth, in pride, in attention, and in discipline that parents dole out. They are virtually born attuned to the emotional exchanges going on around them. "They keep an eagle eye out for differences on how all siblings are treated, and they are quick to pick up differential treatment. What's more, they have notions of whether the treatment they or their siblings get is fair or unfair."

Not only are young children aware of what is going on between their siblings and their parents, they are often profoundly influenced by that dynamic. Dunn's longitudinal studies show that children who feel that they are on the short end of maternal affection and attention relative to siblings (maternal treatment seems to carry more weight than paternal treatment) become worried, anxious, or depressed, as their experiences of deprivation become incorporated into their evaluations of themselves.

And make no mistake, Dunn has found that children as young as two are already incorporating social comparisons into self-appraisals. Further, the greater the perception of differential treatment, the more conflict and hostility marks the sibling relationship. Perceptions of unfairness are also linked to adjustment difficulties, such as contrariness and problems with peers outside the family. These patterns of relating to others can remain remarkably stable over time.

What's even more startling, says Dunn, is that in families where children perceive marked differences in parental treatment, the children experience problems in adjustment—whether or not they are the disfavored one. They have difficulties in relationships. "Yet children are so different, it's hard to treat them the same," Dunn says. "This is the paradox of child development."

Even as adults, people monitor what their siblings get. "I see it with my own grown sons," confides Dunn. "They'll come for a meal and notice which one is getting the most potatoes." Early on, kids develop their own accounts of differential

treatment, and "they carry that mythology around through life." One child, for example, may always escape trouble because parents see him as "the good kid." But siblings are likely to explain it quite differently—they might conclude that he's always trying to sneak around the rules.

Differential treatment by parents is only one factor affecting the durability of the early sibling environment. "Most important is the temperament of each child," says Dunn, how edgy or irritable they are. Openness to experience and flexibility are also key determinants.

What strikes Dunn most is how different the family environment is for each child in the same household. And that helps account for how siblings turn out so different. Children only *seem* to share the same home. In reality, "they inhabit different microenvironments," influenced by age, power, understanding, sensitivity, parental treatment, and the relationships between siblings. The same experience impacts them differently.

Children only *seem* to share the same family environment. In reality, they inhabit radically different microenvironments.

Dunn has found that fewer than a third of siblings even show the same degree of affection towards each other. Even such alleged major influences on children as a mother's mental health may impact siblings differently if, say, one child has a strong relationship with a grandparent.

Carving Out a Place for Me

Sibling relationships tend to be lasting because children develop strategies to compete with each other for parental attention, and that learning becomes encoded in personality, contends Frank Sulloway, a historian of science and psychologist who is a visiting scholar at the University of California at Berkeley. Best known for his investigation of the effects of birth order, Sulloway sees sibling relationships through a starkly Darwinian lens.

Humans are hardly unique, Sulloway insists. "Sibling rivalry is widespread among animals whose young receive parental care, and in this sense it is largely hard-wired." Siblings are a lot like Darwin's finches, not merely highly diverse but driven to find a niche in the sometimes crowded terrain they're born into.

For humans, that's the family environment, and they use their brains—those precociously socially sensitive instruments—instead of their beaks to distinguish themselves one from another, a process known as de-identification. Taking on different family roles based on such factors as age, sex, personality, interests, and ability, they embody the prime evolutionary principle of divergence in order to snare as much parental support as possible.

In Sulloway's view, birth order is one of the major factors driving sibling diversification. Exposed to exclusive parental attention in their earliest years, firstborns, he says, are often most expected to uphold family values and traditions and act as surrogate parents (especially oldest females), fostering the development of conscientiousness. The role of the responsible one may continue well into adulthood, with achievement orientation and expectations that they provide advice and even economic assistance to laterborns.

Lastborns, too, get some privileged parental attention, but by the time they arrive so many family niches are taken they have little to lose by rejecting parental values and becoming risk-takers. Unconventional and even rebellious, they are most likely to be extraverted and open to new ideas. Most political and scientific revolutions, Sulloway contends, are started or championed by lastborns—Copernicus was the youngest of four, Darwin himself the fifth of six children.

Birth order, Sulloway insists, is really proxy for family roles, predicted most by sibling differences in age and the attributes that go along with it, such as size, power, verbal mastery, and overall maturity. For siblings who are closest in age, de-identification is most urgent, forcing siblings adjacent in the family constellation to develop opposing personality traits.

Even if parents go out of their way to ensure that all their kids get equal attention, middle children still lose. "They receive less cumulative investment than do eldest and last-born offspring," Sulloway says. And that explains why they go through life with lower self-esteem, feel more self-conscious, and often feel closer to friends than to parents.

Sometimes disposition trumps birth order in shaping sibling relationships. E.G. Sebastian and his brother, younger by two years, didn't have to seek niches for themselves. Their temperaments took care of that. Growing up in Romania, Sebastian found himself drawn to nature from the start. "Swimming in the river was forbidden, but I swam in it nearly every day, even though my parents spanked me. I rarely did homework and often skipped school. In elementary school, I was a C/D/F kind of kid." His brother, on the other hand, got straight As. "He was conscientious. He cared about school."

There was little competition. Once, as an adult, he happened upon the diary his brother kept as a teenager. "I was surprised to find that his philosophy, his thinking was close to mine." It's just that their personal styles were so different.

"I'm a risk-taker," Sebastian says. "I do things first and think later. He is cautious and overthinks everything. I love to travel. He doesn't; he loves security." The risk-taking Sebastian began an import-export business based in Budapest. He gave it up after he came to visit his brother—who, with their parents, had emigrated to the U.S.—and wound up falling in love and staying in the U.S. The brothers now live about 60 miles apart in the South Carolina low country and visit often. "We are very close, but we are still very different."

Blame Mom, Not Me

As every adult knows, some sibling strategies remain strictly situational, not necessarily incorporated into personality or carried into the world outside the family. (Think whining.) The staying power of sibling strategies accounts for what could be called the Thanksgiving Effect—the tendency of fully functional adults to find themselves drawn, often against their own will, into long-abandoned but still emotionally charged childhood roles at family gatherings.

The imprint of the early family environment tends to run deep because it is a habitual way of thinking about self and others. Few are aware of slipping into an old behavior pattern until it creates unbearable distress. You never measured up at home compared to an older sibling? You may find yourself drawn to a spouse or a boss who is difficult to please.

> **You never measured up at home compared to an older sibling? You may find yourself drawn to a spouse or a boss who is difficult to please.**

It's not fatalistic to think that family position structures relationships, Michael Kerr insists. Kerr, head of the Bowen Center for the Study of the Family in Washington, D.C., maintains that thinking about sibling position actually provides a good way to turn unpleasant sibling relationships around in adulthood. A change of heart occurs when people realize that animosity is not innate to the warring individuals but was set up in the relationships with parents.

This insight helped three brothers who were deadlocked in trying to settle a large family estate. The oldest and middle siblings were at odds over how to value several properties. The oldest was crippled with anxiety because he felt responsible for the outcome, while the second brother felt uncompromisingly entitled to his point of view. Kerr got the men to see that their polarization replicated their relationship with their mother. That allowed the oldest to move away from criticism of his brother while it melted the second brother's attitude, and a compromise was forged.

An End of Life About-Face

Because family roles tend to get encoded in personality and identity, it can take a huge amount of work to develop new patterns of relating to siblings in adulthood. Some universal situations, however, can serve as crucibles in which to recast relationships. In most families, the moment of truth for adult sibling relationships is the aging of parents and decisions about end-of-life parental care.

Such situations not only force siblings into contact but usually require agreement. In some families, the siblings are able to drop their old animosities and adopt a mode of care that is not unfairly burdensome to any one sibling. Other families fracture on the fault lines set decades earlier.

If parental care doesn't make or break siblings, then inheritances certainly do, given the power of final parental dictates to codify inequities in the cold calculus of cash. But for Isadora Alman and her brother, the inheritance only cemented closeness.

"Our father's death was unexpected. My brother traveled across the country for the reading of the will. In it, our father forgave all debts but left my brother and me with very little and strangers with a lot. My brother and I were sitting on opposite sides of the room, but we looked at each other—and laughed at the irony of what a strange guy our dad was. We both got equally screwed."

In the long view, sibling conflict is necessary, inevitable, and an instrument of self-definition that has a correctable course over time. But parents often subscribe to a short view: They prefer peace in the house. They want their children to be close (or at least quiet). What's more, parents invariably claim they treat their kids equally, even though children can't possibly experience their care equally, as they are at different levels of understanding.

Parents are quick to deny differential treatment of their kids; it's painful for them to think about how they may have failed their children.

Parents are quick to deny differential treatment of their kids, says Cal State's Heidi Riggio, because it is difficult and painful for them to think about how they may have failed their children, whose experiences of favoritism are incorporated into identity. "In another culture," she adds, "parents may be willing to admit they treated the eldest son best. But not in America, with its ethos of fairness and equality."

"But if there's no conflict," says family therapist Diane Barth, "then it's not possible for siblings to move on to being more connected as adults. Theirs becomes an artificial relationship." It is the same kind of misunderstanding that believes happiness admits no ripple of discomfort. When siblings learn to fight and to master their own conflicts, Barth explains, that is a formula for resolving conflicts for the rest of their lives. And that's the real path to lasting peace.

Critical Thinking

1. What happens in sibling relationships after the death of a parent?

2. How are roles defined between siblings?

3. Why is sibling rivalry ever present in families and what can parents do to minimize the negative impact?

4. When looking at birth order who is usually considered the "favorite" and why?

5. What happens to sibling relationships as children get older?

From *Psychology Today,* July/August 2010, pp. 54–61. Copyright © 2010 by Sussex Publishers, LLC. Reprinted by permission.

Building on Strengths: Intergenerational Practice with African American Families

Intergenerational kinship and multigenerational families (three or more generations) have been a source of strength for African Americans. This article presents a culturally responsive intergenerational practice model for working with African American families that draws on this legacy. The model looks at intergenerational kinship and multigenerational families through an Afrocentric, intergenerational solidarity framework. It provides a means to understand and support the strengths and resource richness of intergenerational relationships; the Afrocentric paradigm's affirmation of family and cultural strengths; and the power of intergenerational kinship, family solidarity, and support across generations. Building on the six solidarity elements of the intergenerational solidarity framework, this model provides an empowerment-oriented approach for social work practice with African American families that takes into consideration cultural values and practices.

CHERYL WAITES

Family networks, composed of several generations (three or more), have been a source of strength for African American families. Multigenerations providing support and care for family members and fictive kin (non-blood relatives) across the life course have been well documented (Billingsley, 1992; Billingsley & Morrison-Rodriguez, 1998; Hill, 1971, 1993, 1998, 1999; Martin & Martin, 1985; McAdoo, 1998; Schiele, 1996, 2000). Born out of African traditions and adaptation to a harsh environment, multigenerational families have persevered in the face of disparity and oppression spanning 400 years of slavery, years of "Jim Crow," and decades of segregation, marginalization, and intentional and unintentional racism (Christian, 1995). Despite these obstacles, people of African descent have a legacy of intergenerational kinship, resilience, spirituality, and hope (Bagley & Carroll, 1998; Denby, 1996). Multigenerational families and intergenerational kinships have played a significant role in preserving and strengthening African American families.

As our society ages, multigenerational families will be more common, resulting in longer years of "shared lives" across generations (Bengtson, 2001; Bengtson & Roberts, 1991). It has been predicted that there will be almost equal bands of older adults, middle generation adults, young adults, adolescents, and children as we move deeper into the 21st century (U.S. Census Bureau, 2004). This statistic holds true for African Americans. The numbers of African American elders, age 65 and older, are increasing. Between 1980 and 1995, the number of African Americans increased from 2.1 million to 2.7 million (a 29 percent increase). This group is expected to expand to 6.9 million by 2030 and 8.6 million by 2050 (Miles, 1999). Individuals are now more likely to grow older in four-, or even more, generation families; spend an unprecedented number of years in family roles such as grandparent and great-grandparent; and remain part of a network of intergenerational family ties (Bengtson, 2001; Bengtson, Rosenthal, & Burton, 1990; Hagestad, 1996; Riley, 1987). Kin, and non-kin, will be available to provide care and assistance to younger families (King, 1994; Silverstein, Parrott, & Bengtson, 1995) and caregiving for dependent elders (Bengtson et al., 1990). In view of the changing demographics, it is important to revisit cultural values regarding how families interact across generations.

Historically, cultural values, family practices, and strengths, such as special care for children and elders, kinship ties, and collectivism have been part of African American life (Barnes, 2001). Hill (1971, 1999) wrote eloquently about five strengths of African American families: strong achievement orientation, strong work orientation, flexible family roles, strong kinship bonds, and strong religious orientation. Hill and others have pointed to strengths that are linked to history, culture, values, and cultural adaptations and suggested that building on these strengths is a good strategy for working with African American families (Freeman & Logan, 2004; Logan, 2001; McAdoo, 1998; McCullough-Chavis & Waites, 2004; Staples, 1999). Strong kinship ties, intergenerational support, faith, and coming together during times of need have been effective resources for African American families.

Today's social environment, and the challenges individuals and families face, warrant use and revitalization of cultural strengths. Problems such as drug and alcohol addiction, overrepresentation of African American children in foster care, HIV and AIDS, health disparities, high rates of incarceration, unemployment, and poverty are severe and complex. Many individuals and families have demonstrated remarkable resilience; others have suffered. Effective strategies to help families as they contend with pressing issues are rooted in African American cultural strengths. Cultural values and practices that sustained families in the past can be used to empower families today. Use of the power of intergenerational kinships and multigenerational family support can serve to preserve and strengthen vulnerable African American families.

Over the past 20 years, a number of practice approaches have been proposed for culturally competent practice with African Americans and other ethnic and racial groups. Strengths-based, empowerment-oriented, ethnically sensitive, constructionist, Afrocentric, and social justice frameworks have been used to guide practice with African American families. Such frameworks provide models by which social problems are assessed and intervention strategies are outlined. Many recognize multigenerational and extended family strengths. However, there is a need for an approach that builds on and restores the strengths of multigenerational families and intergenerational kinship. This approach may include restoring the influence of the extended family's multigenerational network so that relatives and fictive kin are encouraged to remain involved with family members and step forward to provide support and care. An Afrocentric, intergenerational solidarity approach that acknowledges the family life cycle, as well as the values and traditions that have sustained people of African descent, is a mechanism for promoting family closeness and responsibility. Embracing the legacies and wisdom of past generations and the hope and promise of the future is a framework for best practice. This article describes an intergenerational model that can be used to understand and provide support and assistance to African American families. The model defines families of African descent from an Afrocentric intergenerational perspective. It highlights the history and interconnectedness of African American families and communities and takes into account the temporal nature of the family life cycle.

An Intergenerational Perspective: Theoretical Foundations for Practice

An intergenerational perspective is relevant to social work practice with African American families. It brings an awareness of and attention to kinship, intergenerational relationships, and multigenerational families. Strengths, values, and practices that are transmitted across generations, family life cycle stages, intergenerational support, and current cultural context are central to this perspective (Waites, 2008). It provides a framework for understanding the past, exploring the current environment, and using culturally relevant strategies and practices to empower families.

Intergenerational Solidarity

Family relationships across generations are becoming increasingly important. Changes in family age structures are creating longer years of shared lives (Bengtson, 2001). Bengtson stated that "intergenerational bonds are more important than nuclear family ties for well-being and support over the life course" (Bengtson, 2001, p. 7). With increased longevity, parents, grandparents, and other relatives can be available to serve as resources for younger generations. Kin, across several generations, will increasingly be called on to provide essential family functions; intergenerational support and care will increase over time.

Bengtson and his colleagues (Bengtson & Roberts, 1991; Bengtson & Schrader, 1982) provided a multidimensional construct for understanding intergenerational relationships. Derived from classical social theory, social psychology, and family sociology, their intergenerational solidarity model examines social cohesion between generations. The construct evolved from a longitudinal study consisting of a cross-sectional survey with more than 2,044 participants from three generational families. Data were collected at three intervals, including the great-grandchild generation. From this research, Bengtson and others (Bengston & Mangen, 1988; Bengston & Schrader, 1982; Roberts, Richards, & Bengtson, 1991) constructed an intergenerational solidarity taxonomy for understanding intergenerational relationships. These six elements provide a mechanism for understanding intergenerational relationships and are discussed later in greater detail.

Afrocentric Worldview

An Afrocentric paradigm fits nicely with the intergenerational solidarity framework because it affirms human capacities and family and cultural strengths and promotes intergenerational connections. It presents a worldview that highlights traditional African philosophical assumptions, which emphasize a holistic, interdependent, and spiritual conception of people and their environment (Schiele, 2001).

The Afrocentric paradigm affirms that there are universal cultural strengths and an African worldview that survived the generational devastations caused by the transatlantic slave trade and the oppression that followed. As a result, it is important to understand and respect the customs, practices, and values that are central to African American families and communities. These cultural strengths, as previously described, can be used in micro, meso, and macro interventions to enhance the lives of all people, particularly people of color (Schiele, 2000).

Family Life Cycle

Families are at the heart of the intergenerational perspective. Families have shared history and futures (Carter & McGoldrick, 1999); they move through time together. The sharing of history and futures and the moving through time together are often referred to as family life cycle stages. Theses stages have been identified as leaving home, single young adults, joining of families through marriage, the new couple, families with young children, families with adolescents, launching children and moving on, and families in later life (Carter & McGoldrick, 1999). Relationships with parents, siblings, grandparents, and other family members experience transitions as each group moves along the family life cycle. Multiple family units are formed (for example, families with young children and families in later life), and all are a part of the larger multigenerational family. In this respect, there is a temporal reality associated with multigenerational families, and the family life cycle provides some descriptive information regarding how families move across time.

The stages described by Carter and McGoldrick (1999) laid a foundation for understanding African American families and family life cycle stages. African cultural traditions, environmental realities, and the diversity of family forms—which evolved from cultural traditions and adaptations to hardships—are also relevant. They provide insights regarding intergenerational relationships and temporal stages. A legacy of strong intergenerational kinship, multi-generational families, and extended family networks is reflected in Hill's (1999) flexible family roles. For example, caregiving is an important value for African American families. Grandparents may step in to assist or raise a grandchild. A single parent may depend on support from parents, or grandparents, after a child is born. African American children raised by grandparents often feel filial obligations to care for parents and grandparents (Ruiz & Carlton-LaNey, 1999). Extended family may play important roles and provide support and care to young and older adult relatives. Multigenerations may live in the same residence and pool their resources. For African American families, the family life cycle stages have significant intergenerational patterns of assistance and care that are reciprocal over time. These intergenerational supports, in some cases, may be in need of validation, nurturing, and revitalization to strengthen and support troubled families (Waites, 2008).

Afrocentric Intergenerational Practice

The Afrocentric intergenerational practice model presented here builds on the solidarity construct and the Afrocentric paradigm. It acknowledges the diversity and flexibility of the family life cycle and brings attention to traditions and cultural influences, specifically, caregiving, kinship bonds, the interconnectedness of families, and extended families. It reflects an approach that respects and supports the strengths and resilience of intergenerational kinship. This practice model's basic principles promote a society that values all generations and

- recognizes that each generation has unique strengths—each person, young and older, is a resource
- recognizes the roles of youths, middle generations, and elders in families and communities
- acknowledges conflicts that may occur in inter generational relationships
- encourages collaboration and support across generations

- fosters intergenerational kinship and interdependence
- fosters public policy that recognizes and addresses the needs of all generations
- supports and nurtures family and cultural strengths.

This model is culturally responsive in that it uses strategies that are compatible with culturally competent practice and transforms knowledge and cultural awareness into interventions that support and sustain healthy family functioning (McPhatter, 1997; Waites, Macgowan, Pennell, Carlton-LaNey, & Weil, 2004).

Afrocentric Intergenerational Solidarity Model

The Afrocentric intergenerational solidarity model consists of six solidarity elements and provides indicators of intergenerational cohesion. The infusion of an Afrocentric worldview provides culturally relevant issues, questions, and empowerment-oriented strategies. The first element, *associational solidarity,* focuses on the type and frequency of contact between generations (see Table l). Examining the amount and nature of intergenerational contact is at the forefront. Within an Afrocentric worldview, assessing family traditions and history regarding communication is important. Once information is obtained, a process of nurturing, reinforcing, and revitalizing contact and communication among family members can be undertaken. Intergenerational communication may go beyond phone calls; traditions such as Sunday dinners, regular family visits, family reunions, special events, and other celebrations are mechanisms for connections. Intergenerational communication can lead to strong supportive networks and enhance the amount and quality of intergenerational contact.

The second element, *affectional solidarity,* addresses the expressed closeness, warmth, and trust found in intergenerational kinships. The indicators call for the practitioner to look at emotional ties to family and community, signs of intergenerational conflict, and the overall reciprocity of positive sentiment among family members and across generations. With an Afrocentric view, affiliations with and sentiments toward the extended family, and the African American community as a whole, must also be explored. The goal is to assess and address the issues of affection, trust, and closeness and to support and nurture relational understanding and reciprocity across generations.

The third element, *consensual solidarity,* looks at agreements of values and beliefs. The indicators call for an assessment of intrafamilial concordance. Assessing the transmission and agreement of Afrocentric values, beliefs, and traditions, as well as the cultural strengths, enhances the cultural relevance of practice. Understanding family members' generational differences and their willingness to build intergenerational respect, dialogue, and collaboration is also important. The model suggests that practitioners encourage the understanding and recognition of cultural strengths. In addition, attempts should be made to support family and extended family as they engage in history reminding, consciousness raising, and intergenerational understanding and respect.

Table 1 Intergenerational Solidarity with an Afrocentric Worldview

Construct-Element	Definition	Indicators	Culturally Relevant Issues
Associational solidarity	Frequency and patterns of interaction in various types of activities in which family members engage	• Frequency of intergenerational interaction (that is, face-to-face, telephone, mail) • Types of common activities shared (that is, recreation, special occasion, and so forth)	• Family history, traditions, and practices regarding family communication patterns, and family gatherings and activities • Intergenerational family members' access to one another (that is, transportation, telephone, computer literacy)
Affectional solidarity	Type and degree of positive sentiments about family members, and the degree of reciprocity of these sentiments	• Ratings of affection, warmth, closeness, understanding, trust, and respect for family members • Ratings of perceived reciprocity in positive sentiments among family members	• Preeminence of close parent–child relationship, grandparent relationships, extended family relationships, and so forth
Consensual solidarity	Degree of agreement on values, attitudes, and beliefs among family members	• Intrafamilial concordance among individual measures of specific values, attitudes, and beliefs • Ratings of perceived similarity with other family members in values, attitudes, and beliefs	• Connections with Afrocentric values and practices (that is, respect for elders, special care for children and elders, kinship ties, spirituality, collectivism, and so forth) • Generational values, similarities, and differences
Functional solidarity	Degree of helping and exchanges of resources—giving and receiving support across generations	• Frequency of intergenerational exchanges of assistance (for example, financial, physical, emotional) • Ratings of reciprocity in the intergenerational exchange of resources	• Supportive behaviors and traditions (that is, role of children, parents, grandparents, extended family, the church, lodges and fraternal orders, and so forth in providing support and care)
Normative solidarity	Strength of commitment to performance of familial roles and familial obligations	• Ratings of importance of family and intergenerational roles • Ratings of strength of filial obligations	• Afrocentric holistic, collectivist orientation • Filial beliefs and responsibilities (that is, intergenerational support for at-risk youths, young families, and dependent elders) • Availability of aunts, uncles, children, extended family, church family, and other supports
Structural solidarity	Opportunity structure for intergenerational relationships reflected in number, type, and geographic proximity of family members	• Residential propinquity of family members • Number of family members • Health of family members	• Location of family and extended family members • Migration history • Transportation and travel distances and resources

Source: Bengtson, V. L., & Roberts, R.E.L. (1991). Intergenerational solidarity in aging families: An example of formal theory construction. *Journal of Marriage and the Family, 53,* 856–870.

The fourth element, *functional solidarity,* addresses the frequency of intergenerational exchanges of assistance and resources. The indicators direct the assessment of help giving and receiving and how families assist and support each other. The role of collectivism, extended family support, and community support from churches, lodges, fraternal orders, and so forth are also assessed. Mechanisms to support equable intergenerational care and the use of formal and informal resources are suggested. This may include extended family, fictive kin, church family, intergenerational programs, or other community resources.

Normative solidarity, the fifth element, looks at filial responsibility and obligations. The indicators are family roles and the strength of obligation to those roles. The Afrocentric worldview expands this sense of obligation not only to parents, grandparents, children, and grandchildren, but also to the extended family, fictive kin, and the community as a whole. Intergenerational family and extended family support, and the use of community programs and formal resources, are encouraged.

The sixth and last element, *structural solidarity,* highlights the opportunity for intergenerational interaction as it relates to residential propinquity. For example, some older adults reside with their children or grandchildren in coresidential situations or in the same community. This arrangement affords them great intergenerational access. Some families, however, may move far away and relocate due to employment opportunities elsewhere. Older adults may be unable to travel to family or community events due to distant locations, health issues, or limited access to convenient and affordable transportation. Both latter situations affect opportunities to maintain close contact. The empirical indicators focus on the residential proximity of family members, the number of family members, and health and disability issues. Afrocentric worldviews expand this element so that migration patterns, transportation issues, and travel distances are included. The empowerment strategy focuses on helping families rethink how to address structural proximity barriers. This could take the form of family members organizing and sharing transportation resources or establishing a family "home place" or location where family members can gather for respite, celebrations, and support.

Using This Model

This model is not complicated and can be used in harmony with other empowerment-oriented approaches. A culturally appropriate assessment of intergenerational issues and resources is conducted. Practitioners are directed to explore each of the intergenerational solidarity elements with family members using the practice strategies outlined in Table 2.

Associational solidarity is explored by asking family members questions about their family traditions and how they communicate and keep in touch with each other. Family solidarity is enhanced when there are traditions, activities, and history that serve to keep family members connected—for example, Sunday dinners at a relative's home, regular phone calls, church or religious service attendance, family reunions, birthday celebrations, or Christmas or other holiday activities. The practitioner can work with family members to use a variety of practice strategies (outlined in Table 2) to help family members improve their associational solidarity. This might include encouraging family members to plan and or participate in family events. Participation in family events can lead to more cross-generational communication and contact.

Affectional solidarity questions are posed to family members by first exploring whom they feel particularly close to and why. Helping family members understand their traditions regarding family roles and relationships and how they influence affectional solidarity is an important practice strategy. Affectional solidarity can be nurtured by encouraging a sense of intergenerational kinship—that is, affection for family and extended family members. It encompasses cultivation of intergenerational relationships. The practitioner role is to aid family members in identifying and developing closer ties.

Consensual solidarity is also important and can be explored by discussing family values and by affirming a shared vision for family life. Exploring family members' perceptions and generation differences and similarities provides information regarding family solidarity. Gauging the family's sense of cultural pride and their African American identify is also pertinent. Cultural pride can serve as a unifying force for family solidarity. History reminding to facilitate appreciation of family cultural strengths is appropriate as a practice strategy and might include providing information about cultural history, supporting family opportunities to share thoughts and information about cultural values and beliefs, and engaging family members in activities that will enhance cultural pride. Communities often have Kwanzaa celebrations, concerts, and religious-related programs; watch movies and videos; read books; or engage in culturally inspired storytelling activities. These resources can serve as activities and information that connect the generations and facilitate consensual solidarity.

Functional solidarity is assessed by identification of the "go-to" family members when someone needs assistance. It is also important to identify family roles and resources and how support and care are exchanged across the family and the generations. The practice strategy is to create or restore the family helping network and involves helping family members to embrace shared responsibility and intergenerational support and care for all family members.

Normative solidarity is assessed by exploring expectations regarding family roles. It is also crucial to discuss what happens when someone is not able to perform the designated role. What are the family norms for who should step in? The practice strategy is to affirm, strengthen, and formalize the family members' commitment to one another. This may take the form of encouraging the development of multigenerational networks where children, parents, grandparents, aunts, and uncles all play a role in supporting and caring for family members. Because this responsibility can be demanding, connecting families with community resources such as family support programs, support groups for caregivers, and other programs that serve to strengthen families and extended family helping is crucial.

Structural solidarity is explored by assessing family proximity. Some families use the home of a family member to gather for celebrations or other rituals: It is their home place. Other

Table 2 Afrocentric Intergenerational Solidarity Model—Questions and Practice Strategies

Associational Solidarity Questions
- Tell me about your family's traditions (holiday celebrations, Sunday dinners, family reunions, special events, and so forth).
- How do you participate?
- How does your family keep in touch? How do you keep in touch?

Practice Strategies
- Encourage cross-generation communication, and contact.
- Help family consider methods to communicate and to support each other.
- Encourage family members to participate in family events (family reunions, and so forth) and efforts to remain connected.

Affectional Solidarity Questions
- Tell me about the family members you feel close to.
- What makes you feel particularly close to this person?
- Tell me about your extended family and others who are like family. Do you feel close to them?
- Are their certain relationships or duties that you must honor and respect?

Practice Strategics
- Nurture relationship building, intergenerational kinship, and equable care.
- Encourage supportive family and extended family closeness.

Consensual Solidarity Questions
- Tell me about your family's history—your grandparents, great grandparents, and so forth.
- What were/are important values, beliefs, and traditions in your family?
- Do you and family members have similar values and beliefs regarding___(sex, religion, education, drugs, etc.)?
- Do you feel a connection and pride with the African American community? What type of cultural activities do you and your family participate in?

Practice Strategies
- Engage family in history reminding to facilitate an understanding of cultural and family strengths.
- Facilitate healing by engaging family in activities that will enhance cultural pride and self-esteem.
- Encourage intergenerational respect and help family members acknowledge their shared visions.
- Help family recognize intergenerational resources and strengths.

Functional Solidarity Questions
- How does your family respond when one of its members needs assistance?
- Who are the family members with resources (good, steady job; a home; savings; and so forth) in your family? Are they obligated to help out others in the family? Is there an exchange of resources?
- Do older family members feel obligated to help out younger family members, and is this help reciprocal?

Practice Strategies
- Support flexible family roles and intergenerational kinship.
- Encourage reciprocal intergenerational support and care.
- Assist family in using informal (extended family, church or faith based, and so forth) and formal support systems and recourses.

Normative Solidarity Questions
- What roles do parents, grandparents, children, adult daughters and sons, aunts, uncles, and so forth play in your family?
- In your family, what happens when someone is not able to function in his or her role as parent, son, daughter, caregiver, and so forth?

Practice Strategies
- Encourage and support caregiving and other family commitments.
- Develop multigenerational family support programs for grandparents, and other kin, raising children and for children caring for dependent elders.
- Encourage the development of an extended family support systems.

Structural Solidarity Questions
- Where do your family members live?
- What led them to move to_____? Do you visit?
- How do family members travel when they visit one another? Are there any barriers to visiting?
- Does your family have a "home place," a residence where family members gather for special occasions?

Practice Strategies
- Help family overcome travel and visiting-related barriers.
- Help family members identity a plan for staying connected.
- Develop community intergenerational programs.

families do not have a central location, and some family members may live great distances from the family core of the home place. The role of the practitioner is to help family members explore proximity issues and overcome barriers to traveling and visiting with relatives. This help might include pooling of resources so that all family members can attend the family reunions, church or religious services, and health and wellness care. Providing assistance to families in the use of strategies to support involvement in family and extended family activities could help family members to visit and stay connected.

Use of this model involves the exploration of all solidarity elements. Family members and families may show strengths in a specific area. If not, the practitioner can then use one or all of the strategies suggested in the Practice Strategy sections of Table 2. To follow are three vignettes that present contemporary family issues and suggested strategies.

Vignette One

Denise is a 32-year-old African American single, divorced mother who is trying to cope with caregiving for both her son and her grandmother. Denise's nine-year-old son, David, has been referred to the school social worker due to excessive absences from school. Her 69-year-old grandmother had a stroke, six months ago, and is now residing with Denise and her son David and her 14-year-old daughter. Denise is distraught because her maternal grandmother was "the strong one in the family." All solidarity elements must be assessed. However, there is a pressing need for support and assistance for Denise and her family. This calls for focusing first on normative and functional solidarity. The worker can help Denise examine her current caregiving roles. It is also important for the worker to discuss Denises decision to care for her grandmother—What is her sense of obligation and commitment to this role? Once Denise has explored her caregiving values, beliefs, the realities of her situation, and her intentions, she and the practitioner can develop a plan. This might include exploring family resources, the availability of other family and extended family members for support and caregiving, and more formal resources.

Vignette Two

Mr. Brown is an 84-year-old African American, retired Navy civilian dock worker. His wife of 47 years died 14 years ago after a battling cancer for four years. His only son died in an accident 22 years ago. Mr. Brown has two grand-daughters, ages 30 and 32, and one great-grandson, age 9. They talk on the phone occasionally, but his granddaughters and great-grandson live 2,000 miles away, and he has not been able to visit them. Mr. Brown reports that he is "lonely" and is considering moving into an assisted-living facility. He wants to reconnect with his family before he moves. All the solidarity elements must be assessed. Immediate issues appear to be Mr. Brown's expressed loneliness and his infrequent contact with his granddaughters and great-grandson. This calls for focusing on associational, affectional, and structural solidarity. The worker can help Mr. Brown make contact with his granddaughters and with other family members, especially those family members who

have been supportive in the past. Mechanisms to maintain communication should also be explored. This may consist of organizing regular visiting, where transportation is arranged for Mr. Brown. It could also mean arranging regular phone contact, sharing pictures, and sending cards. Mr. Brown may also benefit from more contact with other family, extended family, and friends from church or any groups that he has participated in over his life course (for example, lodges, fraternal orders, church clubs, civic groups). Also, intergenerational programs, if available, may also be a good resource.

Vignette Three

Joan, a 41-year-old African American woman, is incarcerated because of a drug-related charge. She is in the second year of a three-year sentence and is now drug free. She has three sons, ages 19, 12, and 10. The two youngest sons reside with their paternal grandmother. Joan's oldest son has lived with her mother most of his life. Joan has not seen her sons in two years. The younger children's father died in a car accident; he was driving while impaired. Joan is very concerned about her sons and wants to provide a better life for them. She hopes to arrange visitation, and, so far, her younger son's grandmother has been uncooperative. Her 19-year-old son has refused to visit. Although all solidarity elements should be assessed first, this situation points to affectional and consensual solidarity problems. Joan must be aware that her addiction and past behaviors may have caused apprehension and skepticism on the part of her family. As the practitioner helps Joan to make contact with her children, it will be important for him or her to engage the family in forgiveness, relationship building, and reaffirming of a shared vision across generations for the health and well-being of the children and family. The kinship bonds are in need of revitalization.

Conclusion

In view of contemporary issues facing families and the significance of multigenerational families, culturally relevant models of practice are called for. African American multigenerational families have a legacy of resilience, spirituality, and hope that has served to fortify vulnerable members. As our society ages, the number of multigenerational families will increase, and intergenerational cohesion issues will move to the forefront. This demographic shift, and the opportunity for shared lives, can be an asset for families. An empowerment-oriented framework that provides a mechanism to build on cultural strengths, intergenerational kinship, and support processes by which generations can provide mutual assistance and care during times of need is indicated. This model is a good step in that direction. Many aspects of this model have been a part of culturally responsive work with African American families.

The Afrocentric intergenerational sodality model is a strengths-based approach that works to empower multigenerational families and intergenerational relationships. In this regard, there is an assumption that families and extended families have strengths and that some form of intergenerational kinship can be nurtured. A shortcoming of this model is that the full application of each solidarity component has not been systematically tested. I plan to apply this model to practice interventions and intergenerational programming.

The Afrocentric intergenerational practice model shows promise. Building on Bengtson and others' intergenerational solidarity construct, infused with an Afrocentric worldview, this model provides a culturally relevant approach for work with African American multigenerational families. It facilitates an understanding of how intergenerational relationships can be supported and provides multidimensional guidance regarding intergenerational relationships and multigenerational families. The intergenerational model considers generational transmission from a strengths perspective, looking not only at problems, but also at the assets that multiple generations may provide. It is a framework that taps into the power, resilience, and capital from past and current traditions and relationships. The three vignettes provide examples of how this model might be used. To fully examine this model, additional applications should be studied.

Application of the Afrocentric intergenerational practice model, in conjunction with other empowerment-oriented approaches, is a best practice method. Social workers are called on to work with African American and other families. This work is especially relevant for work with vulnerable African American families in need of nurturance and care. As our society ages, it will be increasing important to understand intergenerational issues and develop resources that help multigenerational families navigate the complex and changing relationships and problems in our contemporary society. As we move through this century, this model may prove to be very relevant to the changing demographics of our aging society.

References

Bagley, C.A., & Carroll, J. (1998). Healing forces in African-American families. In H. I. McCubbm, E. A. Thompson, A. I. Thompson, & J. A. Farrell (Eds.), *Resiliency in African-American families* (pp. 117–143). London: Sage Publications.

Barnes, S. (2001). Stressors and strengths: A theoretical and practical examination of nuclear single parent, and augmented African American families. *Families in Society, 85,* 449–460.

Bengtson, V. L., (2001). Beyond the nuclear family: The increasing importance of multi-generational bonds. *Journal of Marriage and the Family, 63,* 1–16.

Bengtson, V. L., & Mangen, D.J. (1988). Family intergenerational solidarity, revisited. In D.J. Mangen, V. L. Bengtson, & P. H. Landry (Eds.), *Measurement of intergenerational relationship* (pp. 222–238). Newbury Park, CA: Sage Publications.

Bengtson, V. L., & Roberts, R.E.L. (1991). Intergenerational solidarity in aging families: An example of formal theory construction. *Journal of Marriage and the Family, 53,* 856–870.

Bengtson, V. L., Rosenthal, C.J., &. Burton, L. M., (1990). Paradoxes of families and aging. In R. H. Binstock & L. K. George (Eds.), *Handbook of aging and the social sciences* (4th ed., pp. 253–282). San Diego: Academic Press.

Bengtson, V. L., & Schrader, S., S. (1982). Parent–child relationships. In D. Mangen & W. Peterson (Eds.), *Handbook of research instruments in social gerontology* (Vol. 2, pp. 115–185). Minneapolis: University of Minnesota Press.

Billingsley, A. (1992). *Climbing Jacob's ladder: The enduring legacy of African-American families.* New York: Simon & Schuster.

Billingsley, A., & Morrison-Rodriguez, B. (1998). The black family in the 21st century and the church as an action system: A macro perspective. *Journal of Human Behavior in the Social Environment,* (2-3), 31–47.

Carter, B., & McGoldrick, M. (1999). *The expanded family life* (3rd ed.). Boston: Allyn & Bacon.

Christian, C. M. (1995). *Black saga: The African American experience.* Boston: Houghton Mifflin.

Denby, R. W. (1996). Resiliency and the African American family: Model of family preservation. In S. L. Logan (Ed.), *The black family: Strengths, self-help, and positive change* (pp. 144–163). Boulder, CO: Westview Press.

Freeman. E. M., & Logan, S. L. (Eds.). (2004). *Reconceptualizing the strengths and common heritage of black families: Practice, research and policy issues.* Springfield, IL: Charles C Thomas.

Hagestad, G. O. (1996). On-time, off-time, out of time? Reflections on continuity and discontinuity from an illness process. In V. L. Bengtson (Ed.), *Adulthood and aging: Research on continuities and discontinuities* (pp. 204–222). New York: Springer.

Hill, R. (1971). *The strength of black families.* New York: Emerson-Hall.

Hill. R. B. (1993). *Research on the African-American family: A holistic perspective.* London: Auburn House.

Hill. R. B. (1998). Understanding black family functioning: A holistic perspective. *Journal of Comparative Family Studies, 29,* 1–11.

Hill, R. B. (1999). *The strengths of African American families: Twenty-five years later.* New York: University Press of America.

King, V. (1994). Variation in the consequences of nonresident father involvement for children's well-being. *Journal of Marriage and the Family, 56,* 963–972.

Logan, S. L. (Ed.). (2001). *The black family: Strengths, self-help, and positive change* (2nd ed.). Boulder, CO: Westview Press.

Martin, J., & Martin, E. (1985). *The helping tradition in the black family and community.* Washington, DC: NASW Press.

McAdoo, H. P. (1998). African-American families: Strengths and realities. In H. I. McCubbin, E. A. Thompson, A. I. Thompson, & J. A. Futrell (Eds.), *Resiliency in African-American families* (pp. 17–30). London: Sage Publications.

McCullough-Chavis, A., & Waites, C. (2004). Genograms with African American families: Considering cultural context. *Journal of Family Social Work, 8(2),* 1–19.

McPhatter, A. R. (1997). Cultural competence in child welfare: What is it? How do we achieve it? What happens without it? *Child Welfare, 76,* 255–278.

Miles, T. P. (1999). Living with chronic disease and the policies that bind. In T. P. Miles (Ed.), *Full-color aging: Facts, goals, and recommendations for America's diverse elders* (pp. 53–63). Washington, DC: Gerontological Society of America.

Riley, M.W. (1987). On the significance of age in sociology. *American Sociological Review, 52,* 1–14.

Roberts, R.E.L., Richards, L. N., & Bengtson, V. L. (1991). Intergenerational solidarity in families: Untangling the ties that bind. *Marriage & Family Review, 16,* 11–46.

Ruiz, D., & Carlton-LaNey, I. (1999). The increase in intergenerational African American families headed by grandmothers. *Journal of Sociology & Social Welfare, 26(4),* 71–86.

Schiele, J. H. (1996). Afrocentricity: An emerging paradigm in social work practice. *Social Work, 41,* 284–294.

Schiele, J. H. (2000). *Human services and the Afrocentric paradigm.* Binghamton, NY: Haworth Press.

Silverstein, M., Parrott, T. M., & Bengtson V. L. (1995). Factors that predispose middle-aged sons and daughters to provide social support to older parents. *Journal of Marriage and the Family, 57,* 465–476.

Staples, R. (1999). *The black family: Essays and studies.* Belmont, CA: Wadsworth.

U.S. Census Bureau. (2004). *People and households.* Retrieved February 20, 2008, from www.census.gov/population/www/projections/usmterimproj/natprojtab02a.pdf

Waites, C. (2008). *Social work practice with African-American families: An intergenerational perspective.* New York: Routledge.

Waites, C., Macgowan, M. J., Pennell, J., Carlton-LaNey, I., & Weil, M. (2004). Increasing the cultural responsiveness of family group conferencing. *Social Work, 49,* 291–300.

Critical Thinking

1. Building on the six solidarity elements of the intergenerational solidarity framework, how might this framework apply to other types of families?

2. Why is it important to take kinship into consideration when working with families?

3. If you were working in the social service field how would you uncover individual culture within families?

4. Describe what an empowerment-approach is and why it is useful in social work practice.

5. How does this article explain the importance of intergenerational relationships?

CHERYL WAITES, EdD, MSW, is associate dean, School of Social Work, Wayne State University, 4756 Cass Avenue, Detroit, MI 48202; e-mail: ccwaites@wayne.edu.

From *Social Work,* Vol. 54, No. 3, July 2009, pp. 278–287. Copyright © 2009 by NASW Press. Reprinted by permission.

Support and Empower Families of Children with Disabilities

BARBARA VAN HAREN AND CRAIG R. FIEDLER

Special education professionals can play a critical role in enhancing the quality of life not only for a child with a disability but also for that child's entire family. To realize this beneficial impact on the child's family, professionals must operate with the following assumptions (Fiedler, 2000). First, special education professionals must acknowledge that they have a responsibility to work with and support the child's family, because a child who is at risk places a family at risk. Second, professionals must value collaborative relationships with families as the best vehicle for their own professional growth and development and for supporting children with disabilities. Finally, professionals must strive to make families less dependent on their advice and services through family empowerment strategies.

The embodiment of these professional assumptions can be demonstrated by various family-centered support and family empowerment strategies. *Family-centered support services* have been defined as "those practices that (a) include families in decision-making, planning, assessment, and service delivery at family, agency, and systems levels; (b) develop services for the whole family and not just the child; (c) are guided by families' priorities for goals and services; and (d) offer and respect families' choices regarding the level of their participation" (Murphy, Lee, Turnbull, & Turbiville, 1995, p. 25). Empowerment principles promote family strength, competence, and decision making. Empowered families strive for control over their lives and take action to get what they want and need (Turnbull, Turnbull, Erwin, & Soodak, 2006). The following strategies and suggestions can serve special education professionals in their attempts to support and empower families of children with disabilities.

Family Support

1 **Display empathy for families.** Some special education professionals approach families from a judgmental perspective critical of family actions or lifestyles that conflict with their own values or lifestyle choices. Effective family support must be built upon a foundation of empathy, that is, understanding and compassion for a family's situation. Without empathy for families, professionals will lack the motivation to engage in family support and empowerment activities.

2 **Individualize family participation.** Although active family participation is beneficial to a child's educational progress, professionals must be careful to recognize that more family educational participation is not necessarily better for the family as a unit. Due to the demands of simply being a parent of a child with a disability, many parents are unable or unwilling to serve as their child's teacher, therapist, or case manager in following school recommendations for "active participation" with the school program. A supportive professional approach with families would assist them in identifying a level of educational participation that is realistic, given their time and energy resources.

3 **Recognize families as experts and build on family strengths.** On a regular basis, special education professionals must step away from their "expert's role" and actively seek to learn from families by acknowledging that families are experts when it comes to their child. When professionals recognize family expertise, families are supported, their functioning is enhanced, and family strengths begin to emerge. Family strengths can be any characteristic that contributes to a family's sense of well-being or balances individual needs with the needs of the entire family. For example, one family's sense of humor became a principal coping mechanism for the stress associated with raising a son with multiple disabilities.

4 **Value and support family decision making.** In developing educational services for children with disabilities, disagreements between families and special education professionals will sometimes occur. In those instances, support is offered when professionals suspend their own opinions and attempt to reflect on the issue from the family's perspective. If the family's perspective and decision is not clearly contrary to the child's best interests, whenever possible, professionals should attempt to abide by the family's decision and thus promote family self-determination.

5 **Be a professional ally of families.** Families feel tangible support when special education professionals act as allies. Professionals can communicate this ally perspective in a variety of ways: by demonstrating an understanding of the child's uniqueness and individualized needs, showing a willingness to listen to and respect family concerns, being actively involved in professional organizations devoted to protecting rights and improving services for individuals with disabilities, and being willing to express concerns to administrators when families' and special education professionals' educational services are perceived as inappropriate or inadequate.

6 **Engage families in open communication.** Pugach and Johnson (2002) identified *communication* as the cornerstone of any collaborative partnership. Communication between families and school professionals, as well as among family members, provides an open, supportive environment and ultimately enhances educational involvement. With today's technological advances, communication tools have increased in availability and accessibility. Examples to engage in continual dialogue with families include communication via e-mail, teleconferences, cell phones, and pagers. More traditional examples include face-to-face conferencing, telephone calls, handbooks, and newsletters.

7 **Enhance family access.** Families are more apt to feel supported in an educational environment that is flexible, responsive to their needs, and readily accessible to them. For example, the concept of the neighborhood school—the school the child would be educated in if the child did not have a disability—has long been encouraged as a means for the delivery of special education services. One of the key advantages of the neighborhood school for families is accessibility to educational services. If the child with a disability is placed in the neighborhood school, family members can attend parent-teacher conferences, open houses, and other school activities at the same site for the child with a disability as for other children in the family. It also allows children with disabilities to establish relationships with the same individuals they will come in contact with throughout the community. Another example of enhancing educational access is providing a flexible contractual workday for school professionals to be available to meet with families at more convenient times.

8 **Offer family networking.** Support for families can come from a number of avenues. A critical support system can exist between families with common ground. Family connections can result in very transformational experiences and long-lasting relationships. Seeking new information, asking questions, and simply soliciting support can be significantly more comfortable with a peer than with school professionals. Schools should offer parents networking opportunities or a list of potential parental contacts as a resource and support system for those having new experiences in the special education system. For example, many communities have parent-to-parent programs. In these programs, one-to-one matches are made between a trained veteran parent and a referred parent who is experiencing special education or related issues for the first time.

9 **Extend support systems.** Vital members of the family unit include siblings and other extended family members. Often, caregivers include siblings, grandparents, aunts, uncles, and other extended family members or close friends. It is critical that schools open their doors and provide a welcoming atmosphere to all those involved in a child's care. It is also imperative to provide support to these family members. One example of this is Sib Shop, a unique learning and recreational opportunity for brothers and sisters of individuals with disabilities (www.sibling support.org/about/sibshops).

10 **Embrace and celebrate families' successes.** It is critical for special education professionals to recognize the successes experienced by families as they support their child with a disability, regardless of how small the successes may seem. Family members' efforts and ideas should be appreciated and applauded and, thus, serve as a bridge for future success.

Family Empowerment

11 **Enhance families' sense of self-efficacy.** Turnbull, Turnbull, Erwin, and Soodak (2006) proposed an empowerment model that views families as empowered when they possess a high degree of motivation and have sufficient knowledge and skills. Families are highly motivated when they believe in their own capabilities to solve their problems. This is a sense of self-efficacy. Anytime a special education professional provides a family with information, knowledge, or a skill that can address a current problem, the family's sense of self-efficacy is fostered. For example, one special education professional showed a parent how to incorporate letter recognition into the family's daily routine with their first-grade son, who was struggling with beginning reading skills. When the family started to see marked improvement in their son's reading ability over the course of a year, their confidence rose and they became more motivated to tackle other problems.

12 **Model effective problem solving for families.** Effective problem solving is an essential empowerment skill. Empowered families possess the ability to execute a plan of action to resolve problems or barriers to meeting their child's goals or needs. Special education professionals can teach families effective problem-solving steps and look for every opportunity to model those steps in real-life situations with families. The problem-solving process involves the following steps: (a) defining the problem,

(b) generating possible solutions, (c) choosing a solution, (d) implementing the chosen solution, and (e) evaluating the solution.

13 **Increase family coping skills.** Another important component of the empowerment model is the use of coping skills to handle stress in a family's life. Professionals can enhance family coping skills by offering information about and referrals to various community support organizations, such as respite care agencies or parent support groups like United Cerebral Palsy or The Arc. Professionals can also increase family coping skills by encouraging families to focus more on their child's positive characteristics or strengths than on the child's weaknesses. Another example of a coping skill is to help families identify what they can or cannot control in their lives. These last two coping skills are examples of cognitive strategies.

14 **Build family competencies and capacity.** Information is very powerful and essential in a family's movement toward gaining knowledge and achieving empowerment. As suggested by Smith (2001), families can gain valuable insight into their child's education as well as into the school system as a whole. School professionals can encourage this by providing information on educational issues and concerns as well as on processes for educational decision making. Families should also be given the opportunity to observe the child in school environments and to share the information gained as educational partners.

15 **Offer training and professional development to families.** Family members should have opportunities to participate in training and professional development. Such participation offers accurate information and skill-building opportunities, which are cornerstones of empowerment. Families should be vital partners in the development and provision of training. This process should start with a needs assessment, as family members have important insight into their unique needs. Parents should also assist in setting agendas, establishing priorities, and evaluating the effectiveness of professional development opportunities. The ultimate level of empowerment for family members in professional development initiatives is to be encouraged in their own leadership as trainers of others.

16 **Engage family members in all stages of the Individualized Education Program (IEP) process.** Several recommendations for doing so are offered (Lytle & Bordin, 2001; Miles-Bonart, 2002; Smith, 2001) and include providing IEP training for parents and other IEP team participants; minimizing educational jargon to enhance understanding of the process; affording opportunities to increase educators' understanding of the child and home environment as well the parents' understanding of the child's educational setting; ensuring that all appropriate personnel are present at the meeting; and ensuring appropriate follow-through of IEP decisions. A positive parent-educator partnership is most effective when a common

goal is established. This is best expressed as follows: "The common denominator for the IEP is the team's concern for a particular child" (Lytle & Bordin, 2001, p. 44).

17 **Encourage student participation in the IEP meeting.** An IEP team meeting can be an intimidating environment, particularly for students with disabilities. Students, as appropriate, should be encouraged to develop and participate in their own IEP process as an initial step in self-advocacy and empowerment. Key steps in a student-led IEP program (McGahee, Mason, Wallace, & Jones, 2001) include (a) assisting students to understand their IEPs, (b) engaging students in developing an IEP, (c) helping students assess and write sections of their IEPs, (d) preparing students to participate in or lead their IEP meetings, and (e) providing support during the meeting.

18 **Involve families in community collaboration.** Families' lives can be greatly enhanced through community resources and services that are available for assistance. Schools can serve as conduits between families and the numerous services offered. Making family members aware of resources and services and assisting them in the navigation of the systems in their communities will involve them in self-advocacy and empowerment. Though school personnel can and should make family members aware of community supports, they should recognize that families have insight into what will best meet their unique needs.

19 **Foster hope.** Families are typically concerned about their child's future, and large issues loom both in the near and distant landscapes. *Will my child attend a post-secondary educational institution? Will my child be able to live independently? What supports will be needed to assist my child in securing full-time employment? Will my child have a full and rich life in the community with friends to provide socialization and enrichment?* Although special education professionals must be careful not to paint an unrealistic future scenario for any family, optimism and hope about continued progress and increased independence for their child must dominate family-professional interactions. For one family who was especially worried about their daughter's employment possibilities after high school, hope was instilled when a special education professional developed several job placements during the last 2 years of school. Through those diverse job experiences, a clear picture emerged of the kind of work environment and supports necessary to ensure a successful employment experience for this student.

20 **Assist families in articulating their vision for their child's future.** Families are empowered when they know what they want for their children. Professionals can help families to be realistic and optimistic about the services their children need and to recognize what is appropriate for their children. One process that assists families in clearly articulating their children's future vision is the Making Action Plans (MAPS) process (Falvey, Forest,

Pearpoint, & Rosenberg, 1997). With MAPS, a facilitator leads a group of school professionals and family members in discussing the following questions: What is the child's history? What are your dreams for your child? What are your nightmares? Who is your child (brief descriptions)? What are your child's strengths, gifts, and talents? What are your child's needs? What would your child's ideal school day look like?

Benefits abound when families of children with disabilities are supported and empowered through the educational system. The 20 ways described here can prove to be fruitful efforts in enhancing family feelings of support and empowerment.

References

Falvey, M. A., Forest, M., Pearpoint, J., & Rosenberg, R. (1997). *All my life's a circle.* Toronto, Ontario, Canada: Inclusion.

Fiedler, C. R. (2000). *Making a difference: Advocacy competencies for special education professionals.* Boston: Allyn & Bacon.

Lytle, R., & Bordin, J. (2001). Enhancing the IEP team: Strategies for parents and professionals. *Teaching Exceptional Children, 33*(5), 40–44.

McGahee, M., Mason, C., Wallace, T., & Jones, B. (2001). *Student-led IEPS: A guide for student involvement.* Arlington, VA: Council for Exceptional Children.

Miles-Bonart, S. (2002, March). A look at variables affecting parent satisfaction with IEP meetings. *No Child Left Behind: The vital role of rural schools.* Conference proceedings of the 22nd annual National American Council on Rural Special Education (ACRES), Reno, NV.

Murphy, D. L., Lee, I. L., Turnbull, A. P., & Turbiville, V. (1995). The Family-Centered Program Rating Scale: An instrument for program evaluation and change. *Journal of Early Intervention, 19*(1), 24–42.

Pugach, M. C., & Johnson, L. J. (2002). *Collaborative practitioners, collaborative schools.* Denver, CO: Love Publishing.

Smith, S. (2001). *Involving parents in the IEP process* (ERIC Digest E611 DEO-EC-01-6). Retrieved June 28, 2005, from ERIC database.

Turnbull, A. P., Turnbull, H. R., Erwin, E., & Soodak, L. (2006). *Families, professionals, and exceptionality: Positive outcomes through partnership and trust* (5th ed.). Columbus, OH: Merrill/Prentice Hall.

Critical Thinking

1. List some of the ways that schools can help families who have a child with a disability.

2. Can some of the types of supports and empowerment concepts be applied in working with any type of family? What ones are most important to all families?

3. How would a teacher or case manager engage a family who has a child with a disability?

4. How does a community engage families with children who have disabilities?

BARBARA VAN HAREN, PhD, is a director of special education for the Cooperative Services Education Agency (CESA) #1 in Brookfield, Wisconsin. She is also an ad hoc special education instructor at the University of Wisconsin-Oshkosh. Her current interests include participation, development, and implementation of Individualized Education Programs; collaboration; and special education leadership.

CRAIG R. FIEDLER, JD, PhD, is a professor of special education at the University of Wisconsin-Oshkosh. His current interests include special education advocacy, supporting and empowering families of students with disabilities, disability ethics, and inclusion of children and adults with disabilities in the mainstream of school and community life.

From *Intervention in School and Clinic,* Vol. 43, No. 4, March 2008, pp. 231–235. Copyright © 2008 by Pro-Ed, Inc. Reprinted by permission via Copyright Clearance Center.

UNIT 4

Challenges and Opportunities

Unit Selections

Learning Outcomes

After reading this unit, you will be able to:

- Identify the signs of domestic partner abuse.
- Examine the role of power and control in domestic violence.
- Describe how the victim leaves a domestic violent relationship.
- Discuss the care for children who are exposed to domestic violence.
- Identify the claims made when parents leave their children in the car.
- Describe the physical impact of children who are left in cars in extreme temperatures.
- Analyze the court decisions in cases where children are left in cars.
- Explain the role of foster care.

- Recognize the risk factors in children whose parents are alcoholics.
- Describe the development of substance disorders in children of alcoholics.
- Explain the substance use effects model.
- Identify the resilience and protective factors in the children of alcoholics.
- Describe the Family Recovery Project.
- Identify the developmental recovery stages.
- Summarize the effects of recovery on pre-teens and adolescents.
- Identify treatment recommendations.
- Identify the reasons given by partners who cheat.

- Explain how relationship continue after a partner cheats.
- Identify attributes of happily married couples.
- Describe how people cheat on their partners.
- Identify why people cheat.
- Explain what happens to a relationship after infidelity.
- Explain why upper-class women are leaving work to stay at home with children.
- Identify policy implications of women leaving the workforce.
- Describe the impact of women who choose to stay at home influence society.
- Identify how parents can balance their time spent with their family and their career.
- Discuss the challenges parents have dividing time between work and family.
- Describe ways to choose a family-friendly career.
- Describe the changes in salary earning between husband and wives.
- Explain the attributes of the families who find balance in earning differences.
- Describe the impact of betrayal of aging parents.
- Summarize what an aging parent can do if they are financially exploited by a family member.
- Describe how diabetes impacts the entire family.
- Explain the impact on parent's whose child has been diagnosed with diabetes.
- Summarize the child's experience of living with diabetes.
- Define the concept of "The New Normal."
- Identify bereavement outcomes for caregivers.
- Describe the diagnosis and treatment of complicated grief.
- Identify opportunities for intervention with bereaved caregivers.
- Define the concept of a home funeral.
- Examine the family's decision to have a home funeral.
- Summarize the process of a home funeral.
- Describe the impact on families when a spouse or parent is deployed.
- Examine the impact of military deployment on family members left at home.
- Describe the experience of the deployed family member.
- Recognize the stresses place on service members and their families during the deployment.

- Describe the adaptability and resilience of military families.
- Identify how children cope with their parent's deployment.
- Summarize the strengths and challenges faced by military families.
- Describe the uniqueness of military children and their response to death.
- Describe the at risk behaviors for adults in the lives of military children.
- Identify the ways adults can help military children cope with the death of a loved one.
- Describe the impact of divorce on children.
- Summarize how the parent–child relationship survives divorce.
- Explain how divorce can happen without devasting children involved.
- Describe the impact of having a parenting coordinator in divorced families.
- Analyze the different types of parenting coordinators by state.
- Summarize the parenting coordination programs.
- Describe reasons behind couple's delaying divorce.
- Identify common factors in delaying divorce.
- Describe how couples cope with not having the financial stability to divorce.

Student Website
www.mhhe.com/cls

Internet References
Alzheimer's Association
   www.alz.org
Modern Family or Modernized Family Traditionalism?: Master Status and the Gender Order in Switzerland
   www.sociology.org/content/vol006.004/lwk.html
Sociological Perspectives of Work and Family
   www.scribd.com/doc/24528839/
   Sociological-Perspectives-on-Work-and-Family
Child Welfare Information Gateway
   www.childwelfare.gov/
Child Rights Information Network
   www.crin.org/

Stress is life and life is stress. Sometimes stress in families gives new meaning to this statement. When a stressful event occurs in families, many processes occur simultaneously as families and their members cope with the stressor and its effects. One thing that can result is a reduction of the family members' ability to act as resources for each other. Indeed, a stressor can overwhelm the family system, and family members may be among the least effective people in coping with each other's behavior.

In this unit, we consider a wide variety of crises. Family violence is the focus of the first article. "Recognizing Domestic Partner Abuse" presents warning signs and resources for those who experience or those who hope to help those experiencing domestic partner abuse. Each year, children die needlessly because they are left in overheated vehicles. Gene Weigarten discusses the lasting effects when this is the result of "Forgotten Baby Syndrome." The following article, "Role of Foster Family Belonging in Recovery from Child Maltreatment," explores a model of foster care that is intended to reduce the negative effects of child neglect and to enhance the sense belonging of the foster child. Substance abuse is next addressed in "Children of Alcoholics" and "Impact of Family Recovery and Pre-Teens and Adolescents." The first article looks at ways in which children of alcoholics (COA) are put at risk by substance abuse in their families, while it also presents surprising resilience factors that may serve to protect these children from their family dysfunction. The second looks at the nature of family recovery, the traumatic effect of family recovery on the young, and potential treatments.

The next section focuses on the impact of infidelity on the partners and on the relationship. Over half of married partners will cheat at least once in their marriage. The first article "Why Do They Cheat and Lie?" examines this and discusses a number of reasons for why this is so. Next, emotional infidelity is addressed in "Love but Don't Touch." This is a form of unfaithfulness that many see as less serious than sexual infidelity, but others view as just a damaging to a couple's relationship. In this article, Mark Teich addresses a variety of ways of spotting emotional cheating as well as ways of strengthening a relationship after or in anticipation of its happening. A new phenomenon, "Is This Man Cheating on His Wife?," is explored in the final article in this subsection.

The subsection that follows, Economic Concerns, looks at the work/family connection with interesting results. "The "Opt-Out Myth" questions a common belief that women are leaving the workforce to focus on their home life. The view that family and work life must arrive at some form of appropriate balance is the focus of "Making Time for Family Time." "Finding a New Balance" looks at a new and growing phenomenon, couples in which wives make more money than their husbands. This article presents examples of couples who not only cope, but thrive, in this reversal of traditional gender roles. The final article in this subsection, "Trust and Betrayal in the Golden Years," addresses a serious concern faced by too many elderly—the exploitation and abuse of the elderly by their children.

The nature of stress resulting from a life-threatening illness as well as loss and grief are the subject of the next subsection. Life-threatening illnesses can place tremendous strain on couples' relationships. "Dealing Day-to-Day with Diabetes" documents the ways in which families adapt to live with a serious chronic illness. The next article, "The Positives of Caregiving," addresses ways in which mothers are able to respond to the needs of their autistic child in a positive way. The next article, "Bereavement after Caregiving," shows that the stress of caregiving does not end with death. "A Family Undertaking" discusses the final act of love and respect for a loved one in the form of a home funeral.

In the next subsection, the many crises of war are portrayed. "Stressors Affecting Families during Military Deployment" catalogues stressors faced by military families when a member is deployed to a war zone. Military families have long dealt with

© Ingram Publishing

the disruptions associated with having a family member in the military. "Military Children and Families" examines the effects of repeated and lengthy deployments on the children and identifies strengths and challenges of these families—both within the family and community. In "Helping Military Kids Cope with Traumatic Death," Linda Goldman describes the specific needs of children in military families, who face the almost constant threat of traumatic death of loved ones.

Divorce and remarriage are the subjects of the final subsection. The first article in this subsection, "Civil Wars," addresses ways in which the divorcing (and then divorced) couple may use their children as pawns in their battles with each other. The needs of the children must be paramount when a couple divorces—this is too often not the case. In the second article in this section, "Estranged Spouses Increasingly Waiting Out Downturn to Divorce" describes a new phenomenon, that of couples waiting to divorce because of strained finances, or living together after their divorce for the same reason.

Recognizing Domestic Partner Abuse

With its daunting complexities, the path to change takes courage and support.

Domestic abuse. Battering. Intimate partner violence. These are terms that make us wince. And they should: The phenomenon is widespread in the United States, and its effects can be long-lasting and life-threatening. Breaking the pattern of domestic violence can be extremely difficult and may take a long time. It requires courage, planning, and a support network.

The U.S. Department of Health and Human Services defines domestic violence as "a pattern of assaultive and/or coercive behaviors . . . that adults use against their intimate partners to gain power and control in that relationship." It includes not only physical and sexual abuse but also emotional abuse. All can have serious health consequences.

Domestic violence affects people of all ethnic backgrounds; it occurs among the poor and the rich and among the well educated and the poorly educated. Men are usually (though not always) the abusers, and women are usually on the receiving end. In the United States, a woman's lifetime risk of being a victim of such violence is 25%. Women who were abused as children are at an increased risk for being in an abusive relationship as an adult.

First Signs

Women don't consciously choose to have an abusive partner. In fact, the abuser may be charming and well liked by most of the people who know him, but at home he shows a different side. Friends, family, and colleagues are often shocked when his abusive behavior becomes known. In the beginning, it may also be a shock to the abused woman.

Selected Resources

National Domestic Violence Hotline
800-799-7233 (toll free)
800-787-3224 (for the hearing impaired; toll free)

National Sexual Assault Hotline
800-656-4673 (toll free)

National Women's Health Information Center, "Violence against Women"
womenshealth.gov/violence/domestic/
800-994-9662 (toll free)

United Way First Call for Help
800-231-4377 (toll free)

She may have regarded her relationship with this man as the most wonderful, romantic, fairy tale–like experience imaginable, says Susan Neis, executive director of Cornerstone, a shelter that serves five suburbs of Minneapolis.

Changes in the relationship can be difficult to see at first. The abuser's need for control often begins to show itself in little things he says and does. He may criticize the way his partner acts or looks. He may say deeply hurtful things, such as accusing her of being a bad mother. "When somebody says this to you, somebody you're in love with, it's devastating," says Neis, who is herself a survivor of domestic abuse.

Over time, the abuser's words can chip away at a woman's sense of herself. She starts to doubt her perceptions and may even come to believe the horrible things he says about her. She feels isolated, ashamed, and helpless, but at the same time may feel an obligation to keep herself convinced of the fairy tale because "there's nothing else to hold onto," says one 35-year-old woman who received help from Cornerstone.

Control and Power

At the center of domestic violence is the issue of control. The abuser is intent on gaining and maintaining power over his partner through fear and intimidation. Abuse doesn't necessarily involve physical harm. Threats can also be highly effective and should not be minimized, suggests Dr. Judith Herman, clinical professor of psychiatry at Harvard Medical School and training director of the Victims of Violence Program at Cambridge Health Alliance in Cambridge, Mass. A man who says "If you leave me, I'll track you down and kill you and anyone who helps you" can instill as much (or more) fear as one who strikes his partner.

The abusive partner uses various tactics to achieve control. He may intimidate and demean his partner by constantly criticizing her, monopolizing household finances, or telling her what she can wear, where she can go, and whom she can see. He may play "mind games," such as suggesting that she's hypersensitive, hysterical, or mentally unbalanced. Often he isolates the woman from family, friends, and colleagues, either by removing her from them physically or by limiting her employment options and social contacts. Abuse may also take the form of pathological jealousy, such as false accusations of adultery. Soon, the woman may find that she's cut off from all outside connections, no longer in touch with the people and services that could help her.

Isolation may also disconnect her from a sense of what's normal. She may not even think of herself as a victim of domestic violence, says Dr. Megan Gerber, an internist at Cambridge Health Alliance who specializes in women's health and an instructor of medicine at Harvard Medical School. After an incident, the abuser often apologizes and tries to placate his victim. There may be periods of relative calm. It may take a victim a long time to recognize that her partner's behaviors aren't random but form a pattern of abuse.

Intimate Partner Abuse Is a Health Issue

Intimate partner abuse can have profound effects on a woman's health, both physical and mental. Physical harm, including fractures, lacerations, and soft tissue trauma, is one obvious effect. Intimate partner abuse is also linked to chronic health problems and even death—from either suicide because of depression or murder (or manslaughter) by the partner.

The intense, ongoing stress may result in chronic pain or gastrointestinal symptoms. Victims of domestic abuse are more likely to have arthritis, neck pain, pelvic pain, and migraine headaches. They also have an increased risk of menstrual problems and difficulties during pregnancy, including bleeding, low birth weight, and anemia.

Domestic abuse is closely linked with mental illness and substance abuse. A recent study found that 47.6% of battered women were depressed and 63.8% had post-traumatic stress disorder; 18.5% used alcohol excessively; 8.9% used drugs; and 7.9% committed suicide.

Because women in abusive relationships often need emergency room and primary care services, physicians, nurses, and other clinicians are often the first outsiders to learn about the emotional or physical abuse. Women are often reluctant to mention the subject on a patient history form, but if asked by a clinician, they may be relieved to acknowledge it.

Getting Out

Walking away from an abusive relationship is a process more than a single action. Women usually make several attempts—five, on average—before they leave the partner for good. Isolation and fear may prevent a woman from leaving, even when she knows it is probably for the best. She may still love her partner or worry about what will happen to her children if she leaves. She may be unsure how to escape or how to survive financially and care for her children.

Community support can be crucial although a woman in an abusive relationship often has difficulty taking advantage of that support. The abuser may track her computer use, looking for visits to websites and evidence of keyword searches. If that's a concern, says Rita Smith, executive director of the National Coalition Against Domestic Violence in Boulder, Colo., she should use a computer outside the home—for example at a library or a friend's home or work place. As a safeguard, the coalition's own site (www.ncadv.org) features a red "Escape" button that immediately switches the user to an Internet search engine.

Care for the Children

Each year, up to 10 million children witness the abuse of a parent or caregiver. Many women stay in an abusive relationship because they think it's best not to disrupt the children's lives so long as they're not being abused themselves. But children who live with domestic violence are at serious risk for behavioral and cognitive problems. In later life, they may suffer depression and trauma symptoms, and they may tolerate or use violence in their own relationships.

What Can I Do to Help?

You suspect that your friend is in an abusive relationship. For example, she seems anxious and fearful when she recounts arguments with her husband. Or she may mention having to ask him each time she needs money. (While by itself not a sign of abuse, controlling finances can be part of a pattern of abuse.)

Part of you wants to rescue her and take her to a safe place where her husband can't find her. Yet you worry that any action you take could make things worse, increasing the danger she's already in. You know the decision is hers to make, not yours. But you can do a lot to help. Here are some things to consider:

- Think about your relationship with your friend. When and where might you talk with her safely, and what could you say? Does she trust you? Does she feel that she can confide in you without fearing that you'd judge her harshly or dismiss her concerns?
- Ask questions that let her know of your suspicions and concern. One question might be: Are you afraid of your husband? Understand that she might be hesitant to talk about this directly—or might deny or minimize what's happening. Assure her that you'll keep what she says strictly confidential.
- When she talks about the situation, believe what she says and validate her concerns. Let her know you don't think she's crazy or it's all in her head. And let her know that she's not to blame, despite what her partner may have told her.
- Help your friend make use of local resources—public health services, a hospital or clinic, a women's shelter, or a legal assistance program. If she thinks the abuser is monitoring her phone calls, offer her the use of your home phone or cell phone to make these contacts.
- Work with your friend to develop a personal safety plan. One resource for this step is the National Coalition Against Domestic Violence, www.ncadv.org/protectyourself/MyPersonalSafetyPlan_131.html.
- Help her prepare to leave if the danger and abuse escalate. Your friend should have coins with her at all times for phone calls, or a phone card. She should prepare a small bag with clothes, cash, and copies of important documents (birth certificate and passport, for example) and keep it in a safe place. Would you be willing to keep the bag for her in case of need?
- Knowing that someone believes her and is ready to help can be crucial to your friend's safety and eventual escape from the abusive relationship. Be patient, listen, and offer her hope. Recognize that it may take a long time, and often several attempts at leaving, for the relationship to end.

Experts say that women leaving an abusive relationship should take their children with them. Otherwise, it can be difficult to get the children later, because police may not want to remove them from the home if the abusive partner is their biological father. Also, the abuser may later try to get custody by arguing that the woman abandoned her children.

Critical Thinking

1. Why is it important that individuals understand the signs of domestic violence?

2. Is intimate partner violence a health issue and why?

3. What are the reasons for the victim to stay in a relationship where domestic violence is present?

4. What happened to children who are exposed to domestic violence?

5. What can you do if someone you know is in a domestic violence relationship?

6. Knowing the signs of domestic violence, would you be able to recognize them in your partner early to prevent long-term abuse?

The Fatal Distraction: Forgetting a Child in the Backseat of a Car Is a Horrifying Mistake. Is It a Crime?

Every year, at least a dozen children die in overheated cars in the U.S. because parents forgot they were there. Don't assume, says The Washington Post's Gene Weingarten, that it couldn't happen to you.

GENE WEINGARTEN

The defendant was an immense man, well over 300 pounds, but in the gravity of his sorrow and shame he seemed larger still. He hunched forward in his wooden chair, sobbing softly into tissue after tissue, a leg bouncing nervously under the table. The room was a sepulcher. Witnesses spoke softly of events so painful that many lost their composure. When a hospital emergency room nurse described how the defendant had behaved after the police first brought him in, she wept. He was virtually catatonic, she remembered, his eyes shut tight, rocking back and forth, locked away in some unfathomable private torment. He would not speak at all for the longest time, not until the nurse sank down beside him and held his hand. It was only then that the patient began to open up, and what he said was that he didn't want any sedation, that he didn't deserve a respite from pain, that he wanted to feel it all, and then to die.

The charge in the courtroom was manslaughter, brought by the Commonwealth of Virginia. No significant facts were in dispute. Miles Harrison, 49, had been a diligent businessman and a doting, conscientious father until the day last summer—beset by problems at work, making call after call on his cell phone—he forgot to drop his son, Chase, at day care. The toddler slowly sweltered to death, strapped into a car seat for nearly nine hours in an office parking lot in the blistering heat of July.

It was an inexplicable, inexcusable mistake, but was it a crime? That was the question for a judge to decide.

"Death by hyperthermia" is the official designation. When it happens to young children, the facts are often the same: An otherwise attentive parent one day gets busy, or distracted, or confused by a change in his or her daily routine, and just . . . forgets a child is in the car. It happens that way somewhere in the United States 15 to 25 times a year, parceled out through the spring, summer, and early fall. The season is almost upon us.

Two decades ago, this was relatively rare. But in the early 1990s, car-safety experts declared that passenger-side front airbags could kill children, and they recommended that child seats be moved to the back of the car; then, for even more safety for the very young, that the baby seats be pivoted to face the rear. If few foresaw the tragic consequence of the lessened visibility of the child . . . well, who can blame them? What kind of person forgets a baby?

The wealthy do, it turns out. And the poor, and the middle class. Parents of all ages and ethnicities do it. Mothers are just as likely to do it as fathers. It happens to the chronically absent-minded and to the fanatically organized, to the college-educated and to the marginally literate. Last year it happened three times in one day, the worst day so far in the worst year so far in a phenomenon that gives no sign of abating.

The facts in each case differ a little, but always there is the terrible moment when the parent realizes what he or she has done, often through a phone call from a spouse or caregiver. This is followed by a frantic sprint to the car. What awaits there is the worst thing in the world.

In Miles Harrison's case, the judge ultimately decided there was no crime because there was no intent. Prosecutors, judges, and juries reach similar conclusions in many of these cases. But if Harrison's failing is not manslaughter, what is it? An accident?

"That's an imperfect word."

This is Mark Warschauer, an expert in language learning. "The word 'accident' makes it sound like it can't be prevented, but 'incident' makes it sound trivial. And it is not trivial."

Warschauer is a professor at the University of California at Irvine. In the summer of 2003, he returned to his office from lunch to find a crowd surrounding a car in the parking lot. Police had smashed the window open with a crowbar. Only as he got closer did Warschauer realize it was his car. That was his first clue that he'd forgotten to drop his 10-month-old son, Mikey, at day care that morning. Mikey was dead.

Warschauer wasn't charged with a crime, but for months afterward he contemplated suicide. Gradually, he says, the urge subsided, if not the grief and guilt.

"We lack a term for what this is," Warschauer says. And also, he says, we need an understanding of why it happens to the people it happens to.

David Diamond is picking at his breakfast at a Washington, D.C., hotel, trying to explain.

"Memory is a machine," he says, "and it is not flawless. If you're capable of forgetting your cell phone, you are potentially capable of forgetting your child."

Diamond is a professor of molecular physiology at the University of South Florida. He's in D.C. to give a conference speech about his research, which involves the intersection of emotion, stress, and memory. What he's found is that under some circumstances, the most sophisticated part of our thought-processing center can be held hostage to a competing memory system, a primitive portion of the brain that is—by a design as old as the dinosaur's—pigheaded, nonanalytical, stupid.

Diamond recently forgot, while driving to a mall, that his infant granddaughter was asleep in the back of his car. He remembered, he said, only because his wife mentioned the baby. So he understands what could have happened had he been alone with the child. Almost worse, he understands exactly why.

The human brain, he says, is a jury-rigged device in which newer and more sophisticated structures sit atop a junk heap of prototype brains still used by lower species. At the top are the most nimble parts: the prefrontal cortex, which thinks and analyzes, and the hippocampus, which makes and holds on to our immediate memories. At the bottom is the basal ganglia, nearly identical to the brains of lizards, controlling voluntary but barely conscious actions.

Diamond says that in situations involving familiar, routine motor skills, the human animal presses the basal ganglia into service as a sort of autopilot. When our prefrontal cortex and hippocampus are planning our day on the way to work, the ignorant basal ganglia is operating the car; that's why you'll sometimes find yourself having driven from point A to point B without a clear recollection of the route you took, the turns you made, or the scenery you saw.

Ordinarily, says Diamond, this delegation of duty "works beautifully, like a symphony." But sudden or chronic stress can weaken the brain's higher-functioning centers, making them more susceptible to bullying from the basal ganglia. He's seen that pattern in cases he's followed involving infant deaths in cars.

"The quality of prior parental care seems to be irrelevant," he said. "The important factors that keep showing up involve a combination of stress, emotion, lack of sleep, and change in routine, where the basal ganglia is trying to do what it's supposed to do, and the conscious mind is too weakened to resist. What happens is that the memory circuits in a vulnerable hippocampus literally get overwritten, like with a computer program. Unless the memory circuit is rebooted—such as if the child cries, or, you know, if the wife mentions the child in the back—it can entirely disappear."

Diamond stops. "There is a case in Virginia where this is exactly what happened, the whole set of stress factors. I was consulted on it a couple of years ago. It was a woman named, ah . . . "

He puts down his fork and shakes his head. He's been stressing over his conference speech, he says, and his memory retrieval is shot. He can't summon the name.

Lyn Balfour?

"Yeah, Lyn Balfour! The perfect storm."

Raelyn Balfour is what is commonly called a type-A personality. The 37-year-old Army reservist is the first to admit that her inclination to take on multiple challenges at once contributed to the death of her son, Bryce, two years ago. It happened on March 30, 2007, the day she accidentally left the 9-month-old in the parking lot of the Charlottesville, Va., judge advocate general's office, where she worked as a transportation administrator. The temperature that day was only in the 60s, but heat builds quickly in a closed vehicle in the sun. The temperature inside Balfour's car that day topped 110 degrees.

Circumstances had conspired against Balfour. She had been up much of the night, first baby-sitting for a friend with a pet emergency, then caring for Bryce, who was cranky with a cold. Because the baby was still tired, he uncharacteristically dozed in the car, so he made no noise. Because Balfour was planning to bring Bryce's usual car seat to the fire station to be professionally installed, Bryce was positioned in a different car seat that day, directly behind the driver, and thus less visible. Because of a phone conversation with a young relative in trouble, and another with her boss about a crisis at work, Balfour spent most of the trip on her cell, stressed, solving other people's problems.

One more thing: Because the baby sitter had a new phone, it didn't yet contain Balfour's office phone number, only her cell number—so when the sitter phoned to wonder why Balfour hadn't dropped Bryce off that morning, it rang unheard in Balfour's pocketbook.

Balfour was charged with second-degree murder in Bryce's death but was eventually acquitted. The key moment in her trial was when the defense attorney played for the jury a recording of a 911 call made by a passer-by in the first few seconds after Balfour discovered Bryce's body. That tape is unendurable. Mostly, you hear the passer-by's voice, tense but precise, explaining to a police dispatcher what she is seeing. Initially, there's nothing in the background. Then Balfour howls at the top of her lungs, "OH, MY GOD, NOOOO!"

For a few seconds, there's nothing. Then another deafening shriek: "NO, NO, PLEASE, NO!!!"

Unlike most parents who have suffered similar tragedies, Balfour now is willing to talk to the media, anytime. She works with a group called Kids and Cars, telling her story repeatedly. In public, she seldom seems in particular anguish. No one sees her cry. She has, she says, consciously crafted the face she shows. "People say I'm a strong woman, but I'm not. I would like to disappear, to move someplace where no one knows who I am and what I did. But I can't. I'm the lady who killed her child, and I have to be that lady because I promised Bryce."

Balfour has kept her promise in a way suited to her personality: She has become a modern, maternal version of the Ancient Mariner. When speaking to the media, her consistent message is that cars need safety devices to prevent similar tragedies. From time to time, though, she will simply belly up to strangers in, say, a Sam's Club, and start a conversation about children, so she can tell them what she did to one of hers. Her message: *This can happen to anyone.*

111

Critical Thinking

1. If you were one of these parents who were charged with neglect after the death of your child, what would you do, how would you feel, and what would you want others to know?

2. What would you do if you witnessed a parent about to leave his or her child in a car, even if he or she told you it was just for a minute?

3. When working with families, what do you think would be the best way to explain what the impact of leaving a child in a car would be?

Role of Foster Family Belonging in Recovery from Child Maltreatment

DAMEN WAYNE RIGGS, MARTHA AUGOUSTINOS, AND PAUL HOWARD DELFABBRO

A rapidly growing body of research both within Australia and internationally has recognised the broad range of negative life outcomes facing children who are removed from abusive or neglectful contexts and placed into foster care (see Barber & Delfabbro, 2004, for a summary of this research). Such research continues to find that children placed in foster care often experience major physical health problems, challenges in developing attachment relationships with caregivers, developmental delays in speech, motor skills and comprehension, and are at increased risk for mental health problems, drug and alcohol abuse, and a generalised inability to form lasting connections with peers (Wise & Egger, 2009). Nonetheless, research has also shown that foster children (like all children) are resilient, and display considerable skill in ensuring that their physical needs are met, in developing meaningful relationships with caregivers, and living lives that they attribute with value (Harvey & Delfabbro, 2004).

One of the ways in which children learn resilience, particularly following abuse or neglect, is through the experience of relationships with stable and nurturing caregiving figures. Research suggests that foster children who display avoidant, resistant or disorganised attachments to parental figures can learn new ways of attaching to those primary caregivers (i.e., foster carers) who take the place of their birth parents (Dozier, Stovall, Albus, & Bates, 2001). Research also suggests that children who are provided with opportunities to access supportive nurturing relationships after experiences of maltreatment are more likely to experience positive outcomes and display a greater resiliency to future negative life events (Horwitz, Balestracci, & Simms, 2001). More specifically, and in the Australian context, Wise and Egger (2009) found a significant relationship between placement type and well-being outcomes, in that children in family-based foster care as compared to children in residential care were significantly more likely to have attained key family and social relationship objectives. Because those data were not longitudinal, it is not possible to definitively state that family-based care produced these better outcomes, but it is nonetheless fair to suggest from the data that there are significant differences in the experiences of connection and belonging between children in family-based care and residential care, and that this cannot solely be explained by differences in their behavioural presentation (i.e., that children in residential care did report higher levels of health-risk behaviours and criminality).

Of course it is important to recognise that children who experience positive outcomes from foster care are very much the product not only of their own skills and resilience in the face of adversity, but also the skills of those people involved in their daily care. In regard to the existing body of research on care providers' experiences, it has been found that an adult's commitment and motivation to care for children greatly impacts upon the success of the foster placement, both for the child and for the carer. More specifically, this research has found that successful placements and a commitment to long-term care provision typically result from factors including the match between the child and the adult, the enjoyment that the adult derives from care provision, and the level of support and recognition provided to the foster carer (Colton, Roberts, & Williams, 2006; Denby, Rindfleisch, & Bean, 1999).

International research on foster families has identified such families as an important site through which foster children develop a sense of belonging and a positive identity as a person able to succeed in the world (e.g., O'Neil, 2004). Foster children who feel welcomed into a family environment, or who are invited to create a family with foster carers, report that this sense of family is central to their experience of stability in the world (Gardner, 2004). Such findings also suggest that foster families typically provide a safe environment in which healing from previous abuse can occur (Schofield, 2002). Relatedly, current Australian research conducted by the authors has found that the successes that foster children and carers experience in regards to placement stability are often the result of the formation of nurturing familial relations (e.g., Riggs, Delfabbro, & Augoustinos, 2008). From this we have suggested that foster carers who view their engagement in care provision as occurring within a family context are likely to persist in the face of adversity.

Family relations thus provide an important buffer for foster children and carers against histories of abuse, placement disruption or breakdown, and a lack of adequate services and support. Because government agencies mandated to provide such services across Australia face an ongoing lack of funding, it is important that existing funding is used in the best ways possible. Although the considerable body of research on foster care has done much to identify attributes of positive placements, factors that result in placement breakdown (and the negative effects of this), and the considerations that adults undertake before engaging in care provision (see Barber & Delfabbro, 2004, for a summary of this research), only a small body of research has explicitly examined the unique aspects of foster families themselves that may facilitate recovery from trauma for children removed into care.

This paper examines one aspect of a model proposed in the context of UK foster care by Schofield (2002), who suggests that foster children acquire five "life lessons" through their experience of living in a foster family, and that these help to counter the effects of previous maltreatment. Schofield's model suggests that placement in foster care equips foster children with the ability to (a) love, (b) act, (c) think, (d) hope and (e) belong. This paper focuses upon the final lesson—that of belonging—and in particular the five aspects of belonging identified by Schofield: (a) family solidarity, as evidenced by practical and emotional support, (b) family rituals, (c) family identity, (d) family relationships, and (e) family culture, as evidenced by norms, values and aspirations. Through an examination of interview and focus group data collected with Australian foster carers, the analysis provided highlights the ways in which this group of carers have engaged in practices of belonging that may be seen as creating opportunities for healing from abuse for foster children.

Method

The data analysed here are drawn from a broad corpus of individual interviews and focus groups conducted as part of a national research project examining why people choose to become foster carers and how to best attract new foster carers. Ethics approval was sought and granted from both the University of Adelaide and the foster care organisations with whom the foster carers were registered. Ten interviews with couples and 15 focus groups were conducted with men ($n = 31$) and women ($n = 49$) from a range of cultural backgrounds and with a broad range of care experiences across four Australian States using a semi-structured interview schedule. Interviews and focus groups were audiotaped and transcribed orthographically, and all participants were allocated a pseudonym following transcription to ensure anonymity.

Findings published thus far from these data utilising thematic analysis have consistently found that what foster carers require is recognition of the family status of their care provision (for those carers who provide long-term care), and that foster carers have the capacity to understand the care they provide as offering modes of healing from previous trauma for foster children (Riggs, 2008, 2009; Riggs, Augoustinos, & Delfabbro, 2007). With these findings in mind, the model proposed by Schofield (2002) was examined for its relevance to Australian foster families in the sample. Because Schofield's research was conducted with foster children, it was considered inappropriate to attempt to extrapolate evidence about children's capacity to love, hope, think or act from data collected with foster carers. It was, however, deemed appropriate by the authors to examine how foster carers understand their role in nurturing a sense of belonging, particularly because the topic of belonging was identified in early thematic analyses of the data as a salient topic across many of the interviews and focus groups. A decision was made to collapse two of Schofield's categories into one (those of family relationships and family culture), because there was no clear difference between the two made in Schofield's research.

Based on the categories of belonging identified in the Schofield (2002) paper, a content analysis was conducted on the entire dataset utilising the NVIVO data management program (QSR International, Cambridge, Massachusetts, USA). This involved searching for key terms within the dataset, including the four subcategories of belonging and additional terms identified as relating to the category of "family" in previous analyses of the data such as "belonging", "daughter", "son", "love" and "bond". Across all 80 participants, 50 individuals (62.5%) were identified as talking about family (or one of the key terms relating to it) in at least one instance (with a total of 55 instances identified, because some participants spoke about the topic of "family" in more than one discrete instance in their focus group/interview). In focus groups this typically occurred as a discussion between participants of which all members of the group took part. It should be noted that a question related to "family" was not included in the interview schedule, which instead focused on motivations to care provision.

Once identified, all of the paragraphs pertaining to family (and accompanying questions from the researcher) were collected for analysis as individual extracts. These extracts were then carefully examined as to their relationship to the four categories of belonging under examination. Of the 55 references to "family" that were identified, 46 of these were determined as directly related to the four categories, with 10 pertaining to family solidarity, 12 pertaining to family rituals, 15 pertaining to family identity, and nine pertaining to family culture.

Following the tenets of discourse analysis (e.g., Potter, 1996), with a focus on both the rhetorical devices deployed by participants to legitimate particular claims about belonging, and an examination of the broader social contexts upon which the participants appeared to draw, an in-depth analysis as reported below was conducted on eight extracts (two for each of the four aspects of belonging examined here). These extracts were chosen both for the relative diversity of participants represented by the extracts, and for their clarity of attention to the aspects of belonging to which they pertain. Brief demographic information is reported for each participant, because previous analyses of these data (e.g., Riggs & Augoustinos, 2009) have suggested that differences do exist among participants in relation to their experiences of care provision, and thus in the spirit of qualitative research it would appear important to render visible demographic differences even if these are not subject to analysis.

Importantly, the approach to analysis adopted within this paper is less concerned with producing generalisable findings about a particular population, and more concerned with exploring the apparent range of discourses available through which a specific topic is constructed. As such, the analysis presented here, while broadly indicative of the ways in which Australian foster carers from across four States talked about their understanding of belonging within foster families, may not necessarily represent all of the ways in which Australian foster carers understand belonging. Nonetheless, the findings provide important insight into the experiences of foster carers in the Australian context.

Analysis

In the following sections each of the four aspects of belonging as identified by Schofield (2002) are briefly introduced, with representative extracts then provided illustrating how the Australian foster carers in this sample spoke on topics related to each of the aspects. Close attention is given to each of the extracts to elaborate upon the theme of belonging, with specific analytic focus paid to the implications of the understandings of belonging elaborated and their relationship to healing from previous maltreatment for foster children.

Family Solidarity

In her definition, Schofield (2002) suggests that family solidarity among foster carers and children takes the form of kinship relations, which, despite their often non-biological nature (obviously excluding kinship carers), closely resemble those relationships between biologically related family members. Most importantly, Schofield suggests that such solidarity is not temporary, but rather represents a long-lasting bond between family members. Although in biologically related families this sense of solidarity often (although not always, as we see in the instance of children removed from abusive birth family situations) results from the very fact of being born into a family—through the claims to family membership and commitment that are typically made to a child born into a family—claims to solidarity among non-biologically related family members are often enacted in unique ways. In previous research conducted by the authors (Riggs et al., 2008), it was found that many foster carers report a "conception narrative" that marked the founding of their foster family. These types of narrative may be seen to demonstrate a form of family solidarity as suggested by Schofield. The following two extracts further highlight claims to enduring solidarity attested to by the Australian foster carers in this sample. In the first extract Susan, a single heterosexual woman providing long-term care and who had provided care for more than 30 children over 20 years, talks about the ways in which she stays in contact with children previously in her care:

Interviewer: *Are you in contact with the children you have cared for who no longer live with you?*

Susan: *I try to keep in touch, even if it is just on their birthdays. I can remember birthdays like you wouldn't believe. Birthday cards, Christmas cards there has probably only been a couple of families that I wouldn't have wanted to still keep in touch with. I say that once you come through my front door, it is always open. So many of the children I have cared for, who are now adults, have told me how important it is being able to still know where I am and that I am thinking about them.*

Here Susan makes clear reference to the ongoing nature of the relationship she has formed with children in her care and, most importantly, that the children (now adults) understand the permanency and commitment of the relationship. For children who come into care, and who may experience "placement drift" as a result of challenging behaviours or insufficient placement options, a sense of permanency may often be lacking (Barber, Delfabbro, & Cooper, 2001). This can result in a sense of isolation from other people in the world, or an inability to establish meaningful relationships as adults. Carers such as Susan provide foster children with the opportunity to explore the possibility of developing connections and to understand that despite their previous experiences of maltreatment, it is nonetheless possible to engage in long-lasting relationships with other people. In the second extract, Roy talks about the impact that the "little things" make in the lives of foster children, which give them a sense of place in a broader sense:

Roy: *The teenage years if you are there and they are involved in sport you don't have a problem. Karate or whatever if you can support them and take them and pick them up and be there. I noticed that when the boys were younger and they played football, I would be sitting out in the rain, my wife wouldn't come because it was too wet, but I was there, that was all they wanted. They needed someone to talk to afterwards about the game they had just played. Those were the little things I noticed impacted on them more than anything else because you were there. And even when our boys were teenagers, because when they came home, they had a meal cooked and someone was there to talk to them.*

Although Roy constructs his attendance at football games as being "little", we can see that his willingness to be there in the rain, to listen, and to show care, provided an important sense of connectedness for the children in his care. Throughout their interview Roy and his wife spent considerable time elaborating the ongoing commitment they have made to the two boys they raised as foster carers, and the positive outcomes that they believe the boys (now men) have displayed in their lives. Roy's account suggests that being there consistently, and providing children with the knowledge that someone will listen to them, can play a key role in scaffolding repair from maltreatment that allows children to understand the world as a safe place in which other

people are concerned for their welfare. Creating a sense of belonging through demonstrations of care, no matter how "little", show to children in care that they are valued and welcomed into the foster family in which they live. As Roy's words suggest, this process of showing interest has long-lasting effects: his interest and willingness when the children were younger potentially translated into their willingness to share with him and his wife in turn when they were teenagers.

Family Rituals

Rituals of belonging are a typical part of many families, regardless of their structure or formation. Such rituals tell a story about the family to its members, and provide the members with a sense of belonging through shared traditions or practices of meaning making. Rituals may be as simple as annual holidays taken or household practices that are commonly agreed upon by family members. Rituals may also be more complex, in the form of stories told among family members or accounts documented by both foster carers and children to record the history of the child and their location within the foster family. Many of the foster carers who spoke as part of this research identified rituals that they engaged in to develop or maintain connections with foster children, as evidenced by the following two extracts. In the extract below Dawn talks about the ways in which she has aided foster children in having ways of telling their life stories:

Dawn: *Our foster daughter was placed with us pretty much from birth—the birth mother didn't see the baby at all. So I picked her up and bonded like that and I did a diary every day so that when she got a little bit older she had a record. I wanted her to have an idea of what her life was like when she was young, and all the things we did together, and also so she could possibly share this with her birth mother one day. I have since done this for our other children since and it is something they love to look through and tell their own stories about.*

In this extract Dawn, who along with her husband cares for five foster children on a long-term basis, talks about the practical things she has done to facilitate a sense of connection for the children in her care, both with their birth parents, and with their own histories. Many of the foster carers who spoke as part of this research stated that they felt a drive within foster care systems towards placing birth and foster families in antagonistic relations with one another. Yet in the face of this, many foster carers spoke of finding ways to include birth families, or at the very least to ensure that foster children had ways to connect with their birth families. Dawn's commitment to recording the children's life stories holds the potential to demonstrate to foster children the many places to which they can belong, and to allow them to claim membership of both their birth and foster families, rather than expecting them to "choose".

In contrast to this image of foster carers working with birth families, other foster carers spoke of rituals that supported foster children through negative experiences with birth parents:

Mary: *When the social workers decided to force overnight access with her birth mum against our foster daughter's will it was horrible. I used to sing this little lullaby to her and when she returned from access with her birth mum she told us she used to sing the lullaby to herself to comfort herself and we would sing that to ourselves, it was such a strong bond there.*

In this extract Mary, a lesbian foster carer who, with her partner, had provided care to a child for 10 years, spoke of a range of very negative experiences that had resulted from decisions made to support reunification with the birth mother. While this decision was eventually overturned, it had been a negative experience for the foster child, and for Mary and her partner. In this extract Mary speaks of a ritual that had carried them all through these experiences—that of a lullaby they had sung to their foster daughter which held special meaning to them all. This sense of connection had been a source of comfort for the foster child in challenging times, and the "strong bond" between them all as a foster family had ensured that the child had the capacity to heal from the negative experiences. Although it would ideally be the case that decisions were made in practice that prevented foster children from being exposed to further opportunities for maltreatment by birth parents, this may not always be the case. Having means to recover from this (as provided by rituals of care in foster families) is thus an important tool that foster children gain from their connections to foster carers.

Family Identity

As research conducted by the authors would suggest (Riggs, King, Delfabbro, & Augoustinos, 2009), foster children often experience stigma as a result of their identification as "children out of place": as children who, by the very fact of abuse, are located in situations outside of the norm of the nuclear family. Schofield (2002) further suggests that foster families themselves may experience stigmatisation from within society on the basis of their non-normative family status. Research conducted by the authors (Riggs & Delfabbro, 2008) similarly suggests that Australian foster carers in this sample experience a degree of stigmatisation on the basis of the assumption

that they are "just in it for the money". Schofield suggests that developing a sense of family identity can help to counter these experiences of stigmatisation by giving family members a sense of pride in their identification. For foster children this sense of pride may often be evidenced in their desire to identify foster carers as their primary family, or to claim foster carers as their own, as we can see in the following two extracts:

Jude: *Everyone just knows me as his mum unless it is someone I know or I chose to discuss it with. When I phone up the support agency I say I am the children's carer just so they can differentiate whether I am the birth mother or carer, but other than that I am his mum.*

Interviewer: *And did you ask to be called mum?*

Jude: *No it is just something he did. It seemed really important to him to be able to claim me as that, especially with all he had been through.*

In this extract Jude, a single heterosexual foster carer who provides long-term care to a child with a disability, talks about the claim that the child has made to her as his mother. Like many foster carers, Jude stated that being given this title was not by her provocation, but rather was something that the child had done themselves. Australian research on foster care has similarly suggested that many foster children display the need to reach out to foster carers and to name their relationship to them as significant through the allocation of names such as "mum", "dad" or "parent" (Eitzen & McIntosh, 2004). Furthermore, this research suggests that the connection symbolised through this naming must be recognised for the important healing work it does for foster children who seek to establish meaningful relationships with parental figures. Carers such as Jude thus play an important role in providing children in long-term care with the opportunity to claim significant relationships with adults as a means to recovering from previous maltreatment. In the following extract Dan, a gay foster carer raising three foster children, talks of one of his foster children's understanding of their family and their claims to Dan and his partner as parents:

Dan: *With the second child who came to live with us, the first child who we have had for 4 years said "do you want to share my two dads", even though he doesn't always call us that, which we thought was quite cute. He calls us that to other people because that is how he sees us—as his parents—even if we don't necessarily use the language of "dads" at home.*

This extract demonstrates not only the ways in which foster children understand the relationships they have with carers in long-term placements as parent-child relationships, but the capacity of foster children to "educate" other foster children about their place within a foster family. This signifies the importance of both foster carers and other foster children in generating a sense of belonging for foster children who have recently entered a placement. Such welcoming may be considered vital to the development of a sense of belonging that involves support from all family members, not solely the adults in the family.

Family Culture

One of the hallmarks of any family is the culture that it engenders. Somewhat different to family rituals, which are typically taken as referring to the specific practices that family members undertake, family culture refers to the broader beliefs or values that shape the family. Schofield (2002) suggests that, over time, foster families come to develop their own sets of values that represent the coming together of the existing beliefs that both foster children and carers bring to the family, in addition to the ones that they develop together. This sense of a shared culture further structures the narrative of family that foster carers and children hold, as demonstrated in the following two extracts.

Adam: *Recently I have really noticed some of the things that our eldest does that show our shared concern for things in the world. He will bring home his fruit peels or cores because there is nowhere to put them at school and I am like "I never actually told you to do that", so there are some values he has taken on of his own accord. I even saw him tell a guest off at our house recently for putting vegetable scraps in the bin. This person made it out like I had brainwashed him but the reality is he is old enough to have heard my views and made a decision about what the thinks about them, and then to choose whether to agree with them or not.*

In this extract Adam, a gay foster carer of two children, speaks of instances where his teenage foster child engages in behaviours that Adam himself endorses as environmentally responsible. Although, as Adam reports, other adults have considered this to be a form of "brainwashing", Adam suggests instead that these are behaviours that the child has chosen for himself, and which represent a shared view of the world within the foster family. Much like within any family, children in foster families will develop values that come from the things that their parents say, but which will always be tempered by their own perspectives on the world. Respecting the capacity of foster children to make informed decisions, and to develop family cultural practices with foster carers, is an important aspect of acknowledging the forms of

belonging that foster families engage in. In the following and final extract Mark, who cares for two teenage boys with his wife, speaks of the cultural practices that his foster children introduced into their family:

Mark: *Before the boys came to live with us they had never played sport or done anything. I am a great lover of sport but didn't want to push it down their throats. We just took them to league games and they thought they were fantastic. They also taught us about things—they exposed us to new music and interests that we hadn't been aware of before. This year they both won scholarships to a school on the basis of their sporting abilities: there were six scholarships given out and they got two.*

In this extract Mark begins by acknowledging the interests that he and his wife introduced to the children, and which subsequently became a part of their family culture. Importantly, Mark demonstrates some of the significant gains that can be made for foster children who become a part of a foster family culture and the sense of belonging it produces: in this instance the children have secured scholarships to support their education. Mark then moves on to acknowledge the interests that the children have introduced—that of music. Mark speaks of his life as being enriched through his engagement with his foster children, and that their family culture is very much informed by all of the family members, rather than simply being driven by the interests of the adults. In other findings we have suggested that foster carers are potentially uniquely placed to develop forms of non-proprietal family relations with children that move beyond a top-down model, and which instead acknowledge the skills and interests of children as active contributors to the shaping of foster families (Riggs, 2009).

Particularly when children come into care as teenagers, foster carers must engage with their existing interests, and attempt to find ways to connect and engender belonging in ways that encompass all that foster children have already experienced, including life with their birth families. Valuing the interests of foster children can help them to develop a sense of connection through having their experiences shared and validated by significant others.

Conclusions

In this paper we have examined some of the broad ways in which this sample of Australian foster carers appear to work with the children in their care to engender a sense of belonging and family. Following the work of Schofield (2002), we have emphasised four aspects of family belonging: family solidarity, family rituals, family identity and family cultures. We have explored some of the ways in which the Australian foster carers in this sample engage in these modes of belonging and the positive outcomes this produces in relation to recovery from maltreatment. As such, we have emphasised the central role that foster families can play in this recovery, and the unique configurations of foster families that potentially position them as ideal situations in which to enact alternate forms of adult-child relations.

Of course it must be acknowledged that the data reported in this paper may not be representative of the experiences of all Australian foster carers or the children in their care. Moreover, the data speak only to the experiences of foster carers engaged in long-term care provision to children not biologically related to them (who were the majority of the participants in the project), and thus do not tell us anything about the experiences of carers providing short-term care or kinship care. Nonetheless, the findings mirror those produced both within Australia and internationally on the significance of belonging and family to foster children and carers, and they also closely connect to agendas for foster care set by agencies and support organisations in the child protection sector across Australia.

As such, these findings clearly validate agendas that aim, where appropriate, to support the formation of foster families, and to recognise the role that foster carers can play in foster children's recovery from previous maltreatment. This approach is increasingly undertaken in "therapeutic foster placements" across Australia, which, through intensive intervention from health care professionals in collaboration with foster carers, attempt to provide children with spaces in which to heal from trauma (Australian Childhood Foundation, 2009). The findings presented in this paper would suggest that foster families in general may usefully be considered as playing a role in offering a therapeutic space in which children may witness models of parenting that are supportive and which offer the opportunity to belong. In this sense, foster care in Australia may be considered to have an ongoing role in meeting national child protection agendas through the work of foster carers and those who support them. Directing resources to this end would thus seem an appropriate use of child protection budgets aimed at ensuring that practices are undertaken to make the best use of available opportunities and to provide adequate support to those people working directly with children to ensure positive outcomes.

Of course it must be acknowledged that any simplistic notion of belonging to foster families for foster children will likely be confounded by a sense of multiple affinities: to birth families, to friends, to foster families and potentially also to social workers. Importantly, and as indicated in the analysis, some of the foster carers in this sample were aware of these challenges for foster children, and reported being active in their attempts at supporting foster children to integrate a range of (possibly competing) claims to belonging so as to enable them to claim a positive space in the world. This would suggest that an important aspect of future training and recruitment strategies must be a focus on how potential foster carers understand the type of belonging they offer, and how this must have the capacity to address the multiple and complex needs that many foster children will bring with them in relation to their sense of family.

In conclusion, although the findings represented here must be taken tentatively, because they do not include the voices of children, and represent only an extrapolation of understandings of belonging within foster families taken from a broader research project on motivations to care, they nonetheless highlight some of the important work being undertaken by this sample of Australian foster carers in working with children in healing from previous traumas. While this paper does not provide definitive findings on the relationship between placement in a foster family and healing, it most certainly indicates the need for future research on this topic with the aim of better understanding the role that foster families play and the services they require to enable this to occur in the best possible ways.

References

Australian Childhood Foundation. (2009). *Strategies for managing abuse related trauma.* Accessed 8 April 2009, from www.childhood.org.au/smart/

Barber, J. G., & Delfabbro, P. H. (2004). *Children in foster care.* London: Routledge.

Barber, J. G., Delfabbro, P. H., & Cooper, L. (2001). Predictors of the unsuccessful transition to foster care. *Journal of Child Psychology and Child Psychiatry, 42,* 785–790.

Colton, M., Roberts, S., & Williams, M. (2006). The recruitment and retention of family foster-carers: An international and cross-cultural analysis. *British Journal of Social Work, 36,* 1–20.

Denby, R., Rindfleisch, N., & Bean, G. (1999). Predictors of foster parents' satisfaction and intent to continue to foster. *Child Abuse and Neglect, 23,* 287–303.

Dozier, M., Stovall, K. C., Albus, K. E., & Bates, B. (2001). Attachment for infants in foster care: The role of caregiver state of mind. *Child Development, 72,* 1467–1477.

Eitzen, K., & McIntosh, J. (2004). 'Can I call you mummy?' Weighing political correctness against psychological need in foster care. *Journal of Family Studies, 10,* 273–281.

Gardner, H. (2004). Perceptions of family: Complexities introduced by foster care. *Journal of Family Studies, 10,* 170–187.

Harvey, J., & Delfabbro, P. H. (2004). Psychological resilience in disadvantaged youth: A critical review. *Australian Psychologist, 39,* 3–13.

Horwitz, S. M., Balestracci, K. M. B., & Simms, M. D. (2001). Foster care placement improves children's functioning. *Archives of Pediatric and Adolescent Medicine, 155,* 1255–1260.

O'Neill, C. (2004). 'I remember the first time I went into foster care—It's a long story . . .': Children, permanent parents, and other supportive adults talk about the experience of moving from one family to another. *Journal of Family Studies, 10,* 205–219.

Potter, J. (1996). *Representing reality: Discourse, rhetoric and social construction.* London: Sage.

Riggs, D. W. (2008). Towards a 'non-indifferent' account of child protection. *Australian Feminist Studies, 23,* 375–388.

Riggs, D. W. (2009). Developing a 'responsible' foster care praxis: Poly as a framework for examining power and propriety in family contexts. In M. Barker & D. Langdridge (Eds.), *Understanding non-monogamies* (pp. 220–255). New York: Routledge.

Riggs, D. W., & Augoustinos, M. (2009). Institutional stressors and individual strengths: Policy and practice directions for working with Australian lesbian and gay foster carers. *Practice: Social Work in Action, 21,* 77–90.

Riggs, D. W., Augoustinos, M., & Delfabbro, P. (2007). 'Basically it's a recognition issue': Validating a foster parent identity. *Family Matters, 76,* 64–69.

Riggs, D. W., & Delfabbro, P. H. (2008). Economics of care: Recognition and remuneration of foster carers. *Journal of the Association for Research on Mothering, 10,* 94–104.

Riggs, D. W., Delfabbro, P. H., & Augoustinos, M. (2008). Negotiating foster families: Identification and desire. *British Journal of Social Work, 38,* 1–47.

Riggs, D. W., King, D., Delfabbro, P. H., & Augoustinos, M. (2009). 'Children out of place': Representations of foster care in the Australia news media. *Journal of Children and Media, 3,* 112–123.

Schofield, G. (2002). The significance of a secure base: A psychosocial model of long-term foster care. *Child and Family Social Work, 7,* 259–272.

Wise, S., & Egger, S. (2009). *The looking after children outcomes data project: Final report.* Melbourne: Department of Human Services.

Critical Thinking

1. How does foster parenting help create better citizens?

2. Does placing children in stable foster families guarantee that they will develop into stable, law-abiding adults?

Acknowledgments—We begin by acknowledging the sovereignty of the Kaurna people, the First Nations people upon whose land we live in Adelaide, South Australia. This research was supported by an ARC Discovery Grant, DP0666189.

Correspondence: Dr D. W. Riggs, School of Social Work, Flinders University, GPO Box 2100, Adelaide, SA 5001, Australia. E-mail: damien.riggs@flinders.edu.au

Children of Alcoholics
Risk and Resilience

CARA E. RICE, ET AL.

In 2002, over 17 million people in the United States were estimated to suffer from alcohol abuse or alcohol dependence (NIAAA, 2006). These alcohol disorders have devastating effects on the individuals, their families, and society. It has been reported that one in four children in the United States has been exposed to alcohol abuse or dependence in the family (Grant, 2000). A 1992 survey revealed that over 28 million children in the United States lived in households with one or more adults who had an alcohol disorder at some time in their lives, while nearly 10 million children lived with adults who reported alcohol disorders in the past year (Grant, 2000). Children of alcoholics (COAs) are at increased risk for a variety of negative outcomes, including fetal alcohol syndrome, substance use disorders, conduct problems, restlessness and inattention, poor academic performance, anxiety, and depression (West & Prinz, 1987). Furthermore, children of alcoholics are more likely to be exposed to family stressors such as divorce, family conflict, parental psychopathology, and poverty, which, in turn, may contribute to their negative outcomes.

In particular, COAs show increased risk of alcoholism and other substance use disorders. Genetic factors have been identified as increasing the risk of developing substance use problems among COAs (Schuckit, 2000). However, the risk faced by COAs is best understood as resulting from the interplay of both genetic and environmental factors (McGue, Elkins, & Iacano, 2000). We will discuss the factors that influence the development of substance abuse and other negative outcomes in COAs. We will also review three models in the development of substance disorders for COAs. These models are not mutually exclusive, and all three may influence a child. We will also discuss protective factors that may decrease COAs' risk for the development of future negative outcomes.

Prenatal Risk

One pathway for increased risk among COAs is through prenatal exposure to alcohol. Fetal alcohol syndrome (FAS), which can occur if a woman drinks alcohol during pregnancy, is a condition characterized by abnormal facial features, growth retardation, and central nervous system problems. Children with FAS may have physical disabilities and problems with learning, memory, attention, problem solving, and social/behavioral problems (Bertrand et al., 2004).

Pathways of Risk for the Development of Substance Disorders

Multiple pathways have been studied in the development of substance use disorders. Three important ones are the deviance proneness model, the stress/negative affect model, and the substance use effects model (Sher, 1991). Although these models were originally proposed to explain the development of alcohol disorders among COAs, they can also be extended to a consideration of other negative outcomes.

Deviance Proneness Pathway

The deviance proneness pathway theorizes that parental substance abuse produces poor parenting, family conflict, difficult child temperament and cognitive dysfunction. Poor parenting along with conflicted family environment are thought to interact with a child's difficult temperament and cognitive dysfunctions, which raises the child's risk for school failure and for associating with peers who themselves have high levels of conduct problems. Affiliation with these antisocial peers then increases the likelihood of antisocial behavior by COAs, including substance use (Dishion, Capaldi, Spracklen, & Li, 1995). Conduct problems in childhood and later adolescence predict the development of substance use disorders in young adulthood (Chassin et al., 1999; Molina, Bukstein, & Lynch, 2002).

One component of the deviance proneness model is difficult temperament or personality. The temperament and personality traits that are associated with adolescent substance use include sensation seeking, aggression, impulsivity, and an inability to delay gratification (Gerra et al., 2004; Wills,

Windle, & Cleary, 1998). For example, 3-year-old boys observed to be distractible, restless, and impulsive were more likely to be diagnosed with alcohol dependence at the age of 21 (Caspi, Moffitt, Newman, & Silva, 1996). Importantly, these characteristics, which are associated with adolescent substance use, have also been shown to be more common among COAs and children of drug users. (e.g., Carbonneau et al., 1998). This suggests that COAs may be at risk for substance use, in part, because of their personality traits.

One in four children in the United States has been exposed to alcohol abuse or dependence in the family.

Another component of the deviance proneness model is a deficit in cognitive function. Children of alcoholics may also be at risk for substance abuse because of deficits in cognitive functioning that have been called "executive" functions. Executive functioning refers to the ability to adjust behavior to fit the demands of individual situations and executive functioning includes planning, working memory and the ability to inhibit responses (Nigg et al., 2004). COAs have demonstrated poor response inhibition (Nigg et al., 2004), and impairments in executive functioning have found to predict drinking among young adult COAs (Atyaclar, Tarter, Kirisci, & Lu, 1999).

The deviance proneness pathway also suggests that COAs may be at risk because of the poor parenting that they receive. Decreased parental monitoring of the child's behavior, inconsistent discipline, and low levels of social support from parents are associated with increased levels of adolescent substance use and conduct problems (Brody, Ge, Conger, Gibbons, Murry, Gerrard, & Simons, 2001; Wills, McNamara, Vaccaro, & Hirky, 1996). These negative parenting behaviors have been found in substance-abusing families (Chassin, Curran, Hussong, & Colder, 1996; Curran & Chassin, 1996), suggesting that alcoholic parents may engage in poor parenting practices, which may in turn place their children at risk for substance use and/or conduct problems.

Most researchers have assumed that poor parenting leads to behavior problems in children, making it the basis for many prevention and intervention programs. However, developmental researchers have suggested that child behavior also affects parenting (Bell & Chapman, 1986). For example, Stice and Barrera (1995) found that low levels of parental control and support predicted adolescent substance use. However, adolescent substance use, in turn, predicted decreases in parental control and support. Therefore, the link between parenting and adolescent conduct problems and substance use may best be thought of as a system in which parents affect children, and children affect parents.

Stress and Negative Affect Pathway

The stress and negative affect pathway suggests that parental substance abuse increases children's exposure to stressful life events such as parental job instability, familial financial difficulty, parental legal problems, etc. (Chassin et al., 1993; Sher, 1991). These potentially chronic stressors may lead to emotional distress in COAs such as depression and/or anxiety. Substance use may then be used to control this distress.

Research has shown a link between negative affect and substance use in adolescence (see Zucker, 2006, for a review). For example, depression has been found to co-occur with adolescent substance abuse (Deykin, Buka, & Zeena, 1992) and heavy alcohol use (Rohde, Lewinson, & Seely, 1996). Moreover, negative life events have been associated with adolescent substance use (Wills, Vaccaro, & McNamara, 1992). However, not all findings support a negative affect pathway to adolescent substance use problems.

One explanation for the conflicting findings is that not all adolescents with negative affect will be at risk for substance use. Rather, adolescents who suffer from negative affect may only use alcohol and drugs if they also lack good strategies to cope with their negative moods and/or if they believe that alcohol or drugs will help them cope. Therefore, helping COAs to develop coping strategies can potentially serve as an intervention. There may also be gender differences in the extent to which COAs use substance use to cope with stress and negative mood (Chassin et al., 1999).

Substance Use Effects Model

The substance use effects model focuses on individual differences in the pharmacological effects of substances. It is hypothesized that some individuals are more sensitive to the pleasurable effects of alcohol and substance use and/or less sensitive to the adverse effects. For example, Schuckit and Smith (1996) found that male COAs with extremely low levels of negative responses to alcohol were more likely be to diagnosed with alcohol abuse/dependence almost a decade later. It is possible that individuals who do not experience negative effects from drinking may lack the "natural brakes" that limit drinking behavior. Some researchers have also suggested that COAs receive greater stress reduction effects from drinking alcohol (Finn, Zeitouni, & Pihl, 1990). Thus, COAs would be expected to engage in more stress-induced drinking than non-COAs because they derive greater physiological benefit from it. It is important to note, however, that not all studies have supported this finding and more research is needed to draw concrete conclusions concerning COAs' physiological response to alcohol (see Sher, 1991, for a review).

Resilience/Protective Factors

Despite the risks presented by genetic, social, and psychological variables, not all COAs experience negative outcomes. These individuals who, despite high-risk status, manage to defeat the odds, are labeled resilient (Garmezy & Neuchterlein, 1972). Resilience has been extensively studied in a variety of populations, but resilience among COAs remains an area that needs further research (Carle & Chassin, 2004). Sher (1991) hypothesized that factors that can help protect COAs from developing alcoholism include social class, preservation of family rituals, amount of attention received from primary caregivers, family harmony during infancy, parental support, personality, self-awareness, cognitive-intellectual functioning, and coping skills.

COAs show increased risk of alcoholism and other substance use disorders.

Carle and Chassin (2004) examined competence and resilience of COAs and found a significant difference between COAs and non-COAs in competence with regards to rule-abiding and academic behaviors, but no differences in social competence. A small subset of resilient COAs demonstrated at or above average levels of academic and rule-abiding competence. These resilient COAs also had fewer internalizing symptoms and reported increased levels of positive affect than did the general COA population (Carle & Chassin, 2004). This suggests that COAs with average or above average academic and rule-abiding competence as well as low levels of internalizing symptoms and high positive affect may be resilient to the risk associated with having an alcoholic parent.

Another potential source of resilience for COAs may be the recovery of the alcoholic parent. Hussong and colleagues (2005) found support for this idea in a study of social competence in COAs. Results from this study indicated that children of recovered alcoholics demonstrated comparable levels of social competence when compared to children of nonalcoholic parents, suggesting again that not all COAs are at equivalent levels of risk.

Along with recovery of parental alcohol symptoms, previous research has also demonstrated the importance of a number of familial factors in buffering the risk associated with parental alcoholism. For example, parental social support, consistency of parental discipline, family harmony, and stability of family rituals have all been shown to protect COAs from the development of alcohol and drug use and abuse (King & Chassin, 2004; Marshal & Chassin, 2000; Stice, Barrera, & Chassin, 1993).

Although there is evidence to suggest that family factors play a protective role in children's risk for substance use and substance use disorders, there is evidence to suggest that this protection may not be equal for all children (Luthar, Cicchetti, & Becker, 2000). In other words, the protective family factor may reduce the negative effect of parental alcoholism for some children, but may lose its effectiveness at the highest levels of risk. For example, King and Chassin (2004) found that parental support reduced the negative effect of family alcoholism for children with low and average levels of impulsivity and sensation seeking, but not for children with high levels of impulsivity and sensation seeking. In other words, parental support was protective for most children, but not for those with the highest levels of risk. Similarly, Zhou, King, and Chassin (2006) found that the protective effect of family harmony was lost for those children with high levels of family alcoholism. Together these studies provide evidence that consistent and supportive parenting and family harmony are protective for many children of alcoholics, but those children at especially high risk may not benefit from these familial protective factors.

Family relationships, though clearly an important aspect of resilience in COAs, are not the only relationships that appear to contribute to positive outcomes in children of alcoholics. There is also evidence to suggest that, for older children, peer relationships may be as influential as family relationships on adolescents' decision to use substances (Mayes & Suchman, 2006). Therefore, peer relationships may also provide protection against the risk associated with having an alcoholic parent. For example, Ohannessian and Hesselbrock (1993) found that COAs with high levels of social support from friends drank at levels similar to non-COAs, indicating that friendships may also work to reduce the negative effects of parent alcoholism.

Conclusion

Although much work remains to be done in understanding both risk and resilience among COAs, the work that has been done provides important implications for preventive interventions. For example, family factors appear to protect many COAs from negative outcomes. This knowledge supports the need for family-based preventive interventions, which seek to improve both parenting practices and family relationships among families of alcoholics. As research in this area continues to uncover the complex interplay of both the genetic and environmental factors that contribute to COA risk and resilience, prevention researchers will be afforded the opportunity to design and implement interventions to assist this prevalent and heterogeneous population of children.

References

Atyaclar, S., Tarter, R.E., Kirisci, L., & Lu, S. (1999). Association between hyperactivity and executive cognitive functioning in childhood and substance use in childhood and substance use in early adolescence. *Journal of the American Academy of Child and Adolescent Psychiatry, 38,* 172–178.

Bell, R.Q., & Chapman, M. (1986). Child effects in studies using experimental or brief longitudinal approaches to socialization. *Developmental Psychology, 22,* 595–603.

Bertrand, J., Floyd, R.L., Weber, M.K., O'Connor, M., Riley, E.P., Johnson, K.A., Cohen, D.E., National Task Force on FAS/FAE. (2004). *Fetal Alcohol Syndrome: Guidelines for Referral and*

Diagnosis. Atlanta, GA: Centers for Disease Control and Prevention. Available online at www.cdc.gov/ncbddd/fas/documents/FAS_guidelines_accessible.pdf

Brody, G.H., Ge, X., Conger, R., Gibbons, F.X., Murry, V.M., Gerrard, M., & Simons, R.L. (2001). The influence of neighborhood disadvantage, collective socialization, and parenting on African American children's affiliation with deviant peers. *Child Development, 72*(4), 1,231–1,246.

Carbonneau, R., Tremblay, R.E., Vitaro, F., Dobkin, P.L., Saucier, J.F., & Pihl, R.O. (1998). Paternal alcoholism, paternal absence, and the development of problem behaviors in boys from age 6 to 12 years. *Journal of Studies on Alcohol, 59,* 387–398.

Carle, A.C., & Chassin, L. (2004) Resilience in a community sample of children of alcoholics: Its prevalence and relation to internalizing symptomatology and positive affect. *Applied Developmental Psychology, 25,* 577–595.

Caspi, A., Moffitt, T., Newman, D., & Silva, P. (1996). Behavioral observations at age 3 years predict adult psychiatric disorders. *Archives of General Psychiatry, 53,* 1,033–1,039.

Chassin, L., Curran, P., Hussong, A., & Colder, C. (1996). The relation of parent alcoholism to adolescent substance use: A longitudinal follow-up study. *Journal of Abnormal Psychology, 105,* 70–80.

Chassin, L., Pillow, D., Curran, P., Molina, B., & Barrera, M. (1993). The relation between parent alcoholism and adolescent substance use: A test of three mediating mechanisms. *Journal of Abnormal Psychology, 102,* 1–17.

Chassin, L., Pitts, S.C., DeLucia, C., & Todd, M. (1999). A longitudinal study of children of alcoholics: Predicting young adult substance use disorders, anxiety, and depression. *Journal of Abnormal Psychology, 108,* 106–118.

Curran, P.J., & Chassin, L. (1996). Longitudinal study of parenting as a protective factor for children of alcoholics. *Journal of Studies on Alcohol, 57,* 305–313.

Deykin, E.Y., Buka, S.L., & Zeena, T.H. (1992). Depressive illness among chemically dependent adolescents. *American Journal of Psychiatry, 149,* 1,341–1,347.

Dishion, T.J., Capaldi, D., Spracklen, K.M., & Li, F. (1995). Peer ecology of male adolescent drug use. *Development and Psychopathology. Special Issue: Developmental Processes in Peer Relations and Psychopathology, 7*(4), 803–824.

Finn, P., Zeitouni, N., & Pihl, R.O. (1990). Effects of alcohol on psychophysiological hyperreactivity to nonaversive and aversive stimuli in men at high risk for alcoholism. *Journal of Abnormal Psychology, 99,* 79–85.

Garmezy, N., & Neuchterlein, K. (1972). Invulnerable children: The fact and fiction of competence and disadvantage. *American Journal of Orthopsychiatry, 42,* 328–329.

Gerra, G., Angioni, L., Zaimovic, A., Moi, G., Bussandri, M., Bertacca, S., Santoro, G., Gardini, S., Caccavari, R., & Nicoli, M.A. (2004). Substance use among high-school students: Relationships with temperament, personality traits, and personal care perception. *Substance Use & Misuse, 39,* 345–367.

Grant, B.F. (2000). Estimates of U.S. children exposed to alcohol use and dependence in the family. *American Journal of Public Health, 90,* 112–115.

Hussong, A.M., Zucker, R.A., Wong, M.M., Fitzgerald, H.E., & Puttler, L.I. (2005). Social competence in children on alcoholic parents over time. *Developmental Psychology, 41,* 747–759.

King, K.M., & Chassin, L. (2004). Mediating and moderated effects of adolescent behavioral under control and parenting in the prediction of drug use disorders in emerging adulthood. *Psychology of Addictive Behaviors, 18,* 239–249.

Luthar, S.S., Cicchetti D., & Becker, B. (2000). The construct of resilience: A critical evaluation and guidelines for future work. *Child Development, 71*(3), 543–562.

Marshal, M.P., & Chassin, L. (2000). Peer influence on adolescent alcohol use: The moderating role of parental support and discipline. *Applied Developmental Science, 4,* 80–88.

Mayes, L.C., & Suchman, N.E. (2006). Developmental pathways to substance use. In D. Cicchetti & D.J. Cohen (Eds.), *Developmental Psychopathology: Vol. 3. Risk, Disorder, and Adaptation* (2nd ed., pp. 599–619). New Jersey: John Wiley & Sons.

McGue, M., Elkins, I., Iacono, W.G. (2000). Genetic and environmental influences on adolescent substance use and abuse. *American Journal of Medical Genetics, 96,* 671–677.

Molina, B.S.G., Bukstein, O.G., & Lynch, K.G. (2002). Attention-deficit/hyperactivity disorder and conduct disorder symptomatology in adolescents with alcohol use disorder. *Psychology of Addictive Behaviors, 16,* 161–164.

National Institute on Alcohol Abuse and Alcoholism. (2006). NIAAA 2001–2002 NESARC [Data File]. Accessed August 1, 2006. from http://niaaa.census. gov/index.html.

Nigg, J.T., Glass, J.M., Wong, M.M., Poon, E., Jester, J.M., Fitzgerald, H.E., Puttler, L.I., Adams, K.A., & Zucker, R.A., (2004). Neuropsychological executive functioning in children at elevated risk for alcoholism: Findings in early adolescence. *Journal of Abnormal Psychology, 113,* 302–314.

Ohannessian, C.M., & Hesselbrock, V.M. (1993). The influence of perceived social support on the relationship between family history of alcoholism and drinking behaviors. *Addiction, 88,* 1,651–1,658.

Rohde, P., Lewinson, P.M., & Seeley, J.R. (1996). Psychiatric comorbidity with problematic alcohol use in high school students. *Journal of the American Academy of Child and Adolescent Psychiatry, 35,* 101–109.

Schuckit, M.A. (2000). Genetics of the risk for alcoholism. *The American Journal on Addictions 9,* 103–112.

Schuckit, M.A., & Smith, T.L. (1996). An 8-year follow-up of 450 sons of alcoholic and control subjects. *Archives of General Psychiatry, 53*(3), 202–210.

Sher, K.J. (1991). *Children of Alcoholics: A Critical Appraisal of Theory and Research.* Chicago: University of Chicago Press.

Stice, E., & Barrera, M. (1995). A longitudinal examination of the reciprocal relations between perceived parenting and adolescents' substance use and externalizing behaviors. *Developmental Psychology, 31*(2), 322–334.

Stice, E., Barrera, M., & Chassin, L. (1993). Relation of parental support and control to adolescents' externalizing symptomatology and substance use: A longitudinal examination of curvilinear effects. *Journal of Abnormal Child Psychology, 21,* 609–629.

West, M.O., & Prinz, R.J. (1987). Parental alcoholism and childhood psychopathology. *Psychological Bulletin, 102*(2), 204–218.

Wills, T.A., McNamara, G., Vaccaro, D., & Hirky, A.E. (1996). Escalated substance use: A longitudinal grouping analysis from early to middle adolescence. *Journal of Abnormal Psychology, 105,* 166–180.

Wills, T.A., Vaccaro, D., & McNamara, G. (1992). The role of life events, family support, and competence in adolescent substance use: A test of vulnerability and protective factors. *American Journal of Community Psychology, 20,* 349–374.

Wills, T.A., Windle, M., & Cleary, S.D. (1998). Temperament and novelty seeking in adolescent substance use: Convergence of dimensions of temperament with constructs from Cloninger's theory. *Journal of Personality and Social Psychology, 74*(2), 387–406.

Zhou, Q., King, K.M., & Chassin, L. (2006). The roles of familial alcoholism and adolescent family harmony in young adults' substance dependence disorders: mediated and moderated relations. *Journal of Abnormal Psychology, 115,* 320–331.

Zucker, R.A. (2006). Alcohol use and the alcohol use disorders: A developmental-biopsychosocial systems formulation covering the life course. In D. Cicchetti & D.J. Cohen (Eds.), *Developmental Psychopathology: Vol 3. Risk, Disorder, and Adaptation* (2nd ed., pp. 620–656). New Jersey: John Wiley & Sons.

Critical Thinking

1. What are some of the prenatal risks of women who drink?
2. What is the deviance proneness pathway?
3. Describe the Stress and Negative Affect Pathway.
4. What does the Substance Use Effect Model focus on and why is it important?
5. How would you identify resilience and protective factors in children of alcoholics?

CARA E. RICE, MPH, is Project Director of the Adult and Family Development Project at Arizona State University. DANIELLE DANDREAUX, MS, is a doctoral student in applied developmental psychology at the University of New Orleans and is currently employed by the Department of Psychology at Arizona State University. ELIZABETH D. HANDLEY, MA, is a doctoral student in clinical psychology at Arizona State University. Her research and clinical training are focused on at-risk children and families. LAURIE CHASSIN, PhD, is Professor of Psychology at Arizona State University. Her research focuses on longitudinal, multigenerational studies of risk for substance use disorders and intergenerational transmission of that risk.

Preparation of this article was supported by grant AA16213 from the National Institute of Alcohol Abuse and Alcoholism to Laurie Chassin.

Impact of Family Recovery on Pre-Teens and Adolescents

VIRGINIA LEWIS, PhD AND LOIS ALLEN-BYRD, PhD

When discussing parental alcoholism, it is often assumed that the parent's entry into recovery will resolve all problems. However, our research, which examined the impact of family recovery from alcoholism, shows that rather than being a unifying force for all family members, this process is traumatic, with pre-teens and adolescents frequently becoming the "forgotten" members of the family. The effects upon these forgotten members can be explained and understood in the context of recovery stages and family types. The purpose of this article is threefold: (1) to present a very complex process called family recovery, (2) to describe its traumatic impact on pre-teens and adolescents, and (3) to provide treatment suggestions for supporting young people.

The Family Recovery Project

In 1989, Drs. Stephanie Brown and Virginia Lewis were the first researchers to study the processes of family recovery from alcoholism. This research marked a dramatic shift from understanding how alcoholism affects all family members, to identifying the dynamics of family recovery and its influence on all aspects of family and individual functioning.

There were three questions of interest to this project: 1) What happens to the family when one or both parents stop drinking? 2) Is there a normal developmental process of recovery? and 3) What allows some alcoholic families to maintain recovery while others relapse (often repeatedly)?

Methodology

The research methodology was a cross-sectional design, studying 54 volunteer families who ranged in sobriety from a few months to 18 years. The study was multi-perspective (participants' data and researchers' observations) and multi-level (tests that measured individual, dyad, and family dynamics) in order to obtain a comprehensive picture of family recovery dynamics. In addition, two types of data analysis were used—qualitative (research team analyzing video tapes to determine individual and family functioning) and quantitative (a battery of paper/pencil measures administered to each family member). (Specific information on research methodology and results can be found in Brown & Lewis, 1995, 1999; Brown, Lewis, & Liotta, 2000; Petroni, Allen-Byrd, & Lewis, 2003; Rouhbakhsh, Lewis, & Allen-Byrd, 2004.)

Due to the focus of this research, the drinking stage and its impact upon family members were studied retrospectively. Families were asked to describe the drinking years which, when combined with the data collected, provided a before and after sobriety perspective. Although painful for many, this journey into the past was necessary as family recovery cannot be fully understood without knowing what life was like, individually and systemically, during the drinking years.

Important Findings

Information from this research revealed that: a) there are normal developmental stages of recovery, b) there are different types of recovering families, and c) the early years of recovery are very traumatic. These latter two findings were surprising and clinically significant. For example, we found that the type of recovering family impacts stage development and requires different treatment approaches for both type of family and stage of recovery. The concept that the early years of recovery were traumatic came from the families' descriptions that this time was very disruptive, frightening, and dynamic. However, rather than being a negative, this "trauma" was normal, allowing for the disequilibrium and collapse of the addictive processes at the individual and system levels. In its place was a void without a map of how to navigate this necessary state. In time, the void was replaced with new knowledge, coping skills, and real-time functioning, providing the parents stayed in recovery through participation in 12-step programs, remained abstinent, and used various treatment modalities (individual, marital, familial) at different times during the recovery journey.

The early years of recovery are very traumatic.

These findings led to the emergence of two theoretical models: The Family Recovery Model and The Family Recovery Typology Model. Both models are briefly discussed below.

The Family Recovery Model

The Family Recovery Model captures the complex nature of family recovery. This complexity is critical for clinicians to understand because *rather than being the end point, abstinence is the beginning of a long and arduous journey that affects all functioning within a family.*

The Family Recovery Model has two dimensions: time and domain. Time is noted by four developmental stages: (1) drinking, (2) transition, (3) early recovery period, and (4) ongoing recovery period. Each domain is examined at three levels: the environment (family atmosphere); the system (family functioning—roles, rules, routines, communication patterns); and the individual (all family members, their emotions, cognitions, behaviors). The three domains are described in detail in *The Alcoholic Family in Recovery* (Brown & Lewis, 1999).

Developmental Recovery Stages

The following is a brief discussion of the three developmental recovery stages. See Box 1 for a summary of this information.

Transition Stage. This stage, which is characterized by the individual moving from drinking to abstinence, can last for several years during which there may be frequent shifts by the alcoholic between drinking and sobriety. The alcoholic feels completely out of control and the family system is in total chaos. The abstinence sub-stage is referred to as the "trauma of recovery"— there is the relief of sobriety and the utter terror of relapse. For example, although the adults in the family are feeling confused, frightened, and out of control, they are attempting to attend meetings and learning that recovery is possible. Their children, however, typically have no one available to them for support, information, or guidance, leaving them also feeling frightened and confused.

Early Recovery Stage. In this stage, the learning curve is steep for the parents as they are learning self-responsibility and self-care, and are slowly acquiring non-addictive lifestyles. It is a time of tremendous acquisition and application of knowledge. The alcoholic and co-alcoholic (spouse) are breaking addictive interactive patterns and learning to "separate" in order to develop their own individuality. Children and adolescents may cope by withdrawing, acting-out, "adopting" a friend's family, or attending 12-step meetings.

Ongoing Recovery Stage. In this stage, the process of recovery is becoming internalized. Recovery has become a central organizing principle (main force of focus) for the alcoholic and co-alcoholic. Life feels manageable and healthy. Problems, when they do occur, are addressed and resolved whenever possible. Parents can tolerate hearing about their children's pain and anger during the drinking and early recovery years. There is a process of healing between the parents and their now late adolescent or adult children.

Family Recovery Typology Model

The second theoretical model with significant implications for understanding recovery emerged from the finding that there were three types of families who differed dramatically from one another in terms of their recovery process. There were families who, regardless of time in recovery, seemed successful in their recovery processes while others appeared trapped in their dysfunctional patterns despite abstinence by the alcoholic.

The "successful" family style was the Type I family— both spouses were in recovery attending 12-step programs, accepting responsibility for change, and participating in therapy at different points in time. They practiced their sobriety, and recovery was a central organizing principle. The more rigid, stuck, and dysfunctional styles were found in the Type II and Type III families. In the Type II family, only one spouse was in recovery (typically the alcoholic who attended AA meetings), and the family environment and system retained the alcoholic dynamics, influences, and tensions. The alcoholic straddled two worlds: individual recovery and marital/family non-recovery. In the Type III family (of which there were only a few and the alcoholics were all males with short-term recovery), the alcoholics just quit drinking without participation in any 12-step program. Although they "looked" the best on the tests

---

Box 1
Family Recovery Model: Three Developmental Recovery Stages

	Drinking	**Transition**	**Early Recovery**	**Ongoing Recovery**
Alcoholic/Spouse:		Alcoholic moves from drinking to abstinence; may involve frequent shifts between drinking and sobriety, lasting several years.	Alcoholic and spouse are breaking addictive interactive patterns.	The family recovery process is becoming internalized.
Children:		Alcoholics' children typically have no supports, information, or guidance available at this time. They are left feeling frightened and confused.	Alcoholics' children may be left to cope by withdrawing, "acting out," "adopting" a friend's family, or attending 12-step meetings.	By this point, most children are now adult age. A possible healing process between the parents and children may begin.

(probably due to denial of any problems), they were the most rigid and stilted in the interviews.

Effects of Recovery on Pre-Teens and Adolescents

Recovery is a life-long process for families that is very complex, traumatic, and utterly confusing in the early years. One major and disheartening discovery in our research was that pre-teens and adolescents were generally ignored in recovery (similar to their experiences during the drinking years). When one or both spouses became sober and began participating in 12-step programs, they became immersed in working at staying sober. For example, they attended meetings, spoke a new language (recovery terms), and developed new relationships. They were told that their number one focus was to stay abstinent. The result was that their children lacked much-needed effective and active parenting.

For pre-teens and adolescents, the early years of recovery were often worse than the drinking years. For example, they had learned how to "function" in the alcoholic system while the alcoholic was drinking; but with recovery, everything changed with no understanding of what was happening to their family. According to several adult children in the study, they "preferred" the drinking period to early recovery for a variety of reasons. For example, they had learned how to read some of the "signs" associated with drinking, (such as the alcoholic going on a binge, the first drink of the day), and, consequently, knew how to affect damage control. Initial recovery, on the other hand, was fraught with unpredictable, traumatic and out-of-control dynamics resulting in uncertainty on the part of the adolescent on how to deal with these new issues.

The following vignettes demonstrate the impact of alcoholism and recovery on adolescents.

Vignette 1

In one family, the oldest adolescent overdosed on over-the-counter medication (an attempt to break the denial that there was a problem). As she was going to the hospital, she handed her mother a note saying, "Please go to AA, you are an alcoholic." Initially her mother refused, but in time she became sober, both parents went into recovery, and they became a Type I family. For the first few months in the Transition Stage, the teens would come home, find no food on the table, and become angry. "Our parents got their own place (e.g., AA and AlAnon) and new 'parents' (sponsors), and we lost the parents we knew." Six months later, the youngest child left home as he found the changes and abandonment too painful. When this family was interviewed, they were in the Ongoing Recovery Stage and the parents had developed close relationships to their now adult children. This closeness and healing was hard-earned, requiring individual, couple, and family therapy at different times in the recovery years.

Vignette 2

A late adolescent child in the study became very anxious during the research interview. His parents had been in recovery for years and were a Type I family in the Ongoing Recovery Stage. While they were describing the drinking years, he became aware of how much he had denied that there was a problem in the family while growing up. His mother (who kept her alcohol stash in a closet in his room) would frequently drive him to school functions while drunk—behavior he would say was normal or not his problem. He began to frequently stay over at his friend's house thus "adopting" another set of parents in his early teens. Since no one commented, he thought it was normal. As the interview progressed, he said, "This is making me question my reality checks, my perceptions of life." What had been his constructed reality of himself and his family was being shattered. This is threatening for young people launching into adulthood as it questions their identity and their ability to understand reality and their place in the family system. His father said that there was one regret in recovery—that they had abandoned their son to meetings and new people (sponsors, AA members, etc.), and did not help him understand what was happening or how important he was to his parents. This was a common regret expressed by parents who had years of recovery and the ability to reflect on the past (Brown & Lewis, 1999).

Vignette 3

This last vignette is adapted from Lewis and Allen-Byrd (in press) as a brief portrayal of what an adolescent may experience in the transition/early periods of recovery.

Kayla, the oldest child, was the identified caregiver in the family and was gratefully supported by the non-alcoholic parent. She assisted in household decisions and duties, provided parental guidance to the younger children, and had special privileges because of her elevated role and status in the family system. When the parents/family went into recovery, Kayla was, in essence, demoted because as the recovering parent became more actively involved in the family, Kayla's role and functions were no longer needed. Her sense of worth and power, her identity and understanding of her family's reality were taken away when her parents went into recovery leaving Kayla feeling resentful, angry, and bewildered. Without appropriate intervention, adolescents in situations similar to Kayla's will typically act out and/or withdraw from the family.

Treatment Suggestions to Support Young People

With the awareness that family recovery is difficult for pre-teens and adolescents, positive and therapeutic action can be taken. Practitioners can play a vital role in helping children make the transition from drinking into early family sobriety. They can educate the parents, normalize the process of recovery, and provide a safe place for young people to express their fears and feelings. Box 2 provides a number of examples.

The family type will dictate how practitioners can approach parents and provide parenting guidelines. The Type I family will be open and receptive to new ideas and knowledge as both parents are in recovery and accept responsibility for change,

Box 2
Strategies for Facilitating Adolescents' Healthy Transition from Family Drinking to Early Family Sobriety

- Work with parents on basic parenting skills, inform them of the importance of these skills for abating turmoil within the pre-teen and/or adolescent.
- Explain alcoholism and recovery to the pre-teen and adolescent in age-appropriate terms.
- Educate parents on the needs of adolescents who are developmentally leaving the family and may not be interested in becoming involved in the new recovery family structure and dynamics.
- Provide safe parental substitutes for their children.
- Provide opportunities for children and adolescents to become involved in Alateen, Alakid, Alatot.
- Let children know they are not responsible for their parents' alcoholism, recovery, or relapse.
- Encourage parents to ask for help before parent-child problems become a crisis.
- Refer pre-teens and adolescents for individual therapy with a therapist who understands the recovery process and can help the young person navigate through the bewildering and newly emerging family system. The therapy focus should be on helping teens define their own individuality; work through new roles, rules, boundaries; and find their own voice.

(Adapted from Lewis & Allen-Byrd, in press)

growth, and the hope of a healthy family. In the early years, they will require a great deal of external support in the form of sponsors, 12-step members, and therapists.

The Type II and III families present additional issues. In the Type II family, one member is in recovery while the family system remains alcoholic. There is chronic marital and environmental tension that, while unnamed, is typically experienced by the children. For example, the recovering alcoholic becomes the scapegoat as a way to explain problems and tension in the family, or splitting may occur when the adolescent aligns with one parent against the other. Initially the therapist can effect change by working at the marital level and educating the adults on family recovery (e.g., the three domains of recovery, how every member in the family is impacted by alcoholism, and the danger for relapse when only one parent is in recovery).

Hopefully, with intervention, the Type II family will transition into a Type I family. If the "non-alcoholic" parent refuses marital treatment in order to change the alcoholic system into a recovery system, he/she could join a group that educates families about family recovery.

Pre-teens and adolescents may join another group to become educated about family recovery, to find alternative ways to cope with the tensions and changes, and to acquire healthy ways to begin the separation and individuation process. Frequently, without appropriate intervention, the adolescents in Type II and Type III families become involved in the rebellious, acting-out phase of life.

The Type III families (who were typically in therapy for parent-child issues because their children were identified as the "cause" of the family problems) presented unique challenges. Although the alcoholic stopped drinking, nothing else changed. The alcoholic may have cognitive rigidity (black and white thinking), emotional intolerance, and be on a collision course with the adolescent who is acting out and/or attempting to break away from a stifling, straight jacket, family dynamic. During our research Type III families remained the least clear because of their defensive stance in the interviews and paper-pencil measures. For them, the first step is to break individual and systemic denial. The least threatening approach is an educational format where the adults can attend a parent group to learn about the impact of alcoholism on family members, even though no one is currently drinking, and learn healthier parenting skills (e.g., learn what the developmental needs of the pre-teen and adolescent are). There could be a parallel education group for pre-teens and adolescents wherein they could learn the effect alcoholism had on their lives and the toll it took on their personality development, as well as help them become empowered to alter internalized alcoholic processes and develop healthy choices for their future.

Limitations

There were several limitations to the study, noted by the following: (1) the participants were all volunteers; (2) they were educated (high school graduates to all levels of college degrees); (3) they were predominantly Caucasians (multiple attempts were made to recruit a greater ethnic diversity), and (4) small sample size. Further contribution to family recovery could be made by studying single-parent families, court-ordered families, and families from other cultures.

Summary

Family recovery from alcoholism is still an unfamiliar concept in the field of addictions and treatment (Lewis & Allen-Byrd, in press; Brown & Lewis, 1995, 1999). The more knowledgeable practitioners are in the dynamics of recovery, the more effective they will be in helping families and their children move through the normal developmental processes of recovery and launching young people into healthy adulthood.

Practitioners are on the front lines providing vital and appropriate treatment plans and referrals for recovering families with children. Their understanding of the normal processes in the stages of recovery and the knowledge of the different types of families can assist them in creating more successful interventions while minimizing family relapses and preventing adolescents from acting out or withdrawing. Pre-teens and adolescents need a voice and therapists can provide a safe and knowledgeable format for them to be heard and to help guide them through the bewildering times of adolescence in general, and in family systems of recovery, in particular.

References

Brown, S. (1985). *Treating the Alcoholic: A Developmental Model of Recovery.* New York: Wiley.

Brown, S., & Lewis, V. (1995). The alcoholic family: A developmental model of recovery. In S. Brown (Ed.), *Treating Alcoholism* (pp. 279–315). San Francisco: Jossey-Bass.

Brown, S., & Lewis, V. (1999). *The Alcoholic Family in Recovery: A Developmental Model.* New York: Guilford Press.

Brown, S., Lewis, V., & Liotta, A. (2000). *The Family Recovery Guide.* Oakland, CA: New Harbinger Publications.

Lewis, V., & Allen-Byrd, L. (2001). Family recovery typology: A new theoretical model. *Alcoholism Treatment Quarterly, 19*(3), 1–17.

Lewis, V., & Allen-Byrd, L. (in press). Coping strategies for the stages of family recovery. *Alcoholism Treatment Quarterly,* special edition.

Lewis, V., Allen-Byrd, L., & Rouhbakhsh, P. (2004). Understanding successful family recovery: Two models. *Journal of Systemic Therapies, 23*(4), 39–51.

Petroni, D., Allen-Byrd, L., & Lewis, V. M. (2003). Indicators of the alcohol recovery process: Critical items from Koss-Butcher and Lachan-Wrobel analysis of the MMPI-2. *Alcoholism Treatment Quarterly, 21*(2), 41–56.

Rouhbakhsh, P., Lewis, V., & Allen-Byrd, L. (2004). Recovering alcoholic families: When normal is not normal and when is not normal healthy. *Alcoholism Treatment Quarterly, 22*(2), 35–53.

Critical Thinking

1. What are some of the differences between adolescents with substance abuse problems and adults?

2. Looking back on the three vignettes, what would be some advice for the families coping with substance abuse?

3. List some of the important concepts in the article that you feel are essential for therapist to know and explain why you feel they are important.

4. From a research perspective, what do you think about the limitations mentioned and would the recommendations fit other cultures?

VIRGINIA LEWIS, PhD, is co-founder and co-director of the Family Recovery Project and a Senior Research Fellow at the Mental Research Institute (MRI) in Palo Alto, California. **LOIS ALLEN-BYRD,** PhD, is a Research Associate at MRI. Dr. Lewis has co-authored two books on family recovery and both she and Dr. Allen-Byrd have published numerous articles on the subject.

From *The Prevention Researcher,* November 2006, pp. 14–17. Copyright © 2006 by Integrated Research Services, Inc. Reprinted by permission. www.tpronline.com

Why Do They Cheat and Lie?

There are "plenty of excuses made by lots of men after they have had to come clean about their affairs."

Ish Major

I love her. . . . I'm just not in love with her anymore. I'm just not attracted to her any longer. We've lost the spark in our marriage. We lost the connection between us. It was just sex: it didn't mean anything. I was selfish; I didn't think.

These are all-too-common excuses made in the aftermath of an affair—plenty of excuses made by lots of men after they have had to come clean about their affairs. I say "their" affairs because typically it is just that—theirs. Their wants take priority over their wives'. Their needs come first and the needs of the family second. So, is that it? Can we simply chalk it all up to boys being boys? Well, just as there are two people in that relationship, my guess is that there are two very different sides to this cheating story. Let us take a closer look and see exactly who is driving this runaway train.

The overwhelming majority of women in the country say that their absolute biggest fear in a relationship is being cheated on—a fact which makes the actual number of couples who are affected by affairs even more startling. Cheating seems to be a growing trend these days. Studies consistently show that close to 60% of married men cheat. The numbers only are slightly lower for women. Here is an interesting question: "Would you have an affair if you knew you would never get caught?" When married couples were asked this, the numbers balloon to a whopping 80% of both men and women saying yes.

Why is this happening? We really need to take a closer look at the urges and impulses driving this growing trend. I have spoken with thousands of men (single and married) from around the country. Some were card-carrying members of the Cheater's Club: others simply had requested a brochure and were going to "think about it." They give lots of different reasons for their behavior, and have many complaints about their women. Some fair; most not so much. In sifting through and thinking about what they

said, I have been able to distill their reasons down to two simple rationales: men cheat when they feel that their woman does not need them or that they cannot satisfy her. That is it. Most of a man's wandering comes because he is not secure in one or both of these two concepts. However, this does not account for all cheating behavior. Keep in mind, there always will be that select group of immature guys who still tend to feed their egos by driving up the numbers of their sexual conquests. Most mature and/or married men have moved past this stage.

Now, let us examine some of the specific complaints that lead to cheating. One of the most common is that passion has left the marriage. That is to say there is no spontaneity. Men complain that the sex feels routine and mechanical—as if it were a chore on their wives "to do" list or an obligation she had to fulfill. This left the guys feeling less than desirable and, at times, rejected.

A study by iVillage bears out this truth. It found that 63% of married women said they would prefer to catch up on some sleep, watch a movie, or read a book rather than have sex with their spouse. The study goes on to show that 80% of these women report their sex lives as predictable. What is so very interesting here is that the overwhelming majority reports being either extremely or very happy with that predictability. This is in direct opposition to what men feel. This simple fact speaks to the heart of the differences in how men and women think.

Men hate predictability in this arena. They want fun, sparks, spontaneous diesel fuel combustion (or at least an acceptable flex fuel alternative). This goes to the genetic roots of a man. Men are strongly solutions oriented and goal-driven. Men traditionally are hunters and gatherers; they need to explore. Men love a challenge and have a need to conquer. They love to enjoy the spoils of victory—or even the agony of defeat. Most men feel like the wind is taken out of their sails when the end is a foregone conclusion or predictable. Having a conversation about this with your partner is hard. It requires the use of carefully selected words to express your emotions.

It is much easier to seek a challenge elsewhere with someone more spontaneous—someone less predictable, usually meaning less stable and more needy. Remember, guys need to be needed. This is the path that often leads to all air city. That brings us to an interesting point—have you ever noticed the huge difference in the types of people who men and women cheat with? Simply put, men cheat down; women cheat across. Typically, it is not a question of how attractive the woman is. The most insanely beautiful women get cheated on all the time. I often tell people that for every beautiful woman in the world there is at least one guy (ex-boyfriend or former husband) who wants absolutely nothing more to do with her.

It goes back to the question of why men and women cheat and whom they cheat with. If you notice, women rarely cheat with a man who is "less than" the man she already has. He usually is a person of similar or more means, attractiveness, and temperament. Remember, women like routine. Women want as little disruption as possible in their lifestyle in the event their current relationship must end and a new one begins. Women cheat with the idea that the next man will be able to meet her needs better than, or at least just as good as, her current guy.

Men, however, cheat for entirely different reasons. Men cheat for sex . . . usually. It also can be for the emotional gains of attention and adoration—to feel important or wanted again. If you notice, when men cheat, it almost never is with a woman who is as attractive as the one he currently has, or as emotionally and financially stable. For a man, cheating is not about transitioning smoothly to anything, because most men have no intention of ever seriously committing to the women they cheat with. Cheating for men is about meeting a need—period. Once that need is met, he will be able to return home and focus on his girlfriend or wife and family.

Men are extremely adept at compartmentalizing emotions and desires and placing them on a tidy little shelf somewhere in their brain. Sex is just one of those desires. Once the need is met, men no longer have to think about it. Remember, men are goal-driven. Once they find a solution to that problem, they move on. For recent proof, look at Tiger Woods, Jesse James, Gov. Mark Sanford, Sen. John Edwards, and NBA star Tony Parker. All are men of stature, means, and intelligence, and all cheated down.

The second most common complaint men who cheat have is that they just are not attracted to their lady anymore. They report a definite lack of sexual desire. In all fairness, all of us are physically affected by the passing of time, not just women. It is natural but, for men, it is a huge deal because of how men think. Men think in pictures; women in words. Men process the world visually, women through an emotional process. As men get used to what they are seeing, the "newness" of it tends to wear off. That is to say they get less and less excited about seeing it. It becomes just another routine. This is one of the reasons why the number of affairs and divorces tends to spike at the five- to seven-year time frame. Another spike in affairs that is related to the visual aspect of men comes after their lady gives birth—specifically, after witnessing their lady give birth. At that time, a man's visual image of his woman often changes from that of a sexual being to a maternal figure. The point is not lost on men that most women will think this is not only irrational, but totally unfair, and they probably are right.

Okay, that explains the why and how men cheat. Let us see what we can do to prevent this from happening. There are three common mistakes women make when choosing an individual who cheats. The first is not paying attention to their guy's history. Leopards do not change their spots and neither do men. All men have a specific type of woman they like. It usually is abundantly obvious just by looking. Remember, guys are highly visual. Simply put, we like what we like and that usually does not change. Tastes evolve as we mature, but the undercurrent of who a person is and what he really likes remains constant. Women should examine closely the types of women he has dated or married before them. If, as a woman, you feel you are a great departure from that, then you have to be willing to ask yourself the questions: why me and why now? The best predictor of future behavior is past behavior. It only is a matter of time before a man goes back to what he likes. If the images of what he liked bear little resemblance to the images of what he is supposed to be liking now . . . well, that is a recipe for disaster.

The second mistake is failing to pay attention to a man's actions. Men tell by doing, not by saying. I warn women all the time, "Believe all of what men do and nothing of what they say." If a man's actions are matching up with what he is telling you, then it is okay to believe him and proceed accordingly in the relationship. The moment a woman says, "I just do not know where he is coming from sometimes" means his actions and words are not matching up and he is hiding something from her. Her job is to figure out what that is.

The last mistake is one of compromise. Do not compromise on what you really want. What happens a lot of times is that a woman will meet a guy and he may not have all of the characteristics she is looking for but, if one or two are there, she will proceed. Especially if those one or two characteristics are overwhelmingly positive, women oftentimes will overlook the rest that is lacking.

Again, it goes to a woman's nurturing nature. Women want to help us grow and fill in our blanks as men. They hope in the end that we will be appreciative of them for it. It also feeds her ego as well because, if she can do this for you, that means she is a very special woman.

However, things often do not work out that way. So, I encourage women to stick to their guns early and be realistic about what they really want in a man and a relationship. Make sure you have a list of "must haves" and "would be nice to have" when it comes to selecting a partner. Anyone who is not coming pretty close to what you must have should be passed over. Oftentimes we compromise and, while the relationship may stay together long term, the question becomes: how happy are you, really? There are a lot of unhappily married people out there, and very often the reason for that unhappiness is they sacrificed things that were really important to them in a mate early on—only to realize that the partner did not change later. In addition to those three common mistakes, I advise women to pay attention to their intuition. If you feel like he is cheating, then, in some way, shape, or form, he probably is. Also, do not ignore the obvious signs. When a man shows you a lack of attention, cannot account for certain periods of time, is tardy on a regular basis, or displays secretive behavior, your suspicion index has to be going up.

Happily Ever After?

So, does happily ever after really exist? My answer is: absolutely. I have interviewed hundreds of happily married couples around the country, and they all give four keys to finding happily ever after. The first is transparency. Every successful couple—which I am measuring in number of years together and happy—says they began their relationship with transparency.

Webster defines it as: fine or sheer enough to be seen through: free from pretense or deceit; easily detected or seen through; readily understood; characterized by visibility or accessibility of information. The Latin root means "to show oneself."

Think about that: How many of us are confident enough in ourselves to show ourselves completely? How many of us trust our partners enough that they will still like us once we do? Obviously, happily ever after is not for the faint of heart. It is something achieved only by those with strength, courage, and audacity, as well as those who trust—and not necessarily trust in your partner. I am talking about trust in yourself. In order to be transparent (truly and completely) you have to believe that

who you are is enough. You have to know what you really love about yourself and be comfortable enough with all of those parts of you so that you may show them to another person—in their entirety. You cannot worry about them being turned off or judging you. If they are anything less than turned on or accepting or approving or thinking how strong you must be for being able to share, then this probably is not the person who you were going to achieve "happily ever after" with anyway.

The second key is that couples who are happily married did their homework concerning their prospective partner. In particular, they each took a good look at the others' past relationships and asked themselves an honest question: does he or she liking me make sense? They each looked at the particular type of person their mate usually gravitated towards, length of each other's past relationships, reasons those relationships did not last, and how exactly those relationships came to an end. (Was it a good, as in mature, breakup or not?)

Now that is a lot of information to gather and sift through, and I am by no means suggesting you play chief detective and interrogate the heck out of your partner. The tip is you should not have to. This information is readily available when your partner is . . . transparent. Here is another tip: if this information is not being made accessible to you, why not? What is he or she hiding, or ashamed of? There can be no secrets early on if you do not want there to be any secrets later on.

The third key is being committed to setting dates. Happy couples are able to agree on a specific time frame for their relationship milestones. When should we get engaged? When should we get married? When should we have children? If one person compromises too much in one of these areas, it is not unusual for resentment to build. Festering resentment absolutely will destroy a relationship.

The last key is the ability to set goals for the relationship—not just the big picture goals of staying together and happy, but smaller and more immediate ones as well. One woman who had been married for 67 years said she and her husband each set an individual goal of doing something every day to make the other person happy. The hidden pearl of wisdom in what she said were the words "every day." It is a daily work habit. That is the only thing that should become routine about your relationships. People successful in business have a daily work habit as do successful athletes and entertainers. Successful couples are no different. It takes a daily commitment and recommitment if you want to achieve that long-term goal of staying together, forever in love.

Men who cheat often have lots of different excuses to justify what they did. Yet, men who do not cheat only have one reason why not. It typically involves the word "adore," as in "I adore my wife." They go on to explain how simply awful they feel to see their wife have one moment of pain and how they could not imagine being the person responsible for causing her such pain.

Maybe it is just that simple. Maybe instead of focusing on the many things that can go wrong, we should focus on the one thing that is very right—love. It is the reason you chose each other in the beginning. It should be enough of a reason to stay together and stay happy in the end.

Critical Thinking

1. Why does someone who cheats lie about it?
2. What would you do if your partner cheated?
3. Would you feel the need to lie if you were caught cheating on your partner?
4. Can and how do relationships survive cheating?

ISH MAJOR is a psychiatrist and author of *Little White Whys: A Woman's Guide Through the Lies Men Tell and Why,* from which this article is excerpted.

Love but Don't Touch

Emotional infidelity is intense but invisible, erotic but unconsummated. Such delicious paradoxes make it every bit as dangerous as adultery.

MARK TEICH

She was the first girl Brendan ever kissed, the first he made love with, the first he truly loved. They'd lost their virginity together on a magical trip to Amsterdam. He felt they were soul mates and believed that their bond would never be severed. But she had suddenly broken up with him after eight months, and they lost touch until 2000, when he paid her a visit. Their exchange was unremarkable, but they traded e-mail addresses. At first, they merely sent an occasional message, chatting superficially. But the correspondence became more frequent and personal. It was easy—she was sunnier and more passionate than Brendan's wife, Lauren, who was bleary-eyed from caring for their sick son while working full-time to pay the bills. Without the burden of these responsibilities, his old love divided her days between visits to the gym and e-mails to him. Yes, she had a husband: but while Brendan was "witty and creative," she said in her lustful notes, her husband was a drone. What a high it was for Brendan to see himself through this complimentary lens after Lauren's withering view of him: hypercritical, angry, money-obsessed.

At the same time, Lauren found herself drawn to a love interest with roots in *her* past: a man she met through a website devoted to the neighborhood she grew up in. In short order, Lauren was deeply involved in an Internet relationship that kept her mood aloft throughout the day. In every way, her new companion was superior: While Brendan had set out to be a novelist, he now worked for a little health newsletter. It was Lauren's online friend, a research biologist, who spent his free hours writing a novel, and what a gifted writer he was! While Brendan talked about bills past due and criticized everything from her clothes to her weight, her online partner was fascinated by her thoughts and the minutiae of her day. He abounded in the type of wit and imagination Brendan had lacked for years. Sure, her online partner was married, too; he described his wife as remote and inaccessible—a scientist like himself, but so involved with her work that she left the child-rearing to him and almost never came home.

The New Anatomy of Infidelity

Brendan and Lauren never slept with or even touched their affair partners. Yet their emotional involvements were so all-consuming, so blinding, that they almost blew off their marriage for the disembodied fantasies of online love. Infidelity, of course, is older than the Bible. And garden-variety cheating has been on the rise for 25 years, ever since women swelled the workforce. But now, infidelity has taken a dangerous—and often profoundly stirring—new turn that psychologists call the biggest threat marriage has ever faced. Characterized by deep emotional closeness, the secret, sexually charged (but unconsummated) friendships at issue build almost imperceptibly until they surpass in importance the relationship with a spouse. Emotional involvement outside of marriage has always been intoxicating, as fictional heroines such as Anna Karenina and Emma Bovary attest. But in the age of the Internet and the egalitarian office, these relationships have become far more accessible than ever before.

The late psychologist Shirley Glass identified the trend in her 2003 book, *Not Just Friends.* "The new infidelity is between people who unwittingly form deep, passionate connections before realizing they've crossed the line from platonic friendship into romantic love," Glass wrote. Eighty-two percent of the unfaithful partners she'd counseled, she said, had had an affair with someone who was at first "just a friend." What's more, she found 55 to 65 percent of men and women alike had participated in relationships she considered *emotionall*y unfaithful—secret, sexually energized and more emotionally open than the relationship with the spouse.

Glass cited the workplace as the new minefield for marriage; 50 percent of unfaithful women and 62 percent of unfaithful men she treated were involved with someone from work. And the office has only grown more tantalizing, with women now having affairs at virtually the same rate as men. Factor in the explosive power of the Internet, and it's clear that infidelity has become an omnipresent threat. No research exists on how many affairs are happening online, but experts say they're rampant—more common than work affairs and multiplying fast.

> You go on the Internet and ask, 'Whatever happened to so and so?' Then you find him. As soon as you do, all of those raw emotions flood back.

The Slippery Slope

An emotional affair can threaten any marriage—not just those already struggling or in disrepair.

"No one's immune," says Peggy Vaughan, author of *The Monogamy Myth* and creator of the website, DearPeggy.com, where surveys and discussion reflect the zeitgeist. Although those with troubled marriages are especially susceptible, a surprising number of people with solid relationships respond to the novelty and are swept away as well.

Because it is so insidious, its boundaries so fuzzy, the emotional affair's challenge to marriage is initially hard to detect. It might seem natural to discuss personal concerns with an Internet buddy or respond to an office mate having trouble with a spouse. But slowly, imperceptibly, there's an "emotional switch." The friends have built a bubble of secrecy around their relationship and shifted allegiance from their marriage partners to the affair.

Web of Deceit

The perfect petri dish for secret, sexually charged relationships is, of course, the Internet. The new American affair can take place right in the family room; within feet of children and an unsuspecting spouse, the unfaithful can swap sex talk and let emotions run amok.

Often, it's the anonymity of online encounters that invites emotional disclosure, says Israeli philosopher Aaron Ben-Ze'ev, president of the University of Haifa and author of *Love Online*. "Like strangers on a train who confess everything to an anonymous seatmate, people meeting online reveal what they might never tell a real-world partner. When people reveal so much, there is great intimacy." But the revelations are selective: Without chores to do or children to tend, the friends relate with less interference from practical constraints, allowing fantasy to take hold. Over the Internet, adds Ben-Ze'ev, the power of imagination is especially profound.

In fact, says MIT psychologist Sherry Turkle, author of *Life on the Screen: Identity in the Age of the Internet*, it's particularly what's *withheld*—the "low bandwidth" of the information online partners share—that makes these relationships so fantasy-rich and intense. She compares the phenomenon to that of transference in psychotherapy—where patients, knowing little about their therapists, invest them with the qualities they want and need. Similarly, the illicit partner is always partly a fantasy, inevitably seen as wittier, warmer and sexier than the spouse.

So is online love real? "It has all the elements of real love," says Ben-Ze'ev: obsessive thoughts of the lover, an urgent need to be together and the feeling that the new partner is the most

Are You an Emotional Cheat? 7 Telltale Signs

Ever since Scarlett O'Hara flirted in front of Rhett Butler, the jury has been out on extramarital friendships that are sensual, even intimate, yet don't cross the line to actual sex. With emotional affairs so prevalent, psychologists studying the issue have finally drawn some lines in the sand. You may be emotionally unfaithful, they say, if you:

- Have a special confidante at the office, someone receptive to feelings and fears you can't discuss with your partner or spouse.
- Share personal information and negative feelings about your primary relationship with a "special friend."
- Meet a friend of the opposite sex for dinner and go back to his or her place to discuss your primary relationship over a drink, never calling your partner and finally arriving home at 3 A.M.
- Humiliate your partner in front of others, suggesting he or she is a loser or inadequate sexually.
- Have the energy to tell your stories only once, and decide to save the juiciest for an office or Internet friend of the opposite sex.
- Hook up with an old boyfriend or girlfriend at a high school reunion and, feeling the old spark, decide to keep in contact by e-mail.
- Keep secret, password-protected Internet accounts, "just in case," or become incensed if your partner inadvertently glances at your "private things."

wonderful person on earth. You experience the same chemical rush that people get when they fall in love.

"But the chemicals don't last, and then we learn how difficult it is to remain attached to a partner in a meaningful way," points out Connecticut psychologist Janis Abrahams Spring, author of *After the Affair*.

Blasts from the Past

People may be exceptionally vulnerable to affairs when they reconnect with someone from their past, for whom they may have long harbored feelings. "It's very common online," says Vaughan. "You go on the Internet, and the first thing you say to yourself is, 'What happened to so and so?' Then you go find them."

Lorraine and Sam had been high school friends during the Sixties, and even camped out together at Woodstock in 1969. In love with Sam but "awed by his brilliance," Lorraine remained too shy to confess. Then he went off to the University of Chicago while she stayed in New Jersey. She married and had a family, but the idea of Sam still smoldered: If only she had admitted her love!

One day she Googled him and located him in Chicago—and they began to correspond by e-mail. He was a partner in a law firm, had a physician wife and coached his daughter's

Inoculating Your Relationship

The biggest mistake couples make is taking monogamy for granted. Instead, they should take affairs for granted and protect themselves by heading infidelity off at the pass.

As part of a proactive approach, psychologist Barry McCarthy suggests couples discuss the importance of fidelity from the outset, identifying the type of situation that would put each at greatest risk. Is drinking on a business trip your downfall, or the novelty of an exotic individual from a far-off locale? Whatever your weakness, work together to make sure you help each other walk past it.

As for Internet relationships, Peggy Vaughan says the safest way to protect the primary relationship is to "make sure that no online interactions are secret. This means having your partner agree that neither of you will say anything to someone online that you aren't willing for the other one to read. If they resist and invoke privacy rights," she adds, "it is probably because they already have something to hide."

Miami Beach psychologist M. Gary Neuman recommends that in addition to setting limits, you actively build the bond with your partner every day. Among the protective strategies he suggests are exchanging "five daily touch points," or emotional strokes, ranging from bringing your partner a cup of tea to a kiss and hug. He also suggests that partners talk for 40 minutes, uninterrupted, four times a week and go on a weekly date. "It's so easy," Neuman says, "to forget why we fell in love."

—MT

Little League team. "Originally I e-mailed just to say, 'hi,'" she explains. But after a few friendly notes, Sam sent a confession. He'd always been in love with her. But her beauty had daunted him, so he'd settled for a plain, practical woman—his wife—instead. E-mails and then phone calls between Lorraine and Sam soon became constant, whipping both of them into a frenzy of heat and remorse. "I can't stop thinking about you. I'm obsessed," one of Sam's e-mails said. But Sam could never get away, never meet face-to-face. "I feel so guilty," he confessed.

That's when Lorraine stopped sending e-mails or taking his calls. "He was a coward," she says, adding that he disappointed her even more by "begging to continue the affair over the phone."

What kind of person chooses to remain immersed in fantasy? It could be someone who "compartmentalizes the two relationships," psychologist Janis Abrahms Spring suggests. "The person may not want to replace the marriage partner, but may want that extra high."

A woman may languish for years in the throes of her "special friendship," while her male counterpart considers it a nice addition to his life.

Women in Love

Frank Pittman, author of *Private Lies,* says that Lorraine lucked out. If she's like most of those involved in Internet affairs, "the face-to-face meeting would have killed it." And if she'd run off with Sam, it probably would have been far worse. "In the history of these crazy romantic affairs, when people throw everything away for a fantasy, the success rate of the new relationship is very low," he explains.

But Lorraine was just acting true to her gender. It is the woman who typically pushes the relationship from friendship to love, from virtual to actual, says Pittman. It's the woman who gets so emotionally involved she sees the affair as a possible replacement for her marriage—even if her marriage is good—and wants to test that out.

American University professor of psychology and affair expert Barry McCarthy explains that for men, "most affairs are high opportunity and low involvement. For women, an affair is more emotional. President Clinton and Monica Lewinsky are the prototypes," he says.

How does this translate to emotional infidelity, where opportunity may be thwarted but emotion reigns supreme? Some men have begun following female patterns, placing more emphasis on emotion than in the past, while women are increasingly open to sex, especially as they achieve more financial independence and have less to fear from divorce.

Even so, says Peggy Vaughan, women are usually far more involved in these relationships than men. A woman may languish for years in the throes of her "special friendship," while her male counterpart considers it a nice addition to the life he already has. As a result, men and women involved in emotional dalliances often see the same affair in different ways. The woman will see her soul mate, and the man will be having fun. Sometimes, says Ben-Ze'ev, a woman will feel totally invested in an affair, but her partner will be conducting two or even four such affairs at once. (The pattern holds for consummated affairs, too.)

For women, the dangers are great. When an emotional affair results in sex, the man's interest usually cools instantly, says Pittman. Meanwhile, husbands are less forgiving than wives, making it more likely for a woman caught up in such an entanglement to be slammed with divorce.

Total Transparency?

With easy access to emotional relationships so powerful they pass for love, how can we keep our primary relationships intact? Psychotherapist M. Gary Neuman of Miami Beach, author of *Emotional Infidelity,* draws a hard line, advocating a rigorous affair-avoidance strategy that includes such strictures as refusing to dance or even eat lunch with a member of the opposite sex. Vaughan suggests we put transparency in our Web dealings—no secret e-mail accounts or correspondence a partner wouldn't be welcome to see.

Others say such prescriptives may be extreme. "Some Internet relationships are playful," Turkle comments. "People may take on different identities or express different aspects

After Infidelity: The Road Back

An emotional affair can deliver a body blow to a marriage, but it rarely results in divorce. Instead, couples can navigate recovery to make their union stronger than before.

The first step in recovery, says psychologist Barry McCarthy, is honesty. "It is secrecy that enables affairs to thrive. The cover-up, for most people, is worse than the actual infidelity," he says. "So it's only by putting everything on the table that you'll be able to move on."

"The involved partner must be honest about all aspects of the affair," says author Peggy Vaughan. Moving on too fast usually backfires, leaving the injured party reeling and the problem unresolved. "Many people believe that too much discussion just reopens the wound; but, in fact, the wound needs to be exposed to the light of day so that it can heal." The involved partner must answer questions and soothe the injured partner for as long as that person needs.

Psychologist Janis Abrahms Spring says the ultimate goal is restoring trust and suggests couples make a list of the trust-enhancing behaviors that will help them heal. Both partners may need compassion for their feelings, she says, but "the hurt partner shoulders a disproportionate share of the burden of recovery and may require some sacrificial gifts to redress the injury caused." These may range from a request that the unfaithful partner change jobs to avoid contact with the "special friend" to access to that partner's e-mail account.

McCarthy, meanwhile, emphasizes that sexual intimacy should resume as soon as possible, as part of the effort to restore closeness and trust.

"In the course of an emotional affair, you open the window to your affair partner and wall off your spouse," McCarthy says. "To repair the marriage, you must open your windows to your partner and wall off the affair."

—MT

of self; an introvert can play at extroversion, a man at being a woman." The experience may be transformative or casual. "Someone may want just a chess partner, and the technology allows for that."

But if you're going to permit some leeway in the context of your marriage, where do you draw the line? "It's a slippery slope," says Ben-Ze'ev. "You may set limits with your spouse—no phone contact, don't take it off the screen. But people can break the deal. It is a profound human characteristic that sometimes we cross the line."

At best, notes Turkle, a serious emotional affair can alert you to problems in the primary relationship. The injured partner can view it as "a wake-up call" that needs are not being met.

It was perhaps no more than the glimmer of that alarm that enabled Brendan and Lauren to navigate back home. For both, that happened when fantasy clashed with reality—especially when they needed to pull together and care for their sick son. Brendan told Lauren he wanted to take some time to "visit his dad," when his intent was to see his old girlfriend. "I'm so exhausted. Please don't go," Lauren had said, finally asking for help. Using the excuse of a book deadline, she soon began answering e-mails from her online partner only sporadically, then hardly at all.

The illicit partner is always partly a fantasy, she or he is inevitably seen as wittier, warmer and sexier than the spouse.

What had caused them to pull back? On one level it was the need to care for their child, but on another, it was the realization that their online affairs had been a diversion from intimacy, not intimacy itself.

"The idea of actually meeting made me feel ill. I was relieved when Lauren asked me to help at home," Brendan confesses.

"There was so much about my life I never discussed in those e-mails," says Lauren. "In the end, all that witty, arch banter was just a persona, and another job."

Critical Thinking

1. Do you believe in emotional infidelity. Why or why not?
2. How would you respond if you partner was emotionally cheating?
3. If you were being emotionally unfaithful, how would you tell your partner?
4. What can partners do if emotional infidelity happens?

MARK TEICH is publications manager of the Skin Cancer Foundation.

Is This Man Cheating on His Wife?

Alexandra Alter

On a scorching July afternoon, as the temperature creeps toward 118 degrees in a quiet suburb east of Phoenix, Ric Hoogestraat sits at his computer with the blinds drawn, smoking a cigarette. While his wife, Sue, watches television in the living room, Ric chats online with what appears on the screen to be a tall, slim redhead.

He's never met the woman outside of the computer world of *Second Life,* a well-chronicled digital fantasyland with more than 8 million registered "residents" who get jobs, attend concerts, and date other users. He's never so much as spoken to her on the telephone. But their relationship has taken on curiously real dimensions. They own two dogs, pay a mortgage together, and spend hours shopping at the mall and taking long motorcycle rides. This May, when Ric, 53, needed real-life surgery, the redhead cheered him up with a private island that cost her $120,000 in the virtual world's currency, or about $480 in real-world dollars. Their bond is so strong that three months ago, Ric asked Janet Spielman, the 38-year-old Canadian woman who controls the redhead, to become his virtual wife.

The woman to whom he's legally wed is not amused. "It's really devastating," says Sue Hoogestraat, a 58-year-old export agent who married Ric just seven months ago. "You try to talk to someone or bring them a drink, and they'll be having sex with a cartoon."

While many busy people can't fathom the idea of taking on another set of commitments, especially imaginary ones, *Second Life* and other multiplayer games are complicating many lives besides the Hoogestraats.' With some 30 million people now involved worldwide, there is mounting concern that some are squandering, even damaging their real lives by obsessing over their "second" ones. According to a recent survey of 30,000 gamers, nearly 40 percent of men and 53 percent of women who play online games said their virtual friends were equal to or better than their real-life friends. More than a quarter of gamers said the emotional highlight of the past week occurred in a computer world.

A burly man with a long gray ponytail and a handlebar mustache, Ric Hoogestraat looks like the cross between a techie and the Grateful Dead fan that he is. He drives a motorcycle and wears faded black Harley-Davidson T-shirts around the house. A former college computer graphics teacher, Ric was never much of a game enthusiast before he discovered *Second Life.* But since February, he's been spending six hours a night as Dutch Hoorenbeek, his 6-foot-9, muscular, motorcycle-riding cyberself.

In the virtual world, he's a successful entrepreneur with a net worth of about $1.5 million in the site's currency, the linden, which can be purchased through the site at a rate of about 250 lindens per U.S. dollar. He owns a mall, a private beach club, a dance club, and a strip club. He has 25 employees, online persons known as avatars who are operated by other players, including a security guard, a mall concierge, and the "exotic" dancers at his club. He designs bikinis and lingerie, and sells them through his chain store, Red Headed Lovers. "Here, you're in total control," he says, moving his avatar through the mall using the arrow keys on his keyboard.

Virtual worlds like *Second Life* have fast become a testing ground for the limits of relationships, both online and off. The site's audience of more than 8 million is up from 100,000 in January 2006, though the number of active users is closer to 450,000, according to the site's parent company, Linden Lab. A typical "gamer" spends 20 to 40 hours a week in a virtual world.

Though academics have only recently begun to intensively study the social dynamics of virtual worlds, some are saying that they are astonished by how closely virtual relationships mirror real life. On a neurological level, says Byron Reeves, a Stanford University professor, players may not be distinguishing between virtual and real-life relationships. "Our brains are not specialized for 21st-century media," he says. "There's no switch that says, 'Process this differently because it's on a screen.'"

On a Saturday afternoon in July, Ric Hoogestraat decides to go to the beach. So he lights a cigarette and enters *Second Life,* becoming one of 42,752 people logged on at the time. Immediately, he gets an instant message from Tenaj Jackalope, his *Second Life* wife, saying she'll be right there.

They meet at their home, a modern-looking building that overlooks the ocean, then head to his beach club. A full-blown dance party is under way. A dozen avatars, digital representations of other live players, gyrate on the sand, twisting their hips and waving their arms. Several dance topless and some are fully nude. Dutch gets pelted with instant messages.

"What took you so long, Dutch?" a dancer asks.

"Howdy, Boss Man," an avatar named Whiskey Girl says.

Before discovering *Second Life,* Hoogestraat had bounced between places and jobs, working as an elementary schoolteacher and a ski instructor, teaching computer graphics, and spending two years on the road selling herbs and essential oils at Renaissance fairs. Along the way, he picked up a bachelor's degree and took graduate courses at both the University of Wyoming and the University of Arizona. He currently works as a call-center operator for Vangent Inc., a corporation that outsources calls for the government and private companies. He makes $14 an hour.

Hoogestraat learned about *Second Life* in February, while watching a morning news segment. His mother had just been hospitalized with pancreatic cancer—she died two weeks later—and he wanted a distraction. He was fascinated by the virtual world's freewheeling atmosphere. With his computer graphics background, he quickly learned how to build furniture and design clothing. He upgraded his avatar, buying stomach muscles and special hair that sways when he walks. Before long, Hoogestraat was spending most nights and weekends acting out his avatar's life.

When Hoogestraat was diagnosed with diabetes and a failing gallbladder a few months ago, he was homebound for five weeks. Some days, he played from a quarter to 6 in the morning until 2 in the morning, eating in front of the computer and pausing only for bathroom breaks.

During one marathon session, Hoogestraat met Tenaj (Janet spelled backward) while shopping. They became fast friends, then partners. A week later, he asked her to move into his apartment. In May, they married in a small ceremony in a garden over-looking a pond. Thirty of their avatar friends attended. "There's a huge trust between us," says Spielman, who is a divorced mother of two living in Calgary, Alberta. "We'll tell each other everything."

That intimacy hasn't spilled into real life. They never speak and have no plans to meet.

Still, Hoogestraat's real-life wife is losing patience with her husband's second life. "Everybody has their hobbies," says Sue Hoogestraat, who is dark-haired and heavy-set. "But when it's from 6 in the morning until 2 in the morning, that's not a hobby, that's your life."

The real Mrs. Hoogestraat is no stranger to online communities—she met her husband in a computer chat room three years ago. Both were divorced and had adult children from previous marriages, and Sue says she was relieved to find someone educated and adventurous after years of failed relationships. Now, as she cooks, does laundry, takes care of three dogs, and empties ash-trays around the house while her husband spends hours designing outfits for virtual strippers and creating labels for virtual coffee cups, she wonders what happened to the person she married.

One Saturday night in early June, she discovered his cyber wife. He called her over to the computer to show her an outfit he had designed. There, above the image of the redheaded model, it said "Mrs. Hoorenbeek." When she confronted him, he huffily replied that it was just a game.

Two weeks later, Sue joined an online support group for spouses of obsessive online gamers called EverQuest Widows, named after another popular online fantasy game that players call Evercrack.

"It's avalanched beyond repair," says Sharra Goddard, 30, Sue Hoogestraat's daughter. Goddard says she and her two brothers have offered to help their mother move out of the house.

Sue says she's not ready to separate though. "I'm not a monster; I can see how it fulfills parts of his life that he can no longer do because of physical limitations, because of his age. His avatar, it's him at 25," she says. "He's a good person. He's just fallen down this rabbit hole."

Ric, for his part, doesn't feel he's being unfaithful. "I tried to get her involved so we could play together," he says. "But she wasn't interested."

Early in the morning on the day after Dutch and Tanej's virtual beach party, Ric Hoogestraat is back at his computer, wearing the same Harley-Davidson T-shirt he had on the day before. Four hours after logging on, he manipulates his avatar, who is wearing cut-off denim shorts and renovating the lower level of his mall. "Sunday is my heavy-duty work day," he explains.

From the kitchen, Sue asks if he wants breakfast. Ric doesn't answer. She sets a plate of breakfast pockets on the computer console and goes into the living room to watch a dog competition on television. For two hours, he focuses intently on building a coffee shop for the mall. Two other avatars gather to watch as he builds a counter, using his cursor to resize wooden planks.

At 12:05, he's ready for a break. He changes his avatar into jeans and motorcycle chaps, and "teleports" to a place with a curvy mountain road. It's one of his favorite places for riding his Harley look-alike. The road is empty. He weaves his motorcycle across the lanes. Sunlight glints off the ocean in the distance.

Sue pauses on her way to the kitchen and glances at the screen.

"You didn't eat your breakfast," she says.

"I'm sorry, I didn't see it there," Ric responds.

Over the next five hours, he is barely aware of his physical surroundings. He adds potted palms to his cafe, goes swimming through a sunken castle off his water-front property, chats with friends at a biker clubhouse, meets a new store owner at the mall, counsels an avatar friend who had recently split up with her avatar boyfriend, and shows his wife, Tenaj, the coffee shop he's built.

By 4 P.M., he's been in *Second Life* for 10 hours, pausing only to go to the bathroom. His wrists and fingers ache from manipulating the mouse. His back hurts. Yet he feels it's worth the effort. "If I work a little harder and make it a little nicer, it's more rewarding," he says.

Sitting alone in the living room in front of the television, Sue says she worries it will be years before her husband realizes that he's traded his real life for a pixilated fantasy existence, one in which she's been replaced.

"This other life is so wonderful; it's better than real life," she says. "Nobody gets fat, nobody gets gray. The person that's left can't compete with that."

Critical Thinking

1. What are the telltale signs of a man's cheating on his wife?

2. What should the spouse and other family members (depending on their age) do to address the problem of a husband/father's cheating?

The Opt-Out Myth

E. J. GRAFF

On October 26, 2003, *The New York Times Magazine* jump-started a century-long debate about women who work. On the cover it featured "The Opt Out Revolution," Lisa Belkin's semipersonal essay, with this banner: Why don't more women get to the top? They choose not to. Inside, by telling stories about herself and eight other Princeton grads who no longer work full-time, Belkin concluded that women were just too smart to believe that ladder-climbing counted as real success.

But Belkin's "revolution"—the idea that well-educated women are fleeing their careers and choosing instead to stay home with their babies—has been touted many times before. As Joan C. Williams notes in her meticulously researched report, "Opt Out or Pushed Out? How the Press Covers Work/Family Conflict," released in October 2006 by the University of California Hastings Center for WorkLife Law, where she is the director, *The New York Times* alone has highlighted this "trend" repeatedly over the last fifty years: in 1953 (Case History of an Ex-Working Mother), 1961 (Career Women Discover Satisfactions in the Home), 1980 (Many Young Women Now Say They'd Pick Family over Career), 1998 (The Stay-at-Home Mother), and 2005 (Many Women at Elite Colleges Set Career Path to Motherhood).

And yet during the same years, the U.S. has seen steady upticks in the numbers and percentages of women, including mothers, who work for wages. Economists agree that the increase in what they dryly call "women's participation in the waged workforce" has been critical to American prosperity, demonstrably pushing up our GDP. The vast majority of contemporary families cannot get by without women's income—especially now, when upwards of 70 percent of American families with children have all adults in the work force, when 51 percent of American women live without a husband, and when many women can expect to live into their eighties and beyond.

The moms-go-home story keeps coming back, in part, because it's based on some kernels of truth. Women *do* feel forced to choose between work and family. Women *do* face a sharp conflict between cultural expectations and economic realities. The workplace is still demonstrably more hostile to mothers than to fathers. Faced with the "choice" of feeling that they've failed to be *either* good mothers or good workers, many women wish they could—or worry that they should—abandon the struggle and stay home with the kids.

The problem is that the moms-go-home storyline presents all those issues as personal rather than public—and does so in misleading ways. The stories' statistics are selective, their anecdotes about upper-echelon white women are misleading, and their "counterintuitive" narrative line parrots conventional ideas about gender roles. Thus they erase most American families' real experiences and the resulting social policy needs from view.

Here's why that matters: if journalism repeatedly frames the wrong problem, then the folks who make public policy may very well deliver the wrong solution. If women are happily choosing to stay home with their babies, that's a private decision. But it's a public policy issue if most women (and men) need to work to support their families, and if the economy needs women's skills to remain competitive. It's a public policy issue if schools, jobs, and other American institutions are structured in ways that make it frustratingly difficult, and sometimes impossible, for parents to manage both their jobs and family responsibilities.

So how can this story be killed off, once and for all? Joan Williams attempts to chloroform the moms-go-home storyline with facts. "Opt Out or Pushed Out?" should be on every news, business, and feature editor's desk. It analyzes 119 representative newspaper articles, published between 1980 and 2006, that use the opt-out storyline to discuss women leaving the workplace. While business sections regularly offer more informed coverage of workplace issues, the "opt out" trend stories get more prominent placement, becoming "the chain reaction story that flashes from the *Times* to the columnists to the evening news to the cable shows," says Caryl Rivers, a Boston University journalism professor and the author of *Selling Anxiety: How the News Media Scare Women* (April 2007).

There are a number of problems with the moms-go-home storyline. First, such articles focus excessively on a tiny proportion of American women—white, highly educated, in well-paying professional/managerial jobs. Just 8 percent of American working women fit this demographic, writes Williams. The percentage is smaller still if you're dealing only with white women who graduated from the Ivies and are married to high-earning men, as Belkin's article does. Furthermore, only 4 percent of women in their mid-to-late thirties with children have advanced degrees and are in a privileged income bracket like that of Belkin's fellow Princeton grads, according to Heather Boushey, a senior

economist with the Center for Economic and Policy Research. That group is far more likely than average women to be married when they give birth (91 percent, as opposed to 73 percent of all women), and thus to have a second income on which to survive. But because journalists and editors increasingly come from and socialize in this class, their anecdotes loom large in our personal rearview mirrors—and in our most influential publications. Such women are chastised for working by Caitlin Flanagan (a woman rich enough to stay home and have a nanny!) in *The Atlantic,* and for lacking ambition by Linda Hirshman in *The American Prospect.* But such "my-friends-and-me" coverage is an irresponsible approach to major issues being wrestled with by every American family and employer.

The stories are misleading in a second important way. Williams's report points out that "opt-out stories invariably focus on women in one particular situation: after they have 'opted out' but before any of them divorce." The women in those articles often say their skills can be taken right back onto the job. It's a sweetly optimistic notion, but studies show that, on average, professional women who come back after time away—or even after working part-time, since U.S. women working part-time earn 21 percent less per hour worked than those who work full-time—take a hefty and sustained pay cut, and a severe cut in responsibility level. Meanwhile, nearly 50 percent of American marriages end in divorce, according to the latest census figures. While numbers are lower for marriages in the professional class, divorce remains a real possibility. Williams points to Terry Martin Hekker, one of the opt-out mothers, who in 1977 published an op-ed in *The New York Times* entitled, "The Satisfactions of Housewifery and Motherhood in 'An Age of Do-Your-Own-Thing.'" In 2006, Hekker wrote—again in the *Times,* but demoted to the Sunday Style section—about having been divorced and financially abandoned: "He got to take his girlfriend to Cancun, while I got to sell my engagement ring to pay the roofer."

In other words, interview these opt-out women fifteen years later—or forty years later, when they're trying to live on skimpy retirement incomes—and you might hear a more jaundiced view of their "choices."

The opt-out stories have a more subtle, but equally serious, flaw: their premise is entirely ahistorical. Their opening lines often suggest that a generation of women is flouting feminist expectations and heading back home. At the simplest factual level, that's false. Census numbers show no increase in mothers exiting the work force, and according to Heather Boushey, the maternity leaves women do take have gotten shorter. Furthermore, college-educated women are having their children later, in their thirties—after they've established themselves on the job, rather than before. Those maternity leaves thus come in mid-career, rather than pre-career. Calling that "opting out" is misleading. As Alice Kessler-Harris, a labor historian at Columbia University, put it, "I define that as redistributing household labor to adequately take care of one's family." She adds that even while at home, most married women keep bringing in family income, as women traditionally have. Today, women with children are selling real estate, answering phone banks, or doing office work at night when the kids are in bed. Early in the twentieth century, they might have done piecework, taken in laundry, or fed the boarders. Centuries earlier, they would have been the business partners who took goods to market, kept the shop's accounts, and oversaw the adolescent labor (once called housemaids and dairymaids, now called nannies and daycare workers).

Which brings us to an even deeper historical flaw: editors and reporters forget that Belkin's generation isn't post-feminism; it's mid-feminism. Women's entrance into the waged work force has been moving in fits and starts over the past century. Earlier generations of college-educated women picked either work *or* family, work *after* family, or family *after* work; those who graduated in the 1980s and 1990s—Belkin's cohort—are the first to expect to do both at the same time. And so these women are shocked to discover that, although 1970s feminists knocked down the barrier to entering the professions in large numbers, the workplace still isn't fixed. They are standing on today's feminist frontier: the bias against mothers that remains embedded on the job, in the culture, and at home.

Given that reality, here's the biggest problem with the moms-go-home storyline: it begins and ends with women saying they are *choosing* to go home, and ignores the contradictory data sandwiched in between.

Williams establishes that "choice" is emphasized in eighty-eight of the 119 articles she surveyed. But keep reading. Soon you find that staying home wasn't these women's first choice, or even their second. Rather, every other door slammed. For instance, Belkin's prime example of someone who "chose" to stay home, Katherine Brokaw, was a high-flying lawyer until she had a child. Soon after her maternity leave, she exhausted herself working around the clock to prepare for a trial—a trial that, at the last minute, was canceled so the judge could go fishing. After her firm refused even to consider giving her "part-time" hours—forty hours now being considered part-time for high-end lawyers—she "chose" to quit.

More than a third of the articles in Williams's report cite "workplace inflexibility" as a reason mothers leave their jobs. Nearly half mention how lonely and depressed those women get when they've been downgraded to full-time nannies. Never do such articles cite decades of social science research showing that women are happier when occupying several roles; that homemakers' well-being suffers compared to that of working women; or that young adults who grew up in dual-earner families would choose the same family model for their own kids. Rarely do such articles ask how husband and wife negotiated which one of them would sacrifice a career. Only by ignoring both the women's own stories and the larger context can the moms-go-home articles keep chirping on about choice and about how such women now have "the best job in the world."

Underlying all this is a genuinely new trend that the moms-go-home stories never mention: the all-or-nothing workplace. At every income level, Americans work longer hours today than fifty years ago. Mandatory overtime for blue- and pink-collar workers, and eighty-hour expectations for full-time professional workers, deprive everyone of a reasonable family

life. Blue-collar and low-wage families increasingly work "tag-team" schedules so that someone's always home with the kids. In surveys done by the Boston College Sloan Work and Families Research Network and by the New York-based Families and Work Institute, among others, women and men increasingly say that they'd like to have more time with their families, and would give up money and advancement to do it—if doing so didn't mean sacrificing their careers entirely. Men, however, must face fierce cultural headwinds to choose such a path, while women are pushed in that direction at every turn.

Finally, the opt-out articles never acknowledge the widespread hostility toward working mothers. Researching the book I wrote for Evelyn Murphy in 2005, *Getting Even: Why Women Don't Get Paid Like Men—and What to Do About It*, I was startled by how many lawsuits were won because managers openly and publicly told women that they couldn't be hired because they were pregnant; or that having a child would hurt them; or that it was simply impossible for women to both work and raise kids. Many other women we talked with had the same experience, but chose not to ruin their lives by suing. One lawyer who'd been on the partner track told us that once she had her second child, her colleagues refused to give her work in her highly remunerative specialty, saying that she now had other priorities—even though she kept meeting her deadlines, albeit after the kids were asleep. She was denied partnership. A high-tech project manager told me that when she was pregnant in 2002, she was asked: Do you feel stupider? Her colleague wasn't being mean; he genuinely wanted to know if pregnancy's hormones had dumbed her down. Or consider the experience of Dr. Diane Fingold, an internist at Massachusetts General Hospital in Boston and an assistant professor at Harvard Medical School, where she won the 2002 Faculty Prize for Excellence in Teaching, the school's highest teaching award. Her credentials are outstanding, yet when she asked to work three-and-a-half fewer hours a week so that she could manage her family demands—"just a little flexibility for a short period in my life!"—her practice refused. She was enraged. "I thought hard about leaving medicine altogether," she said. Her husband is a successful venture capitalist whose "annual Christmas bonus is what I make in a year!"

Had Fingold left, in other words, she would have fit neatly with Belkin's hyperachievers. But she loves practicing and teaching medicine, and realized she couldn't reenter at the same level if she walked away entirely. So she moved to another practice that was willing to accommodate her part-time schedule until, in a few years, she can return to full-time. Had she chosen the Belkin course, would she have opted out—or been pushed out?

Experiences like Fingold's bear out what social scientists are finding: strong bias against mothers, especially white mothers, who work. (Recent research shows bias against African American mothers of any class who don't work, a subject that deserves an article of its own.) Consider the work being done by Shelley Correll, a Cornell sociology professor, described in an article in the March 2007 *American Journal of Sociology*. In one experiment, Correll and her colleagues asked participants to rate a management consultant. Everyone got a profile of an equally qualified consultant—except that the consultant was variously described as a woman with children, a woman without children, a man with children, and a man without children. When the consultant was a "mother," she was rated as less competent, less committed, less suitable for hiring, promotion, or training, and was offered a lower starting salary than the other three.

Here's what feminism hasn't yet changed: the American idea of mothering is left over from the 1950s, that odd moment in history when America's unrivaled economic power enabled a single breadwinner to support an entire family. Fifty years later we still have the idea that a mother, and not a father, should be available to her child at every moment. But if being a mom is a 24-hour-a-day job, and being a worker requires a similar commitment, then the two roles are mutually exclusive. A lawyer might be able to juggle the demands of many complex cases in various stages of research and negotiation, or a grocery manager might be able to juggle dozens of delivery deadlines and worker schedules—but should she have even a fleeting thought about a pediatrics appointment, she's treated as if her on-the-job reliability will evaporate. No one can escape that cultural idea, reinforced as it is by old sitcoms, movies, jokes—and by the moms-go-home storyline.

Still, if they were pushed out, why would smart, professional women insist that they chose to stay home? Because that's the most emotionally healthy course: wanting what you've got. "That's really one of the agreed-upon principles of human nature. People want their attitudes and behavior to be in sync," said Amy Cuddy, an assistant professor in the management and organizations department at Northwestern Kellogg School of Management. "People who've left promising careers to stay home with their kids aren't going to say, 'I was forced out. I really want to be there.' It gives people a sense of control that they may not actually have."

So yes, maybe some women "chose" to go home. But they didn't choose the restrictions and constrictions that made their work lives impossible. They didn't choose the cultural expectation that mothers, not fathers, are responsible for their children's doctor visits, birthday parties, piano lessons, and summer schedules. And they didn't choose the bias or earnings loss that they face if they work part-time or when they go back full time.

By offering a steady diet of common myths and ignoring the relevant facts, newspapers have helped maintain the cultural temperature for what Williams calls "the most family-hostile public policy in the Western world." On a variety of basic policies—including parental leave, family sick leave, early childhood education, national childcare standards, after school programs, and health care that's not tied to a single all-consuming job—the U.S. lags behind almost every

developed nation. How far behind? Out of 168 countries surveyed by Jody Heymann, who teaches at both the Harvard School of Public Health and McGill University, the U.S. is one of only five without mandatory paid maternity leave—along with Lesotho, Liberia, Papua New Guinea, and Swaziland. And any parent could tell you that it makes no sense to keep running schools on nineteenth century agricultural schedules, taking kids in at 7 A.M. and letting them out at 3 P.M. to milk the cows, when their parents now work until 5 or 6 P.M. Why can't twenty-first century school schedules match the twenty-first century workday?

The moms-go-home story's personal focus makes as much sense, according to Caryl Rivers, as saying, "Okay, let's build a superhighway; everybody bring one paving stone. That's how we approach family policy. We don't look at systems, just at individuals. And that's ridiculous."

Critical Thinking

1. Why do you think working women are choosing to leave the workforce and stay at home with their children?

2. How do employment policies impact the decision for these women to stay at home?

3. Do you feel it is more difficult for women to re-enter the workforce?

4. What can be done to protect women in the workforce who have children?

E. J. GRAFF is senior researcher at Brandeis University's Schuster Institute for Investigative Journalism. From "The opt-out myth: most moms have to work to make ends meet. So why does the press write only about the elite few who don't?" *Columbia Journalism Review* 45.6 (March–April 2007): 51(4).

Making Time for Family Time

Advice from early-career psychologists on how they juggle family and career.

Tori DeAngelis

Starting your psychology career is one of the most exciting—and stressful—times of your life. It's also a period when many early-career psychologists take on new personal responsibilities, such as marrying, starting families and caring for aging parents.

Pulling this off is a lot like spinning plates, and the field's expectations don't make it any easier, says Carol Williams-Nickelson, PsyD, associate executive director of the American Psychological Association of Graduate Students (APAGS), herself working at APA and raising a family.

"There's still a pretty strong undercurrent, especially for women, that career needs to come first if you want to advance," she says.

Other factors make this scenario even more complex, other early-career experts say. For some women, it's the ticking biological clock; for many men, it's changing roles in relation to family and work.

Capt. Jason Prinster, PhD, whose internship led into his current job heading the mental health clinic at the Nellis Air Force Base in North Las Vegas, reflects this attitude.

"Three years from now, my wife could be the one making more money, and I could be the one taking the kids to work and working part time," Prinster says. "I don't think my dad ever had that thought 30 years ago."

Yet to some extent, work places still stigmatize men who openly say they value family as much as work, which puts such men in a bind, Williams-Nickelson adds.

Given these complexities, it helps to get advice from people on the front lines. Early-career experts recommend that you:

- **Communicate.** It's Psych 101, but it's true: Good communication greases the wheels of family sanity, other early-career experts say. A case in point is Jay Robertson-Howell, PsyD, a psychologist at Seattle University's counseling and psychological services center who is raising two young children with his partner, veterinarian Travis Robertson-Howell, DVM. He and Travis make sure to talk not only about each other's needs, but also the needs of the family and their professional concerns, Robertson-Howell says. As time

pressures mount, it's easier to avoid hard topics: "We constantly have to remind ourselves to keep at it," he says.

- **Negotiate.** A central tenet of good communication is agreeing on the particulars of duties and schedules, other early-career psychologists say. While couples arrange these basics in different ways, it's important for both people to discuss and agree on the arrangements and be willing to tweak them as necessary, Prinster says.

Balancing work and family is a lot like spinning plates, and psychology's expectations don't make it any easier.

For instance, Prinster and his wife, Colleen, had many discussions before deciding to split their duties along fairly traditional gender lines, with Colleen staying home with their two children and Prinster bringing home the paycheck. "We talked a lot about our respective roles and made peace with that, at least while the kids are young," Prinster says. "That's really helped. I don't feel guilty working all day, because I know we've already talked about what she expects and what I expect."

- **Schedule time for your family and yourself.** Make sure to ink in family time as an explicit part of your schedules, adds Kristi Sands Van Sickle, PsyD, who is starting her career as an assistant professor at the Florida Institute of Technology and is raising a young daughter with her husband, retired business executive Paul Van Sickle.

"We carve out family time so that even if I'm really busy, we have one day on the weekend when we're all together," says Van Sickle. The two also plan regular visits with Paul's two children from a previous marriage, who live about an hour away. "It's important to put in extra effort to make sure they feel included," she says.

Schedule time for yourself, too, for exercise, hobbies or just to regroup, advises Robertson-Howell. "Sometimes we get going so fast in this society that we forget about that."

- **Trim the excess.** Just as important as good communication is a strategy many of our parents advised us to use: Boil things down to the basics, Prinster says. He and Colleen went from being a couple that pursued many individual interests before they had children, to a team that pursued their family's interests, he says.

"I work to make money to support my family, and I spend time with my wife and kids," Prinster says. "Beyond that, only the things that are really, really important get the resources." That applies to money, too: Colleen works at their children's cooperative preschool in exchange for reduced tuition, and they cut out cable TV—a sensible move, because "we don't have time for TV!" Prinster says.

- **Pick a job that makes sense.** Some early-career psychologists consciously choose jobs that may lack outward razzle-dazzle but offer reasonable hours, decent pay and good boundaries. To spend more time with his partner, David, and their young twins, Seth Williams, PsyD, left a job that expected him to be on "24/7, 365" to one with more reasonable hours and expectations.

"If the kids are sick, I can leave any time if there's nothing life-or-death hanging on it," says Williams, associate director of clinical training at the online graduate school Capella University. He got lucky with his supervisor, too: She has a family and "walks the talk" of work-family balance, he notes.

- **Get more creative.** While there's nothing wrong with traditional job trajectories, other early-career experts say it's worth thinking outside the typical career box to accommodate family needs.

Although her graduate program emphasized academic careers, Eileen Kennedy-Moore, PhD, chose to write books and have a small clinical practice instead. The combination allowed her to work and meet the needs of her four children.

"It gave me flexibility," Kennedy-Moore explains. "If a kid was sick one day, I could handle that and just work harder the next day." It also proved a smart career move: Her books have been published by major publishing houses, and she's garnered many therapy clients and speaking engagements as a result.

- **Find support.** Relying on trusted others is vital, whether it's fellow moms or dads to vent with, or relatives or babysitters who can give you breaks, Van Sickle says.

But your most important support may be your spouse, so nurture that relationship, she recommends. "Paul is my anxiety barometer," she says. "He's better at reading when I'm feeling anxious and overwhelmed than I am."

- **Put family first.** You only have one chance to raise your children, says Williams-Nickelson, who has two young daughters with her husband, psychologist and attorney David Nickelson, PsyD, JD. An avid careerist before she had children, she was overwhelmed by the strength of her feelings toward her girls and now knows they will be her top priority for a long time.

"I feel like I've given a lot to my career and to the profession, and now it's time to give to my kids," she says.

Williams-Nickelson adds that she now understands what mentors advised her in the years before she had children.

"You can have it all," they told her. "Just not all at once."

Critical Thinking

1. What are some of the ways working parents can make time for family?
2. Why is it important to put family first?
3. Identify types of resources needed for working families.
4. Does the type of work matter when measuring the amount of family time spent by parents?

Finding New Balance

A growing percentage of wives earn more than their spouse, and their families are doing just fine.

JEAN CHATZKY

Like many other families, Tara and Charles Dai found their world quaking from the recession. Eighteen months ago, Charles, a computer consultant, was laid off. With the job market so contracted, they decided he'd stay home and care for the children, ages 4 and 7.

"Now he's Mr. Mom and I'm the primary breadwinner," says Tara, 39, a health care consultant in Flemington, N.J., and developer of *Stork Tunes,* a CD for moms-to-be.

The shift wasn't easy for either of them. "I felt pressure at first and took on more hours," she says. "He was caught up in the I'm-only-useful-if-I'm-making-money thing. He had trouble understanding that making dinner, handling family finances and taking care of the kids is helpful."

Today, says the Shriver Report, a 2009 study by Maria Shriver and the Center for American Progress, only one of five families with children at home have dads who work and moms who stay home. According to the Bureau of Labor Statistics, 25.9% of wives in 2007 were earning more than their husbands in households where both spouses work. That's up from 17.8% two decades ago. Since December 2007, men have accounted for three-quarters of all job losses.

When earning more money shifts the status quo at home, learning new ways to cope with the money/gender gap can help.

When earning power shifts the status quo, learning new ways to cope can help.

For Men

A Successful Wife Helps Your Career

It seems counterintuitive, but Sharon Meers, coauthor of *Getting to 50/50: How Working Couples Can Have It All By Sharing It All,* says men have a higher probability of job success if their wives work. "Think about it," she says. If you know that your wife can pay the mortgage for a while, and your job goes sour, you can leave it to go back to school or get retraining.

Talk About What's Happening

After 20-odd years, the Mommy Wars—the sniping about whether moms who work or moms who don't are better for the kids—have wound down. But the Daddy Wars are just beginning. Men are starting to talk about it at websites such as rebeldad.com, run (from home) by Brian Reid, whose wife is a law professor. Most men aren't comfortable chatting in a coffee shop, but they may be more at ease going online and expressing their feelings there.

Maintain Some Financial Autonomy

For years, I've told stay-at-home mothers they should have some money of their own. It forces you to actively manage it. And being married doesn't mean you have the same financial priorities. Everyone needs to be able to buy a cup of coffee or a pair of shoes without asking.

For Women

You're Not Hurting the Kids

For their book, Meers and co-author Joanna Strober surveyed more than 1,000 working mothers. They found that, for women, the significant issue centers not on a belief that men are supposed to be the moneymakers but on a belief that if they have to go out and become the primary breadwinner for the family, their children are going to suffer.

"There is zero evidence to support this," Meers says. "Clearly, no one should ignore their children, but employment in and of itself, and in the amounts that mothers do, leads to only positive outcomes for children."

Specifically? Employment tends to raise mothers' self-esteem and lower the incidence of depression, both of which are good for children. A higher level of income tends to lower stress for the entire family as well.

"Although the airwaves are filled with people who will tell you the opposite," Meers says, "you need to know—your children will be absolutely fine."

Accept Your Spouse's Parenting Skills

Even as she amped up her work hours, Tara Dai had trouble letting go of some child-related tasks that mothers were "supposed" to do, such as taking the kids to the pediatrician and helping them with their homework.

In fact, Meers says, it's in these areas that entertaining a new perspective can be the most enlightening. "The style differences can be really helpful," she says. "When one parent is about to go bananas because a child won't eat or something, the other parent will have another way of dealing with it."

Bank Online

Research has shown that for two-thirds of people, money represents power. The more you share this belief, the better the likelihood that changing income dynamics will wreak havoc at home. Why? Because it puts the higher earner in charge—and marriages work best when power is balanced.

To even the playing field, take a step back from the paycheck. Have it direct-deposited into a bank account that you both can access online so you both can keep track of your money in real time.

If you maintain individual accounts as well (more below on why this is a good idea), decide together how much money will be transferred from the main joint account into those accounts and how often such transfers will be made.

Finally, have those transfers executed automatically every time you get paid.

For Couples

Get Some New Friends

When I moved to the suburbs after my first child was born, I was in the minority. About one-third of women worked outside the home and two-thirds didn't. I quickly noticed that most of the new friends I made were "train friends"—other women who were commuting, just like me. They were the women with whom I felt most comfortable. Meers says I was onto something and suggests couples follow suit.

"If you want to live in a more egalitarian marriage, one of the first things to do is find other people who believe what you believe and hang out with them," she says. "It's a lot easier to resist the forces that will make you feel uncomfortable."

Silence the Peanut Gallery

Not everyone, particularly in your parents' or grandparents' generation, is going to accept how you and your spouse choose to run your life. They may even come right out and tell you you're doing the wrong thing. Insist, sooner rather than later, that they respect your decisions.

Wealthy Wives

These well-known wives make more money than their husbands:

- Meredith Vieira and Richard Cohen
- Heidi Klum and Seal
- Gisele Biindchen and Tom Brady
- Rachael Ray and John Cusimano
- Katherine Heigl and Josh Kelley
- PepsiCo president Indra Nooyi and Raj Nooyi
- Tina Fey and Jeff Richmond
- Michigan Gov. Jennifer Granholm and Dan Mulhern
- Danica Patrick and Paul Hospenthal
- Stephenie Meyer and Christian Meyer
- Meryl Streep and Don Gummer
- Sarah Palin and Todd Palin

"My mom is from India," Meers says. "She comes from a conservative culture, and she was not excited about me being a managing director at Goldman Sachs with a little child." Meers told her: "I love you. I want you to be very involved with my son, but it's hard with your anxiety." Translation: Rein it in if you want to see the kid.

Outsiders (and even relatives are outsiders) need to understand that this is not a negotiation; this is your choice. And unless they support it, they risk losing their place in your lives.

Finally, Delegate the Dirty Work

Aaron Rochlen, associate professor in counseling psychology at the University of Texas, recently completed a study of couples with working moms and stay-at-home dads.

Charles Dai lost his job in the recession. Today, wife Tara is the breadwinner; he's stay-at-home dad.

One finding: Although the fathers say they get a lot of satisfaction from child-care duties, they're not "too thrilled" with having to maintain the cleanliness and orderliness of the house.

Guess what? Neither are mothers. For everyone's sanity, if you can afford it, hire help.

Critical Thinking

1. What are some of the reasons for the change in families where mothers are earning more?

2. How do you think men adjust to the role of staying home with the children when their wives work?

3. What do you think of the belief that the children suffer if it is the father who stays home?

JEAN CHATZKY is the financial editor for NBC's Today show. Get more personal finance tips from Jean at JeanChatzky.com.

Trust and Betrayal in the Golden Years

Just when they're needed most, a growing number of children are turning on aging parents—taking away their nest eggs and their independence.

KYLE G. BROWN

Concerned about her mother's mental health, Sarah took decisive action. She helped 82-year-old Celia move to a retirement community, she set up accounts for her at a local health-food store and an upscale clothing boutique. She also took over her financial affairs.

But at the mention of her daughter, Celia says: "I swear to God, she should be in jail."

Since 2004, when an Alberta court granted her daughter guardianship of her mother and control of her $400,000 in savings and stocks, Celia claims Sarah has taken almost all of her possessions—and left her without a bank account, or even identification. (Both of their names have been changed to protect their privacy.) While her daughter claims to be acting in her best interests, Celia feels betrayed and helpless.

And she is hardly alone. Toronto lawyer Jan Goddard, who has worked on elder-abuse issues for 17 years, says financial exploitation of seniors is now "endemic across the country." This can range from snatching a few dollars from grandma's purse to transferring property.

Brenda Hill, the director of the Kerby Rotary House Shelter in Calgary, agrees. "We've had people who have had their homes sold, who have been virtually on the street with no food and no money because their children have taken all their assets," she says. "It happens quite often."

And the problem is likely to get worse before it gets better. People 65-plus are the fastest-growing segment of the Canadian population—but cuts to health services in the 1990s have meant that fewer seniors are living in public institutions.

This, in turn, has placed increased pressure on family members, which a Statistics Canada report in 2002 suggested could lead to a rise in the abuse of older adults.

South of the border, taking money from mom and dad is also seen as a serious issue. So much so, that the Elder Financial Protection Network predicts that it will become the "crime of the century."

Ageism is partly to blame. As is a culture of entitlement—where the money parents spend can be seen as a "waste" of the child's future inheritance.

Charmaine Spencer, a gerontologist at B.C.'s Simon Fraser University, says both are particularly prevalent in North America. Although she adds, "I have not seen a single culture in which abuse of the elderly does not take place—it's financial and psychological abuse, and when that doesn't work, it's physical."

But addressing such exploitation is anything but straightforward. How do legal and medical professionals determine when adult children are taking advantage of aging parents—and when they are enforcing necessary restrictions on those no longer able to care for themselves? How do they intervene, either to stop abuse or to help elderly parents cope with newly dependent roles, when seniors are enmeshed in painful power struggles with grown sons and daughters?

Take one of Ms. Goddard's eightysomething clients. The increasingly frail woman complained that she needed more support than her son—who lives in her house—was providing. She decided to revoke his power of attorney.

But, according to Ms. Goddard, when the woman told her son about the meeting, he was furious. The next day, she called Ms. Goddard to cancel everything. As she spoke nervously on the phone, Ms. Goddard could hear the woman's son in the background, telling her what to say.

Though lawyers like Ms. Goddard can call in the police in such situations, getting seniors to make formal complaints against their children can be difficult. Ultimately, she says, clients have to face the repercussions of confronting their families and "keep wavering whenever they go back home."

Seniors' own shame can also keep them from reporting that their children are taking advantage of them. Although abuse seems to cut across socio-economic lines (even New York socialite Brooke Astor made headlines recently because of her son's alleged neglect), older adults often feel guilty talking publicly about private matters.

As for those who do brave action against their children, many do not make it very far. While money is in their children's hands, victims of financial abuse cannot afford the fees to take a case to court—which can run at a minimum of $10,000. And legal aid is rarely awarded to seniors involved in civil cases.

Ms. Hill tells the story of a Calgary widow who sold her house and moved into her daughter's home. Her children transferred money from her account to theirs, borrowed her bank card and charged her for "services" such as rides and errands.

A few months later, the woman fled to the Kerby Rotary House Shelter with a small fraction of her savings. But at the age of 87 she could not face the idea of spending what little time and money she had left in the courts. Now, she resides in a seniors' lodge with just enough cash to live out her days—though her daughter will never be brought to justice.

Dr. Elizabeth Podnieks, the founder of the Ontario Network for the Prevention of Elder Abuse, conducted the first national survey on elder abuse in 1990. She says that even when lawyers do take seniors' cases, complainants have difficulty convincing the court that they are the victims of theft and exploitation. For example, their memory is often called into question, as they struggle to recall "giving" money to defendants.

Family members who question their parents' ability to look after their finances may consult a capacity assessor—a health professional with special training in assessing mental capacity.

Tests vary from province to province, but Larry Leach, a psychologist at Toronto's Baycrest centre for geriatric care, says they generally set out to answer the tricky question of whether elderly adults "appreciate all the risks of making an investment and giving gifts to people."

If a parent is deemed incapable, the government may then become the guardian of property until a family member applies to the courts to gain guardianship.

This is what soured the relationship between Celia and her daughter. In 2004, Celia was diagnosed with dementia and deemed "unable to care for herself." Her daughter then won guardianship over Celia's affairs.

Celia hotly disputes the doctor's findings—but now the onus is on her to prove that she is mentally fit or to appoint a new guardian.

Meanwhile, she is no longer speaking to Sarah. Once in charge of her own health-food store, she feels humiliated taking "handouts" from her daughter. "I can't do anything. Where can I go with no money?" she says.

As for more cut and dried cases, where neither dementia nor family dynamics is in play, Dr. Podnieks says: "Older people don't understand why the police can't just 'go in and get my money back.' They know it's a crime, you know it's a crime, the abuser knows it's a crime—so where is the law, where is the protection?"

Detective Tony Simioni, who is part of the Edmonton Police Force's Elder Abuse Intervention Team, says senior abuse is about 20 years behind child abuse, both in terms of public awareness and government and police resources. "Financial-abuse cases rarely see the top of the agenda," he says. "It's low on the totem pole of crimes."

Still, Judith Wahl, who has been working at the Advocacy Centre for the Elderly in Toronto for more than 20 years, remains optimistic. She believes that public education campaigns on elder abuse are making an impact. The rising number of reported incidents, she says, is partly due to a growing willingness to talk openly about abuse.

A 75-year-old Winnipeg woman is a case in point. She was coerced for years into paying her daughter's bills, rent and grocery tabs.

"I would come home and cry and sort of tear my hair, and think, 'Where do I turn to for help? Who do I go to?'" she says.

But eventually her friends encouraged her to contact a seniors support centre. With their help, she gained the confidence to confront her daughter—and to grant her son power of attorney.

These days, she gives gifts to her granddaughter, but when her daughter asks her for more, she tells her to talk to her "attorney."

Critical Thinking

1. What do you think is the motivation behind betraying a elderly parent?

2. If you were working with Celia, what would be some advice for her in her daughter's betrayal?

3. What are some suggestions to advocacy groups who work with the elderly to help caregivers recognize the impact of this type of betrayal?

KYLE G. BROWN is a freelance writer based in Calgary.

Dealing *Day-to-Day* with Diabetes
A Whole Family Experience

Karen Giles-Smith, MS, RD

When a child is diagnosed with diabetes, it's a time of upheaval for the entire family. Gayle Hood, a dietitian and mother of two young boys, was devastated when one of her sons was diagnosed with type 1 diabetes. Hood experienced myriad emotions: denial, fear, sadness, guilt, and anger. "I knew life would never be the same from that moment on," she says. "I was right. We have a new 'normal' now."

Unless they've experienced it themselves, most people don't realize how diabetes affects families. A basic understanding of what families of children with diabetes go through and a willingness to offer encouragement and support can help these families adjust to their "new life."

A Devastating Diagnosis

Life was relatively carefree for the Hood family—Gayle, her husband Mike, and their two sons, Matt and Jacob—until nearly one year ago when Matt, then aged 8, was diagnosed with diabetes. The diagnosis was unexpected; neither side of the family has a history of diabetes. When Matt began drinking large amounts of water and getting up several times during the night to use the bathroom, Gayle subconsciously recognized the symptoms. She took Matt to the doctor but didn't allow herself to seriously consider the possibility of diabetes until the pediatrician said, "Matt has glucose in his urine. I'm on the phone right now with the hospital. They're expecting him in the pediatrics unit." As Gayle gathered their belongings, she replied, "That's what I was afraid of," and began to cry.

Gayle called Mike at work. He heard the distress in her voice but didn't fully understand the implications of the diagnosis. When Mike arrived at the hospital and saw the physicians and nurses crowded around Matt's bed, he also realized life would never be the same. He likens it to the sobering feeling many men experience the moment their baby is born.

"This is something families live with 24 hours a day," says Gayle. "When I counseled diabetics, I saw them once, and as a clinical dietitian, that was the most important time to me. But health professionals have to see the bigger picture." The bigger picture is the family dynamics—the milieu of emotions and worries and the ways families deal with the initially overwhelming aspects of learning about and living with diabetes.

The Parents' Experience

Parents of children newly diagnosed with diabetes are given all the facts about managing diabetes from a clinical standpoint. However, according to Alicia McAuliffe-Fogarty (formerly Alicia McAuliffe), PhD, who has type 1 diabetes and is the founder and director of the Circle of Life Camp, Inc., a nonprofit camp for children and young adults with diabetes, the social and emotional aspects of diabetes are probably underemphasized.[1]

Denial, guilt, and fear are often the first feelings parents face. McAuliffe-Fogarty's mother explains her reaction when her daughter was diagnosed with diabetes at the age of 11: "Not my little girl! I had nursed her forever, three years to be exact. She ate all the right homemade food, had sun and fresh air. What could we have done differently? We wracked our brains as to how we could have done this to her. We feared the same for her sister. We feared for her future as well as ours. How could fate be so cruel?"[1]

Gayle had had a similar reaction. "All I could think about was why this was happening to our family," she says, "and I was worried about giving Matt the insulin shots." In fact, during the first few days at home, Gayle was terrified that she might harm Matt by giving him the wrong amount of insulin.

Mike worried about the future. He wondered how he and his family would cope. In the hospital, he watched a video of parents of children with diabetes explaining that life can be normal again. During the video, Mike wondered how they would ever reach that point.

According to McAuliffe-Fogarty, who wrote the book *Growing Up With Diabetes: What Children Want Their Parents to Know,* parents have more difficulty accepting and adjusting to diabetes than children. "It is more difficult to fit diabetes into an adult lifestyle and to relearn a new routine while unlearning old habits," she says. McAuliffe-Fogarty recalls one parent saying, "At first, you feel like your entire life has been taken away and you are a slave to diabetes."[1]

McAuliffe-Fogarty counsels parents to move past feelings of guilt and anger as soon as possible and focus on their children and managing their diabetes. An optimistic attitude about diabetes and making sure diabetes doesn't limit the child helps him or her live a normal life. McAuliffe-Fogarty tells parents,

Gayle's Recommended Readings

A First Book for Understanding Diabetes by H. Peter Chase, MD

Growing Up with Diabetes: What Children Want Their Parents to Know by Alicia McAuliffe

Helping the Student with Diabetes Succeed: A Guide for School Personnel, The National Diabetes Education Program (Available at: www.ndep.nih.gov/resources/school.htm)

Safe at School (information packet), American Diabetes Association, 1-800-DIABETES

Taking Diabetes to School by Kim Gosselin and Moss Freedman

"Your child is able to do anything as long as she fits her diabetes regimen into her schedule."[1]

The Child's Experience

When some children are diagnosed with diabetes, they become angry and feel sorry for themselves or deny they have diabetes—and they should be allowed to feel this way. Deanne Kelleher, RD, a pediatric endocrinology dietitian with Sparrow Health System in Lansing, Mich., says children's feelings of self-pity come and go, but it's important not to give in to pity parties, especially with teens. "I allow the tears initially, then encourage them to move on," says Kelleher. "They'll say it's not fair that they have to manage their diabetes, and I say, 'No, it's not fair, but it's lifesaving therapy," Kelleher also stresses the importance of listening to the family and letting them lead the education. "It helps me get the family's perspective—how they're doing and how they're handling things," she says. "I just ask them to tell me about it. I've learned a lot from my patients."

Parents, too, must listen to their child's concerns, questions, and feelings. McAuliffe-Fogarty says, "Children lean on their parents for support and encouragement, and for a child living with diabetes, this is even more important." She tells parents, "You taught your child how to crawl, walk, and talk. Now you must teach her to live, to survive, and to thrive."[1]

The Hood Family: Surviving and Thriving

After becoming comfortable with the basics, such as insulin injections, calculating carbohydrates and exchanges, and interpreting food labels, Gayle says the most helpful part in managing Matt's diabetes was working with the endocrinology team to set up a flexible routine. "It's important to consider the family as a whole," says Gayle, "instead of only treating the clinical symptoms."

A Typical School Day

- 6:30 AM: Matt gets up and tests his blood sugar level.
- 7 AM: Gayle gets up and the family eats breakfast. Gayle counts the carbs that Matt eats and inputs the data into his pump.
- 7:30 AM: Gayle packs school lunches and a snack for Matt. She writes the amount of carbs in the snack on the snack bag and the amount of carbs in Matt's lunch on a piece of paper for him to carry in his pocket.
- 8 AM: The boys go to school.
- 10 AM: In class, Matt tests his blood sugar, eats his snack, and enters the data into his pump.
- 12 PM: Matt tests his blood sugar, eats lunch, and walks to the school office. The secretary checks the note in Matt's pocket and makes sure Matt enters the correct data into the insulin pump. She may need to refigure the carbs if Matt didn't eat all of his lunch.
- 3 PM: Matt tests his blood sugar before he gets on the bus. If his blood sugar is low, he takes fast-acting glucose and the teacher calls Gayle to pick him up. If Matt feels "low" during the bus ride, the driver gives Matt a snack from the stash Gayle has supplied.
- 4 PM: Matt has a snack at home and enters the data into his pump.
- 6 PM: Matt tests his blood sugar, eats dinner, and inputs the data into his pump.
- 8 PM: Matt tests his blood sugar, eats a snack, and inputs the data into his pump.
- 9 PM: The boys go to bed.
- 3 AM: Gayle tests Matt's blood sugar while he sleeps if changes have been made to the pump settings during the day or if a high or low blood sugar is suspected.
- Every 72 hours: Change infusion set.

Additional glucose checks may be needed if Matt is feeling "high" or "low."

- Once per week: Data from the meter/pump is uploaded to the pump company's website where the pediatric endocrinologist's office can access the data and suggest any necessary changes to the care plan.

Together, the endocrinology team and the Hood family made accommodations in Matt's care plan for his activities and sports, family traditions, and the family's lifestyle, such as who would manage what (eg, grocery shopping, meal preparation, counting carbs). "At Christmastime, we put less candy and more fun stuff in their stockings," Gayle says. "And instead of giving the boys giant Easter baskets, we have a scavenger hunt." She explains that, especially with children, it's important to be lenient with what they're allowed to eat. "They shouldn't have to feel left out, deprived, or that they have to hoard candy bars."

When working with families, Kelleher gets a comprehensive idea of what goes on at home to customize the education: How is food viewed in the family? Are any foods considered a treat or a reward? What were mealtimes like before the diagnosis? "Parents' No. 1 concern," says Kelleher, "is that they're stuffing their child with food when the child doesn't want to eat." To make it possible for children to honor their feelings of hunger and fullness, Kelleher develops a more flexible insulin plan—based on what they're actually going to eat—as early as possible. She also teaches children how to manage insulin to enjoy a birthday treat or a snack at school. "Kids with diabetes don't need special snacks," Kelleher says. "With proper guidance, planning, and family support, we can help them feel not so different from other kids."

The ABCs of Diabetes

Even though Gayle has a background in nutrition and counseled type 2 diabetics as a clinical dietitian, she was floored by how much she had to learn about diabetes management after Matt was diagnosed. For many months, Gayle's full-time "job" was to educate herself and others to ensure Matt received proper care at home and school. "The most important thing you can do for your child is to educate the adults surrounding [him or] her, so your child is not excluded or treated differently," McAuliffe-Fogarty says. "Also, educate your child about diabetes and the misconceptions surrounding the condition so [he or] she is prepared . . . When schools, peers, and the general public are educated and understand diabetes, their misconceptions are dispelled, they are less afraid of it, and they will feel more comfortable around people with diabetes."[1]

Kelleher agrees: "Part of my responsibility is to make sure we educate as many people in the patients' lives as possible: the nanny or the day care provider, siblings, Grandpa and Grandma, and the schoolteacher."

To educate the school employees, Gayle did her homework and a lot of legwork. Armed with information about how to help the school staff and students feel comfortable caring for and being around Matt, Gayle visited the school several times to talk to school staff and Matt's classmates.

Gayle met with several staff members individually: the principal, secretary, Matt's third grade teacher, art teacher, music teacher, gym teacher, and bus driver. She had to start at square one since there hadn't been a student with newly diagnosed diabetes in need of insulin injections for as long as the principal could remember. To make matters more complicated, there wasn't a school nurse at the elementary school. Gayle explained Matt's needs and provided the staff with detailed verbal and written instructions for school days and field trips. She also added information about diabetes to the school's 504 (laws prohibiting discrimination against someone with a disability) and medical management plan. (Visit www.diabetes.org for more information.)

When Matt started third grade in the fall, Gayle visited the school every day at lunch to give Matt an injection until the special education teacher, the only staff member willing to wield a needle, took over. "I let the teacher practice on me," says Gayle.

How Parents Can Help Educate Schools

- Ask for the school district policy on medication administration, blood glucose testing, and injections.
- Meet with the teacher and principal one week or more before the school informs them that your child has diabetes. Explain daily management and effects of high and low blood glucose.
- Obtain the daily class schedule: recess, gym class, lunch time, snack time, etc.
- Establish a box of emergency snacks in locations such as the main office, homeroom, gym teacher's desk, and on the bus.
- Teach how to give injections to someone at the school, particularly if there is no school nurse. Even if your child has a pump, someone still needs to know how to administer glucagon in an emergency.
- Meet with any staff member at the school that your child has regular contact with: music teacher, art teacher, librarian, playground supervisors.
- Talk to the bus driver. Make sure he or she knows that your child must be able to eat on the bus, if necessary.
- Find out where blood glucose testing will occur (may be in the office or classroom).
- Get the menu from the school cafeteria to determine carbohydrates.
- Educate your child's classmates about diabetes.
- Prepare a 504 plan and a medical management plan.

"Practicing on an orange isn't the same, and I wanted to be sure she was comfortable." The special education teacher called Gayle every day to ask how many units Matt needed, which depended on his blood glucose before lunch and how many carbs he ate. In October, Matt switched from insulin shots to the pump, and Gayle visited the school twice every day—at 10 am and 12:30 pm—to help Matt enter data into the computerized pump until he felt confident doing it while supervised by the school secretary. Gayle says the school staff has been supportive and followed through responsibly several times, such as calling her when Matt's low blood sugar didn't improve after a snack. The school staff also makes sure substitute teachers receive information about Matt's condition, including the symptoms to watch for and what to do.

To make sure Matt's classmates didn't think something was "wrong" with him, Gayle read them the book *Taking Diabetes to School*. The book is written from the perspective of a child with diabetes in a way that's easy for children to understand: "Doctors and nurses don't know how or why I have diabetes. I didn't do anything wrong (like eat too many sweets), and it's nobody's fault! Doctors and nurses do know you can't catch diabetes from me. It's okay to play with me and be my friend."[2]

Education can prevent value judgments that may hurt a child's feelings and self-esteem. Word choices, for instance, make a big difference. Instead of calling a child "a diabetic," the child is "a person with diabetes." Instead of calling diabetes a "disease" (although technically, it is), it can be referred to as "a condition." And glucose readings should be called "low," "normal," or "high" instead of "good" or "bad." Without this type of age-appropriate education, children may believe Matt did something wrong to have diabetes, that he's sick and may die, or that he should be treated differently or avoided.

"I feel like I'm broadcasting [Matt's diabetes] to the world," says Gayle. "I communicate with everyone: all of Matt's coaches and the staff at all the summer day camps. But if I don't let everyone know, they might think he's just acting goofy when his blood sugar is low. It's a delicate balance. I want Matt to be treated normally, but the adults taking care of him need to know about his diabetes."

The New Normal

"I've been able to deal with everything pretty well," says Gayle, "because I have a type A personality. But to avoid getting overwhelmed, I have to think ahead and be very organized." Mike says he feels things are "pretty normal" now, but it's tough to be spontaneous. "You always have to remember to bring the meter, glucose tabs, and a cooler with you and eat on a fairly regular schedule," says Mike. "I'm not very organized, so I'm grateful that Gayle is."

Events that are fun and exciting for Matt are usually stressful for Gayle. "I still worry when there's a substitute teacher or when Matt goes on a field trip, to a birthday party, or stays at a friend's house overnight," she says. "But I let him go and have fun and be a kid." Something as simple as a trip to a nearby beach requires a lot of time planning and packing. Gayle developed a checklist of 18 items to pack. The list helps her remember everything, which gives her peace of mind.

Matt has learned to do some age-appropriate self-care, such as blood glucose monitoring, ketone testing, and entering his blood glucose levels into the computerized insulin pump. It took him more than three months to muster the courage to do his own finger sticks, but now it's as routine as brushing his teeth. Matt has a mind-over-matter approach to his diabetes management, recently telling his mom, "If you believe something won't hurt, it won't."

Gayle treats Matt the same as always and encourages others to do the same. "I don't allow diabetes to be used as an excuse or a crutch. I want him to be a normal kid," she says, "and to do all the things other kids can do. He's a kid with diabetes, but he's still a kid."

References

1. McAuliffe A. *Growing Up with Diabetes: What Children Want Their Parents to Know.* New York: John Wiley & Sons, Inc.; 1998.
2. Gosselin K, Freedman M. *Taking Diabetes to School.* Plainview, N.Y.: Jayjo Books; 1998.

Critical Thinking

1. Describe how diabetes impacts the entire family.
2. Explain the impact on parent's whose child has been diagnosed with diabetes
3. Summarize the child's experience of living with diabetes
4. Define the concept of "The New Normal"

KAREN GILES-SMITH, MS, RD, is the manager of nutrition communications for the Dairy Council of Michigan and a freelance writer.

The Positives of Caregiving: Mothers' Experiences Caregiving for a Child with Autism

MICHAEL K. CORMAN

The documentation and representation of the experiences of caregivers of children with autism and other developmental disabilities has been one dimensional at best, with a pervasive focus on the stresses, burdens, and parental coping associated with caregiving (Grant, Ramcharan, McGrath, Nolan, & Keady, 1998). Much of this focus is warranted. For example, sources of stress (stressors) for caregivers of these children are numerous and might include the autistic traits themselves (DeMyer, 1979; Tomanik, Harris, & Hawkins, 2004), social stigmas from the general public and health practitioners (Gray, 1998, 2002a, 2002b), and the social support system that is intended to alleviate stress (Corman, 2007a; DeMyer, 1979; Gray, 1998).

This multitude of stressors can have an immense effect on individuals in the family, including parents and siblings (DeMyer, 1979; Kaminsky & Dewey, 2001; Schopler & Mesibov, 1994), extended family members (Gray, 1998), and, depending on how caregivers cope, the possible life gains that the individual with autism can make (Schopler & Mesibov, 1994). For example, parents often experience a combination of emotional problems (such as depression, isolation, and feelings of being a failure as a parent), physical problems (fatigue, ulcers, headaches, fluctuation in weight, dermatitis, and other physical health conditions), career problems (limited or no employment—specifically for mothers and career changes), and negative effects on the marriage (marital discord often ending in divorce; Gray, 1998, 2002a). Parents also report feelings of guilt, isolation, doubts of their ability to care for their child, anger toward the symptoms of autism, increased physical and psychological tensions, frustrations, lack of life satisfaction, and feelings of exhaustion and old age (DeMyer, 1979; Gray, 2002b). Last, because of the unique and often complex symptomatology associated with autism, such as a lack of verbal communication, variant cognitive functioning, and severe behaviors, comparative studies have reported that the burden of caregiving for children with autism is greater than that of parenting a child with other disabilities (Weiss, 2002), such

as mental retardation, Down's syndrome, cystic fibrosis, and chronic and fatal physical illness.

Caregiving for a child with autism is stressful! But what about the positive side of caregiving? The narrow focus on the stressful and negative aspects of the caregiving experience offers only partial insights into the experiences of caregiving for children with chronic conditions. There is a need for research to examine the other side of the spectrum, the positive and often joyous side of parenting children with disabilities. The purpose of this article is to provide insight into that positive side by exploring the experiences of mothers of children with autism through in-depth interviews. Although these mothers portrayed an experience that was often stressful, they also discussed many joys of caregiving. This article attempts to strike a balance with the majority of research that focuses on the negatives of caregiving; it will show that caregiving for children with autism is not solely stressful. These findings have theoretical and practical implications. First, this article provides a brief overview of the literature on the positives of caregiving for individuals with chronic conditions.

Literature Review

Most caregiving research focuses solely on the negative aspects of the experience (Chappell, Gee, McDonald, & Stones, 2003), which may be indebted to the pathological models of stress that guide such inquiries. For instance, Pearlin, Lieberman, Menaghan, and Mullan's (1981) framework of the stress process focuses on the stressors (antecedents to stress) associated with caregiving and pays specific attention to the many related relationships, and the developing and changing nature of these relationships over time, that eventually lead to stress (see also Pearlin, Mullan, Semple, & Skaff, 1990). Lazarus and Folkman (1984) offered a framework that focuses on the more individual and psychological components of what they called the *stress-coping process*. They suggested that it is how stressors are appraised, in addition to individual resources, that determines whether or not an event is stressful (Lazarus & Folkman, 1984). Although these conceptualizations are useful for exploring the stressful aspects of caregiving and how individuals cope, they are limited in that they fail to address any positives of caregiving in a systematic way; positives have been left by the wayside (Kelso, French, & Fernandez, 2005). As Grant et al. (1998) suggested, such a singular view fails to account for other important dimensions.

Research on caregiving has only recently considered gratification and the role of positives in the caregiving experience. For example, in Susan Folkman's (1997) seminal study of caregiving for men with HIV/AIDS, she discussed how positive states of mind can co-occur with negative states. She reported that "despite high levels of distress, people also experience positive psychological states during caregiving and bereavement" (p. 1207). Folkman described four psychological states associated with coping: (a) positive reappraisal, (b) goal-directed problem-focused coping, (c) spiritual beliefs and practices, and (d) the infusion of ordinary events with positive meaning. All four states have an underlying characteristic, that is, the appraisal of positive meanings occurring within a stressful event, which she referred to as *meaning-based coping*.

Grant et al. (1998) explored the positives of caregiving by interviewing 120 caregivers of individuals with intellectual disabilities. They described rewards and caregiver gratification as emerging from three sources: (a) the relationship between caregiver and care receiver, (b) intrapersonal characteristics of the caregiver, and (c) the desire for positive outcomes or the avoidance of negative affect. They also found that many of the gratifications expressed by caregivers were related to, or a product of, successful coping strategies, supporting Folkman's (1997) findings.

More recently, Chaya Schwartz (2003) defined caregiver gratification as "fulfilling parental duties, a better idea of 'what's important in life', learning about inner strengths, aware of personal limitations, learning to do new things, satisfaction from doing what's right, personal growth, [and] becoming more self-confident" (p. 580). In her study of 167 primary caregivers of individuals with mental, developmental, or physical disabilities, she found that caregivers who were younger, unemployed, and had poor health were more likely to experience caregiver gratification. In addition, she found the only characteristics of the child that factored into experiencing gratification were the age of the child (younger children) and the type of disability (having a physical rather than a mental disability). Last, subjective (perceived stress) rather than objective burden (the level of care required) was associated with less caregiver gratification (Schwartz, 2003). Schwartz speculated that the gratification parents experienced might be a product of how they perceived or created meaning in their caregiving role.

In the field of autism, research has only provided marginal insights into the more rewarding aspects of caregiving. For instance, in a study about narratives published on the Internet by parents, Amos Fleischmann (2004) found that in addition to the demanding aspects of caregiving, a majority of Websites focused on the positive essence of individuals with autism and the caregiving experience, with an emphasis on parents'

positive relationship with their child and joyous experiences derived from caregiving. Fleischmann's study is supported by other research on the contributions people with disabilities make to their families: families might benefit in terms of strengthened family ties, compassion and fulfillment, and happiness (Pruchno, 2003).

Despite the shortcomings of Pearlin et al. (1981, 1990) and Lazarus and Folkman's (1984) models, they allow for a scope that looks beyond adjustment and toward positives (Kelso et al., 2005). This is apparent in Folkman's (1997) work on caregiving for individuals with HIV/AIDS (see also Folkman & Moskowitz, 2000a, 2000b). Using these insights, the positives of caregiving are defined in this article as experiences or events that caregivers appraise as positive and sometimes joyous. It is important to note that if this definition seems ambiguous, it is because the positives of caregiving remain relatively uncharted, lacking conceptual clarification (Grant et al., 1998). Based on mothers' reflections, this article explores the positives of caregiving for a child with autism. In doing so, a more complete understanding of these parents' lived experiences emerges, with important contributions to the broader constellation of caregivers of children with chronic conditions.

Method
Participants

Results reported in the next section were drawn from a larger study that explored mothers' experiences of caregiving for a child with autism, before and after their child was placed outside of the home (either in foster care, a group home setting, or a treatment-care facility, hereafter referred to as *placed* or *placement*). Interviews occurred between November 2005 and February 2006. Nine mothers participated in total; 6 lived in British Columbia, and 3 lived in Alberta, Canada. The average age of mothers was 46, with a range between 35 and 62 years old. For 7 out of the 9 mothers, family income ranged between $30,000 and more than $100,000. One mother responded "middle class," and another chose not to answer. As of the first interview, the children with autism were between the ages of 8 and 18, with the average being 14 years old. The age of these children at the time of placement was 6–15, with an average of 11 years old. Mothers were purposively chosen because they are usually the primary caregivers (Gray, 2003) and are therefore more likely to be involved in the day-to-day ups and downs of caregiving. Furthermore, a unique sample of mothers was chosen; their experiences were so stressful that their child was ultimately placed outside of the home (see Corman, 2007a). Although this study did not aim to be generalizable, it was assumed that if this sample experienced positives, caregivers in less stressful circumstances (e.g., caregivers of a child with less severe autistic characteristics and other disabilities) would also experience them. Therefore, these findings are potentially transferable to other constellations of caregivers.

A diagnosis of autism was reported by 7 out of the 9 mothers during the initial contact, with the remaining 2 mothers reporting a diagnosis of pervasive developmental disorder (PDD) and PDD not otherwise specific (PDD-NOS). Mothers also reported co-occurring conditions, including Landau-Kleffner syndrome, obsessive compulsive disorder, mental handicap, epilepsy (for three children), and Down's syndrome. Two of the mothers had a female child, and 7 had a male child. Although I refer to a generalized *autism,* it is important to note that there is no all-or-nothing form of autism but rather a continuum of severity, known as autism spectrum disorders (Wing, 1988). Based on mothers' descriptions, these children would most likely fall within the moderate to severe end of the spectrum.

Research Design

In-depth, semistructured interviews were conducted based on transcendental phenomenology (Moustakas, 1994), a qualitative research strategy and philosophy that allows researchers to identify the essence of experience as it relates to certain phenomena as described and understood by participants of a study (Creswell, 2002). Mothers were interviewed at their homes and asked to retrospectively talk about their caregiving experiences. Questions were geared toward exploring the positives and joys of caregiving, the demands of caregiving, and how mothers coped, focusing on the times before and after out-of-home placement. The portion of the interviews reported in the analysis below are based on the questions that explored the positives during the early years prior to placement (approximately 0–8 years of age, depending when the placement process was activated) and after their child left home. Interviews lasted on average 2.24 hours with a range of 1.5–3 hours. The interviews and the numbers of mothers interviewed continued until sufficiency and saturation of information were reached.

Interviews were transcribed in their entirety and analyzed based on a modified approach offered by Moustakas (1994), specifically intended for the analysis of qualitative data. Eight steps were followed: (1) identifying patterns in the data based on the lived experiences of participants, (2) reducing the data by identifying unique aspects of experience, (3) organizing the data into core themes that represent the experience of participants, (4) validating step 3 by reviewing the complete transcript of participants, (5) constructing an individual textural description of the experience presented by each participant, (6) based on step 5, constructing a clear account of the dynamics of the experience, (7) combining steps 5 and 6 to create a textural-structural description of each participant that incorporated the experiences of participants, and (8) combining individual textual descriptions of each participant into one that represents the experience presented by the group as a whole.

To assist in the process just described, insights offered by Moerer-Ur-dahl and Creswell (2004) were followed. Initially, significant statements within each participant's transcripts were identified, with a primary focus on understanding how individuals viewed different aspects of their experiences as they related to the positives and joys of caregiving. The goal here was to ground or contextualize the positives of caregiving to gain a better understanding of the distinct character of positives as described by mothers. The data were then broken down into themes based on the experiences of mothers. Once themes were developed, a detailed description of the experience of each

mother as it related to the themes that emerged was provided. Conclusions were then drawn in accordance with the lived experiences expressed by participants. The product of this process was the grouping of statements into the themes discussed in the next section.

Results
Pockets of Child Development

All parents expressed the positives during the early years of their child's development as "pockets" because they were "kind of few and far between." Positives discussed by mothers included their child developing, seeing their child happy, times devoid of negative autistic traits or maladaptive behaviors (as perceived by the mother) that are often associated with autism, spending time with their child, unique and/or positive personality traits of their child, and knowing or discovering what was wrong with their child. I discuss each in the following paragraphs.

Developmental Gains

With a diagnosis on the autism spectrum, parents are often left in ambiguity because of the nature of the disability; they do not know how much their child will develop in the years to come. As a result, mothers described feelings of joy when their child started to make developmental gains. For example, one mother discussed how she was "very pleased" when her child progressed in developmental areas, such as "when he started to speak." Another mother commented on her child's success in learning new tasks; "Oh yeah, his success still makes me feel good, no matter what. Like I remember when he learned how to wave good-bye. That made me cry that day [laugh]." Another mentioned the "little milestones that parents take for granted, I think are tremendous."

Another mother discussed how watching her child was "hugely satisfying . . . it makes it all worth it when you start to see a little bit of language or a behavior, or a skill emerge." For some mothers, this gave them hope for their child's future. One mother explained, "I think . . . a little bit of joy with a child that's seriously handicapped goes a long way. It gives you a lot of hope."

Child Being Happy

All mothers experienced positives derived from seeing their child happy. Although this might seem like a common experience of all parents, it is important to contextualize this side of caregiving in that many mothers viewed their child as being chronically unhappy. One mother put it best, "just to see him happy, because all through his life he's lived either withdrawn or anxious, or afraid of doing things." When mothers saw their child happy, they were especially happy. For example, joy arose for one mother when she watched her child enjoy his favorite activity. She explained:

> You see this bright-eyed little boy at the top of the slide, that was his favorite activity was going down the slides. So when you see him at the top of the slide with this big grin on his face, those kinds of times were really exciting for me. . . . I just knew that he enjoyed that.

Seeing her child happy made her feel "really good...That is sort of what we hope our kids are going to feel." Another mother described, "when he's happy and having a really good time, then I'm happy. It's like I'm just a normal parent."

Times Devoid of Negative Autistic Traits or Maladaptive Behaviors

Mothers also talked about times devoid of negative behaviors (negative autistic traits), which they thought of as "normal" times. For instance, one mother described how when her child "didn't throw his food ... [or] didn't have any feces smearing in the bathroom," these were more positive times. Others experienced positives when their child "hadn't pinched another child or hit another child." One mother went on to explain, "So any time he was cooperating ... times that he was being and not bothering anybody .... If I heard that he sat for five minutes in his desk, or he sat in circle time without poking the next person." During these times, some mothers expressed being "really happy."

Spending Time with Your Child

Despite many of the difficulties, all mothers described the positives of spending time with their child. For instance, one mother discussed how she and her child would go swimming together and go down to the beach to spend time together. Her child "loved it" and always "liked hanging off me." She described how there were so many "nice times" that they spent together. Another mother described how she felt "just connected" to her child because of the times they spent together, specifically "the caregiving part ... being hands on, physically connected." She talked about how she "really enjoyed" the connection she had with her child: "We're connected on a different level." This mother concluded:

I guess having a child with autism, you connect with them on a completely different level than I think you would with other children because you don't have language. He's also mostly nonverbal, so physical connections are really important; it's the way you communicate that's beyond words I guess, so I think that's part of it.

For this mother, what might be viewed as a demanding aspect of caregiving was in fact very joyous for her.

Unique and/or Positive Personality Traits of Their Child

Individuals with autism often have a variety of challenges, including maladaptive behaviors, difficulty in communicating with others, difficulty listening and following directions, and other co-occurring medical conditions. However, individuals who have autism are heterogeneous; the severities of impairments vary from person to person (Gray, 2003; Seltzer, Shattuck, Abbeduto, & Greenberg, 2004). Nonetheless, the positive side of this uniqueness often goes unrecognized. All mothers in this study recognized the uniqueness of their child. In doing so, they expressed many positives derived from the unique personality traits of their child.

For example, mothers discussed how their child was "real sweet" and showed affection. Another mother talked about her child being a "very warm individual .... We were blessed that way, I guess; very cuddly, quite attached to your close family members." Other personality traits included being "very funny, like she's got a good sense [of humor] ... she's quite a little monkey," and being "a very good-natured kid ... he still has a happy disposition." Despite the negative traits mothers dealt with throughout their caregiving experience, which sometimes worsen or change as their child ages into adulthood (Gray, 2002a), mothers described the many unique personality traits of their child as a positive side of caregiving.

Knowing or Discovering What Was Wrong with Their Child

Common perceptions of receiving a diagnosis on the autism spectrum suggest that the experience is devastating, and often it is (Mansell & Morris, 2004). In fact, for many of the mothers in this study, the autism diagnosis represented the loss of the child that was or could have been. One mother explained how "the day that I found out [I was floored] because there's nothing like that in my family, and we've always been high achievers ... and I don't know where that [diagnosis] came from."

Although some mothers described receiving the diagnosis of autism as very burdensome—"it was sad, it's pretty devastating, to have a child who's not typical"—for others, the receipt of the diagnosis was not a stressful experience but a positive one. With a diagnosis, mothers were relieved to finally know what was wrong with their child after having entered into multiple systems of care in search for answers and supports. For example, after receiving a diagnosis, one mother described how "all of a sudden you know ... because up until this point everybody's been asking me 'Why is he doing this? What's he doing?' And I'd be going 'I don't know; I don't know'. I really had no answers for anybody." With a diagnosis, answers started "coming out." With these answers, mothers described a positive experience derived from knowing and understanding.

Furthermore, the receipt of a diagnosis allowed the mother to gain access to specialized services and supports for her child, such as intervention therapy, and herself, such as respite, and set out a pathway of care for her child.[1] The ability to take action was positive, and often a relief, because now the mother was able to help her child. One mother expanded upon this point:

I'm very much a doer, and so when you have a diagnosis, then you can look at putting the pieces together to move forward and do something; especially I hear so much about early development and early intervention. It was right around the time that the money was being made available for early intervention, and I didn't want to waste a minute, especially knowing that that money would dissolve when he was 6.

The Impacts of Positives

Parents did not just describe the positive side of caregiving, they also discussed how the positives interacted with negative and stressful experiences (i.e., their stress-coping process). For example, the positives associated with their child developing gave mothers hope. One mother, like many parents of children with autism, worried about her child's future (Ivey, 2004). When her child started to make developmental milestones, she began to have a more positive outlook for her child's future. This hope impacted the concerns and worries she had for her child's future. She went on to explain how the positives "are the things that keep you going . . . a little bit of joyful experience gives you . . . the ability to go on."

On a more general note, one mother described how the positives of caregiving had an impact on her stress-coping process.

Well they (the positives) kept me going . . . it wasn't all negative. It kind of gave me hope to continue on, like every day is a new day kind of thing . . . . It gave me a reason to get up in the morning so I wouldn't be waking up going "oh no, I have to deal with another day" sort of thing . . . any time you have any kind of joy or positive feelings then that . . . just gives you a really good feeling that you can continue over the next period of time.

Another mother explained:

[The positives] just keep you going. Without the moments of comic relief, without the joys, without those moments of connection where he catches your eye directly for 1 minute and you actually have his gaze directly, without those things, you'd go stir crazy. Those are the things that feed you. I get a huge amount of strength from the tiniest little things.

Despite the demands of caregiving, mothers experienced a multitude of positives during their caregiving years, many of which brought joy to their lives.

Positive Reflections on Their Overall Caregiving Experience

All mothers spoke about personal transformation as a result of their caregiving years. This transformation included learning from their experience and growing as a person. It is important to note that these positive reflections are not linked to any specific event but were a product of their caregiving experience as a whole. Furthermore, it is important to contextualize this positive side of caregiving: All mothers eventually placed their child with autism due to a number of factors, including their child's maladaptive behaviors increasing drastically, "getting more intense" and more difficult to deal with over time, a failure in the support system that was intended to alleviate stress, and a general inability to cope with the demands of caregiving, leading to mothers experiencing severe distress and feeling that they "couldn't go on" (Corman, 2007a). However, despite this experience of severe distress, all mothers ultimately reflected positively on their caregiving experience as a whole.

For example, one mother explained the learning involved in caregiving where she not only "learned a lot about autism, but I learned a lot about people, and I would have missed that . . . it was a really wonderful thing." Another explained how "the biggest positive is just the learning that came out of that for us as a family, but for me in particular as a person. But I think

it's shaped all of us, it certainly has shaped [my husband and daughter] as well as me."

Others described caregiving as making them stronger as a person. One mother mentioned how she "became a fighter, just kind of like an advocate for the family but also for [my child with autism] . . . So, yeah, definitely it makes you stronger. And it makes you tougher in a way." Her experience also made her realize what is "important . . . So, you realize what's really important and don't sweat the small stuff." Another mother described her child with autism as being one of her greatest teachers in life:

I mean, I don't even know who I would be if I hadn't had May . . . it's kind of a weird thing, but in my life, she's been kind of one of my key teachers. She's kind of forced me to kind of examine parts of myself that I don't know if I ever would have got to if I didn't have her. And, she forced [my husband] and I to kind of deal with issues that might have taken us years . . . It's been a struggle, and sometimes I've hated her for it, [but] nobody has taught me so much.

Mothers also discussed how the caregiving experience made them more empathetic:

My husband and I were asked one time about the biggest thing that we got from Sam. I think it was the gift of patience 'cause I have patience unlimited, you know . . . 'cause once somebody's dumping milk out in your front yard [laugh], it's amazing how much patience you have.

Discussion and Conclusion

Despite the demanding aspects of caregiving for children with autism, and it is often very demanding, caregivers experience many positives and joys from their role as caregivers. However, the majority of research focuses on the negative and more stressful aspects of the caregiving experience. Breaking away from this preponderance of research in the field of autism, this article highlights some of the positives of caregiving that mothers experienced during the early years of their child's development and overall reflections on their caregiving experience after their child left home. When asked to discuss the positives of care-giving, all mothers expressed a multitude of positives directly related to their caregiving role (Chappell et al., 2003; Folkman, 1997; Grant et al., 1998; Schwartz, 2003). Others derived positives from finding the "positive essence" in their child (Fleischmann, 2004) and achievements of their child (Grant et al., 1998). More unique positives included discovering what was wrong with their child in the face of not knowing.

Implications for Practice

Many practical implications arise from this study. Although caregiving for children with autism is demanding, this article suggests that the positives and joys that emerge from this role are not only important but also have a specific function. Whereas current research describes the positives of caregiving as a *product* of successful coping—the adaptational function of positives (see Folkman, 1997; Grant et al., 1998)—parents in this study discussed how positives had an impact *on* their stress-coping process, rather than being simply a product of it. In other words, positives also occur outside of the stress-coping process, and interact with it, affecting how mothers experience stressors and negative outcomes, potentially impacting their ability to cope at different times. This finding expands on the function of positives within the caregiving experience; they go beyond adaptational function to being a core aspect of caregivers' experiences.

Furthermore, the importance and function of the positives and joys of caregiving is most apparent when they are not present. In the larger study that contributed to this article, all mothers described severe distress and solely negative outcomes during the time leading up to and immediately following the placement of their child, a time devoid of any positives or joys of caregiving. One mother described it best: "When the stresses got to be too much, the joy of everything started to disappear." Does a lack of positives impact caregiver well-being and a caregiver's ability to cope? Cummins (2001) explained that most caregivers are able to describe positives derived from their caregiving role; when they are unable to do so, the demands of their role are likely to be intolerable. Grant et al. (1998) further explained that without the positives of caregiving, it may not be possible for caregivers to feel as if they are able to continue encountering the stressful circumstances corollary to their role. As such, it might be concluded that the positives of caregiving are an integral part of parents' ability to cope, to the point that when they are not present, parents may not be able to continue caregiving. Policy and practice implications directly follow from these findings in that a lack of positives might be an indicator of the current state of a caregiver's well-being or lack of well-being. It might be an indicator for professional services and supports that additional supports are needed to proactively assist those in crisis or on the brink of crisis. Furthermore, policies need to be developed that are proactively geared toward preventing a crisis or assisting those on the brink of a crisis rather than solely intervening once the crisis emerges. Of equal importance, this examination of positives provides future families of children with autism and other disabilities a better understanding of the experience of caregiving as a whole—an experience that is very demanding at times but also has many positives.

How families cope with the demands associated with caring for a child with autism not only influences the well-being of the family but also possible life gains that an individual with autism can make (Schopler & Mesibov, 1994). Current research on caregiving for children with autism attempts to promote the use of successful coping strategies and resources to improve the quality of life of the caregiver and care receiver (Dunn, Burbine, Bowers, & Tantleff-Dunn, 2001; Gray, 1994, 1998). One practical implication that might inform research, policy, and practice on successful coping is the need to promote and draw attention to the positives of caregiving both within service agencies and for those caregiving for children with autism and other disabilities. If services and supports are able to enhance the positive aspects of caregiving by drawing

attention to them, parents might be able to cope more successfully with the difficulties of caregiving. In addition, it might be beneficial for services and supports to facilitate the joys of caregiving by drawing attention to the strengths of the caregiver and the positive contribution their child with a disability makes to their family (Pierpont, 2004). The strengths-based perspective and active interviewing are two resources that service providers might draw upon to help facilitate and draw attention to the positives of caregiving.

The strengths-based perspective is one orientation that might assist those whose work intersects with individuals with disabilities and their families in drawing attention to and facilitating the identification of the positive and joyous aspects of caregiving. This perspective shifts away from pathological conceptions of persons with disabilities and the experiences of caregiving to more qualitative and holistic understandings, aligned with the positives of caregiving discussed earlier. By focusing on strengths (see Cohen, 1999; Early, 2001), this perspective has the potential to assist service providers in gaining a more complete understanding of the caregiving experience and perceiving their experiences in a more positive light, which has the potential to increase caregivers' quality of life and the quality of care they provide (Berg-Weger, Rubio, & Tebb, 2001).

In addition to the strengths-based perspective, and complementary to it, insights offered by the reflexive and linguistic turns in sociology could be of use to service providers and researchers alike as a resource or tool to draw upon to explore the positives of caregiving and draw attention to them. One approach aligned with this shift is "the active interview," which is a methodological and analytical approach to interviewing that conceptualizes the interview as an active meaning-making process between interviewee and interviewer, who both participate in the coproduction of knowledge. The interviewer (i.e., service provider), in the context of exploring the positives of caregiving, might invite or "incite" the interviewee (i.e., caregiver) to talk about and reflect on the positives of caregiving. Traditionally, this approach might be viewed as leading the respondent, resulting in a social desirability bias (Esterberg, 2002; see also Cummins, 2001). However, the active interview suggests that interviewers are inevitably embedded and implicated in the meaning-making processes of respondents. Holstein and Gubrium (2002) explained:

> This is not to say that active interviewers merely coax their respondents into preferred answers to their questions. Rather, they converse with respondents in such a way that alternate considerations are brought into play . . . encouraging respondents to develop topics in ways relevant to their own everyday lives . . . to provide an environment conducive to the production of the range and complexity of meanings that address relevant issues. (pp. 120–121)

Furthermore, in the context of the positives of caregiving, the active interview is not solely concerned about the positives; it suggests that there is usefulness in inviting individuals to think about the positives and honor participants in the meaning-making process. As such, I suggest that this approach can provide a more fruitful examination of the caregiving experience as a whole by assisting researchers and service providers in exploring and gaining a better understanding and appreciation of the positives of caregiving. This process might also facilitate families and caregivers in talking about and reflecting upon their experiences in a more positive and joyous light (Berg-Weger et al., 2001).

Directions for Future Research

The findings from this study suggest that future research should focus on the factors that lead to positives of caregiving, which might identify and assist in the development of services, supports, and specific interventions that will potentially facilitate improved outcomes for individual caregivers, care receivers, and the family as a whole. As such, there is a need to explore links among positives, social supports, coping, and appraisal processes of caregivers of children with autism and other chronic conditions. Furthermore, future research should investigate these links to determine how the facilitation of positives might affect caregivers' lived experiences. Also, as mentioned earlier, it is important to examine positives and joys not only in relation to stressors but also as a significant factor throughout the entire stress-coping process.

Last, this study focused on the retrospective experience of mothers whose children were under 18 years old. However, for the first time in history, large numbers of people with autism are reaching old age (National Advisory Council on Aging, 2004; Seltzer et al., 2004). As a result, parents now "face a lifetime of caregiving responsibilities" (Kim, Greenberg, Seltzer, & Krauss, 2003, p. 313). However, very little is known about this constellation of caregivers and care receivers. There is need to explore the experiences of individuals with autism, their caregivers, and families as they age over the life course.

Note

1. In British Columbia and Alberta, for instance, institutional services and supports are attached to a diagnosis of autism (see Corman, 2007b).

References

Berg-Weger, M., Rubio, D., & Tebb, S. (2001). Strengths-based practice with family caregivers of the chronically ill: Qualitative insights. *Families in Society: The Journal of Contemporary Human Services, 82*(3), 263–272.

Chappell, N., Gee, E., McDonald, L., & Stones, M. (2003). *Aging in contemporary Canada.* Toronto, Canada: Pearson Educational Publishers/Prentice Hall.

Cohen, B. (1999). Intervention and supervision in strengths-based social work practice. *Families in Society: The Journal of Contemporary Human Services, 80*(5), 460–466.

Corman, M. K. (2007a). *Primary caregivers of children with autism spectrum disorders—An exploration of the stressors, joys, and parental coping before and after out-of-home placement.* (Masters Thesis, University of Victoria, Canada, 2007). Available from the Electronic Theses and Dissertations Website: http:// hdl.handle.net/1828/1227.

Corman, M. K. (2007b, August). *Panning for gold—An institutional ethnography of health relations in the process of diagnosing autism in British Columbia.* Paper presented at the meeting of The Society for the Study of Social Problems, New York.

Creswell, J. (2002). *Research design: Qualitative, quantitative, and mixed methods approaches* (2nd ed.). Thousand Oaks, CA: Sage Publications.

Cummins, R. (2001). The subjective well-being of people caring for a family member with a severe disability at home: A review. *Journal of Intellectual & Developmental Disability, 26*(1), 83–100.

DeMyer, M. (1979). *Parents and children in autism.* Washington, DC: V. H. Winston & Sons.

Dunn, M., Burbine, T., Bowers, C., & Tantleff-Dunn, S. (2001). Moderators of stress in parents of children with autism. *Community Mental Health Journal, 37*(1), 39–52.

Early, T. (2001). Measures for practice with families from a strengths perspective. *Families in Society: The Journal of Contemporary Human Services, 82*(2), 225–232.

Esterberg, K. G. (2002). *Qualitative methods in social research.* Boston: McGraw-Hill.

Fleischmann, A. (2004). Narratives published on the Internet by parents of children with autism: What do they reveal and why is it important? *Focus on Autism and Other Developmental Disabilities, 19*(1), 35–43.

Folkman, S. (1997). Positive psychological states and coping with severe stress. *Social Science & Medicine, 45*(8), 1207–1221.

Folkman, S., & Moskowitz, J. T. (2000a). Positive affect and the other side of coping. *American Psychologist, 55*(6), 647–654.

Folkman, S., & Moskowitz, J. T. (2000b). Stress, positive emotion, and coping. *Current Directions in Psychological Science, 9*(4), 115–118.

Grant, G., Ramcharan, P., McGrath, M., Nolan, M., & Keady, J. (1998). Rewards and gratifications among family caregivers: Towards a refined model of caring and coping. *Journal of Intellectual Disability Research, 42*(1), 58–71.

Gray, D. (1994). Coping with autism: Stresses and strategies. *Sociology of Health & Illness, 16*(3), 275–300.

Gray, D. (1998). *Autism and the family: Problems, prospects, and coping with the disorder.* Springfield, IL: Charles C. Thomas Publisher.

Gray, D. (2002a). Ten years on: A longitudinal study of families of children with autism. *Journal of Intellectual & Developmental Disability, 27*(3), 215–222.

Gray, D. (2002b). 'Everybody just freezes. Everybody is just embarrassed': Felt and enacted stigma among parents of children with high functioning autism. *Sociology of Health & Illness, 24*(6), 734–749.

Gray, D. (2003). Gender and coping: The parents of children with high functioning autism. *Social Sciences & Medicine, 56*, 631–642.

Holstein, J. A., & Gubrium, J. F. (2002). Active interviewing. In D. Weinberg (Ed.), *Qualitative research methods* (pp. 112–126). Oxford, UK: Blackwell.

Ivey, J. (2004). What do parents expect? A study of likelihood and importance issues for children with autism spectrum disorders. *Focus on Autism and Other Developmental Disabilities, 19*(1), 27–33.

Kaminsky, L., & Dewey, D. (2001). Sibling relationships of children with autism. *Journal of Autism and Developmental Disorders, 31*(4), 399–410.

Kelso, T., French, D., & Fernandez, M. (2005). Stress and coping in primary caregivers of children with a disability: A qualitative study using the Lazarus and Folkman process model of coping. *Journal of Research in Special Educational Needs, 5*(1), 3–10.

Kim, W., Greenberg, S., Seltzer, M., & Krauss, W. (2003). The role of coping in maintaining the psychological well-being of mothers of adults with intellectual disability and mental illness. *Journal of Intellectual Disability Research, 47*(4-5), 313–327.

Lazarus, R., & Folkman, S. (1984). *Stress, appraisal, and coping.* New York: Springer Publishing.

Mansell, W., & Morris, K. (2004). A survey of parents' reactions to the diagnosis of an autistic spectrum disorder by a local service: Access to information and use of services. *Autism, 8*(4), 387–407.

Moustakas, C. (1994). *Phenomenological research methods.* Thousand Oaks, California: Sage Publications.

Moerer-Urdahl, T., & Creswell, J. (2004). Using transcendental phenomenology to explore the "ripple effect" in a leadership mentoring program. *International Journal of Qualitative Methods, 3*(2), 1–28.

National Advisory Council on Aging. (2004). *Seniors on the margins: Aging with a developmental disability.* Canada: Minister of Public Works and Governmen Services Canada.

Pearlin, L., Lieberman, M., Menaghan, E., & Mullan, J. (1981). The stress process. *Journal of Health and Social Behavior, 22*(4), 337–356.

Pearlin, L., Mullan, J., Semple, S., & Skaff, M. (1990). Caregiving and the stress process: An overview of concepts and their measures. *The Gerontologist, 30*(5), 583–594.

Pierpont, J. (2004). Emphasizing caregiver strengths to avoid out-of-home placement of children with severe emotional and behavioral disturbances. *Journal of Human Behavior in the Social Environment, 9*(1/2), 5–17.

Pruchno, R. (2003). Enmeshed lives: Adult children with developmental disabilities and their aging mothers. *Psychology and Aging, 18*(4), 851–857.

Schopler, E., & Mesibov, G. (1994). *Behavioral issues in autism.* New York: Plenum Press.

Schwartz, C. (2003). Parents of children with chronic disabilities: The gratification of caregiving. *Families in Society: The Journal of Contemporary Human Services, 84*(4), 576–584.

Seltzer, M., Shattuck, P., Abbeduto, L., & Greenberg, J. (2004). The trajectory of development in adolescents and adults with autism. *Mental Retardation and Developmental Disabilities Research Reviews, 10*(4), 234–247.

Tomanik, S., Harris, G., & Hawkins, J. (2004). The relationship between behaviours exhibited by children with autism and maternal stress. *Journal of Intellectual & Developmental Disability, 29*(1), 16–26.

Weiss, M. (2002). Hardiness and social support as predictors of stress in mothers of typical children, children with autism, and children with mental retardation. *Autism, 6*(1), 115–130.

Wing, L. (1988). The continuum of autistic characteristics. In E. Schopler & G. Mesibov (Eds.), *Diagnosis and assessment in autism* (pp. 91–110). New York: Plenum Press.

Critical Thinking

1. How can the positives outweigh the negatives in caregiving for those with autism?

2. Have you personally witnessed examples of positive as well as negative caregiving? If so, did one experience outweigh the other?

3. What do you think can be learned by the experience of caregiving for those with autism?

MICHAEL K. CORMAN, MA, is a doctoral student in the Department of Sociology at the University of Calgary and a part-time faculty member in the Department of Sociology & Anthropology at Mount Royal College in Calgary, Alberta. His research and teaching interests include the sociology of health and illness, aging, institutional ethnography, caregiving and autism spectrum disorders, health care work, and critical research strategies. Correspondence regarding this article can be sent to the author at mkcorman@ucalgary.ca or University of Calgary, Department of Sociology, Social Sciences 913, 2500 University drive NW, Calgary, AB, T2N 1N4 Canada.

Author's note—I would like to thank Dr. Neena L. Chappell for her continued support throughout the larger study that contributed to this article and the preparation of this manuscript.

Bereavement after Caregiving

Richard Schulz, PhD, Randy Hebert, MD, MPH, and Kathrin Boerner, PhD

O f the approximately 2.4 million deaths that occur in the United States each year, nearly 70% are the result of chronic conditions such as heart disease, cancer, stroke, and respiratory diseases. The large majority of decedents are older persons suffering from one or more disabling conditions which compromised their ability to function independently prior to death. As a result, a typical death is preceded by an extended period of time during which one or more family members provide unpaid care in the form of health and support services to their disabled relative.[1] A recent survey estimates the out-of-pocket cost of caring for an aging parent or spouse averages about $5500 a year.[2]

Our understanding of bereavement is undergoing fundamental changes as a result of recent prospective studies of bereavement that focus on circumstances surrounding the death of a loved one. One important finding to emerge in recent years concerns the impact of family caregiving on caregiver response to death of a loved one.[3,4] Family members involved in care provision before death show remarkable resilience in adapting to the death of their relatives. Symptoms of depression and grief decline rapidly after the death and return to near normal levels within a year of the death.[5] This may be due to multiple reasons, including having time to prepare for the impending death and life afterward, relief from the burdens of caregiving, an end to the suffering of their loved one, and the absence of guilt over having done the "work of caregiving."

Despite the generally positive prognosis for most bereaved caregivers, a sizable minority continues to experience high levels of stress and psychiatric problems after death. Approximately 10% to 15% of people experience chronic depression.[6] In our own work with caregivers of patients with dementia, we found that 30% of caregivers were at risk for clinical depression 1 year post-death, and 20% experience complicated grief.[4,5] As described below, complicated grief is distinct from both depression and normal grief reactions.

Understanding the variability in response to death and the role of caregiving factors as predictors of bereavement outcomes is critical to developing effective interventions for this group. To address this issue, we distinguish among 2 types of predictors of pathologic depression and grief outcomes among caregivers: Factors associated with the caregiving experience prior to death, and factors associated with depression and grief assessed postbereavement. The rationale for making this

Approximately 20% of bereaved caregivers will experience a variety of psychiatric symptoms including depression and/or complicated grief, a disorder characterized by persistently high levels of distress that impair functioning in important life domains. We identify prebereavement risk factors for poor adjustment after the death of a loved one along with preventive strategies that can be implemented prior to death as well as diagnostic procedures and therapeutic strategies that can be used to identify and treat individuals who develop complicated grief disorder after death.

Schulz R, Hebert R, Boerner K. Bereavement after caregiving, *Geriatrics*, 2008:63(1):20–22.

distinction is that each factor provides a different opportunity for intervention. Identifying which caregiving factors contribute to poor bereavement outcomes provides us with important leads about interventions that could be delivered during caregiving. Likewise, postbereavement factors linked to poor bereavement response may help identify intervention options that can be delivered after death.

Caregivers at Risk for Poor Bereavement Outcomes

The most common finding across multiple studies is that prebereavement levels of mental distress such as depression and anxiety are predictive of postbereavement adjustment. A related finding is that high levels of burden, feeling exhausted and overloaded, lack of support, and having competing responsibilities such as work or caring for younger children are all associated with negative postbereavement outcomes.[3,7,8] The fact that increased burden is a risk factor for poor bereavement outcomes may explain in part the higher mortality rate observed among caregivers of terminal patients who do not use hospice services when compared to those who do.[9] Demographic factors also play a role. Individuals with lower income, lower education, and those who are African Americans are also more likely to exhibit greater depression and complicated grief after the death.

Table 1 Questions to Identify Caregivers at Risk for Negative Postbereavement Outcomes

Do you feel overwhelmed by the responsibilities of providing care to your relative?

Do you feel isolated from family and friends?

Do you feel prepared for the death of your loved one?

In the past month have you felt depressed, sad, or anxious much of the time?

Table 2 Symptoms of Complicated Grief

Trouble accepting the death

Inability to trust others since the death

Excessive bitterness related to the death

Feeling uneasy about moving on

Detachment from formerly close others

Feeling life is meaningless without the deceased

Feeling that the future holds no prospect for fulfillment without the deceased

Feeling agitated since the death

A recent randomized trial of dementia in caregivers showed that psychosocial-behavioral interventions designed to decrease caregiver burden and distress had the added benefit of preventing complicated grief after the death of their loved one.[4] This suggests that adverse effects of bereavement can be addressed through preventive treatments delivered to family caregivers prior to the death of their loved one. Individuals at risk for negative postbereavement outcomes can be identified by asking a few questions to determine how stressful caregiving is, the availability of support from family and friends, how depressed and anxious they feel, and whether or not they feel prepared for the death of their loved one (see Table 1). Treatment options for caregivers thus identified include interventions to reduce caregiver burden, such as hospice care, behavioral and pharmacologic treatment of depression and anxiety, and referral to religious counselors.

Diagnosis and Treatment of Complicated Grief

One of the hallmarks of poor response to death is persistent (ie, 6 months or longer) complicated grief. This disorder is distinct from normal grief reactions or depression. It is characterized by an intense longing and yearning for the person who died and by recurrent intrusive and distressing thoughts about the absence of the deceased, making it difficult to concentrate, move beyond an acute state of mourning, form other interpersonal relationships, and engage in potentially rewarding activities. Complicated grief is a source of significant distress and impairment and is associated with a range of negative psychiatric and physical health consequences.[10]

Formal diagnostic criteria for complicated grief disorder have been proposed for inclusion in the *Diagnostic and Statistical Manual of Mental Disorders, Fifth Edition (DSM-V).*[11] A diagnosis of complicated grief disorder requires that the bereaved person must have persistent and disruptive yearning, pining, and longing for the deceased. The individual must experience 4 of the 8 symptoms at least several times a day and/or to a severely distressing disruptive degree (see Table 2). Symptoms of distress must endure for at least 6 months and significantly impair functioning in important life domains.

Complicated grief often occurs along with other disorders such as major depression and post-traumatic stress disorder (PTSD) and is associated with suicidality and self-destructive behaviors,[12] but it is a distinct disorder requiring treatment strategies different from those used with major depression and PTSD. A recent randomized trial found higher and faster rates of improvement among persons with complicated grief using loss-focused, cognitive behavioral therapy techniques when compared to rates obtained with a standard interpersonal therapy approach used to treat depression.[13] Components of effective treatment included repeated retelling of the story of the death, having an imaginary conversation with the deceased, and working on confronting avoided situations. In general, although traditional treatments for depression after bereavement such as referral to a psychiatrist or psychologist for medications and/ or psychotherapy can be effective in treating depression and to some extent, complicated grief, there is added benefit to treatments that are specifically tailored to address symptoms of complicated grief.[6]

Hundreds of studies carried out in the past 2 decades have documented the negative health effects of caregiving, showing that caregivers are at increased risk of psychiatric and physical morbidity.[14] The challenges of caregiving become even more extreme as the care-recipient nears death. When the death does occur, the caregiver enters bereavement already compromised with high levels of depression and anxiety and sometimes physical exhaustion brought about by the caregiving experience. Even with these vulnerabilities, caregivers, for the most part, adapt well to the death of their loved one. Psychiatric symptomatology typically improves and caregivers are able to effectively reengage in activities that may have lapsed while caregiving.

Opportunities for Intervention

Despite this generally positive picture of caregiver adaptation to bereavement, a minority of caregivers exhibit adverse bereavement outcomes in the form of high levels of depression and/or complicated grief. High levels of burden, physical exhaustion, lack of social support, along with traditional predictors, such as prebereavement anxiety and depression, are all associated with negative postbereavement outcomes. Although empirical support for the efficacy of bereavement interventions to enhance adaptation to bereavement is mixed at best,[13,15] researchers have generally not tested preventive approaches in which interventions are delivered prior to death. In addition, new treatment strategies described above specifically designed to treat complicated grief hold promise for helping individuals who are not able to effectively cope with the death of a loved one.

References

1. Emanuel EJ, Fairclough DL, Slutsman J, et al. Assistance from family members, friends, paid care givers, and volunteers in the care of terminally ill patients. *N Engl J Med,* 1999; 341(13):956–63.

2. Gross J. Study finds higher outlays for caregivers of older relatives. *New York Times,* November 19, 2007:A18.

3. Schulz R, Boerner K, Hebert RS, Caregiving and bereavement. In Stroebe MS, Hansson RO, et al, eds. *Handbook of Bereavement Research and Practice: 21st Century Perspectives.* Washington, DC: American Psychological Association Press; in press.

4. Schulz R, Boerner K, Shear K, et al. Predictors of complicated grief among dementia caregivers: a prospective study of bereavement. *Am J Geriatr Psychiatry,* 2006;14(8):650–658.

5. Schulz R, Mendelsohn AB, Haley WE, et al. End of life care and the effects of bereavement on family caregivers of persons with dementia. *N Engl J Med.* 2003;349(20): 1936–1942.

6. Hensley PL, Treatment of bereavement related depression and traumatic grief. *J Affect Disord.* 2006;92(1):117–124.

7. Hebert RS, Dang Q, Schulz R. Preparedness for the death of a loved one and mental health in bereaved caregivers of patients with dementia: findings from the REACH study. *J Palliat Med.* 2006;9(3):683–693.

8. Boerner K, Schulz R, Horowitz A. Positive aspects of caregiving and adaptation to bereavement, *Psychol Aging.* 2004;19(4):668–675.

9. Christakis NA, Iwashyna TJ. The health impact of health care on families: a matched cohort study of hospice use by decedents and mortality outcomes in surviving, widowed spouses, *Soc Sci Med.* 2003;57(3):465–475.

10. Prigerson HG, Bierhals AJ, Kasi SV, et al. Traumatic grief as a risk factor for mental and physical morbidity, *Amer J Psychiatry.* 1997;154(5):616–623.

11. Zhang B, El-Jawahri A, Prigerson HG, Update on bereavement research: evidence-based guidelines for the diagnosis and treatment of complicated bereavement. *J Palliat Med.* 2006;9(5):1188–1203.

12. Latham AE, Prigerson HG. Suicidality and bereavement: complicated grief as psychiatric disorder presenting greatest risk for suicidality. *Suicide Life Threat Behav.* 2004;34(4): 350–362.

13. Shear K, Frank E, Houck PR, et al. Treatment of complicated grief: a randomized controlled trial. *JAMA.* 2005;293(21):2601–2608.

14. Schulz R, Beach S. Caregiving as a risk factor for mortality: the caregiver health effects study. *JAMA.* 1999;282: 2215–2219.

15. Schut H, Stroebe MS. Interventions to enhance adaptation to bereavement. *J Palliat Med.* 2005;8(suppl 1):S140–147.

Critical Thinking

1. Why is grief harder for caregivers, and what can professionals, family members and others do to help?

2. Describe the elements of complicated grief and how they are similar to PTSD?

3. What are some of the poor bereavement outcomes caregivers face?

Dr SCHULZ is Professor of Psychiatry, Director, University Center for Social and Urban Research, University of Pittsburgh, Pittsburgh, Pa. **Dr HEBERT** is Assistant Professor of Medicine, Division of General Internal Medicine, University of Pittsburgh. **Dr BOERNER** is Senior Research Scientist, Jewish Home Lifecare, Research Institute on Aging, New York, NY.

Disclosures: Drs Schulz, Hebert, and Boerner disclose that they have no financial relationship with any manufacturer in this area of medicine.

A Family Undertaking

HOLLY STEVENS

When Harriet Ericson died in January 2007 at age 93, she went to the grave in the same manner in which she lived her final years—lovingly tended by her son Rodger Ericson of Austin, Texas. A former U.S. Air Force chaplain and Lutheran pastor (ELCA), Ericson bathed, anointed and dressed his mother's body, then laid it in a casket he had built himself and named "hope chest" to reflect the family's faith in the resurrection. The next day, with the help of his daughters and grandsons, he lifted her casketed remains into the bed of his pickup truck and secured the precious cargo for a road trek to Minnesota, where a family grave plot was waiting.

Except for the preparation of the grave, Ericson took care of all the details that would usually be handed to a commercial mortician. Ericson was, in effect, his mother's funeral director—and it was all completely legal.

Referred to as home funerals by most who practice them, these homespun arrangements arc protected by law in 44 states. "A home funeral can help people gently integrate the death into their lives and faith." says home funeral educator Donna Belk, who helped Ericson prepare for his mother's passing. "When the body stays at home for up to a few days, family and friends remain connected to the entire process; the gradual changes that occur in the body over this time frame coincide with the family's adjustment to its loss." Even in the six states that require the involvement of a commercial provider—Connecticut, Indiana, Louisiana, Michigan, Nebraska and New York—some families have been able to work with morticians so as to participate more fully in the process.

The term *home funeral* does not mean that a funeral ritual is necessarily held in the home. It refers to an approach to the entire process from the moment of death to final disposition:

A home funeral is a noncommercial response to death.

A home funeral is a noncommercial, family-centered response to death that involves the family and its social community in the care and preparation of the body for burial or cremation and/or in planning and carrying out related rituals or ceremonies and/or in the burial or cremation itself. A home funeral may occur entirely within the family home or not. It is differentiated from the institutional funeral by its emphasis on minimal, noninvasive care and preparation of the body; by its reliance on the family's own social networks for assistance and support; and by the relative or total absence of commercial funeral providers in its proceedings. (From *Undertaken with Love: A Home Funeral Guide for Congregations and Communities,* by the Home Funeral Committee Manual Publishing Group.)

A home funeral can include a religious ceremony in a church. The family may choose to have the body present at the ceremony or not, and may have the casket open or closed. For Christians, a home funeral can address the same religious purposes served by other funeral arrangements carried out within a religious setting: to treat the body with reverence and honesty, to proclaim the hope of resurrection and our risen life in Christ, to commend the deceased into God's care, and to mark our common bond with all who are alive with us and who have died before us.

A home funeral protects the sanctity of the process by removing the material pressures that have shaped American funeral etiquette since the Civil War, when affluent families began paying embalming surgeons to find their fallen sons on the battlefield and inject them with enough arsenic for the body to be preserved for the trip home. At that point a commercial industry began to grow, one that was beholden less to the precepts of the church than to the material and seemingly insatiable whims of consumers—even at life's end.

Is it any wonder that common funeral myths point back to an industry that makes its profits by catering to and encouraging material impulses? In my work as a funeral consumer advocate, families tell me time and again that they had no idea that embalming rarely is required by law or that they can buy an inexpensive casket from a source other than the funeral home or even construct their own.

"I have no problems with people requesting and using the services of funeral homes as long as morticians are not pushing or deceiving the grieving family into expenses that are not necessary," Ericson told me. He said that an employee of Service Corporation International, the nation's largest funeral home chain, told him that every cemetery in America requires an outer liner for cremated remains. When Ericson responded that he knew that was not so, the salesperson qualified his answer:

"Well, not every cemetery, but yes, every cemetery in the country that SCI owns."

Religious leaders are often lured into complacency by the promotional favors they receive from funeral directors. In his book *Does This Mean You'll See Me Naked?* (Rooftop Publishing), funeral director Robert Webster recalls that a former boss, also a funeral director, would welcome a new minister to town with a pen and pencil set. On the next visit, the funeral director would deliver tickets to Cincinnati Reds games; at other times, he'd press a crisp $100 bill into the pastor's hand or send a fruit basket. "These people help us to stay in business," Webster's boss told him. "Go out of your way to treat them well."

In a home funeral involving a parishioner, the pastor can take the lead in helping families integrate the care of the body, the funeral ceremony and the interpretation of the death into a religious context. By contrast, in a typical arrangement with a funeral home, says Ericson. "It was not uncommon for me as a pastor to receive $75 for my services—visitation of the family at the time of death, arranging the religious service with the family, preparing the bulletin, getting the church in order, preparing a personalized yet theologically sound sermon, and conducting the burial/committal service—while the mortician charged an extra $75 to have the service at my church."

In my faith community, New Garden Friends Meeting in Greensboro, North Carolina, a committee assists families in our congregation that want to care for their own dead. We've identified our legal rights and responsibilities in assisting with home funerals. We bring the simple, noninvasive skills involved in caring for the body at home. We bring ease and acquired wisdom to the process, offering families an option for spiritual and emotional closure at life's end.

In Raleigh, North Carolina, the Islamic Burial Society of North America teaches groups of Muslim men and women to care for their dead in keeping with the precepts of the Qur'an. Because Muslim and Orthodox Jewish burial practices are similar, the project has fostered friendships between members of the two faiths as they work together to return death rituals to their religious communities. Death care has a way of reminding us both of our mutual human limitations and of the place of faith as a source for hope and sustenance in the face of great loss.

Granted, even if most families knew that in most states they may care for their own dead without the involvement of a licensed funeral director, home funerals would be unlikely to put any professional undertakers out of work anytime soon. Americans have become so removed from their dead that even in a home funeral they hesitate to touch the body. The practice requires more involvement from the family, although the support of an experienced congregation can greatly case the load. Occasionally, circumstances prohibit a vigil and make a home funeral impractical.

Families have found the home funeral process to be enormously healing.

Most people who have experienced home funerals tell me that they found the process to be enormously healing; it enabled them to participate creatively in honoring the one who died and to integrate the experience into the context of their faith in ways that commercial funeral homes and crematories cannot replicate. As Ericson says, "Home funerals mean less traipsing behind the undertaker, who is geared toward efficiency and profit."

I see more faith communities embracing home funerals and other less commercial practices at life's end. Some church-owned cemeteries have dropped vault requirements to allow ecologically minded parishioners to simplify their return to dust after death. In the Pocono Mountains, the Eastern Pennsylvania Conference of the United Methodist Church leases a portion of its forests to an organization that creates family burial sites for cremated remains at the roots of selected hardwood trees.

For the first time since embalming surgeons began to set up shop on Civil War battlegrounds, Americans are reassessing how funeral practices relate to congregational life. The growing interest in home funerals and other natural end-of-life practices offers religious institutions the opportunity to support alternatives that are embedded more deeply in community and resistant commercial culture. The home funeral movement calls on religious leaders to honor an etiquette that is simpler, more affordable and ultimately more sacred.

Critical Thinking

1. What are some of the benefits of having a home funeral for the family?
2. How should a family decide to have a home funeral or not?
3. What are the legal issues surrounding home funerals?
4. What is the evolution of home funerals?
5. Why would families choose to have a home funeral?

HOLLY STEVENS is a funeral consumer advocate and coordinator of the Undertaken with Love project at homefuneralmanual.org.

Stressors Afflicting Families during Military Deployment

Gina M. Di Nola

Operation Iraqi Freedom is a stressful time for many military families. Help is available, if one knows where to look. The U.S. Army has implemented a program to address the needs of family members–the Family Readiness Group or FRG. Before any program or group can assist spouses, it is necessary to name and understand the issues families face. In doing so, leaders can be better prepared to help family members handle the stressors associated with the current deployments in support of Operation Iraqi Freedom (OIF) and the Global War on Terrorism (GWOT).

History of the FRG

Involvement of spouses in the military started with the Revolutionary War. In May of 1780, Esther Reed (her husband was an aide to George Washington) and 39 wives started the first wives' club, which became known as "the Association". The Association performed fundraising for supplies, cooking, mending, nursing, and equipment caddying in exchange for rations to feed their families (1).

During World War II, the Association became known as the "waiting wives club", an established support system for family members back home. The club eventually evolved and was institutionalized after the Persian Gulf War (2) to today's family support group known as the Family Readiness Group (FRG). The FRG serves as the link between units and their spouses; it is the support system for family members, especially during wartime or deployment.

Role of the FRG

The FRG plays an important role in the military. The effectiveness of family support groups has been apparent since the Vietnam War (2). After the First Gulf War, the U.S. Army mandated that all units have an established family support group, or FRG (3). "Commanders have an obligation to provide assistance to establish and maintain personal and family affairs readiness . . . . Examples include Family Readiness Groups . . . ." (3). The role of the FRG is to keep families informed and updated during times of deployment, training, or military exercises. Although it doesn't practice the same formalities and structures as the military, the FRG is beneficial during the difficult times that military spouses must face.

Stressors during Deployments

There is no doubt that deployments cause much stress to the service member and the family. Operation Desert Storm/Shield was the largest military mobilization since the Vietnam War (4). Three categories of stressors were identified in a study done during Operation Desert Storm (5): emotional (missing the soldier, safety concern for the soldier), deployment-related (managing budget, Powers of Attorney, and increase in child-care costs), and general life events (non-English speakers, new to installation, etc.). The list of stressors noted at that time were loneliness, financial insecurities, children's discipline, and an overall feeling that the military was not concerned for their well-being. Some spouses did not use programs available to them for fear of being classified as unable to handle their problems. Others were not able to seek family support because they were not stationed near them. Family roles had to be changed and required adjustment by both parents and children.

Other factors affecting spouses during Operation Desert Storm were rumors. In 1992, the US Army War College reported that "family support groups helped, in some cases, to reduce rumors" (6). However, in a subsequent study conducted by the U.S. Army Research Institute (ARI) and the Walter Reed Army Institute of Research (WRAIR), "unit leaders' support for families was strongly related to rumors . . . ." The case study demonstrated that family support groups may facilitate the spread of rumors and any attempts to control rumors actually enhanced them (6).

Another stresser faced by families is spousal aggression. A study done between 1990 and 1994 revealed that there was a significant probability of aggression for soldiers who had deployed than those who did not (7). In 1996 Caliber Associates interviewed 96 couple participants in the Army's Family

Advocacy Programs. Half of the abusers had been deployed an average of 110 days and cited deployment as the triggering stressor (8). Between 2002 and 2004, Fort Bragg, NC alone reported 832 victims of domestic violence (9), which were deployment-related.

Children's reactions to deployments vary with age and developmental stage. Children's system levels are similar to the stress level experienced by their parents or caregiver. One would think the source of the stress would be the immediate family. Instead of being informed by their parents, active-duty children received most of their information from teachers. Media coverage also added to the concerns of safety of the deployed service member. There is an additional stress factor—concern for the service member's safety (10). Active duty children worried that the military parent would die during the deployment (11). Watanabe and Jensen state that children who were not prepared for the deployment fared not as well as those who were (12).

Current OIF Stressors

The National Military Family Association surveyed military spouses in 2005. Stress levels were measured for the various points of the deployment cycle. Fifteen percent experienced heightened stress levels upon notification of the deployment and 18 % upon the departure of the service. During the deployment or absence of the service member, 62 % felt the greatest stress. The respondents emphasized the need for good communication between the unit and the families. Some family members felt that "when entering a second or third deployment, they carry the unresolved anxieties and expectations from the last deployment(s)" (13).

Redeployment and reintegration were also times of much stress for families. The constant deployment left little time for adjustment for each phase of the deployment cycle. Family members expressed an interest in knowing what to expect prior to, during, and after the redeployment phase. Yet few participated in formal training or briefings offered by the installation (13).

Stressors and the FRG

Stressors may vary with each deployment, and everyone copes differently. By establishing family support groups, families were thought to be better equipped to handle the challenges of the military lifestyle, up to the point where the support group becomes a stressor. Whether it is the Army's Family Readiness Group, the Air Force's Key Spouse Program, the Navy's Ombudsman Program, or the Marine Corps's Key Volunteer Network, group dynamics within the support system can affect the coping mechanism of the family members.

The commitment of support group leaders was questioned in a survey conducted recently of 100 family members of deployed soldiers in 2007. Commitment concerns that were stated by the family members included lack of communication from leaders, slow dissemination of information from leaders, cliques within the family support groups (or the FRG), gossip, drama in the group, and limited group activities. Of those who did not like their FRG, 20 % still attended the meetings. Three percent of the participants did not know how to contact their leader in the event of an emergency. One family member suggested that a social worker be present at the meetings. Although 74 % remained on or near the installation, only 54 % attended support group meetings.

Conclusion

According to Webster (2006), readiness is defined as being "prepared mentally or physically for some experience or action." According to the Army's Training and Doctrine Command Public Affairs Office, "Family readiness is the state soldiers, spouses and family members proactively prepare for, and in which they are able to cope with mobilization, deployments and prolonged separations." (14). Independence, financial responsibility, etc. are a few of the attributes of readiness for today's family. Yet, no one knows how ready the family will be until the family separation or deployment occurs.

Deployments are inevitable while serving in the military. Families have many programs or resources available to them to help them cope with the challenges of the deployments, yet many do not use them. The intent of the FRG was to provide families these resources. Unfortunately, the dilemma can stem from the FRG. Addressing the stressors that families face is the first step to attaining readiness. With current and prolonged deployments in support of OIF or GWOT, time is of the essence.

References

1. Crossley A, and Keller CA: The army wife handbook: Updated and expanded, Second edition, Sarasota, FL, ABI Press, 1993.
2. Rosen LN, Durand DB: Coping with the unique demands of military family life. In The military family: A practice guide for Human Service providers, ed. Martin JA, Rosen LN, Sparacino LR, Westport, CT: Praeger, 2000; 55–72.
3. Department of the Army: Army Regulation 600–20: Army Command Policy. 2006.
4. Black Jr WG: Military-induced family separation: A stress reduction intervention. Social Work 1993; 38; no. 3.
5. Rosen LN, Durand DB, Martin JA: Wartime stress and family adaptation. In The military family: A practice guide for Human Service providers, ed. J. A. Martin, Rosen LN, Sparacino LR, Westport, CT, Praeger, 2000: 123–138.
6. Schumm WR, Bell DB, Knott B: Predicting the extent and stressfulness of problem rumors at home among army wives of soldiers deployed overseas on a humanitarian mission. Psychol Rep 2001; 89; 1: 123–34.
7. McCarroll JE, Ursano RJ, Liu X, Thayer LE, Newby JH, Norwood AE, Fullerton CS: Deployment and the probability of spousal aggression by US Army soldiers. Mil Med 2000; 165; 1: 41–4.
8. Brannen SJ, Hamlin II ER: Understanding spouse abuse in military families. In The military family: A practice guide for

Human Service providers, ed. Martin JA, Rosen LN, Sparacino LR; 169–183. Westport, CT: Praeger, 2000.

9. Houppert K: Base crimes: The military has a domestic violence problem. Retrieved on February 6, 2008 from www.motherjones.com/cgibin/print_article.pl?url=www.motherjones.com/news/featurex/2005/07/base_crimes.html

10. Stafford EM, Grady BA: Military family support. Pediatric Annals 2003; 32:2: 110–115.

11. Ryan-Wenger NA: Impact of the threat of war on children in military families. American Journal of Orthopsychiatry 2001: 71; 2: 236–244.

12. Watanabe HK, Jensen PS: Young children's adaptation to a military lifestyle. In The military family: A practice guide for Human Service providers, ed. Martin JA, Rosen LN, Sparacino LR: 209–223. Westport, CT, Praeger, 2000.

13. National Military Family Association: Cycles of deployment: An analysis of survey responses from April through September, 2005: 20. San Diego, Defense Web Technologies, 2005.

14. US Army's Training and Doctrine Command: Family Readiness Group Leader's Command Information Pocket Guide, 2003: Fort Monroe, VA, Headquarters, U.S. Army Training and Doctrine Command, 2003.

Critical Thinking

1. What are some of the reasons military families do not use support groups?

2. What are some ways communities can support families who have deployed members?

3. How can family of the deployed person provide emotional support to each other?

4. What are some existing programs for families coping with deployment?

5. What has the military done to assist with family readiness?

Military Children and Families

Strengths and Challenges during Peace and War

The gathering of military men should be thanking their children, their fine and resourceful children, who were strangers in every school they entered, thanking them for their extraordinary service to their country, for the sacrifices they made over and over again . . . Military brats . . . [spend] their entire youth in service to this country and no one even [knows]. (Conroy, 1991, p. xxv)

NANSOOK PARK

A common saying in the military is that when one person joins, the whole family serves. Military families may often be in the background of public discourse on the military, but they are critical to its success. Although aspects of military life can be difficult for families, positive family functioning boosts a service member's morale, retention, and ability to carry out missions (Shin-seki, 2003). According to a recent report, service members reported positive family relationships as a source of resilience and problems at home as a source of stress and interference (Mental Health Advisory Team 6, 2009). Any efforts to build a strong, effective, and sustainable military force must also consider military families, improving the relationships of the soldier with his or her family members and strengthening the family itself (cf. Gottman, Gottman, & Atkins, 2011).

Since the start of the Global War on Terror, military children and families have faced multiple tests associated with unprecedented lengthy and multiple deployments; shorter stays at home between deployments; and greater risks of death, injury, and psychological problems among service members. Although many military children and families rise to the occasion and do well (Wiens & Boss, 2006), these challenges can take a toll on their health and well-being (Chandra, Burns, Tanielian, Jaycox, & Scott, 2008; Flake, Davis, Johnson, & Middleton, 2009). Despite urgent needs to better understand the impact of deployment on military children and families and to provide appropriate support for them, there is a dearth of research. Programs and interventions exist, but definitive conclusions about what really works are by and large lacking.

Programs that try to assist military children and families often focus only on the prevention or reduction of problems. As important as it is to address problems, it is just as important to recognize the strengths and assets of military children and families and to promote and bolster them. A full and accurate picture of military children and families is needed upon which to base interventions. One of the best ways to prevent or solve problems is to identify what goes well and to use this as the basis of intervention (Park, 2004, 2009; Park & Peterson, 2008; Park, Peterson, & Brunwasser, 2009; Peterson & Park, 2003).

Over the years, studies of military children and families by psychologists have been isolated from and neglected by mainstream psychology. Most studies are done by researchers who are present or former members of the military or immediate members of military families. Studies are too rarely published in the mainstream psychology journals. This state of affairs needs to change to meet the surging needs of military children and families.

This article describes what is known about military children and families: their demographics, their challenges, and their strengths, during both peace and war times. Also addressed are issues and gaps in the existing research and practice. The thesis is that greater attention to the strengths and assets of military children and families is needed in order to design and implement effective programs to support them. This approach echoes the premise of the U.S. Army Comprehensive Soldier Fitness (CSF) program described elsewhere in this special issue (Cornum, Matthews, & Seligman, 2011). The fitness of soldiers extends beyond mere physical prowess to include psychosocial well-being, a key component of which is the well-being of their families (Peterson, Park, & Castro, 2011; Rohall, Segal, & Segal, 1999). Currently, collaborative efforts between psychologists and the U.S. Army are extending the CSF program to family members.

The Changing Demographics of the Modern U.S. Military Family

In the United States today, there are several million men and women wearing the uniform of the country's military. In broad terms, this is a young (50% below age 25) and male (85%) population, with individuals from rural, less affluent, and ethnic minority (African American and Latino/a) backgrounds overrepresented (U.S. Department of Defense, Defense Manpower Data Center, 2008). Almost all have a high school degree or equivalent, and 70% have at least some college credits. About half of them are married, with about 10% of the armed forces in dual-career marriages (i.e., married to another member of the military).

In contrast to the U.S. population as a whole, members of the military tend to marry earlier, a fact that researchers need to take into account in comparing military and civilian families because marriage at a younger age can be associated with more problems than marriage at an older age (Amato, Booth, Johnson, & Rogers, 2007). Among married individuals in the armed forces, more than 70% have one or more children, and there are at least 1.85 million children with one or both parents in the military (65% active duty and 35% Reserves or National Guard; Chandra et al., 2008; Segal & Segal, 2004).

Research on military families as well as formal programs to support them often uses a narrow definition of what a *family* entails: mother and father—one of whom wears a uniform—and their biological children. The so-called nuclear family is not the only type that exists, especially in the contemporary United States. Single-parent families have increased in recent decades, as well as blended families and intergenerational families. With the increase of women in the military, dual-career military families have increased (Segal & Segal, 2004). Each type of family has unique difficulties and assets.

In this article, the phrase *military children and families* is used to refer broadly to all individuals who are connected to a military family—traditional and nontraditional families, extended and binuclear families, spouses and significant others, sons and daughters, stepsons and stepdaughters, brothers and sisters, parents and grandparents, and so on. The focus is on military-connected children, but the functioning of all family members bears on the well-being of these children.

Strengths and Challenges among Military Children and Families

Military life presents both challenges and opportunities to grow for children and families (Hall, 2008). To provide effective services for military children and families, we need a better understanding of these challenges and strengths framed in terms of the culture and function of the military during peace and during war.

During Peace

Even during peaceful times, military children and families face recurrent separations, frequent and often sudden moves, difficult reunions, long and often unpredictable duty hours, and the threat of injury or death of the military service member during routine training and peaceful missions (Black, 1993). On average, active duty military families move every two to three years within the United States or overseas (Croan, Levine, & Blankinship, 1992). Secondary school-age students move three times more often than their civilian counterparts do (Shinseki, 2003). These frequent relocations disrupt children's schoolwork, activities, and social networks, requiring ongoing adjustment to new schools and cultures. Children can grow up feeling rootless and may have difficulties building deeper relationships or maintaining long-term commitments (Wertsch, 1991). Especially during adolescence, interruption of peer relationships can be detrimental to a child's psychosocial development (Shaw, 1979). Also, separation from a parent because of military assignments can have negative impacts on a child's school performance and mental health (Jensen, Grogan, Xenakis, & Bain, 1989). Due to different school and state requirements for course credits and course materials, frequent moves pose additional challenges for academic achievement and graduation by transferring students. These problems are especially pronounced for students with special needs (Hall, 2008).

Nevertheless, the available evidence suggests that military children typically function as well as or even better than civilian children on most indices of health, well-being, and academic achievement. They have similar or lower rates of childhood psychopathology, lower rates of juvenile delinquency, lower likelihood of alcohol or drug abuse, better grades, and higher median IQs than do their civilian counterparts (Jensen, Xenakis, Wolf, & Bain, 1991; Kenny, 1967; Morrison, 1981). According to a large-scale survey of military adolescents (Jeffreys & Leitzel, 2000), military children are in general healthy, have good peer relationships, are engaged in school and community, do well at school, and are satisfied with life. On average, military children report high optimism and positive self-images (Watanabe, 1985).

Compared with civilian children, military children have greater respect for authority and are more tolerant, resourceful, adaptable, responsible, and welcoming of challenges, and they have a greater likelihood of knowing and befriending someone who is "different" (Hall, 2008); they engage in fewer risky behaviors (Hutchinson, 2006); they exhibit greater self-control (Watanabe, 1985); and they show lower levels of impatience, aggression, and disobedience and higher levels of competitiveness (Manning, Balson, & Xenakis, 1988). Most military children are happy to embrace the term *military brat* and one or another of its backronyms such as "brave, resilient, adaptable, and trustworthy."[1]

Difficult life events do not automatically lead to problems in children. In some cases, challenges provide an opportunity to grow. For instance, relocation can be a positive experience. Children and families have the opportunity to meet new people and make new friends, to visit different places, and to experience diverse cultures (O'Connell, 1981).

If families have positive attitudes toward relocation, social support, previous relocation experience, and active coping styles, they do better when they move (Feldman & Tompson, 1993; Frame & Shehan, 1994). As stressful as parental separation can be, military children are afforded the opportunity to take on responsibilities and to be more independent and mature. Although the inherent hierarchy and structure of military culture can produce resentment among some military children and decrease their independent thinking, it can also foster discipline. Furthermore, military values that emphasize service, sacrifice, honor, teamwork, loyalty, sense of purpose, sense of community, and pride can work as resilience factors to overcome the difficulties of military life (Paden & Pezor, 1993).

During War

The major challenge for military children and families during war is a lengthy deployment of the uniformed family member to a combat zone. Children not only miss the deployed parent, but they also experience obvious uncertainty surrounding his or her safety, especially in single-parent or dual-career families. There are other issues as well. Children may be asked to take on greater responsibilities, and daily routines may change (Pincus, House, Christenson, & Adler, 2001). Families may move to be closer to other relatives. Unlike relocation during times of peace, war-time relocation of families may require them to move off base into the civilian community where they lose the existing military support system (MacDermid, 2006).

Nearly 900,000 U.S. children have had at least one of their parents deployed since 2001, and currently 234,000 children have one or both parents at war (Zoroya, 2009). Long and frequent deployments of service members put military children and families at risk for psychosocial problems (American Psychological Association, Presidential Task Force on Military Deployment Services for Youth, Families, and Service Members, 2007). According to U.S. Department of Defense data, between 2003 and 2008 the number of military children receiving outpatient mental health care doubled, and during that period inpatient visits by military children increased by 50%, with a 20% jump from 2007 to 2008 ("Department of Defense Reaches Out to Children of Soldiers," 2009). This indicates potentially a cumulative toll of parental deployments on military children and urgent needs for proper mental health services for this population.

Although scarce, several studies have looked at the impact of parental deployment on children during current wars. Although military children and families cope relatively well with shorter separations (less than six months), longer and multiple deployments create measurable distress (Chandra et al., 2010; Flake et al., 2009). Parental deployment can affect physical health, academic performance, behavior problems, depression, and anxiety of military children. Adolescent children of deployed parents show significantly higher levels of stress, systolic blood pressure, and heart rate than their civilian counterparts (Barnes, Davis, & Treiber, 2007). Children of deployed service members also show decreases in their academic performance, school engagement, and overall school adjustment (Engel, Gallagher, & Lyle, 2010). More than one third of school-age children showed high risk for psychosocial difficulties during parental deployment, 2.5 times the national norm (Flake et al., 2009). Children of deployed parents, especially older youth and girls, reported more problems with school, family, and mental health. The longer the parental deployment is, the greater these problems are, during and after deployment (Chandra et al., 2010).

Risk factors exacerbating the negative effects of deployment on military children and families include a history of family problems, younger families, less educated families, foreign-born spouses, families with young children, those with lower pay grades or reduced income, those without a unit affiliation such as National Guard and Reserve families, families with children who have disabilities, families with pregnancies, single-parent families, and families with mothers in the military (American Psychological Association, Presidential Task Force, 2007).

Although military deployment poses risks, especially for some families, it is equally important to remember that many military children and families show resilience and growth. During the deployment of a family member, parents report that their children are closer to family and friends, and that they are more responsible, independent, and proud. Seventy-four percent of the spouses of service members report personal growth, despite also reporting increased loneliness, stress, and anxiety (U.S. Department of Defense, Defense Manpower Data Center, 2009b).

Resilience plays an important role in all phases of deployment. Resilience mitigates stress and improves adjustment to deployment by children and families. Families that function most effectively are active, optimistic, self-reliant, and flexible (Jensen & Shaw, 1996; Wiens & Boss, 2006). Families that function well find meaning in military life and identify with the work of their uniformed family member (Hammer, Cullen, Marchand, & Dezsofi, 2006; Marchant & Medway, 1987). Family preparedness for deployment as well as community and social support lead to better adjustment (Wiens & Boss, 2006).

Huebner (2010) found that adolescents who adapted well during parental deployment showed the ability to put the situation in perspective; positive reframing; the embracing of change and adaptation as necessary; effective coping skills; and good relationships with family, friends, and neighbors. For example, one adolescent reported, "I have really good neighbors that understand the situation going on. And I'm always welcome at my neighbors" (Huebner, 2010, p. 14).

During deployment, the well-being of military children needs to be approached not just at the level of the individual child but also in terms of larger social systems—the extended family, neighborhoods, schools, and communities. The community environment affects children's adjustment and coping during wartime deployment, and parental stress strongly relates to a military child's psychosocial functioning during deployment (Flake et al., 2009; Huebner, Mancini, Bowen, & Orthner, 2009). The challenges faced by military children are exacerbated by family and community inability to recognize and provide proper support and assistance. If the family as a whole adjusts well to deployment, then so do children. If we care about military children's well-being, it is imperative to ensure family well-being because they are so closely connected.

All things considered, military families on average have done well and show resilience during peace and even war. Problems of course exist for some military families, but rarely to a greater extent than among civilian families. Contrast this conclusion with the notion of the *military family syndrome,* which refers to a constellation of out-of-control offspring, authoritarian fathers, and depressed mothers (Lagrone, 1978). This alleged syndrome has been refuted repeatedly by relevant evidence (e.g., Jensen, Gordon, Lewis, & Xenakis, 1986; Jensen et al., 1991; Morrison, 1981), but it seems to be as resilient as the healthy military family that it fails to acknowledge. The fact that military families overall have done well in the past deserves greater dissemination in the present than seems to occur in today's popular media. If nothing else, the historical strength of the military family can serve as a source of pride and inspiration.

Strengths-Based Approaches

Military children and families often do well, but they are not invulnerable (Cozza, Chun, & Polo, 2005). Rather, they do well because they have compensating strengths and assets (Bowen, Mancini, Martin, Ware, & Nelson, 2003: Palmer, 2008). It behooves us to identify what these may be, to enhance them, and to use what is learned to design interventions for all military children and families, those with or without problems. As noted, one way to prevent or solve problems is to base interventions on what is going well.

The previous section reviewed the strengths and assets of military children and families. More family support programs that address strengths as well as problems are needed. Existing programs need not be replaced but expanded. A focus on what goes well does not mean that what goes poorly should be ignored. Indeed, strengths-based interventions complement and extend problem-focused interventions (Park, 2004, 2009; Park & Peterson, 2006, 2008; Park et al., 2009; Peterson & Park, 2003). A comprehensive approach to the support of military families may be more effective than a problem-focused strategy, and it would certainly reduce the stigma that surrounds the seeking of "mental health" care.

Programs and resources, formal and informal, already exist in both military and civilian sectors to support military children and families. Targeted programs and services are helpful, but we need further assistance, support, and engagement of the broader community.

The *Military Child Education Coalition* (MCEC) programs to support military children are worthy of attention. They embody the strengths-based focus advocated here. MCEC has been working directly with different branches of the military, school districts, and parents to facilitate transition of transferring military children (MCEC, 2001). MCEC offers regular training for school counselors and teachers, involves civilian students in their programs, and makes available relevant information to schools as well as parents. Underlying all of the MCEC programs is the assumption that military families are resilient and resourceful, but that accessible information, consistent school rules, and support help reduce the annoyances associated with student relocation.

The Student 2 Student program of MCEC is a unique student-led, school-based program for transitioning students from military families. This program provides social as well as instrumental support for students relocating to and from different schools. A team of advisors, volunteer students, and school liaison officers from each school are trained to develop and implement specific plans that fit their particular school setting and to implement, recruit, and train others at their school. These programs benefit all transitioning students, military connected or not.

As another example, MCEC's initiative "Living in the New Normal: Helping Children Thrive through Good and Challenging Times" engages and empowers the whole community. It is designed to reach everyone involved with military-connected children. It provides resources and trains adults to help children with deployment-related challenges to develop resilience. Further, the program brings together all sectors of the community to identify the unique assets of that community and to develop specific plans to utilize those assets to provide sustained support not only for military children and families but also for all community members. The MCEC programs stand in contrast to many other interventions for military families, which are often brief and highly targeted, because they involve larger social units (schools and communities) on an ongoing basis.

Issues and Recommendations

There is a significant shortage of evidence-based programs. Indeed, many programs for military children and families are not evaluated at all. In the absence of evidence for their effectiveness, they are but well-intended interventions. When resources are limited and demands are great, it is even more critical to identify programs that are effective and efficient, and to understand the active ingredients that make programs successful (Lester, McBride, Bliese, & Adler, 2011). Following appropriate evaluation, successful programs can be disseminated with confidence, and ineffective programs can be modified or eliminated. A better job needs to be done coordinating and disseminating information about existing programs, increasing their accessibility to the entire military community, and reducing stigma associated with seeking mental health care.

More generally, the research literature on military children and families is too scant, especially in light of contemporary concerns with their well-being while the United States is at war. Several observations about this literature are offered, followed by recommendations for further research and interventions.

Much of the relevant research on military families is not methodologically rigorous. Studies are often hampered by small and nonrepresentative samples and often lack appropriate comparison groups. They are often cross-sectional and starkly descriptive. Potential confounds are often not measured and thus cannot be taken into account, leaving studies inconclusive.

Studies of military children need to use multiple informants. Studies usually depend on what the nonmilitary parent says and may reflect a reporting bias. Consider that one investigation found greater problems among military children than among civilian children according to parental report but *not* according to the direct report of the children (Jensen et al., 1991). Chandra et al. (2010) noted similar discrepancies between conclusions based on parental report and child report.

The lack of explicit theory is conspicuous, although there is an important exception: the cycle of deployment model, which distinguishes different phases through which military families pass when a family member is deployed: (a) predeployment (from notification to departure), (b) deployment (from departure to return), (c) reunion (termed *redeployment* in the military), and (d) postdeployment. Each phase has its own characteristics and requirements (Pincus et al., 2001).

Research on the effects of deployment on military children and families usually focuses only on the period of actual deployment. Redeployment and postdeployment are poorly understood and in need of greater explication. Although reunion can be joyous, it also requires changes and adjustments in roles and routines for all family members, and these can be stressful and confusing (American Psychological Association, Presidential Task Force, 2007). Furthermore, many families have to start preparing for the next deployment again. For both families and service members alike, the postdeployment stage is particularly long and complex (MacDermid, 2006). Many returning service members experience combat-related mental health problems, injuries, and disabilities. These can burden children and families. There is simply not enough research about the long-term effects on children and families of living with a parent who is experiencing such difficulties and how to help them. Longitudinal studies are needed.

Also, a developmental perspective should be utilized in understanding the effect of deployment on children in order to provide developmentally appropriate services. Children at various developmental stages face different developmental tasks and have different levels of cognitive, emotional, and social skills. As a result, children may respond quite differently at each deployment cycle depending on their developmental stages (Paden & Pezor, 1993).

As already noted, most military family studies assume a traditional family and thus do not adequately sample the relevant populations. Considering the diversity of military family types, future studies should examine the impact of military life, especially deployment, on children from different types of families. Future studies should also compare the effects on children of maternal versus paternal deployment.

Although studies have been done spanning different military eras, they rarely use the same measures or procedures, precluding strong conclusions about similarities and differences among different military cohorts (e.g., those serving during Vietnam, Somalia, Desert Storm, and Operation Iraqi Freedom/Operation Enduring Freedom versus those serving during more peaceful times). Military families, no less than their civilian counterparts, are complex. The challenges they face are likely not across the board but rather are influenced by a host of interacting factors—branch of service, age, education, ethnicity, pre-existing problems and assets, community integration (e.g., living on base or off base), exposure to combat, and number of deployments—that are rarely studied in terms of their interactions.

Studies making direct comparisons across branches of the service are also rare, although those studies that do exist often find differences in family functioning across Army, Navy, Air Force, Coast Guard, and Marines. Another neglected contrast related to family functioning is whether the uniformed family member is active duty or Reserve or National Guard. As is well known, a large number of Reserve and National Guard members currently serve; almost 700,000 members of the Reserve and National Guard have been activated since 9/11, parents of about 35% of military children (U.S. Department of Defense, Defense Manpower Data Center, 2009a). Reserve and National Guard families live off base among civilians and are less integrated into a military community, factors that limit their access to military support systems and programs. Many have either left or put on hold their civilian careers because of their "suddenly military" status. The effects on children and families are largely unknown, although one suspects that they include notable instability and stress.

Recent reports suggest that Reserve children and families may be at greater risk for mental health and adjustment issues (Chandra et al., 2008; Mental Health Advisory Team 6, 2009). Children from Reserve families report a lack of understanding and support from their peers and teachers more than children from active-duty families. And what about the children and families of civilian contractors and Federal Agency employees serving in war zones, so heavily relied upon during the current wars? No study has addressed the challenges they face.

There are members of the military family who are often neglected in research and intervention. Siblings can play an important role in bolstering the well-being and resilience of military children and deployed service members. Sibling relationships in general are among the most crucial in a person's life (Bank & Kahn, 1982). Increased attention to military children who do or do not have siblings would be important. Given frequent relocations, siblings may be even more important for military children than for civilian children, providing stability, familiarity, and support not readily available elsewhere.

Another glaring absence in the literature is consideration of the brothers and sisters of service members. The siblings of service members are of course affected by the deployment, injury, or death of those who serve, but virtually nothing is known about challenges they face and how to help them. Studies of civilians make clear that sibling loss adversely affects health and well-being. Surviving siblings often experience anxiety, guilt, sadness, and anger (Bank & Kahn, 1982). They report health that is even worse than that of surviving spouses (Hays, Gold, & Pieper, 1997).

"Siblings of troops often are forgotten mourners" (He-fling, 2009). According to a recent report, there are several thousand surviving siblings from current wars. Many are in their 20s or 30s (Hefling, 2009), but considering that many service members who have lost their lives were young, a large number of surviving siblings are also in their teens or even younger—children themselves. When a service member dies, the spouse, the children, and the parents are generally expected to be most affected. Sibling death may be overlooked as a significant loss (Moss, Moss, & Hans-son, 2001). As a result, siblings may not receive the support they need.

Finally, more research is needed to understand the impact of deployment and grief on military parents and grandparents (Rando, 1986). Their coping and adjustment are important for their own sake as well as in terms of the impacts on the health and well-being of all other family members (Fry, 1997).

CSF Program for Military Family Members

Currently, a major effort is under way to extend the CSF program to all Army family members. Psychologists and the U.S. Army are collaborating to enhance the resilience and well-being of military family members. This project is based on the premise that family members play an important role in the soldier's performance, resilience, and well-being. Parallel to the CSF for soldiers, the family CSF program will include both assessment and program modules built on a strengths-based approach.

The Global Assessment Tool for families, now under development, measures a person's strengths and problems in four life domains: emotional, social, familial, and spiritual (Peterson et al., 2011). The contents of assessment and training modules for families are designed to address both common personal and family-related issues with special attention to unique challenges and experiences faced by military families. The assessment tool is planned to be available through a military website for family members, and the outcome will be confidential. Upon completion of the survey, participants will receive instant feedback on strengths and issues in each life domain. Depending on the results, tailored information and various training modules, from self-development online programs to more intensive group or personal interventions, will be made available.

At this early stage of the project, the target participants are adults in the military family—spouses or caretakers of military children. Strengths and problems among military children will be measured by the caretaker's report, and separate training modules are planned to provide adults with tools to promote the resilience and well-being of military children. A larger community of military family members will be reached in an efficient and cost-effective way with computer technology in conjunction with other strategies to deliver assessment and programs (Gottman et al., 2011). The family component of the CSF program has just begun. The initiative will be revised on the basis of the results of ongoing research and evaluation. It is conceivable that in the future, additional direct assessment and programs for military children will be added to the CSF program.

Conclusion

Throughout history, military children and families have shown great capacity to adapt to and grow from challenges, during peace or during war. However, with U.S. involvement in current wars, military families face multiple challenges that put them at high risk of distress and mental health problems. Their needs are greater than ever. The well-being of military children and families is desirable in its own right and as a means to many other valued ends, for individuals and the larger society.

There is an urgent need for better understanding of both the challenges and the strengths and assets of military children and families to help them not only survive but also thrive. Studies and programs need to take a comprehensive approach that is strengths based *and* problem focused. Studies and programs must focus not just on the individual but also on larger social contexts. We need more high-quality research and more evidence-based programs. Programs need to be rigorously evaluated and better disseminated to reach all those who are in need. Current efforts to expand the CSF program to military family members are another example of a systematic collaboration between psychology and the military to achieve the goal of a healthy, resilient, and productive military community.

Psychology as a field is in a unique position to accomplish all of these goals (Seligman & Fowler, 2011). Military children and families deserve sustained attention from psychology. One hopes that more psychologists will join and indeed help lead this worthy endeavor. About one third of the population has a direct relationship with someone in the military, and virtually everyone has an indirect relationship (Black, 1993). Military families live in our neighborhoods. Their children go to our schools. Much can be learned from them. Building and sustaining healthy, resilient, and thriving military children and families will bring benefits not just to them but ultimately to all Americans. The military family *is* the American family.

Note

1. The origin of the term *military brat* is not agreed on, although some have traced it to an acronym for British Regiment Attached Traveler (i.e., a soldier's child).

References

Amato, P. R., Booth, A., Johnson, D. R., & Rogers, S. J. (2007). *Alone together: How marriage in America is changing.* Cambridge, MA: Harvard University Press.

American Psychological Association, Presidential Task Force on Military Deployment Services for Youth, Families, and Service Members. (2007). *The psychological needs of U.S. military service members and their families: A preliminary report.* Washington, DC: American Psychological Association.

Bank, S., & Kahn, M. (1982). *The sibling bond.* New York, NY: Basic Books.

Barnes, V. A., Davis, H., & Treiber, F. A. (2007). Perceived stress, heart rate, and blood pressure among adolescents with family members deployed in Operation Iraqi Freedom. *Military Medicine, 172,* 40–43.

Black, W. G. (1993). Military-induced family separation: A stress reduction intervention. *Social Work, 38,* 273–280.

Bowen, G. L., Mancini, J. A., Martin, J. A., Ware, W. B., & Nelson, J. P. (2003). Promoting the adaptation of military families: An empirical test of a community practice model. *Family Relations, 52,* 33–44. doi: 10.111 l/j. l741-3729.2003.00033.x

Chandra, A., Burns, R. M., Tanielian, T., Jaycox, L. H., & Scott, M. M. (2008). *Understanding the impact of deployment on children and families: Findings from a pilot study of Operation Purple Camp participants* [Working paper]. Santa Monica, CA: Rand Corporation.

Chandra, A., Lara-Cinisomo, S., Jaycox, L. H., Tanielian, T., Burns, R. M., Ruder, T., & Han, B. (2010). Children on the homefront: The experience of children from military families. *Pediatrics, 125,* 16–25.

Conroy, P. (1991). Introduction. In M. E. Wertsch, *Military brats: Legacies of childhood inside the fortress* (p. xix–xxvii). St. Louis, MO: Brightwell.

Cornum, R., Matthews, M. D., & Seligman, M. E. P. (2011). Comprehensive soldier fitness: Building resilience in a challenging institutional context. *American Psychologist, 66,* 4–9. doi:10.037/a0021420

Cozza, S. J., Chun, R. S., & Polo, J. A. (2005). Military families and children during operation Iraqi Freedom. *Psychiatric Quarterly,* 76, 371–378. doi:10.1007/slll26-005-4973-y

Croan, G. M., Levine, C. T., & Blankinship, D. A. (1992). *Family adjustment to relocation* (Technical Report No. 968). Alexandria, VA: U.S. Army Research Institute for the Behavioral and Social Sciences.

Department of Defense reaches out to children of soldiers. (2009, October 22). *U.S. Medicine.* Retrieved from www.usmedicine. com/articles/Department-of-Defense-Reaches-Out-to-Children-of-Soldiers.html

Engel, R. C, Gallagher, L. B., & Lyle, D. S. (2010). Military deployments and children's academic achievement: Evidence from Department of Defense education activity schools. *Economics of Education Review, 29,* 73–82.

Feldman, D. C, & Tompson, H. B. (1993). Expatriation, repatriation, and domestic geographical relocation: An empirical investigation of adjustment to new job assignments. *Journal of International Business Studies, 24,* 507–529. doi: 10.1057/ palgrave.jibs.8490243

Flake, E. M., Davis, B. E., Johnson, P. L., & Middleton, L. S. (2009). The psychosocial effects of deployment on military children. *Journal of Developmental and Behavioral Pediatrics, 30,* 271–278. doi: 10.1097/ DBP.0b013e3181aac6e4

Frame, M. W., & Shehan, C. (1994). Work and well-being in the two-person career: Relocation stress and coping among clergy husbands and wives. *Family Relations, 43,* 169–205. doi: 10.2307/585323

Fry, P. S. (1997). Grandparents' reactions to the death of a grandchild: An exploratory factor analysis. *Omega: Journal of Death and Dying, 35,* 119–140.

Gottman, J. M., Gottman, J. S., & Atkins, C. (2011). The Comprehensive Soldier Fitness program: Family skills component. *American Psychologist, 66,* 52–57. doi:10.1037/a0021706

Hall, L. K. (2008). *Counseling military families: What mental health professionals need to know.* New York, NY: Routledge.

Hammer, L. B., Cullen, J. C, Marchand, G. C, & Dezsofi, J. A. (2006). Reducing the negative impact of work-family conflict on military personnel: Individual coping strategies and multilevel interventions. In C. A. Castro, A. B. Adler, & T. W. Britt (Eds.), *Military life: The psychology of serving in peace and combat* (Vol. 3, pp. 220–242). Westport, CT: Praeger Security International.

Hays, J. C, Gold, D. T., & Pieper, C. F. (1997). Sibling bereavement in late life. *Omega: Journal of Death and Dying, 35,* 25–42.

Hefling, K. (2009). *Siblings of troops often are forgotten mourners.* Retrieved October 21, 2009, from www.armytimes.com /news/2009/09/ap_military_grieving_siblings_092409/

Huebner, A. J. (2010, January). *Impact of deployment on children and families: Recent research updates.* Presentation at the National Guard Professional Development Conference: Family Program Professional Development, Orlando, FL.

Huebner, A. J., Mancini, J. A., Bowen, G. L., & Orthner, D. K. (2009). Shadowed by war: Building community capacity to support military families. *Family Relations, 58,* 216–228. doi: 10.111 l/j.1741-3729. 2008.00548.x

Hutchinson, J. W. (2006). Evaluating risk-taking behaviors of youth in military families. *Journal of Adolescent Health, 39,* 927–928. doi: 10.1016/j.jadohealth.2006.05.015

Jeffreys, D. J., & Leitzel, J. D. (2000). The strengths and vulnerabilities of adolescents in military families. In J. A. Martin, L. N. Rosen, & L. R. Sparacino (Eds.), *The military family: A practice guide for human service providers* (pp. 225–240). Westport, CT: Praeger.

Jensen, P. S., Gordon, G. A., Lewis, R. L., & Xenakis, S. N. (1986). The military family in review: Context, risk, and prevention. *Journal of the American Academy of Child Psychiatry, 25,* 225–234. doi: 10.1016/ S0002-7138(09)60230-2

Jensen, P. S., Grogan, D., Xenakis, S. N., & Bain, M. W. (1989). Father absence: Effects on child and maternal psychopathology. *Journal of the American Academy of Child and Adolescent Psychiatry, 28,* 171–175. doi:10.1097/00004583-198903000-00004

Jensen, P. S., & Shaw, J. A. (1996). The effects of war and parental deployment upon children and adolescents. In R. J. Ursano & A. E. Norwood (Eds.), *Emotional aftermath of the Persian Gulf War: Veterans, families, communities, and nations* (pp. 83–109). Washington, DC: American Psychiatric Press.

Jensen, P. S., Xenakis, S. N., Wolf, P., & Bain, M. W. (1991). The "military family syndrome" revisited: "By the numbers." *Journal of Nervous and Mental Disease, 179,* 102–107. doi: 10.1097/00005053199102000-00007

Kenny, J. A. (1967). The child in the military community. *Journal of the American Academy of Child Psychiatry, 6,* 51–63. doi:10.1016/S0002-7138(09)61289-9

Lagrone, D. M. (1978). The military family syndrome. *American Journal of Psychiatry, 135,* 1040–1043.

Lester, P. B., McBride, S., Bliese, P. D., & Adler, A. B. (2011). Bringing science to bear: An empirical assessment of the Comprehensive Soldier Fitness program. *American Psychologist, 66,* 77–81. doi: 10.1037/a0022083

MacDermid, S. M. (2006). *Multiple transitions of deployment and reunion for military families.* Retrieved from the Military Family Research Institute, Purdue University website: www.cfs.purdue.edu/mfri/DeployReunion.ppt

Manning, D. T., Balson, P. M., & Xenakis, S. N. (1988). Prevalence of type A behavior in American combat soldiers and their children. *Military Medicine, 153,* 358–360.

Marchant, K. H., & Medway, F. J. (1987). Adjustment and achievement associated with mobility in military families. *Psychology in the Schools, 24,* 289–294. doi:10.1002/1520-6807(198707)24:3<::AID-PITS2310240315>3.0.CO;2-A

Mental Health Advisory Team 6. (2009, November 6). *Mental Health Advisory Team (MHAT) 6 Operation Enduring Freedom 2009 Afghanistan* (Report chartered by the Office of the Command Surgeon US Forces Afghanistan (USFOR-A) and Office of the Surgeon General United States Army Medical Command). Retrieved from www.armymedicine.army.mil/reports/mhat/mhat_vi/MHAT_VI-OEF_Redacted.pdf

Military Child Education Coalition. (2001). *United States Army secondary education transition study.* Arlington, VA: Military Family Resources Center.

Morrison, J. (1981). Rethinking the military family syndrome. *American Journal of Psychiatry, 138,* 354–357.

Moss, M. S., Moss, S. Z., & Hansson, R. O. (2001). Bereavement and old age. In M. S. Stroebe, R. O. Hansson, W. Stroebe, & H. Schut (Eds.), *Handbook of bereavement research: Consequences, coping, and care* (pp. 241–260). Washington, DC: American Psychological Association, doi: 10.1037/10436-010

O'Connell, P. V. (1981). *The effect of mobility on selected personality characteristics of ninth and twelfth grade military dependents* (Unpublished doctoral dissertation). University of Wisconsin, Milwaukee.

Paden, L. B., & Pezor, L. J. (1993). Uniforms and youth: The military child and his or her family. In F. W. Kaslow (Ed.), *The military family in peace and war* (pp. 3–24). New York, NY: Springer.

Palmer, C. (2008). A theory of risk and resilience in military families. *Military Psychology, 20,* 205–217. doi:10.1080/08995600802118858

Park, N. (2004). Character strengths and positive youth development. *Annals of the American Academy of Political and Social Science, 591,* 40–54. doi:10.1177/0002716203260079

Park, N. (2009). Building strengths of character: Keys to positive youth development. *Reclaiming Children and Youth, 18,* 42–47.

Park, N., & Peterson, C. (2006). Moral competence and character strengths among adolescents: The development and validation of the Values in Action Inventory of Strengths for Youth. *Journal of Adolescence, 29,* 891–910.

Park, N., & Peterson, C. (2008). Positive psychology and character strengths: Application to strengths-based school counseling. *Professional School Counseling, 12,* 85–92.

Park, N., Peterson, C, & Brunwasser, S. M. (2009). Positive psychology and therapy. In N. Kazantzis, M. A. Reinecke, & A. Freeman (Eds.), *Cognitive and behavioral theories in clinical practice* (pp. 278–306). New York, NY: Guilford Press.

Peterson, C, & Park, N. (2003). Positive psychology as the evenhanded positive psychologist views it. *Psychological Inquiry, 14,* 141–146.

Peterson, C, Park, N., & Castro, C. A. (2011). Assessment for the U.S. Army Comprehensive Soldier Fitness program: The Global Assessment Tool. *American Psychologist, 66,* 10–18. doi:10.1037/a0021658

Pincus, S. H., House, R., Christensen, J., & Adler, L. E. (2001). The emotional cycle of deployment: A military family perspective. *Journal of the Army Medical Department, 4/5/6,* 615–623.

Rando, T. (1986). Death of the adult child. In T. Rando (Ed.), *Parental loss of a child* (pp. 221–238). Champaign, IL: Research Press.

Rohall, D. E., Segal, M. W., & Segal, D. R. (1999). Examining the importance of organizational supports on family adjustment to military life in a period of increasing separation. *Journal of Political and Military Psychology, 27,* 49–65.

Segal, D. R., & Segal, M. W. (2004). America's military population. *Population Bulletin, 59,* 1–40.

Seligman, M. E. P., & Fowler, R. D. (2011). Comprehensive Soldier Fitness and the future of psychology. *American Psychologist, 66,* 8286. doi:10.1037/a0021898

Shaw, J. A. (1979). Adolescents in the mobile military community. In D. X. Freedman et al. (Eds.), *Adolescent psychiatry* (Vol. 7, pp. 191–198). Chicago, IL: University of Chicago Press.

Shinseki, E. K. (2003). *The Army family* (White paper). Retrieved from www.whs.mil/library/Dig/AR-M620U_20080912.pdf

U.S. Department of Defense, Defense Manpower Data Center. (2008). *The changing profile of the Army 1985–2008.* Alexandria, VA: Author.

U.S. Department of Defense, Defense Manpower Data Center. (2009a). *Reserve components: Noble Eagle/Enduring Freedom/Iraqi Freedom.* Alexandria, VA: Author.

U.S. Department of Defense, Defense Manpower Data Center. (2009b). *2008 surveys of military spouses: Impact of deployments on spouses and children.* Alexandria, VA: Author.

Watanabe, H. K. (1985). A survey of adolescent military family members' self-image. *Journal of Youth and Adolescence, 14,* 99–107.

Wertsch, M. E. (1991). *Military brats: Legacies of childhood inside the fortress.* St. Louis, MO: Brightwell.

Wiens, T. W., & Boss, P. (2006). Maintaining family resiliency before, during, and after military separation. In C. A. Castro, A. B. Adler, & T. W. Britt (Eds.), *Military life: The psychology of serving in peace and combat* (Vol. 3, pp. 13–38). Westport, CT: Praeger Security International.

Zoroya, G. (2009, June 25). Troops' kids feel war toll. *USA Today.* Retrieved from www.usatoday.com/news/military/2009-06-24-military-kids_N.htm

Critical Thinking

1. What are some of the strength and challenges military families face?

2. How do children cope when a parent is deployed more and at greater lengths?

3. What do you see as the need for more research on this issue?

4. What can friends of these families do to help with coping?

5. Why do you think that children have more trouble with coping?

I would like to acknowledge Daniel Fifis, retired school psychologist at Fort Jackson Schools, Columbia, South Carolina, whose generosity and dedication to military children and families have touched so many, including me. I thank Christopher Peterson, Albert Cain, Mary Keller, Jennifer Kirkpatrick, and Joyce Hodson for their help during preparation of this article. Special thanks go to Patricia K. Shinseki, who shared valuable insights and resources about military children and families and provided inspiration through her deep concerns and caring for them.

Correspondence concerning this article should be addressed to Nansook Park, Department of Psychology, University of Michigan, 530 Church Street, Ann Arbor, MI 48109-1043. E-mail: nspark@umich.edu

Helping Military Kids Cope with Traumatic Death

Linda Goldman, MS, LCPC, FT

Ordinary fears are a normal part of a child's developmental growth, and children create internal and external mechanisms to cope with these fears. But a child's ordinary fears can be transformed into very real survival fears in the face of severe trauma. After children experience the death of a parent, they often feel alone and different. Frightened because their once comfortable world now seems unpredictable and unsafe, they may react in ways that we as adults can truly not judge, understand, or anticipate. The impact of a dad's or mom's death in the military can be so traumatically disturbing that the terror involved with the death and the way the parent died may override a child's ability to grieve in a natural way, and share sadness and frustration.

Events can cause panic, stress, and extreme anxiety in kids' lives, and the feelings are heightened with each new instance reported in the media. The terror that grips our children in these circumstances emerges from situations that suddenly overwhelm them and leave them feeling helpless, hopeless, and unable to cope. Trauma is defined by the Encarta® World English Dictionary as "an extremely distressing experience that causes severe emotional shock and may have long-lasting psychological effects." This unexpected and shocking event destroys a child's ability to cope and function in a normal way.

Children can suffer from a state of trauma that can develop into Post-Traumatic Stress Disorder, in which present events trigger memories of trauma resulting in panic, anxiety, disorientation, fear, and all the psycho-physical feelings associated with the traumatic memory.

Signs of Traumatized Children

Seven-year-old Joey's dad was killed in Iraq. He constantly questioned Mom. "Tell me exactly what happened. Did my Dad suffer?" Joey had nightmares and regressed to bedwetting. Tyler's dad was killed by a stray bullet during military combat. His father would always tell him "Nothing can stop me from coming home." Tyler constantly worries about where the bullet hit him, did it hurt him, was he unprotected, and did he die instantly. He began having stomachaches and panic attacks, worrying his mom could get killed too. Jonathan's dad was killed in a firefight in Iraq. Instead of being honored as the son of a military hero, he was often victimized on the playground by a school bully. Jonathan kicked him and both boys were punished. His grades dropped from straight A's to F's after his dad died.

Many young people may experience physical, emotional, cognitive, and behavioral symptoms. These signals range from stomachaches and nightmares to poor grades, isolation, depression, regression, and hostility.

Caring adults need to recognize the signs of grieving and traumatized children, and they need to be aware of the techniques and resources available to help bring safety and protection back to the child's inner and outer world. For example, listening to children's thoughts and feelings, and providing a safe means of expression helps teachers, parents, and educators reinforce their ability to ensure a safe and protected environment.

Traumatized children tend to recreate their trauma, often experiencing bad dreams, waking fears, and recurring flashbacks. Young children have a very hard time putting these behaviors into any context of safety. Many withdraw and isolate themselves, regress and appear anxious, and develop sleeping and eating disorders as a mask for the deep interpretations of their trauma. Young children engage in post-traumatic play by compulsively repeating some aspect of the trauma.

The most common identifying factors that children are re-experiencing the event are play reenactment, nightmares, waking memories, and disturbing thoughts and feelings about the event. Sometimes kids avoid reminders of the traumatic event and show little conscious interest.

Many traumatized children exhibit hyper arousal by increased sleep problems, irritability, inability to concentrate, startle reactions, and regressive behaviors.

When caring adults can identify traumatized kids, they can normalize grief and trauma signs and develop ways kids can express their feelings and emotions. Parents, educators, and other caring professionals can model, present, and support comfortable ways to bring safety and protection back into kids' lives.

Young children developmentally live in an egocentric world filled with the notion that they have caused and are responsible for everything. George's dad was deployed to Iraq twice. Over and over George explained to his teacher. "It's my fault my dad died. I should have made him stay home from Iraq." Some kids may also feel survival guilt. They may think, "Why am I living when so many others have died?" Adults can reframe guilt and magical thinking from "What could I have done?" to "What can I do now?"

At-Risk Behaviors

Children may begin to exhibit at-risk behaviors after a traumatic event. The frequency, intensity, and duration of these behaviors are important factors to consider. Children may experience post-traumatic stress, revisiting the traumatic event through outside stimulus like photos, music, and the media, or by reliving the sights and sounds of the tragedy in their minds. Expect children to re-experience a degree of their original trauma on the anniversary of their parent's death.

The following behaviors may be indicators that a child may benefit from professional help:

- Sudden and pronounced change in behavior
- Threat of suicide or preoccupation with suicide, evidenced through artwork or writing
- Harmful acts to other children or animals
- Extreme confusion or incoherence
- Evidence of substance abuse—drugs, alcohol, etc.
- Sudden change of grades
- Avoidance or abandonment of friends
- Angry or tearful outbursts
- Self-destructive behavior
- Inability to eat or sleep
- Over-concern with own health or health of a loved one

- Giving away important possessions
- Sudden unexplained improvement in behavior or schoolwork
- Depression, isolation, or withdrawal

Activities That Help Kids Express Thoughts and Feelings

Helping children to establish a sense of order in an ever-changing and chaotic world is important. Not only do we want our kids to realize they are survivors of a difficult event, but they also need to know that their life still has continuity and meaning. Parents and educators working with traumatized children should keep to the daily routine as much as possible. This allows kids to feel a renewed sense of security.

Establishing family activities also has a reassuring effect on children. Preparing meals together, eating dinner as a family, reading stories aloud, or playing family games can help to reestablish a sense of normalcy to kids' lives. It is important to initiate safe places for kids to express their ideas. This can be done by finding quiet times at home, in the car, or on a peaceful walk. Being with children without distractions can produce a comfortable climate to begin dialogue. Bedtime should be a reassuring time, too. Often, this is the time children choose to talk about their worries. Parents can consider an increase in transition time, storytelling, and book reading to create a peaceful, uninterrupted nighttime environment.

Hope for the Future

The sudden death of a mom or dad in military service can shatter a child's emotional and physical equilibrium and stability. Too many boys and girls experience fear, isolation, and loneliness after a parent's traumatic death. Faced with a myriad of losses ranging from parental death, moving, change of school, reduced income level, and public mourning, many children are left in a world where they see no future and no protection.

One goal of trauma work with children is to restore safety and protection to children who have experienced the loss of a parent in combat. Another goal is to provide parents and youth workers with information, understanding, and skills related to the issues creating trauma. With these tools we can help our children become less fearful and more compassionate human beings, thereby increasing their chances of living in a future world of increased inner and outer peace.

Critical Thinking

1. What is one recommendation from Goldman for helping military children cope with death that stood out for you, and why?

2. How do military children cope differently than other children coping with death?

3. What are some ways at which caregivers can help military children cope with death?

4. Have you or someone you know had to cope with the death of a loved one in the military?

5. How should communities assist families affected by the death of a loved one?

LINDA GOLDMAN is the author of *Life and Loss, Children Also Grieve, Raising Our Children to Be Resilient,* and *Breaking the Silence: A Guide to Help Children with Complicated Grief.* She works with traumatized children in her practice near Washington, D.C. Email: Linda. goldman@verizon.net, Web: www.childrensgrief.net

A Divided House

In an era of bitter divorce battles, parents often use children as hammers to bash each other, manipulating not only the legal system but also their children's affections. Can a broken parent-child bond be restored?

MARK TEICH

In 1978, after Cathy Mannis and her future husband moved into the same cooperative at U.C. Berkeley, they ran into each other often. She was not immediately smitten. "I detested him at first, and I should have stayed with that feeling," recalls Cathy Mannis of her now ex-husband. "He was overweight and always very critical. Then he lost weight, became cuter, and started paying attention to me. He was going to be a doctor and he seemed so trustworthy; he said he would never desert his family as his own father had done to him." They started dating, and she ultimately cared for him enough to marry him. "I thought he'd be a good father, and I was dying to be a mother. I thought we'd have a good life."

She worked full-time as a legal secretary to put him through medical school. She also bought the two of them a town house with money she'd saved before marriage. When she gave birth to a boy, Matt (not his real name), she was as happy as she'd ever been. Over time, she saw signs that her husband was cheating on her, but she always forgave him.

Their second son, Robby, was born autistic, and things went downhill fast. The boy had speech and learning problems and was frequently out of control. Her husband was appalled. "He's dumber than a fish," he said.

Still, they had one more child, Harry (the name has been changed), hoping to give Matt a sibling without Robby's problems. Harry turned out normal, but he bonded most closely with Robby; they became inseparable.

When Cathy once again became convinced her husband was cheating—he inexplicably never came home one night—she finally threw him out. He filed for divorce before she could forgive him again.

Cathy was granted primary custody of the kids, and her ex soon married the woman he'd been seeing on the side. Because of all she had to do to help Robby as well as her other two kids, Cathy could no longer hold a full-time job. Meanwhile, her ex declared two bankruptcies and, at one point, even mental disability, all of which kept alimony payments to a trickle.

Eventually Cathy was so broke that her electricity was turned off; she and the boys ate dinner by candlelight. Then she became so ill she had to be hospitalized for life-threatening surgery. She had no choice but to leave the kids with her ex. "He promised to return them when my health and finances improved," she says.

That was almost seven years ago. Her health has long since returned and she has a good job she can do from home, but the only child ever restored to her, despite nonstop court battles, was Robby. In fact, her ex got the courts to rule that the children should be permanently separated, leaving the other two children with him, since Robby was a "threat" to his younger brother's well-being.

Through all those years, Cathy says she faced a campaign of systematic alienation from Matt and Harry. "When I called to speak to them, I was usually greeted with coldness or anger, and often the boys weren't brought to the phone. Then my ex sent letters warning me not to call them at home at all. Whenever the kids came to stay with me, they'd report, 'Dad says you're evil. He says you wrecked the marriage.'" Then he moved thousands of miles away, making it vastly more difficult for her to see her children.

As time has passed, the boys have increasingly pulled away. Matt, now grown and serving in the military, never speaks to Cathy. Thirteen-year-old Harry used to say, "Mommy, why can't I stay with you? All the other kids I know live with their moms," before leaving visits with her. Now he often appears detached from her and uninterested in Robby, whom he once adored. His friends at his new home think his stepmother is his mom, because that's how she introduces herself. "She told me she would take my kids, and she did. The alienation is complete," rues Cathy. "All I ever wanted was to be a mom."

Divorcing parents have long bashed each other in hopes of winning points with kids. But today, the strategy of blame encompasses a psychological concept of parental alienation that is increasingly used—and misused—in the courts.

On the one hand, with so many contentious divorces, parents like Cathy Mannis have been tragically alienated from the children they love. On the other hand, parental alienation has been seized as a strategic tool in custody fights, its effects exploited in the courtroom, often to the detriment of loving parents protecting children from true neglect or abuse. With the impact of alienation so devastating—and false accusations so prevalent—it may take a judge with the wisdom of Solomon to differentiate between the two faces of alienation: a truly toxic parent and his or her victimized children versus manipulation of the legal system to claim damage where none exists.

The maligning of an ex need not be conscious—or even particularly extreme—to inflict lasting damage on a parent-child relationship.

A Symptom of Our Time?

Disturbed by the potential for alienation, many divorce courts have today instituted aggressive steps to intervene where they once just stood by. And with good reason: Alienation is ruinous to all involved. "In pathological or irrational alienation, the parent has done nothing to deserve that level of hatred or rejection from the child," explains University of Texas psychologist Richard Warshak, author of *Divorce Poison: Protecting the Parent-Child Bond from a Vindictive Ex.* "It often seems to happen almost overnight, and neither the rejected parent nor even the rejecting child understands why."

Often, in fact, it's the emotionally healthier parent who gets rejected, Warshak adds. That parent tends to understand that it's not in the child's best interests to lose the other parent. In contrast, the alienating parent craves revenge against the ex—then uses the child to exact that punishment. "It's a form of abuse," Warshak says. "Both parent and child are victims."

The alienating parent could vilify the ex to rationalize the dissolution of the relationship, explains Atlanta family therapist Frank Pittman, MD "Even though they managed to stay married to that person for 10 or 15 years, they now see him or her as the devil's spawn. It's the only way they can justify the breakup of their marriage, because otherwise, it would be their own fault." Once they've convinced themselves of that, it's easy enough to see why their children should be kept away from the other parent.

The maligning of an ex need not be conscious—or even particularly extreme—to inflict lasting damage on a parent-child relationship. "The child can hear negative comments inadvertently," notes Diane McSweeney, a marriage, family, and child counselor for the San Diego Unified School District. "Mom is on the phone with a friend, or Dad is talking to his girlfriend and the child happens to hear negative things. I don't think most people mean to insult the other parent to the child, but they're caught up in their grief for their failed marriage and don't appreciate that the kid can hear everything."

Alienation is especially damaging when one parent can't contain the anger—Mom cheated, or Dad hasn't visited or paid child support—and the wounded parent starts venting to the child. "They're just so desperate to talk to someone, and there's no one else they trust left to talk to. They would never do that to

---

Divorce without Devastating the Kids

Clearly, some parents—those who are physically or emotionally abusive—should be separated from their children. But these are the rarity, and in virtually all other cases, children would do better if their divorced parents stayed amicable partners in raising them. To keep a divorce as healthy as possible for children, follow these rules:

- **Never put** the other parent down. Divorce uproots children's feelings of stability badly enough—trashing or eliminating one of the parents magnifies the instability exponentially.
- **Rather than using** kids as a sounding board, divorced parents who are struggling with each other should seek outside emotional help.
- **Hold any charged** or volatile discussions far out of earshot of the children.
- **Do everything in** your power to accept your ex's next mate, since this person will also play an important role in your child's future stability and happiness.

Parents Who Alienate May Use the Following Tactics

- **Limiting the time** a child can spend with the other parent, and even violating court-ordered visitation schedules.
- **Making false** or unfounded accusations of neglect or abuse, especially in a legal forum. The most damaging expression of this is the false accusation of sexual abuse.
- **Creating fear** of rejection and threatening to withhold affection should the child express positive feelings about the absent parent.
- **Saying negative things** about the other parent in front of or within earshot of the child.
- **Blaming the other** parent for the collapse of the marriage.
- **Moving far away,** making it difficult for the other parent to have a regular relationship with a child.

---

their child in any other situation, but now they are in no shape or form ready to parent," says McSweeney. "The child is then thrown into confusion, feeling the need to take sides. 'I love Mom, but Mom hates Dad, so how can I love them both?' Or, 'I'll make Dad mad if I keep loving Mom, so I have to choose him over her.' "

"I was an adolescent when my parents were divorced," recalls Michelle Martin. "You were either on my mother's side or against her, and if you were on her side, you had to be against my father. She was so angry at him for walking out on her, felt so much shame and betrayal, that you couldn't possibly have a relationship with him if you wanted one with her."

Decades later, Michelle recalls her father (who has since died) as a gentle, caring man. But from the moment he left, her mother systematically worked to convince her that he had been abusive. "She really could not have portrayed him more negatively. 'How can you love him?' she'd say. 'You can't count on him.' He'd call, and she'd tell him my siblings and I didn't want to talk to him, then she'd tell me he didn't want to talk with us."

Afraid to lose her mother's love on top of having had her father walk out, Michelle ended up buying the brainwashing. Eventually, her father married another woman and moved away. At first he came into town regularly to visit, but the ever-renewing hostility gradually became too much for him, and the visits became few and far between.

Her father's reluctance to criticize her mother allowed Michelle's misconceptions to continue unabated, keeping up the walls her mother had created between them. It wasn't until she was 17 that her father finally said to her, " 'You know, a lot of the things you've been told about me were untrue.' It was instantly eye-opening." By her early twenties she'd reconnected with her father, but they only had about 15 years together; he died when she was 38. "I'd lost all those years with a wonderful man, as well as with the members of his family that I loved."

Strategies of War

There's another side to the alienation phenomenon: the hard-edged legal one. Although it is a psychological issue, parental alienation can be truly addressed only in the legal system. Remedy for alienation, say experts, requires an order from a court to allow a manipulated child time to bond with the alienated parent. It is critical, therefore, that there be proof that alienation has in fact occurred. If a parent seeking custody can document the phenomenon, the system—if it is working—will adjust a custody arrangement to promote relationship repair.

The courts worked fairly for Larry Felton, an orthodontist in Detroit (identifying details changed). His wife, an architect who had put her career on hold to raise their daughter, Emily, left Larry and later divorced him. Immersed in his practice, he settled for the once a week plus every other weekend visits the court imposed. "I was devoted and determined to make it work. I wasn't going to let anything keep me from having a relationship with my daughter," he says.

But when Emily grew older and he asked for a little more time with her, things turned ugly. By unilateral decree of his ex, he stopped getting even the limited time that was his due. By the time the court got involved, Emily had grown distant and withdrawn, blaming him for all that had happened. She resisted seeing him at all.

He might have lost his bid for more time with his daughter if not for a key piece of evidence. His ex called to tell him she was canceling yet another weekend with Emily. Then, thinking

she'd disconnected the phone when she had not, she said to the daughter and Felton's answering machine, "Your father is evil, a bad man, but we need him for his money. At least he's good for that."

After hearing the tape, the judge awarded primary custody to Larry in hopes of reversing the alienation that had been ongoing for years. Seven years later, 17-year-old Emily has reaped the benefits. Though it took time to earn her trust back, her father now has a solid relationship with her, and her time with her mother is more positive. "I think it saved her," Felton says.

Things are hardly ever so clear-cut in court. Often, judges don't have access to proof like Felton's incriminating voice mail. In the end, after listening to expert witnesses from both sides, decisions are often based on impressions and even the testimony of the children, the very ones who are brainwashed and may be least reliable of all.

"Even when a judge acknowledges that alienation occurred, the court can end up siding with the alienating parent because of the child's wishes," Warshak says. "Otherwise, they fear, the child in his anger might hurt himself or someone else."

In fact, it takes a sophisticated judge to realize what psychologists might see as obvious: Deep down, the child has never really stopped loving the other parent. He or she has just been brainwashed like a prisoner of war or a cult victim, programmed to accept destructive beliefs until critical thinking can be restored.

"Even if they say they don't want to see the parent, underneath they might be longing to reconnect," says Warshak. "These kids need more time with that parent rather than less. Only then will they have a chance to see that the poisoned thoughts are wrong." In the most extreme cases, children are permitted to see the alienating parent only during therapy sessions until the alienation has been resolved.

Other times judges listen mostly to the parent who says he or she has been wronged—and that too can be misleading. According to John E. B. Myers, a professor of law at the University of the Pacific McGeorge School of Law in Sacramento, California, false accusations of parental alienation do "tremendous harm to many children and their parents, particularly mothers seeking custody in family court."

According to Myers, fathers accused of sexual or other abuse by mothers often hide under the protective mantle of "parental alienation" in court, pitting accusation against accusation. The alleged alienator may be dismissed as manipulative, an assumption not always representing truth. The charge could paint a protective parent as a liar trying to poison a child instead of keeping him from harm.

University of California at Davis law professor Carol Bruch adds that the theory of parental alienation fails to account for the anger often felt by children of divorce, especially the kind of contentious divorce that results in custody fights in the first place. "Sometimes the child's feelings are prompted by the behavior of the noncustodial parent. That parent may not be abusive, but just deficient in some way. A parent can become estranged from a child without any provocation whatsoever from the other parent." The estranged parent could accuse the custodial parent of alienating behavior through blindness to his or her own role.

It takes a sophisticated judge to realize what psychologists might see as obvious: that deep down, the child has never stopped loving the other parent.

Loss and Repair

With knowledgeable experts and astute judges, real alienation can be discerned from false accusations. When alienation is accurately recognized, appropriate intervention on the part of the court can certainly help families heal the damage.

Without the right intervention, however, the result is a scenario of loss and unresolved grief like that of Cathy Mannis. Ironically it is Robby, Cathy's autistic son, who is most acutely in touch with his pain.

"What his father did, first trying to institutionalize him as dangerous, then separating him from his brothers, gave him a devastating signal that he was not worthy, that he deserved punishment rather than help and love," explains Stephen Stahl, MD, PhD, Robby's psychiatrist and a professor of psychiatry at the University of California at San Diego.

Now 18, Robby feels rejected by both his father and his younger brother, both of whom have very little to do with him anymore. "My father never cared about me, so I don't care about him anymore," he says. "But I loved being with Harry every day and every night. I try to call him a lot, but my stepmom is often mean to me or hangs up on me. I almost never get to see him, and he doesn't call. It all makes me so sad."

Parents' grief is also profound. "The child is alive but still lost to you, so close but yet so far, there but not seeing you, and you're uncertain if you'll ever have the relationship back again," Warshak says. "You can't grieve the final loss, because you can never accept that it's final."

As for Cathy Mannis, she recently had Harry with her in San Diego for a one-week court-ordered visit. She and Robby were both thrilled to have the chance to reconnect with him. But as wonderful as that week was, it only set Mannis up for further heartbreak. "He left on Sunday," she says, "and I won't see him again for four months."

Critical Thinking

1. What are some of the ways parents alienate the other parent to their children?

2. How should the court influence parent behavior?

3. What can be done to heal the parent-child relationships in divorced families?

MARK TEICH is a writer in Stamford, CT.

Civil Wars

Psychologists who work as parenting coordinators help moms and dads keep the peace.

CHRISTOPHER MUNSEY

Research suggest that it's not divorce in itself that most harms children, but the tension between divorcing parents, some of whom repeatedly appear before judges to battle over drop-off times or visitation rights.

One review of studies in *Children and Divorce,* for example (Vol. 4, No. 1, pages 165–182), found that children whose parents bitterly fight over divorces scored as significantly more disturbed on standardized measures of maladjustment.

"In a lot of these cases, the individual parents 'parent' fine. It's when they interface that all hell breaks loose," says Matt Sullivan, PhD, a Santa Clara, Calif., psychologist, who works with many divorcing clients.

But help is at hand: Through the growing practice area of parenting coordination, psychologists are helping feuding parents call a truce, communicate and work out their disagreements with the goal of better-adjusted children and less-burdened courts.

"It can be helpful for parents to have someone who can help them work out how they're going to keep conflict away from the kids, and help them focus on what the kids need, as opposed to what's going on between the two of them," says Judge Judith Bartnoff of the District of Columbia Superior Court, who has seen the benefits of parenting coordination in several custody disputes.

With their communication skills, psychologists are uniquely qualified for parenting coordination, says Robin Deutsch, PhD, of Harvard Medical School who has served in the role and provided training as well. "Psychologists can help people stuck in ineffective communication patterns learn to communicate better," she says. "It's the bread and butter of what [we] know how to do."

A Growing Field

Parenting coordination typically starts with a court-ordered parenting agreement establishing a detailed custody schedule, with exact drop-off and pickup times listed, plus arrangements for vacations and holidays. When a dispute arises—such as which sport a child should play—the parenting coordinator can step in, halt the angry back-and-forth between the parents and gather feedback from all parties involved.

Besides hearing from the adults involved, a parenting coordinator pays close attention to the child's needs. After gathering the different perspectives, the coordinator—depending on the state where the parents live—either makes the decision, or recommends a solution.

Eight states have passed laws setting up parenting coordination procedures since 1989: Minnesota, Oklahoma, Idaho, Oregon, Colorado, Texas, Louisiana and North Carolina. Meanwhile, a number of other states rely on existing laws that give judges leeway to appoint parenting coordinators (see sidebar).

Demanding Work

Sullivan and co-author Karl Kirkland, PhD, recently completed a survey of 54 parenting coordinators. They found that 44 percent of the responding parenting coordinators were licensed psychologists. Other mental health professionals such as master's level social workers and licensed professional counselors also do the work, with attorneys forming the third-largest share.

For all the different ways parenting coordination is carried out, psychologists say common issues arise for practitioners who move into the area of practice: chiefly, the need for balance, and avoiding falling into dual roles, Deutsch says. Parenting coordinators can't become therapists to their clients, and they have to make decisions fairly, Deutsch says.

"Maintaining impartiality is very important," she says.

From a practitioner's perspective, parenting coordination can be lucrative, without the hassle of third-party payers. In most cases, parents pay the parenting coordinator on a fee-for-service basis, says Sullivan, adding that many coordination agreements spell out the hourly cost of the service, how the parents will split the costs, and what happens if fees go unpaid. Some programs offer pro bono parenting coordination to low-income parents, such as one based in Washington, D.C.

The work is also attractive to many psychologists because of its flexible scheduling. And the field is growing, as more judges turn to the idea of using parenting coordinators to help defuse the most problematic cases, several observers say.

It can be very demanding though, judging from the comments of several psychologists experienced in parenting

State by State

Here's a snapshot of how parenting coordination works and is developing in several states and the District of Columbia:

- **California:** If both parents agree, a judge can appoint a parenting coordinator, using a statute already on the books. Called "special masters," these coordinators make legally binding decisions when disputes arise between parents.

- **Maryland:** Although efforts are under way to draft legislation to define parenting coordination, judges in several Maryland counties began turning to parenting coordinators several years ago, says Paul Berman, PhD, a psychologist who also serves as the professional affairs officer for the Maryland Psychological Association. If both parties sign off, the judge can name a parenting coordinator once a child custody order has been signed. In his work, Berman is empowered to decide what's best, presenting his decision in writing to both parents.

- **Massachusetts:** Legislation establishing a parent coordination program hasn't moved out of committee in the state legislature in the past two years, but judges do appoint parenting coordinators, says parenting coordinator Robin Deutsch, PhD, relying on their traditional discretion to take action in the best interest of children. If both parents agree, the state allows judges to appoint a parenting coordinator at the time of divorce to help resolve disputes that the parties can't resolve on their own.

- **District of Columbia:** As part of a pilot project of APA, Argosy University, the D.C. Bar and the D.C. Superior Court, family law judges can appoint a licensed clinical psychologist as a special master, who works in a team format with advanced doctoral students from Argosy University in Washington, D.C., to provide parent coordinator services to caregivers who otherwise couldn't afford it, says Giselle Hass, PsyD, an associate professor at Argosy who serves as clinical director for the program.

  Besides helping caregivers learn to communicate effectively with each other, the students can help connect them with resources for themselves and their children, Hass says. Those resources might include helping arrange the evaluation of a child for a possible developmental disability, referring a caregiver for treatment of a mental health issue or helping connect with free legal help.

- **Texas:** Under a state statute, a judge can order a parenting coordinator to get involved if parents agree or if there is evidence of high conflict. However, Texas parenting coordinators do not have authority to make decisions, says Lynelle Yingling, a marriage and family therapist in Rockwall, Texas. Instead, parenting coordinators talk with both parents and help parents develop solutions, Yingling says.

—C. Munsey

coordination. Getting in the middle of disputes where the parties are often very angry at each other requires a thick skin.

"It's just tough work," says Sullivan. "These are difficult people to work with." He adds that having a "directive, take-charge" personality helps a psychologist succeed as a parenting coordinator. "It takes a particular brand of psychologist to fit this role."

Critical Thinking

1. What are the benefits to families who have parenting coordination available?

2. What are some of the limitation of these programs?

3. Of the five different states discussed in this article, which one to you feel has a good program and why?

4. Should parenting coordination happen in all divorces and why?

5. What are some of the roles and responsibilities of parenting coordinators and would you want to have a job as a parenting coordinator and why?

APA's Pilot Parenting Coordination Program

An APA-initiated program enables family law judges in Washington, D.C., to appoint licensed clinical psychologists as special masters who work with Argosy University doctoral students to smooth out disputes between caregivers. Since the program started in January 2005, parenting coordinators have handled 19 cases.

In June, APA's Practice Directorate honored several people who consulted on and helped develop the program including APA's Shirley Ann Higuchi, JD; Dr. Robert Barrett, of the American School of Professional Psychology at Argosy University—Washington, D.C., campus; Judge Judith Bartnoff of the District of Columbia Superior Court; and Dr. Bruce Copeland, formerly of Washington, D.C.

—C. Munsey

Estranged Spouses Increasingly Waiting Out Downturn to Divorce

Donna St. George

In the Great Recession, breaking up is hard to do.

With housing values depressed and jobs disappearing, divorce has become a luxury beyond the reach of some couples. There is often not enough money to pay for separate households or to hire lawyers, fight over children and go to court.

What has always been painful is now desperate and confounding, with a growing number of couples deciding to wait out the economic storm while others take new approaches—such as living together as they separate.

"I have lots of files sitting in the drawer, where people can't move forward," says David Goldberg, a divorce lawyer and mediator in Gaithersburg. He has been working in family law for 44 years and says he has never seen a time like this one.

Lately, he said, "I have a lot of clients who have ended up in bankruptcy."

The difficulties of divorce in the downturn are familiar to Paulene Foster, a 42-year-old federal worker from Olney, who says her precarious finances forced her to wait a year. If that wasn't enough, she also shared a house with her estranged husband—him in the basement, her upstairs. Strapped months went by as the couple were saddled with a suburban townhouse that would not sell.

"It was a mess," Foster said.

Her divorce, filed last month with a $105 check after going to a *self-help law clinic* in Montgomery County, comes as the national rate of failed marriages has declined slightly—not necessarily because divorce-minded couples are happier than before but, some experts suggest, because they don't have the money to call it quits.

At one Woodbridge law firm, 20 to 25 percent of clients seeking a divorce live under the same roof as their estranged spouse to save money as they await court action.

Other couples say they are stymied by the grim reality that they owe more on the family home than they could get if they sold it.

How do they start over if debt is all that's left to divide?

Heather Hostetter, who has a divorce practice in Bethesda, said that many couples used to divorce with enough equity in a house so that both spouses could re-create lives not so different from their old ones.

"It used to be you could go own another home," she said. "Maybe it's a little smaller, maybe it's not in the same neighborhood.

"Now you see people who go from homeowners to renters."

Divorce and Bankruptcy

Facing harsher circumstances, Marissa Fuller, who works in child care in Fairfax City, says her husband's job loss and then his underemployment had an accumulating impact. They had relationship troubles. They fell short on bills month after month. She tired of begging utility companies to turn back on the family's water and electricity.

In January, she filed both for bankruptcy and divorce, sure that the economic tension and the discord that came with it took a toll. "That really made the marriage crumble," she said. Fuller found housing through a nonprofit program and is saving for her own apartment, but she says the math of providing for two children on her salary seems nearly impossible.

Experts say that divorce claims slightly more than 40 percent of marriages. *Rates calculated by the National Marriage Project* show a modest decline in divorce during 2008, the first year of the recession, when 838,000 cases were granted in 44 states—at a time when growing economic strain might have produced a spike in divorce. A year earlier, 856,000 divorces were finalized. Scores of studies show a link between tough times and divorce.

W. Bradford Wilcox, director of the National Marriage Project at the University of Virginia, says some families are pulling together amid the economic turmoil, and others that want to split up are postponing until they see a rebound in the economy and in home values. A divorce can cost as little as $100 on a do-it-yourself basis with little in dispute and $10,000 to $20,000—or more—for a divorce that ends up in court.

Still, dividing into two households can prove the more daunting task—the same income being used to cover an extra housing payment, extra utility bills, separate groceries. This can be tricky when a home has no equity or line of credit to draw from.

In Manassas, lawyer Kirk Wilder says that in some cases, the house is so void of value that neither party wants to be stuck with it. "It used to be, 'Well, I want the house,'" he said. "Now it's, 'You take the house.' That's a huge change."

The economics of breaking up are a little better in the District and parts of Northern Virginia, where spouses can live in the same house during the required separation period, as long as they share little more than the space around them. No sex. No meals. No togetherness.

"They don't do each other's laundry, they don't eat together, they don't go to the kids' soccer game together," says Pat Hammond, a lawyer in Prince William County who advises clients with increasing frequency about how to get divorced without moving out of the house. "If they live in a three-bedroom townhouse, and they have four kids, it ain't going to work."

A Place to Sleep

Steve Halbert, an Arlington County resident who divorced in 2008, attests to the difficulty of the proposition.

His wife lived in one bedroom; he lived in another. He tried to work as much as possible to stay out of the house. "If you're in the same room, then a fight is waiting to happen," he said. For all of the struggle, his mortgage is still upside down 18 months later—and he still does not have a way to refinance his house and clear his ex-wife's name from the mortgage loan.

Halbert, a commercial real estate appraiser, says he earns half of what he did in the boom days and now pays alimony. "There used to be a lot of disposable income," he said, "and now it's, 'Be glad you have a place to sleep.'"

Prince William lawyer Larry Fabian says perhaps a quarter of his clients live together while they seek a divorce, which was almost unheard of five or so years ago. "It's really difficult," he says of their experiences. "It's pretty much the worst of all worlds."

Then again, some would say it is even harder in Maryland, which requires a full year of separate residences for mutual and voluntary divorce. That requirement is economically difficult for some; impossible for others.

Jesslyn Haskins, 42, a nurse and mother of three in Upper Marlboro, says a judge threw out her divorce case because she and her ex-husband had shared the same house during their separation. She says she then left, moving in with friends and ultimately getting an apartment, as relations grew more bitter and the mortgage went unpaid. Now divorced, she says she lives in the house and pays the mortgage but is in jeopardy of foreclosure because of missed back payments.

The National Marriage Project's Wilcox says working-class couples, who already have high rates of divorce, are especially vulnerable to a recession-related breakup because they are hit harder by unemployment, which is a significant predictor of divorce. Men, in particular, see themselves as breadwinners and are prone to feelings of worthlessness and depression during lengthy periods without a job, Wilcox says. "We would predict this recession is having a pretty big impact on working-class couples," he says.

In terms of divorce, the recession bears similarities to the Great Depression, says Johns Hopkins University sociologist Andrew Cherlin, noting that in the 1930s, divorce rates fell amid the worst of the economic crisis, only to rise as the country recovered. "Troubled economic times breed troubled marriages," he says. "But whether those marriages end in divorce right away is another thing."

Cherlin said the recession has probably created "a backlog of unhappy married couples who would like to get a divorce soon but can't afford it," and he predicted a surge in cases during the first several recovery years. "The longer this severe economic downturn continues," he said, "the larger the backlog will be."

Critical Thinking

1. How would you cope with having an estranged spouse live with you?

2. What do you think the impacts of these relationships are on children?

3. What are some other alternatives estranged spouses have other than living under the same roof?

UNIT 5

Families, Now and into the Future

Unit Selections

Learning Outcomes

After reading this unit, you will be able to:

- Demonstrate ways to interview family members.
- Develop an approach to interview family members.
- Describe a family interview.
- Discuss some of the variations between families.
- Describe how the author used his own unconventional family.
- Apply the concept of unconventional families.
- Recognize the attributes of happy families.
- Describe how families can be happier.
- Explain the positive effect that rituals have on family ties.
- Discuss the sense of togetherness that rituals provide.
- Identify the way that rituals provide families with intergenerational processes.
- Discuss the evolution of marriage in today's American society.
- Explain some common beliefs around marriage.
- Synthesize the nature of martial relationships.

Student Website
www.mhhe.com/cls

Internet Reference

National Institute on Aging
www.nih.gov/nia

*W*hat is the future of the family? Does the family even have a future? These questions and others like them are being asked. Many people fear for the future of the family. As previous units of this volume have shown, the family is a continually evolving institution that will continue to change throughout time. Still, certain elements of family appear to be constant. The family is and will remain a powerful influence in the lives of its members. This is because we all begin life in some type of family, and this early exposure carries a great deal of weight in forming our social selves—who we are and how we relate to others. From our families, we take our basic genetic makeup, while we also learn and are reinforced in health behaviors. In families, we are given our first exposure to values, and it is through families that we most actively influence others. Our sense of commitment and obligation begins within the family as well as our sense of what we can expect of others. Much that has been written about families has been less than hopeful and has focused on ways of avoiding or correcting errors. The articles in this unit take a positive view of family and how it influences its members. The emphasis is on health rather than dysfunction.

Knowledge is the basic building block of intelligent decisions regarding family relationships. Information is important in planning for our family's future. One way to gather this information is through interviews, and "Get a Closer Look" explains just how this can be done. The complex family form seen in "Meet My Real Modern Family" demonstrates that families come in all shapes and sizes and can be healthy, supportive places of personal growth. "Relative Happiness" presents a number of ways in which families can become healthier and happier. Family

© 2009 Jupiterimages Corporation

rituals are examined as being a powerful force for family cohesion and change, and the nature of family rituals is described in "The Joy of Rituals" and "Rituals in Relationships." Finally, what is understood to be "traditional" marriage is, in fact, a recent phenomenon. Marriage is an evolving institution, and "Where Is Marriage Going?" discusses the direction that marriage may take in the future.

Get a Closer Look
12 Tips for Successful Family Interviews

IRA WOLFMAN

How do you get relatives talking? A good family history interview isn't easy to conduct. You need to combine the best attributes of caring friend, hard-nosed reporter, and sensitive psychologist. But do it well and you may be rewarded with wonderful stories.

Interviews are different from normal conversations. One person has a goal: to get information from another person (let's call him or her the "talker"). You want the talker to feel comfortable, but you also need to direct the conversation to the points you are interested in.

You also have to be flexible. Sometimes an unexpected topic can turn out to be wonderful. Other times you'll need to lead your talker back to the main point—without hurting his or her feelings. This can be difficult, but you will become better at it as you go along—practice will make you skilled. Be patient with yourself and expect some mistakes. To make things easier, keep these tips in mind:

1. Before any interview, give advance warning.
Explain what you want to do, why you want to do it, and why the talker is important to you and your research. You can call or write a letter or e-mail. Here's an example of the kinds of things you should say:

Dear Aunt Gus:

I'm working on a history of our family, and it would be very helpful if I could sit down and talk with you. I'm particularly interested in your memories of my great-grandparents (your mother and father) and the family's early years in Minnesota. I'd also love to look at any old photographs or documents you have.

I won't need much more than an hour of your time and would like to hold our talk at your home. Any weekend day would be fine. Can you let me know a date that is convenient for you?

Thanks so much for your help.

By writing this letter, you've given your relative a chance to start thinking about the topics you're interested in, and you may have even jogged her memory. Of course, not all your relatives will be close by, and your arrangements may be more difficult than "any weekend day." That just makes your writing—and planning—even more important.

2. Prepare before your interview.
Find out whatever you can about the talker *before* the interview. Where does she fit in the family? What documents might she have? What other genealogical jewels might she have?

Gather as much information as you can ahead of time about her relationship to everyone in your family. Your parents can probably help you with this.

3. Think out all your questions beforehand.
Interviewing requires structure. Write your questions on a sheet of paper, organized by subject. One easy way to organize what you want to ask is by year: Start with your relative's earliest years and then move on from there.

"So, Aunt Gus, you lived in the house in a town outside Minneapolis till you were 10—about 1922, right? Then where did you move?" Or "You say Great-grandpa worked as a tailor in St. Paul. Did you ever visit his shop? Where was it? What years did he have the business there?" As this interviewer did, it's a good idea to summarize what you already know so that your subject can verify your facts. Then move on to a request for more detail.

Sometimes the simplest questions can hit the jackpot. I asked my great-uncle Max, "How old were you when you went from Poland to America?" I didn't get an answer; I got a story:

I must have been about 15 when I went to Warsaw to get a visa to emigrate. I got the visa, but then the counselor at the examination said, "Listen, boy, you are underage. You can't go without your father." He crossed out my stamp.

I went back to our town and told my father. He said, "Don't worry, we'll take care of that."

My father was a religious man, but he also knew how to get things done. He called a policeman from our town and asked him to make me older.

Ready, Set, Research . . .
Your Family Tree

- Interview your parents about their family history. Practice interviewing with them.
- Make appointments to interview other family members.
- Prepare your questions. (For a list of good questions for family interviews, see www.workmen.com /familytree.)
- Type up your notes from interviews. Ask the relatives you interviewed to review them and correct or add to them.
- Write a thank-you note to every family member you interviewed.

I got new papers. Now I turned from 15 to 18 or 19. I went back to Warsaw, and I was able to leave. And on February 20, 1920, I took the boat Susquehanna *from Danzig to New York.*

Remember to also ask open-ended questions. "What do you remember most about the apartment on Division Street?" or "Tell me about your relationship with your brothers" may yield something unexpected and wonderful.

4. Bring a video or tape recorder if possible. A small tape recorder usually doesn't disturb anyone, and it catches every bit of information, including the way your talkers sound and exactly how they answer questions. If you plan to videotape, be sure someone comes with you to run the camera. You need to focus on your talker.

5. In any case, bring a notebook and a pen. Even if you have [an audio tape or video] recorder, always take handwritten notes. Recorders can break down.

During the interview, write down names and dates and double-check them with your subject. Facts are important, but the most important information your talkers offer are their stories. Try to capture the way they talk and their colorful expressions: "That ship was rolling on the ocean like a marble in your hand."

There's another good reason to bring pen and paper with you. You won't have to interrupt when you think of a question; just write a note to yourself so you'll remember to ask it at an appropriate time.

6. Start with easy, friendly questions. Leave the more difficult or emotional material for later in the interview, after you've had time to gain your talker's trust. If things aren't going well, you may want to save those questions for another time.

It's also a good idea to begin with questions about the person you're interviewing. You may be more interested in a great-grandfather if he is the missing link in your family chart. But first get some background information about your talker—your aunt, for example. This serves two purposes. First, it lets her know she's important to you, that you care about her, and that her life is interesting, too. Second, as she talks, she may reveal some other information that you would never have known about otherwise.

7. Bring family photographs with you. Look for photos, artwork, or documents that will help jog your subject's memory. Bring the pictures out and ask your talker to describe what's going on. "Do you remember when this was taken? Who are the people? What was the occasion? Who do you think took the picture?" You may be amazed at how much detail your relative will see in a photograph and also at the memories that come spilling forth.

8. Don't be afraid of silence. You might feel uneasy and want to rush in with another question when your talker stops speaking. *Don't.* Silence is an important part of interviewing and can sometimes yield to interesting results. Because people often find silence uncomfortable, they often try to fill it if you don't—and in doing so, they may say something you might not have heard otherwise.

Sometimes silence is also necessary for gathering thoughts. Don't forget—you are asking your subjects to think back on things they may not have considered for years. Calling up these memories may spark other thoughts, too. Allow your subject time to ponder. You may be thrilled by what he or she remembers.

9. Ask the same question in different ways. People don't know how much they know, and rephrasing a question can give you more information. This happens all the time. "I don't know," a relative will tell you, sometimes impatiently. They do know—they just don't know that they know. The most common version of this occurs when an interviewer asks, "What was your father's mother's name?" The relative answers, "I never knew her. I don't know." Then a few minutes later, in response to "Whom were you named after?" this answer comes; "My father's mother."

Try to find a couple of ways to ask important questions. You may feel like you're being repetitive, but you never can be sure what you will learn.

10. Be sensitive to what you discover. Sometimes people become emotional talking about the past. They may remember long-dead relatives or once-forgotten tragedies. If your talker is upset by a memory, either remain silent or quietly ask, "Is it all right if we talk some more about this? Or would you rather not?" People frequently feel better when they talk about sad things; you should gently give your relative the *choice* of whether or not to go on.

11. Try not to interrupt. If your talker strays from the subject, let him or her finish the story and then say, "Let's get back to Uncle Moe" or "You said something earlier about . . ." By not interrupting, you make the conversation friendlier, and the story may lead you to something you didn't expect.

Of course, there is always the exception to the rule. If a story goes on forever and seems useless, the best way to handle it may be to say, "Gee, Aunt Gus, could you hold the rest of that story for later? I'd like to get the facts out of the way and then come back to that."

12. Ask for songs, poems, unusual memories. You may discover something wonderful when you ask your subject if she recalls the rhymes she used to recite while jumping rope as a little girl or the hymns she sang in church. Probe a little here—ask about childhood games and memories, smells and tastes and sounds.

Critical Thinking

1. In what way would you use the suggestions from the article in your interview of a family member?

2. Discuss the importance of family interviews.

3. What are some of the challenges associated with interviewing family members?

4. What are some good questions to ask family members during the interview?

5. Are there any other tips you would add to a successful family interview that were not mentioned in the article?

Excerpted from *Climbing Your Family Tree.* Copyright © 1991, 2002 by Ira Wolfman and the Statue of Liberty–Ellis Island Foundation, Inc. Text by **IRA WOLFMAN.** Used with permission of Workman Publishing Co., Inc., New York. All Rights Reserved.

Meet My Real Modern Family

As a gay man, the author never expected to have children. Now he and his husband have four between them. How science, friendship, and love created an unconventional clan.

ANDREW SOLOMON

Children used to make me sad. With the happy children in my adult life, I felt guilty, even mean, about being sad. The origin of that sadness was opaque, but I think it came most from how the absence of children in the lives of gay people had been repeatedly held up as my tragedy. When I came out, the prevailing view was that I was shortsightedly choosing sexual fantasies over producing a family. I was encouraged by my parents and the world to marry a woman and procreate. I spent years drifting between relationships with men and with women; I was mildly bisexual in a fluid era, but if children hadn't been part of the equation, I wouldn't have bothered with the other half. Even though I was in love with some of the women I dated, I felt mildly fraudulent in those intimacies. While I was becoming true to myself, the world changed. What I couldn't know then was whether I truly wanted children, or whether I just wanted to prove wrong everyone who had pitied me.

Shortly after I met John, who is now my husband, we ran into his friends Laura and Tammy and their toddler, Oliver, at the 2001 Minnesota State Fair. John and Laura had been co-workers, and Laura had observed him for years before she and Tammy had asked him to be their child's biological father. Though not especially close to them, he had agreed, signing legal documents in which he foreswore paternal rights and they foreswore claims to support. He had offered to be in the child's life to the extent he was able, if the child so wished, but in deference to Tammy's position as adoptive mother, he had so far remained uninvolved. Nevertheless, the women asked him to be a sperm donor again, and Lucy was born in 2004, by which time John was living with me in Manhattan.

The question of having biological children in unorthodox ways was familiar to me. A few years before I met John, during a trip to Texas, I attended a dinner that included my college friend Blaine. I had adored her for more than 20 years, but then, everyone adores Blaine; she is serenely beautiful and poised, and I had never felt indispensable to her as I do with more difficult friends. Blaine had divorced and shortly thereafter lost her mother, and she alluded to her yearning to become a mother

herself. I said I'd be thrilled to father her child. The idea that she might actually want to have a baby with me was unimaginable; I suggested it with the rhetorical politesse with which I'd invited new acquaintances in remote countries to stop by for a drink if they ever found themselves in Greenwich Village. When I got home, however, I wrote her a letter, saying that I thought she would be a glorious mother, and that if she didn't have a child with me, I hoped she'd have one with someone.

When Blaine came to my 40th birthday party in New York three years later, in 2003, we realized that we both wanted to have that child together. I wasn't ready to tell John, who was still living in Minneapolis. When I did tell him, he exploded. He had been a sperm donor, he argued; I would have a child who would bear my last name. I would be involved in an ongoing, profound relationship with Blaine that he feared would lethally triangulate our own. I did not know how hard it is to reinvent family, and he could not envision how fulfilling this particular reinvention might be. I nearly backed out but felt I couldn't renege on my word, based on a wish I could likewise not forsake. John, whose benevolence invariably triumphs, finally relented, and Blaine and I conceived through IVF. Blaine, meanwhile, had met her partner, Richard, putting a reasonable if unusual balance in place.

> I did not know how hard it is to reinvent family, and he could not envision how fulfilling this particular reinvention might be.

Falling in love with John had meant not only the discovery of great happiness, but also the elimination of great unhappiness. Marrying him was my way of acknowledging our love as more a presence than an absence, which was especially urgent as we moved forward with the Blaine plan. I am a dual national, and Britain had recently passed an encompassing civil-partnership law, so we had a June ceremony in the English country-side, presided over by a registrar, a minister, and a rabbi. In my

FAMILY TREE
BLACK LINE family unit
COLORED LINE biological relationship

CLOCKWISE FROM UPPER LEFT **Tammy** (she and Laura are mothers to Oliver and Lucy; Andrew's partner, John, is the biological father of both children); **Laura** (she was also the surrogate for Andrew and John's son, George); **Andrew** (married to John, he is the biological father of little Blaine and George); **little Blaine** (the daughter of Andrew and his college friend Blaine, who conceived through **IVF**); **Blaine** (Andrew's college friend and the mother of little Blaine); **Oliver** (Laura and Tammy's son; John's biological child); **Richard** (Blaine's partner); **Howard** (Andrew's father); **George** (Andrew and John's son, whom Laura carried; Andrew is the biological father); **John** (Andrew's partner, George's dad, and the biological father of Oliver and Lucy); **Lucy** (daughter of Tammy and Laura; John's biological child).

wedding toast, I said, "The love that dared not speak its name is now broadcasting." If all my gay childhood traumas had led me to this day, I thought, maybe they were not so bad as they had seemed. Oliver, then 7, served as John's ring bearer. Blaine, four months pregnant with our child, came with Richard, and John ventured that we'd had the first gay shotgun wedding.

John and I headed to Texas for little Blaine's delivery, by Caesarean section, on Nov. 5, 2007. I watched the obstetrician pull my child out of her mother, and was the first person to hold her, and was as shocked as I was elated. I had to affirm paternity before my name went on the birth certificate; the hospital clerk advised me, as an unmarried father, to ask for genetic testing, referring knowingly to the "love child." I spared him the details.

Little Blaine was to live in Texas with her mother, and we were to visit each other often. I was grateful that John welcomed the daughter he had dreaded—grateful, too, that he and Blaine had come to cherish each other. Blaine's 86-year-old father, whose values I had thought this might challenge, accepted me as a son; my father was overjoyed by his granddaughter. My pleasure in fatherhood aligned with the satisfaction of giving scope to Blaine's genius for motherhood. Blaine had my own mother's elegance of thought and appearance, echoed her ability to find hilarity in the dailiness of life, demonstrated the same madcap imagination largely hidden by discretion and obdurate reserve, and shared her gene for intelligent empathy tinged with sadness.

Still, I wanted a child in my own house with John. It's good news that being gay is no longer crazy (removed from the DSM, psychiatry's bible, in 1973) or illegal (fully decriminalized in 2003), but we carry the legacy of its being both, and couldn't have children to assert progress, social or personal. John had wanted to marry; I hadn't, particularly; and then the reality had entranced me. I exacted a child as fair trade,

believing John, too, would end up entranced. John said, "How much happier do you need to be?" I said, "If we don't have a child because you've vetoed the idea, it will infect the rest of our marriage." The conversation stalled there, but John's compassion ultimately carried the day. For my birthday six months later, in October 2007, he gave me a carved antique cradle tied up with a bow, and said, "If it's a boy, can we call him George, after my grandpa?"

A lawyer laid out the advantages of having one woman provide the egg and another the womb, so that neither would have full claim as mother, and we began the blind-dating egg hunt. Our first choice was a charming woman who, several months into preparations, tested positive for cocaine. Even as I championed another prospect, whose egg we finally used, I felt sorry that I would never see what might come of mixing John's genes with my own. I was thankful we could get an egg, but sad that neither of us could produce one; glad we could have a child at all, and regretful about the aura of manufacturing that clung to the venture. Children are always products of emotion and biology, but it's disorienting when those elements become asynchronous.

John had proposed that I be biological father of this child and said that he might sire the next, if there were one. When we told Laura and Tammy our plan, Laura said, "We couldn't have had Oliver and Lucy without you, and we'll never be able to thank you enough for that, but I could be your surrogate to show how much you mean to us." There followed medical screenings of Laura, the egg donor, and me; samples (the bright hospital room, the leatherette briefcase of dated girlie magazines provided by the staff); fertility treatments for Laura; embryo transfers; and ultrasounds. Children had been a buffer for Laura against pain and fear, giving purpose to her calm authority; now, she bravely converted that vulnerability into generosity.

We got pregnant on our second IVF protocol. Pregnancy supersedes irony; you never know anyone as admiringly as you do when she is carrying your child, and I marveled at the way Laura wove the life she was building for us into the life she had built for herself. Through the proceeding, we drew inexorably closer to Laura and Tammy and the kids. Oliver and Lucy referred to the expected baby as their brother, and I was shy of their enthusiasm. However, I liked Oliver's zaniness and Lucy's exuberance, and I loved how John's wit and gentleness echoed in them. We went to Minneapolis for the late stages of the pregnancy and ended up staying a month, seeing them every day. When Oliver and Lucy learned that little Blaine called us Daddy and Papa John, they said they wanted to call us Daddy and Papa, too. I was not prepared for the idea that all of these children were in various degrees mine, but the generosity with which John had come to embrace an inclusive notion of family and celebrate the Blaines modeled my path to acceptance. Having set out to have two children, I was suddenly contemplating four. To bring us closer had been part of Laura's purpose in helping us, and it worked. By little Blaine, by the imminent George, by Oliver and Lucy, I had been changed, and children made me happy.

On April 9, 2009, at 9:45 P.M., at Abbott-Northwestern Hospital in downtown Minneapolis, we got a view of George's pate, and then Laura pushed six times, and out he popped, into John's arms. I cut the cord. We summoned Oliver and Lucy from the waiting room; we called Blaine and my father. John was instantly enraptured, as I knew he would be. For nine months, we'd felt the favor Laura did us almost as though someone had offered to carry an increasingly heavy bag of groceries up an increasingly steep staircase, but that day we understood that she had made a life for us. We saw clearly for the first time something wild and heroic in her, an acreage of heart and valor beyond anything our male experience had taught us.

Planning to have a baby had been my department; caring for one was John's. I had taught him about determination, about doing things instead of simply imagining them; now he taught me about experiencing those things. We had been advised that if the Defense of Marriage Act were repealed, we should have a marriage legally recognized where we live, so we had a second wedding in Connecticut, two years after our English one. We incorporated a naming ceremony for George, appointing godparents and honorary aunts. It was momentous to hear the Danbury city clerk declare us "husband and husband" and just as consequential to have all four children together for the first time. I keep on my iPhone a portrait from that day, a visual aid for elucidating how we are all related. I wrote this story to usurp that image.

When John and I were invited to the White House Easter Egg Roll last spring, we explained that we were an extended nuclear family, and the whole lot of us went. When my stepsister got married in October, all four children were pages or bridesmaids. We spent most of December together in the candyland of a New York Christmas, and it was revisionist Rockwell, the four kids around the tree at my father's house. Loving John had helped me to become whole, and loving these children rooted me in that wholeness. I had feared ahead of time that I might

not love my children enough: now I am enthralled by George's fascination with the moon; by little Blaine announcing, when she saw that I had cut my finger, "You need a mommy," and fetching a Band-Aid; by Oliver and Lucy debating whether to leave a ginger cookie for Santa or give it to John and me.

Little Blaine has learned to say, soulfully, "I miss you, Daddy," even when we are together, which used to break my heart. During a vacation in June, I took her for a walk, leaving Blaine and Richard in a restaurant with John and George. As I was pointing out sights, she said, "Oh, Daddy, I'm so happy," and when I picked her up, she leaned her head on my collarbone and said, "I miss you." The next morning, out on a boat, she threw her arms around her mother, and said, "I miss you," and I realized that for her, "miss" and "love" meant one idea. I have come to use the words interchangeably myself. I miss my children even when I'm beside them, and acknowledging that ache seems the best way to contain it. Although he would never forsake the kids we have, John maintains that he could have been happy without children, but now that I know this joy, I feel I could not. I dwell too much in abstraction and the future, and parenting has taught me the present time that children require, where contentment, even rapture, reside.

All happy families are the same, and yet, when my brother says he loves his wife and children, everyone is delighted; when I speak of loving my family, people are often shocked and occasionally disgusted. Our affection becomes political—thrilling in a way, but I'd prefer to have intimacy untainted by purpose. That photo on the iPhone often seems euphemistic, because what it shows looks easy. It is exhilarating to be Christopher Columbus landing on the wilder shores of love, but sometimes one would prefer to live where the luxury hotels have already been built and Internet access is wireless. Most people expect to have children, and there are susceptibilities attached to that; I had expected not to have children, and the reversal contains stranger ones. I have had to separate the relief of escaping that tragic childlessness to which my parents gave so much airtime and the reality of human beings for whom I am variously responsible. It must be easier when there is a script.

Once George arrived, the urgent question arose of how all these relationships might constellate. John and I have complete charge of George; Blaine and I had agreed in advance that we would make the major decisions about little Blaine together; Laura and Tammy have separate parental authority, and we do not set the course for Oliver and Lucy, nor Laura and Tammy for George. The three arrangements are different, and as most parents suppress sibling rivalry, we struggle to avoid situational comparison. I would not obscure the frictions sparked by conflicting priorities and boundaries, disparate resources, myriad parenting styles—but they are dwarfed by the fact that it all somehow functions. We have earned the familial relationships into which others stumble, and there is a veteran's peace in our mutual devotion.

John and I sent out birth announcements that included a picture of us with George. One of John's cousins returned it with a note that said, "Your lifestyle is against our Christian values. We wish to have no further contact." Some people scorn the idea of calling five adults and four children in three states a family, or believe that the existence of our family undermines theirs. I do not accept competitive models of love, only additive ones. I espouse reproductive libertarianism, and would propose that when everyone has the broadest choice, love itself expands. I would never want to be smug about the affection we all found in one another. It is not a better love than others, but it is another love, and just as species diversity is crucial to sustain the planet, this diversity strengthens the ecosphere of kindness.

I espouse reproductive libertarianism, and would propose that when everyone has the broadest choice, love itself expands.

Even the most liberal courts note, apparently in approval, that gay people do not make their children gay. If one suggests that black people should be able to reproduce so long as the kids are white, one sees how much prejudice is enmeshed in even ostensibly pro-gay arguments about family. It's disorienting to recognize that the more conventional our choices are, the more radical we are, that my days of party hopping and

sexual adventuring were tolerable, but that our arguing about how much to babyproof, thinking about preschools, buying a swing set, and joining a church constitute an assault on family values. There's a bizarre and hateful inversion in this. American modernity is built on our liberation from a pernicious 1950s model of the nuclear family that was never true in the first place, and those who attempt to preserve that model are not conservatives, but regressives.

The change has already happened; it's only the law that lags. The road less traveled, as it turns out, leads to pretty much the same place.

Critical Thinking

1. How would you compare your family to the author's "unconventional family"?

2. What do you think the author means by unconventional?

3. Why is there so much variation in families?

SOLOMON's *last book*, The Noonday Demon, won the National Book Award; his new book on extraordinary families, *Far From the Tree, will be out in 2012.*

Relative Happiness

Your family may not be storybook, but you can cheer up the house by breaking bread, finding fun, and following a few proven plotlines.

AMY ROSENBERG

When I was a child, I loved the *All-of-a-Kind Family* books. Five sisters sharing a bedroom in a small New York apartment at the turn of the last century—what could be more fun? To me, growing up in the suburbs with an older brother with whom I was never very close, and with parents who were active in numerous clubs and organizations that often kept them out of the house, the idea of a large family doing things together was extremely appealing. I envied even a housecleaning scene in which the girls' mother hid buttons for them to find as they dusted the living room. Everything was tackled with team spirit, and so everything—even the chores—seemed like play. The family possessed an infectious energy that you couldn't help but absorb through the books' pages. Simply put, they were happy.

Of course, the current era demands a different kind of family life. You and your partner may both be working long hours while staying electronically tethered to the office afterward. Your kids, too, are probably deep into their devices. On the weekends, homework—your kids' or your own—takes over, and errands swallow up whatever time is left. Then, when you finally manage to corral the whole clan for some quality time together, someone is too exhausted to enjoy it, someone else resents the forced fun, and no one really knows how to talk to anyone else.

It's hard to feel in control when you're busy managing the daily scramble. But you should at least be cognizant of the power you have to set the tone of your home, even if it's most often set by default, by all those electronic interferences. For starters, you can impose limits on interruptions and distractions. And then, on top of that, you can consciously decide to do what came naturally to the *All-of-a-Kind Family,* one that constantly shared adventures, despite being poor. Because they were steeped in Jewish culture, they adhered to family rituals that further increased warmth and closeness. Happiness wasn't their goal; it was a by-product of their lifestyle.

You have the power to set the tone of your home, even if it's most often set by default.

Tolstoy wrote that all happy families are alike, but an unhappy family is unhappy after its own fashion. This may or may not be true, but happy families share certain behaviors and that unhappy ones can change. Examining what works for others might help you figure out ways to start increasing the levels of joy among your own clan.

A truly happy family supports and encourages the growth of each of its members. Reaching that ideal state requires the group to respect one another's space while simultaneously fostering togetherness. Such a family paradoxically provides predictable comfort and dramatic highs and lows, both of which come from caring deeply for the people under your own roof.

Communicate Well and Often

Catie and Kevin O'Keefe, a couple in their late 50s who live in Washington, D.C., where they raised their three children, swear that effective communication is the key. When their kids, now 26, 23, and 19, were younger, Catie and Kevin (who, incidentally, own a communications company together) emphasized the importance of interacting with one another. "We ate dinner together every night," says Kevin. "That was a given. We asked each other, 'What did you do today?' We had discussions about everyday kinds of things. It brought us closer together."

Barbara Fiese, a psychologist who studies family routines and health at Syracuse University, finds that "eating together helps open up the lines of communication. Concerns leak out, and it becomes an opportunity to solve problems as a team."

The Landsgaards, a large clan living in a small town in Mississippi, also insist on eating together—no easy feat with six children ranging in age from 3 to 10 years old. "Everyone feels free to express themselves around the table," says Kristen

Landsgaard, mother of the family, "even the babies. I home-school the older kids, so I have breakfast and lunch with all of them, and my husband always joins us for dinner. We all connect that way."

Eating together is an opportunity for families to solve problems as a team.

For Naomi Pabst and Don Daly, who live in lower Manhattan with their 3 children—Anatola, 11, Ian, 4, and Ariana, 1, one-on-one time with each child is as crucial as group sessions. "Maintaining five different schedules in a chaotic city means we really have to take the opportunity to have one-on-one time when it arises," Naomi says. "We have to make the in-between moments count." She often has her most heartfelt conversations with her elder daughter while walking with her from one activity to another.

The O'Keefes also encouraged their kids to verbally resolve conflicts. "We let our kids talk things out among themselves," Kevin explains. And when talking was hard, they found other ways. "Our middle child always found it easier to write letters than to speak. When she was a teenager and we set a curfew for her, she disagreed with our rules. She wrote us a letter that made a great argument for a later curfew, and we changed our minds."

The letter episode demonstrates one of the most important aspects of communication in any relationship: listening with an open mind and letting each person communicate in his or her own way. It's tempting, as a parent trying to maintain a sense of authority or avoid unwanted precedents, to set hard and fast rules and stick to them unwaveringly. But truly understanding others' points of view is crucial. As clinical psychologist and family dynamics expert Ellen Weber Libby points out, "You have to have confidence that other family members, even kids, have healthy instincts about what they need for themselves."

"For us," Kevin says, "it was about respect. We were able to communicate well with our kids because we respected them as individuals, and they, in turn, respected us. Because we listened to them and told them exactly what we expected of them, they didn't want to disappoint us."

Now that their children are older and living away from home, daily dinner-table communication is not an option for the O'Keefes, but the family still finds ways to stay connected. They speak on the phone often and get together for holidays. As the eldest, Patrick, puts it, "We always ask each other about our activities when we talk. We rely on one another to tell when big events are coming up and then we do our best to remember to ask about it the next time we talk."

Build Rituals

FOR DAVE NUSCHER and Dave Sullivan, of Belmont, Massachusetts, regular rituals are the glue that holds their family together. Rituals lend structure to the Nuscher-Sullivans' days, creating a framework to support communication and respect.

The two Daves adopted their 9-year-old son, Perry, when he—was just under a year old. As a non-traditional family, they had to work perhaps harder than others to get the ball rolling; simply starting the international adoption process was a test of their commitment to the idea of having a family. But they had already been together for five years and they knew they had a strong enough foundation. "We felt confident that we'd be good dads," says Nuscher, "and we wanted to provide a child with the same kind of happiness we both had growing up."

When they brought their son home from Cambodia, all the established habits and roles had to undergo adjustment, just as with any new parents. "From the very beginning, we found that having a routine helped Perry get settled and it helped us, too," says Nuscher. "From the time he was 9 months old until he was 2 or 3, we sang him the same two songs and read him the same two books every single night."

Now that Perry is older, the daily routine maps out a division of labor in which each family member knows what's expected of him, and the logistics of each day run as smoothly as possible. Nuscher, director of editorial and creative services at Tufts University, manages all the finances. As a computer science instructor at Harvard and Boston Universities, Sullivan has a slightly more flexible schedule; he helps Perry get ready for school and out the door. Perry, for his part, knows exactly what jobs he must complete each morning (prepare for school, feed the guinea pigs) in order to earn 30 minutes of video-game time.

Other, more special rituals give them quality time together. Once a week, they take turns choosing a restaurant to go to for dinner. On Saturdays, Perry and Nuscher go to the library and play sports; on Sundays, Perry and Sullivan go to church together. And equally important is the alone-time built into the daily structure. "We can predict when we'll have time together and when we'll have time to ourselves," says Nuscher. "That's really important to us." It's important in general, according to Feise. "You want everyone in the family to have a sense of place and individual identity," she says. "That is what lends each person the belief that they have something to contribute."

The Landsgaard family also relies on daily routine to sustain a sense of security. "For us," Kristen says, "the most important ritual is saying the rosary together every night before bedtime. We're all together in the same room at the same time then, and everyone is quiet. There's a real sense that we're all there for each other."

Some families hold fast to less frequent, often more elaborate traditions that are equally effective for creating a sense of closeness and shared excitement. Larry Rosen, a professor of psychology at California State University, Dominguez Hills, and author of *Rewired: Understanding the iGeneration and the Way They Learn,* offers as an example his family's construction of an extravagant gingerbread house each year. Twenty years ago, he says, when he had two teenagers, a preteen, and a baby, he cut out a newspaper article about the art of edible homes, and he and his kids got to work. It became a project central to the family's holiday experience, starting about a month or so before Christmas with a group discussion about possible themes and designs. "Now," Rosen says, "it's become an inviolable thing." His children, ranging in age today from 18 to 35, all return home during the holidays, and everyone sets aside a full 48 hours to complete the house. "It's not really about the house, though," observes Rosen. "It's about the fact that we spend two days a year together as a family. Our closeness is partly grounded in the ritual."

Stay Flexible

AS IMPORTANT AS routine is, *too* rigid families with inflexible attitudes suffer under the weight of predictability. The Pabst-Dalys keep a mind-bogglingly complex schedule. Three days a week, Naomi Pabst commutes three hours round-trip between Manhattan and New Haven, Connecticut, where she is a professor of African-American studies at Yale University. Don Daly, who owns his own real estate business, usually oversees getting the children to school and day-care. Anatola, a serious gymnast, has four-hour practices four evenings a week and weekly commitments with a performing arts group. And Daly and Pabst insist on having dinners all together each night, even if it means late bedtimes. "It takes a lot of order and precision to coordinate each day, and we have to organize things meticulously," Pabst says. "But within that, we're spontaneous. We think of ourselves as orderly, but never regimented. It's crucial for us to be able to go with the flow."

While the family has rituals, such as celebrating every holiday and having a pancake brunch together every weekend, they make a point of also doing things on the spur of the moment. They might, for example, hop in their car for an unplanned weekend trip to Vermont or accept an impromptu invitation to a friend's house, even when doing so disrupts the usual evening, homework, or morning routine. "We like to keep a sense of adventure and fun," says Pabst. "It's part of working to keep the family dynamic alive, fresh, and bright."

Be confident that family members, even kids, have healthy instincts about what they need for themselves.

Focusing on that dynamic allows Pabst and Daly to keep their own relationship vibrant. "Our secret ingredient," Pabst says, "is that Don and I are madly in love with each other. We have a deep regard for one another, and we work hard to keep ourselves emotionally available. Even if I'm taxed to my limit, I'll still take the time to pay attention to him in loving ways, and he'll do the same. The spontaneity is part of that."

Therein, according to Ellen Weber Libby, lies one of the keys to creating a happy family. "The parents' relationship is the beginning. Children mirror tensions they see and feel in their parents, and those tensions affect their relationships with one another. When they see their parents loving each other and committing to each other, the whole family is strengthened."

Nevertheless, Libby says, if parents are no longer committed to each other, it doesn't make sense to project a false love, or to stay together for the sake of trying to keep children happy. "Kids feel so much more relaxed when a house isn't filled with unspoken tension," she says. "If parents are not working well together, their children may be better off if they separate." Divorced parents can still express respect for their ex-spouses, respond honestly and openly to their kids' needs, and engage in fun activities with their kids, she points out. "Being from a single-parent family does not have to mean being unhappy."

Have Fun and Reach Out Together

ANOTHER ESSENTIAL INGREDIENT in a happy family life is taking the time to do new things together—even if doing so means dragging reluctant teenagers along. "When you enjoy each other," says Libby, "you create joint experiences that serve as a bond. You get to know each other as individuals, and kids learn important things like compromise and respect for others' desires."

As Patrick O'Keefe explains, "When you're young, it's hard to tell your friends that you're going out of town for the weekend with your parents and sisters. We went often, and I always felt like I was missing out on things. Most of the time though, it ended up being really fun. On our boat we had no TV, no friends, and no video games, so we would entertain each other and get rest. Each weekend made us closer, and I think the seclusion from the rest of our confusing adolescent worlds was crucial to the growth of all of us individually and as a unit."

Doing things as a family also gives parents a chance to impart values to kids and to model appropriate behaviors through their own behavior. As Richard Weissbourd, a child and family psychologist at Harvard University, argues, parents today tend to *overemphasize* their children's happiness. "What would really be helpful to kids is seeing their parents caring for others; that should he a priority. That's how kids themselves learn to care for others." Choosing activities you can do together that will benefit others—volunteering at a soup kitchen, for example, or helping in a community cleanup—allows kids to see parents caring about the world around them, and also gives them a sense of their own place in that world.

For Pabst and Daly, that kind of togetherness is inspiring, and helps them keep their own senses of wonder while reinforcing the sense of wonder in their kids. "We always want them to have a feeling of abundance in the world, and to be grateful for that abundance, and to give freely to others because of it," Pabst says. "When they're older, we plan to figure out ways to enjoy time together while also contributing to the communities around us. That just feels like the right thing for a family to do."

Critical Thinking

1. How would you describe your own family's happiness?

2. What kind of attributes have you identified from the article that are in your family?

3. Do you agree with the opinion of the author on happiness in families? Why or why not?

4. In thinking about happy families are there any attributes that are missing from the author's list?

5. Are all families who are happy alike? Why or why not?

AMY ROSENBERG is a writer living in New York City.

From *Psychology Today,* July/August 2010, pp. 62–69. Copyright © 2010 by Sussex Publishers, LLC. Reprinted by permission.

The Joy of Rituals
Simple Strategies for Strengthening Family Ties

Reading Bible stories before bedtime, sitting down to Sabbath dinner, and saying grace before each meal brings warmth and joy to many families. Now, researchers are discovering that such activities enhance child development as well.

DAWN MARIE BARHYTE

Rituals are repeated and shared activities that carry meaning and provide an emotional reward to family members. Although routines are also repetitious family behavior and vital to family life, they lack the symbolic content and compelling nature that rituals possess. Unlike rituals, routines are purely instrumental rather than symbolic; they are activities family members *have* to do rather than *want* to do.

Meg Cox, expert on rituals and author of *The Heart of a Family—Searching America for Traditions that Fulfill Us*, believes that a ritual is anything—big or small—that families perform together deliberately. She says they must be repetitious and provide some dramatic flourish that elevates the activity above the ordinary grind.

Even simple activities can be transformed into satisfying and memorable rituals, such as always singing a certain song whenever you give your child medicine, or declaring an evening study break for hot cocoa on cold winter weeknights. Cox writes, "The more we understand [rituals], the more their power will enrich our lives."

William J. Doherty, professor of family social science at the University of Minnesota, and author of *The Intentional Family* adds, "Children are natural ritualists. They crave connection and love predictability. Family rituals give children a sense of steady love and connection, and give order to their lives."

Shared Experience

Rituals are significant not so much for the act itself but for the results they yield; the sense of togetherness that grows out of shared experience and the feeling of rightness that comes from its repetition.

According to research, these repeated positive experiences form strong connections between neurons in the brain and foster a sense of security in children. They also help kids learn what to expect from their environment and how to understand the world around them.

Other studies have shown that young people who are best equipped to face the challenges of life and stay centered are those who feel close to their families. That closeness comes from the routine reassurances and shared experiences found in everyday rituals.

At one time or another, all families experience stress. Rituals have the capacity to provide stability even during trying times. Researchers have found that rituals are integral family resources that can act as a coping mechanism during those challenging moments. Professor Doherty adds that family rituals are what children can fall back on when under stress. He says that regular meals with parents provide emotional protection from every major risk factor.

Little Celebrations

When you think of family rituals, you probably picture the grand annual events such as Thanksgiving, Christmas, Hanukah, birthdays, weddings, or baby dedications. But you may want to consider adding some everyday rituals that can serve as glue that binds families together right in the midst of our harried lives. These common, often repeated happenings can become extraordinarily vital and act as a powerful buffer against this complex world. These rituals will build a bridge that connects the past to the future and allows children to pick up the torch and pass it on to the next generation.

According to Meg Cox, "Scientists tell us that many animals have rituals, and anthropologists report they haven't found any human societies without them, which alone is compelling evidence that rituals must be a human necessity."

Psychologists insist that rituals help us keep track of where we came from and essentially who we are. While this is key for all family members, it's profoundly significant for children who are forming their own identities. Rituals become a road map for kids, offering a comforting sense of predictability and order to life. When children have a clear sense of where they come from, they have a better sense of where they are going. Knowing what to do and being able to predict what comes next helps a boy or girl feel competent, and feeling competent is key to emotional well-being.

Grounded by Constancy

Children delight in rituals, look forward to them, learn from them, and feel comforted and grounded by their constancy. Positive family rituals leave indelible imprints on children's minds and form treasured memories ready to be passed on from generation to generation. For instance, knowing that every fall the family will load themselves into the minivan and go pumpkin or apple picking makes the season something to look forward to and savor.

Knowing that, each night, dad will talk to his child about his or her day and read a story at bedtime gives often-lonely children something to which they can look forward. In fact, developing a bedtime ritual is an excellent way to unwind and quietly embrace the day's happenings.

Whether it's reading a story, saying a prayer, or giving a hug and kiss, these nightly rituals offer security and comfort that fold gently into pleasant slumber.

The challenge, of course, lies in making the decision to create this time and saying no to any intrusions. With the myriad of demands on our time, it will require some effort. But the payoff will be well worth it.

Takes Work

Once you have good family rituals in place, keeping them alive takes work. If it's centered on a specific day, like Sabbath dinner, and you're not able to do it one week, don't let it slip away. Squeeze it in later in the week if you have to do so.

With some attentiveness, your family rituals will survive the demands of life and may endure for generations to come. Know that no matter what life brings, rituals will act as a safety net for your family members. Establishing your own distinctive activities now and faithfully repeating them will offer a much-needed shelter in unsettling times. Rituals are like keepsakes that live in your heart.

Springboard for Action

If you are inspired but feel at a loss at the thought of starting your own family ritual, here are some ideas to use as a springboard for action.

- If you're like many families today and can't manage family dinners seven nights a week, try for **breakfasts together or special fruit-juice treats in the evening.** These relaxed moments of sharing nourishment and conversation provide a much-needed platform for reconnecting.
- Recognition night. A fun way to celebrate your child's achievements in the classroom or extracurricular activity is to serve an **"Honoree Dinner"** on a special plate reserved for that occasion with all the healthy foods they crave.
- Designate one night a week as **"Family Night"** created solely for family members to connect, interact, and communicate while having wholesome fun. One week you could play board games, another rent a DVD and serve popcorn, and yet another allow various family members to plan the meal and help cook it as a team.
- Hold an **"Unbirthday"** where you surprise your child by unexpectedly celebrating the fact that they exist. Include their favorite foods, a cake, and small tokens of affection.
- Create a **"Give a Helping Hand Day"** to help children cultivate altruism and focus on others less fortunate. As a family, participate in some community service like volunteering at a nursing home or soup kitchen, or collecting food for a local food pantry.

Life is hard. Rituals can help soften the edges and bring a sense of togetherness back into the lives of every family member. Why not start one today?

Critical Thinking

1. What are some rituals in your family and how do you know they are rituals?
2. What kind of rituals would you like to create with your own children?
3. Why do you think that rituals must be consistent?
4. Why are rituals so important to families?
5. Describe the shared experience of rituals.

Freelance writer **DAWN MARIE BARHYTE** of Warwick, New York, is a stepmother of two and grandmother of six. She's a former junior volunteer coordinator at St. Anthony Community Hospital and teacher at the First Baptist Child Care Center.

Rituals in Relationships

Rituals, including the rites of organized religion, are critical parts of life. They provide context, meaning, rhythm, and connection.

DOLORES T. PUTERBAUGH

Watch a Smoker handle a new pack of cigarettes. Better yet, watch that same individual handle several fresh packs. There is a ritual in preparing to smoke: perhaps a tap-tap-tap of the unopened pack on the base of the palm: then flipped and the other end tapped three times. Opening the pack always is done the same way: Is all of the foil removed or only one portion? Is the cigarette put directly into the mouth or, is it. too, subject to tapping? A smoker experiencing withdrawal will begin to calm down in anticipation of the nicotine fix just by going through the initial ritual motions of handling the pack of cigarettes.

Absent any formal structure for ritual, such as organized religions or public meetings, humans will create ritual behaviors. Sometimes rituals are large: the multihousehold gathering at Thanksgiving, or attending an annual parade. Rituals may be private, or nearly so: I have heard addiction counselors assert that much of illegal drug use is ritualized behavior that has become, not only part of the addiction, but a replacement for healthy rituals that alford real meaning and connection. Some rituals are invisible to all but the participants: the intimacy of a Sunday morning church-breakfast-newspaper sequence that never varies, or weeknight family dinners. Rituals span the simplest gesture and the highest of sacraments.

Rituals, including the rites of organized religion, are critical parts of life. They provide context, meaning, rhythm, and connection. Research indicates thai families with strong, positive ritual patterns produce well-adjusted children, while families without them often are chaotic and tend to have higher incidences of bad behavior. All rituals, however, are not created equal. In families where routines, such as dinner, are enforced rigidly with a lot of negative emotions and aggressive behavior, the ritual's effects are not positive and lead to more unhealthy family interactions. A family dinner where parents fight or nag their children creates toxic ripples that spread out into other circles of each member's life.

What makes a ritual? Rituals are predictable sets of behaviors with agreed-upon rules, repeated over time. Generally, most participants know their roles in the rituals, although these may evolve. The ritual is important as an individual experience as well as its value as a piece of a pattern. A family that visits the cemetery every Memorial Day finds meaning in each annual visit as well as in reminiscing about past years' visits and the expectation that the visits will continue.

A ritual may be hidden to all but its participants, who, in all likelihood, generally do not identify what they are doing as a ritual; it simply is part of being "us." Outsiders (such as psychological researchers videotaping family dinners) may perceive painfully tiresome conversations where a family experiences a reaffirmation of connections and roles. Barbara Fiese, professor and chair. Department of Psychology at Syracuse University, recounts a story of investigators' boredom with a family's dinner-time rehashing of which members liked jelly on their peanut butter sandwiches: the family later explained that they were divided as jelly-nonjelly enthusiasts, and these were predictors of other characteristics (e.g., jokers vs. organizers). The family used their PBJ shorthand to characterize friends and family. The jelly-nonjelly references in conversation were important ritual assertions of family members' strengths and mutual reliance.

Therapists use rituals with families and couples to encourage deeper connections or healing from emotional wounds. A family project can be ritualized to evoke certain meanings: a marriage strained by addictions or adultery can create a ritual that symbolizes a fresh start and the reinvention of the relationship. Smaller pieces of the initial ritual can be inserted into daily life. Marriage enrichment programs, such as Marriage Encounter or Retrouvaille, provide daily activities of discussing thoughts and feelings about a prearranged topic to continue the connective work of the weekend retreat into the real world of married life.

Rituals help define our roles and facilitate questions of purpose and meaning within parameters that should not confine but, instead, direct exploration. Yet, there is a limit to how much time it is healthy to spend in the throes of an existential crisis of meaning.

Rituals promote emotional security by providing consistent environmental cues that trigger specific emotional responses. We all stand and salute the flag: the entire congregation kneels in unison: the bleachers are filled with face-painted fans doing the wave. The contextual aspect of rituals tells us what to do, what to expect, and this can alleviate anxiety. That is not to say that everyone is walking around on the cusp of free-floating anxiety. An interesting life requires a balance between the novel and the predictable. The ratio may differ, depending on age, personality, and temperament, but some of each is necessary. Thus, we always may sit in the same bleacher seats, eat the same snack, complain about the umpire (critical predictable aspects of the ritual). and, yet, the outcome of the game remains open (novelty). Too much novelty yields anarchy and chaos: life can become as unpredictable as a perpetual episode of "The Twilight Zone." Conversely, a lack of novelty leads to dullness, boredom, and, quite possibly, instigation of bad behavior just to make something—anything—happen.

Context Matters

Context is important in small-scale rituals as well as large. If, for example, a married couple always has coffee together in the morning—no matter how hectic their schedules, or whether they get up at vastly different hours—that mug of coffee, in the context of morning (whatever stage of morning it may be for each) and the small talk that surrounds it, creates a specific environment and holds meaning for that couple: it is part of the rhythm of their daily, weekly, yearly life. Taking the time for connection, however brief and seemingly pointless it may be to others, asserts each one's commitment to the relationship.

Through ritual behaviors, we find meaning, from daily life to the transcendent. What does it signify to be a friend, spouse, parent, or child? Rituals help define our roles and facilitate questions of purpose and meaning within parameters that should not confine but, instead, direct exploration. Yet, there is a limit to how much time it is healthy to spend in the throes of an existential crisis of meaning. After that, we have to choose meaning and develop it within some sort of context. Rituals should not become a substitute for self-examination, reason, ethical exploration, and intellectual development. That would be silly, superstitious, and a degradation of one's humanity. Instead, rituals, through their symbolism of higher concepts, are meant to evoke awareness of those transcendent meanings.

Finding meaning in ritual requires mindfulness, a psychological term currently in vogue. It means, among other things, "Hey you! Wake up and pay attention!" Certainly, some people seem to sleepwalk through even the most profound rituals. For them, the ritual simply has become a set of rehearsed motions that may provide part of the benefit of ritual in terms of context and sociological cues, but the opportunity for greater benefits is lost.

Families can use rituals, as well as the shift of roles within rituals, to affirm continuity while incorporating change. A child may move into a new role within the context of family dinner (old enough to say Grace? Big enough to clear some dishes?), but the ritual of dinner and sharing the events of the day remains.

Rituals also provide the means to forge connections. In blended and adoptive families, for instance. I often "prescribe" the project of creating a family coat of arms for the new unit. Family members must collaborate on each part of the assignment. Planning and execution are group tasks. What animal best symbolizes this new family, and why? What colors "go" with this family? What are the family's strengths, and how can they represent those with symbols on the coat of arms? This is not a one-hour process. Ideally, it takes place over a few evenings or weekend afternoons. The entire family gathers to present and explain the final creation. I usually suggest that the finished project migrate throughout the home. Each member should have a chance to have the coat of arms in his or her room, as well as posting it in common areas.

Many families have rituals that help define what it means to be a member of that family, although if you walked up with a recorder and notebook and said you wanted to take notes on their ritual behavior they would not necessarily identify what they are doing as a ritual. Repetitive discussions, such as the PBJ inventory previously mentioned, are one form of ritual. A friend recounted that his family "worries." They get together and "worry" about some member or another; apparently, they talk the situation through again and again, reinforce or ante up one another's concerns, and define themselves as caring for their members through shared "worrying." To be a member of this family means sometimes you will be one of the worriers and sometimes you will be the object of worry. The worst scenarios would be that you never become an object of worry (which would mean that you no longer are a valued member of the family) or you are excluded (or withdraw yourself) from the worrying team. That would entail being cut off from your family's life.

Humans deal with the passage of time and changes through ritual. In recent years, the trend has been to mark as many passages as possible (except for the long delay between youth and retirement, when we try our best to pretend that absolutely no change is occurring). Children graduate from preschool, kindergarten, primary school, middle school, and high school. Rehearsal dinners no longer art—meals shared by the wedding party after a walk-through with clergy; anyone and everyone involved in the wedding (including third cousins and their dates) expects to be served a ritual (and catered) meal. Existential angst over life and death, and the meaning of life in the face of death, are mediated through rituals—wakes, vigils, funerals, family gatherings. These rituals provide rhythm across seasons, as well as mark passages.

A child is born, and the family enters into the particular welcoming and initiation rituals of their beliefs. The child matures, and new rituals emerge that link the child's life with the lives of others in the community as well as older family members. Some are formal (a baptism, a bris) and others are not. A child wears a parent's baptismal gown and profound continuity is ritualized. Another studies dance starting at age six, like her mother, and multiple generations become part of the rhythm of maturity and change. The rituals of daily, weekly, and yearly life provide harmonies that support the melody of each individual's progress through life. Try changing the way Christmas morning is orchestrated and watch a teenager who has been doing her best to evade family dinners raise strenuous and indignant objections. The predictable rhythms of life's rituals make it safe to shake things up in other areas. How is she supposed to take those first tentative flights on fragile wings if you keep shaking the nest?

Rituals can help maintain a sense of normalcy when other parts of life are in chaos. Keeping rituals afloat in times of disasters, illness, or other tragedies eases tension and can alleviate the temptation to surrender to hopelessness. A family that gathers around a camp stove and says grace before eating MREs in the days without electricity after a hurricane is a family that has not surrendered its core values and meaning. The storm will pass; the roof will be repaired; the electricity will come back on line; and essential aspects of what it means to be a member of this particular family will be unscathed. In the meantime, the inclusion of important family rituals despite material disarray will help the children (and adults) recover from trauma.

Those enamored of the concept of self-esteem will be reassured by the sizable body of research indicating that children whose families have firm but flexible ritual patterns tend to develop greater confidence and self-esteem. This is not necessarily the "I feel good about myself because . . . well, just because" self-esteem that many youngsters have been spoon-fed since the 1970s. Rather, it is a sense of one's worth and place as a result of loving and being loved by other people. By being a valued part of a family, children develop sufficient confidence to go out into the world.

Rituals support families separated by distance, nurture love in marriage, and safely stretch family boundaries as children mature and pull away. It is my observation, although by no means scientifically corroborated, that this is the aspect of ritual least understood and, therefore, most neglected, by the typical family. Most families perform admirably on the big rituals: they pull out all the stops for birthdays, anniversaries, and holidays. Pivotal events, like weddings, become projects of incredible size and scope. However, as anyone knows who has witnessed fistfights or bridal party melt-downs before the reception, extravaganzas do not create connection—they only shine a laser scope on whatever connection exists. Anyone hoping for great experiences in the major rituals of passage would do well to invest energy in the nearly invisible gestures that ritualize connection in daily life.

Small daily gestures and routines are vital rituals for couples and families. Predictability is critical; the meaning ascribed to the behavior by all parties is central. If one person finds ritual pleasure in making tea for the other at wake-up time, but the tea drinker takes it for granted, finds it embarrassing (it's the 21st century; isn't this old-fashioned?) or otherwise discounts it, the opportunity for connection through the ritual is squandered. The tea-brewer is, through private ritual, reaffirming a connection and caring for the other person; the tea-drinker, who is being served hot tea in the morning, ironically, is the loser in this equation for not accepting the ritual offering of daily recommitment and connection. It still may be meaningful to the brewer, but only as a private reaffirmation, not as a shared experience.

> **It can be difficult to dedicate the time and effort to create and sustain rituals, and it is not surprising that a population that lacks the will to keep New Year's resolutions for more than a week or two is dismayed at the commitment required of ritual.**

Dinnertime Routines

Dinnertime probably is the most common daily routine for families and, as a result, is taken for granted, unappreciated, and neglected. Frequently, rushing to the next activity or television thwart any potential for context, meaning, rhythm, and connection. It may devolve into a daily routine with no ritual significance. Eating dinner while watching television may be part of a routine, but it lacks the intimacy and purpose of ritual. There are exceptions: one family of my acquaintance regularly watched "Survivor" and served meals based on the "reality" location. They dressed up in thematic costumes for the show and gathered to connect, discuss, debate, and break bread (or coconuts). They created a meaningful family ritual around what easily might have been only a mutually detached experience.

If a family or couple wants to capitalize on the value of rituals, almost any activity or exchange can become richer. The use of symbols—who knew a PBJ sandwich could serve as a psychological trait marker, bonding shorthand, and the context of ritual?—and positive emotions are the most critical factors. The repetitive nature of rituals—the aspects of routine and predictability—is important as well. Some researchers have found that rituals and routines often are used deliberately, with appreciation for their power, by single-parent families and families in homeless shelters. In both situations, the awareness that their family life has the potential for greater strain and chaos can awaken the determination to overcome risks by extra commitment to special celebrations, storytelling, and connective rituals in difficult circumstances.

Sometimes, though, what pass as rituals in many homes merely are loosely held habits. It can be difficult to dedicate the time and effort to create and sustain rituals, and it is not surprising that a population that lacks the will to keep New Year's resolutions for more than a week or two is dismayed at the commitment required of ritual. In therapy, I often ask couples about their rituals. I am saddened by how many do not seem to understand what rituals are, much less appreciate the richness rituals can bring to family life. "Well, we usually go out for drinks on Friday," offers one. "And we read the paper every Sunday morning," says the other. These may be rituals, or they merely may be casual habits that just as easily would be tossed aside if a group of friends planned a girls' night out on Friday, or if the opportunity to join a Sunday morning softball league came along.

If their Friday outing for drinks and nachos were a ritual, they would refer to it throughout the week, establishing its connective value and its context in the rhythm of their life. Each would look forward to it and internally experience it not only as a pleasant, relaxing time, but as a symbolic event that helps define who they are as a couple. The Friday nachos-and-beer would entail a leaving-behind of the workweek and a dedication to their life as a couple during the weekend. Even if they were meeting friends, it would be "our" time—that's a much different experience than just going out because there is nothing on television and no one can think of anything else to do. Nachos? Sure, whatever.

Critical Thinking

1. What are the differences between routines and rituals?

2. Give an example of a routine and a ritual.

3. What are the essential elements of a ritual?

4. What are some family events that are associated with rituals?

5. How do families decide on roles in the ritual process?

DOLORES T. PUTERBAUGH, American Thought Editor of *USA Today*, is a psychotherapist in private practice in Largo, Fla.

Where Is Marriage Going?

Anthony Layng

It was bad enough when the divorce rate in the U.S. reached epidemic proportions and single parenting became commonplace. Now, more and more Americans are developing a tolerance for same-sex marriage. New York recognizes such marriages, and the California and Connecticut Supreme Courts struck down those states' laws banning marriage for same-sex couples, allowing them to join Massachusetts in accepting homosexual unions. Even though Californians recently voted to stop granting marriage licenses to same-sex couples, the sanctity of marriage seriously seems to be undermined and in danger of further deterioration.

Most Americans believe that marriage is an inherently sacred institution, the purpose of which is procreation and the socialization of children. That is why the idea of same-sex marriage, the prevalence of single mothers raising children, and the frailty of modern marriages are considered such a threat to "proper" marriage. Such pessimism particularly is prevalent among biblical literalists and other Christian fundamentalists who feel that any alteration of traditional marriage constitutes a moral decline, and many others agree.

However, examining the history of marriage encourages quite a different conclusion. The ethnographic study of tribal societies suggests what marriage meant to our ancestors thousands of years ago. Obviously, having children is an ancient concern, but most tribal people did not view marriage as something sacred. Many tribes had no ritual to acknowledge the start of a marriage, nothing we would equate to a wedding. Among the traditional Cheyenne, courtship involved a girl allowing a suitor to sleep with her in her parents' tepee, entering stealthfully after dark and leaving before the others in the tepee awakened. All the couple needed to do to be considered married was to have the young man sleep late enough to be discovered by her parents. Similarly, some Pacific islanders, such as the Ulithi, allowed couples to "announce" that they wished to be considered married simply by cohabiting. Coming-of-age rituals were far more common in tribal societies than weddings, and yet marriage was, with very few exceptions, the norm in all these societies.

Somehow, the belief that marriages are arranged in heaven, an extremely romantic idea, has become equated with considering marriage as sacred. Again, taking a historical perspective as provided by our knowledge of traditional societies, marriages frequently were arranged by parents or other relatives. Among the Sambia of New Guinea and the Tiwi of northern Australia, many marriages involved infant brides. In numerous warlike tribes such as the Yanomamo of Venezuela, men obtained wives by capturing them from enemy villages.

Granted, marriage in this country often is associated with religious concepts and usually initiated with a sacred ritual. Yet, from the perspective of the history of humanity, this is a rather recent development. Even newer are our present matrimonial motives. Instead of marrying to ensure that our offspring will care for us when we are too old to provide for ourselves, we now consciously limit the number of children to how many we can afford. No longer does marrying and having children provide assurance that the elderly will be cared for. Understandably, most modern couples, for a variety of reasons, choose to limit their fecundity to one or two children or remain childless. Unlike tribal people, those of us who elect to avoid marriage nevertheless may be admired and influential. However, our tribal ancestors structured their lives around marriage. Who you were, your role in society, and your prestige all largely were determined by your place in the kinship system. Whom you and your kin married could ensure or alter your status in society. One rose and fell in the social order by strategic marriage. Of course, infant marriage and marriage by capture no longer are acceptable. Arranged marriages remain legal, but are considered unsuitable. Now, it seems, the only legitimate motivation for marriage is romantic love and seeking emotional fulfillment. Marriage to enhance status still occurs, but generally is frowned upon. We are quite critical of the wealthy senior socialite who marries her young tennis instructor, or the twenty something beauty who marries a famous elderly celebrity. Such unions are considered laughable or crass.

Tribal people married to gain prestige by having many children (hopefully, several sons) to ensure their future welfare. Additionally, given the strict sexual division of labor in these societies, at least one man and one woman were necessary components of a normal household. This had been the case since our ancestors lived as hunters and gatherers. Even in traditional agrarian societies, the labors of men and women produced very different things, and both were required for running a successful household and providing for children. Now that men and women are obtaining nearly equal educations and more and more couples are, of necessity, gainfully employed, any domestic division of labor likely is to be dictated by personal inclinations and circumstances rather than gender. No longer is the husband inevitably the breadwinner and the wife a stay-at-home mother. Marriage in the U.S. is a very flexible institution today. The nature of a marital relationship is not determined primarily by custom but is left to each couple to work out according to personal needs and preferences. It no longer necessarily involves a hierarchical arrangement between spouses. Contemporary husbands and wives frequently consider themselves to be equal partners. Even parenting has lost its imperative tie to marriage since it has become acceptable for single people to raise children today.

The nature of a marital relationship is not determined primarily by custom but is left to each couple to work out. . . .

It is under these circumstances, given how marriage has evolved to its present form, that homosexual men and women have begun to find same-sex marriage attractive. Clearly, each marriage is an ever-adapting relationship, altering over time as circumstances change. Similarly, the institution of marriage has evolved and will continue to do so. Since the earliest marriages in very primitive societies, this custom has taken various forms, always adjusting as society evolved. That process particularly is evident today because social change has been accelerating. Current legislative attempts to prohibit such change are understandable, but unsuitable and unlikely to succeed, as our technology, beliefs, and customs have a long dynamic history, and marriage is subject to the same forces of social change as the rest of our culture.

Critical Thinking

1. How do you view marriage in today's society?
2. What has changed in marriage?
3. What has had the greatest impact on marriage?
4. How does society impact marriage?
5. What are the common beliefs around marriage and how does media impact those beliefs?

ANTHONY LAYNG is professor emeritus of anthropology at Elmira (N.Y.) College.

Test-Your-Knowledge Form

We encourage you to photocopy and use this page as a tool to assess how the articles in *Annual Editions* expand on the information in your textbook. By reflecting on the articles you will gain enhanced text information. You can also access this useful form on a product's book support website at www.mhhe.com/cls

NAME: _____   DATE: _____

TITLE AND NUMBER OF ARTICLE:
_____

BRIEFLY STATE THE MAIN IDEA OF THIS ARTICLE:
_____

LIST THREE IMPORTANT FACTS THAT THE AUTHOR USES TO SUPPORT THE MAIN IDEA:

_____

WHAT INFORMATION OR IDEAS DISCUSSED IN THIS ARTICLE ARE ALSO DISCUSSED IN YOUR TEXTBOOK OR OTHER READINGS THAT YOU HAVE DONE? LIST THE TEXTBOOK CHAPTERS AND PAGE NUMBERS:

_____

LIST ANY EXAMPLES OF BIAS OR FAULTY REASONING THAT YOU FOUND IN THE ARTICLE:

_____

LIST ANY NEW TERMS/CONCEPTS THAT WERE DISCUSSED IN THE ARTICLE, AND WRITE A SHORT DEFINITION:

We Want Your Advice

ANNUAL EDITIONS revisions depend on two major opinion sources: one is our Advisory Board, listed in the front of this volume, which works with us in scanning the thousands of articles published in the public press each year; the other is you—the person actually using the book. Please help us and the users of the next edition by completing the prepaid article rating form on this page and returning it to us. Thank you for your help!

ANNUAL EDITIONS: The Family 12/13

ARTICLE RATING FORM

Here is an opportunity for you to have direct input into the next revision of this volume.
We would like you to rate each of the articles listed below, using the following scale:

1. **Excellent: should definitely be retained**
2. **Above average: should probably be retained**
3. **Below average: should probably be deleted**
4. **Poor: should definitely be deleted**

Your ratings will play a vital part in the next revision.
Please mail this prepaid form to us as soon as possible.
Thanks for your help!

RATING	ARTICLE	RATING	ARTICLE
	1. Marriage and Family in the Scandinavian Experience		25. Children of Alcoholics: Risk and Resilience
	2. The Significant Dynamic Relationship between Globalization and Families		26. Impact of Family Recovery on Pre-Teens and Adolescents
	3. Matches Made on Earth: Why Family Values Are Human Values		27. Why Do They Cheat and Lie?
	4. Family Partnerships That Count		28. Love but Don't Touch
	5. This Thing Called Love		29. Is This Man Cheating on His Wife?
	6. She's Out There		30. The Opt-Out Myth
	7. 24 Things Love and Sex Experts Are Dying to Tell You		31. Making Time for Family Time
	8. Against All Odds		32. Finding New Balance
	9. The Expectations Trap		33. Trust and Betrayal in the Golden Years
	10. Fats, Carbs and the Science of Conception		34. Dealing Day-to-Day with Diabetes: A Whole Family Experience
	11. Baby Survival Guide: 7 Truths That'll Keep You Sane		35. The Positives of Caregiving: Mothers' Experiences Caregiving for a Child with Autism
	12. Can Marriage Be Saved?		36. Bereavement after Caregiving
	13. The Polygamists		37. A Family Undertaking
	14. Good Parents, Bad Results		38. Stressors Afflicting Families during Military Deployment
	15. Do We Need a Law to Prohibit Spanking?		39. Military Children and Families: Strengths and Challenges during Peace and War
	16. Children of Lesbian and Gay Parents: Psychology, Law and Policy		40. Helping Military Kids Cope with Traumatic Death
	17. Parenting Gay Youth: Creating a Supportive Environment		41. A Divided House
	18. The Forgotten Siblings		42. Civil Wars
	19. Oh, Brother!		43. Estranged Spouses Increasingly Waiting Out Downturn to Divorce
	20. Building on Strengths: Intergenerational Practice with African American Families		44. Get a Closer Look: 12 Tips for Successful Family Interviews
	21. Support and Empower Families of Children with Disabilities		45. Meet My Real Modern Family
	22. Recognizing Domestic Partner Abuse		46. Relative Happiness
	23. The Fatal Distraction: Forgetting a Child in the Backseat of a Car Is a Horrifying Mistake. Is It a Crime?		47. The Joy of Rituals: Simple Strategies for Strengthening Family Ties
	24. Role of Foster Family Belonging in Recovery from Child Maltreatment		48. Rituals in Relationships
			49. Where Is Marriage Going?

ABOUT YOU

Name _____ Date _____

Are you a teacher? ☐ A student? ☐
Your school's name _____

Department _____

Address _____ City _____ State _____ Zip _____

School telephone # _____

YOUR COMMENTS ARE IMPORTANT TO US!

Please fill in the following information:
For which course did you use this book?
_____

Did you use a text with this ANNUAL EDITION? ☐ yes ☐ no
What was the title of the text?
_____

What are your general reactions to the Annual Editions concept?
_____

Have you read any pertinent articles recently that you think should be included in the next edition? Explain.
_____

Are there any articles that you feel should be replaced in the next edition? Why?
_____

Are there any World Wide Websites that you feel should be included in the next edition? Please annotate.
_____

May we contact you for editorial input? ☐ yes ☐ no
May we quote your comments? ☐ yes ☐ no

NOTES

NOTES

NOTES

NOTES

NOTES

NOTES

NOTES

NOTES